INTERNATIONAL DEVELOPMENT IN FOCUS

Voices to Choices
Bangladesh's Journey in Women's Economic Empowerment

Jennifer L. Solotaroff, Aphichoke Kotikula, Tara Lonnberg, Snigdha Ali, Rohini P. Pande, and Ferdous Jahan

WORLD BANK GROUP

Contents

Figures

Foreword

I sing the song of equality
In my view, gender disparity is essentially a triviality.
Everything that is great in the world,
all the works, beneficial and good,
half must be credited to woman,
and to man half only we should.

—Kazi Nazrul Islam

In the last decade, Bangladesh has made important strides in many dimensions of gender equality, creating opportunities for women and girls from all walks of life. It reduced fertility rates, achieved gender parity in schooling, and paved the way for millions of women to work in the garments sector. According to the World Bank's recently released Human Capital Index, girls in Bangladesh today have a better chance than boys of completing school and surviving to the age 60.

But to what extent have these changes translated into even greater voice and decision-making power for women? *Voices to Choices* examines the experience of Bangladesh's women—their journey since the previous World Bank report, *Whispers to Voices: Gender and Social Transformation in Bangladesh*—and looks at how to build on past progress to improve economic empowerment.

Every day, in the workplace and in the home, Bangladeshi women contribute to the country's economic development. But pronounced gender gaps remain. Despite a 10-percentage-point increase in women's labor force participation rate in the last decade, women in Bangladesh are half as likely as men to enter the labor force. More than one-third of women who do work are unpaid contributing family helpers. Although the rate of female entrepreneurship has been growing, women-led businesses continue to be small and concentrated in specific sectors.

Social and economic barriers prevent many women from accessing and deciding on the use of assets, including land, housing, and livestock. Lifting these barriers will help Bangladesh achieve its ambition of accelerated growth and development. This is because women's economic empowerment is linked to poverty reduction: when women earn, they will invest more in their children and communities.

This book focuses on different domains of women's economic empowerment to determine why these gaps persist and suggests policy options to narrow them. Drawing on good practices from around the globe, the authors prioritize recommendations that can yield sustainable results in the short and long term.

The government of Bangladesh, the private sector, development partners, and other stakeholders all have a vital role to play to create an enabling environment for women in Bangladesh to make decisions about their families, finances, and businesses. Bangladeshi women are starting to engage in many areas of the economy and are breaking the glass ceiling in arts and culture, literature, sports, politics, and other fields. And they can do more.

It is my hope that with the full participation of women, Bangladesh will sing its own song of equality and rise to the aspirations of its national poet, Kazi Nazrul Islam, of a country where everything that is great, all works beneficial and good, are shared by its men and women, boys and girls alike.

Qimiao Fan
Country Director
Bangladesh, Bhutan, and Nepal
The World Bank

Acknowledgments

This book was prepared by a core team led by Jennifer L. Solotaroff of the South Asia Social Development Unit, Social, Urban, Rural, and Resilience Global Practice (GSU06) and the World Bank Gender Group. Core team members included Rohini P. Pande (GSU06), Aphichoke Kotikula, World Bank Gender Group (GTGDR); Tara Lonnberg (GSU06), Snigdha Ali (GSU06), and Ferdous Jahan (GSU06). Syed Usman Javaid, Pakistan Country Management Unit (SACPK); Anne Shrestha, Water Global Practice for South and East Asia Region 2 (GWAGP); Tonmoy Islam (GSU06), and Md. Wahidur Rahman Qabili (GSU06) conducted quantitative data analysis. James Sujit Malo and F. H. Yasin Shafi provided written inputs. Zahin Takrim Hussain, Bangladesh Country Management Unit (SACBD); Janet Bably Halder (SACBD), Habiba Jeba (SACBD), and Dolly Teju (GSUO6) provided administrative support. Mehrin Mahbub, Joe Qian, Shilpa Banerji, and Yann Doignon, South Asia Region External Communications (SAREC); and Samera Chowdhury (GSU06) offered guidance and inputs on communications and dissemination activities. Special thanks to Faustina Pereira, International Human Rights Law and Development Specialist, for her guidance and review of relevant chapters. Thanks also are due to Md. Mamun-Ur-Rashid and his staff at Development Research Initiative (dRi) for primary qualitative data collection; and to Bakhtiar Sohag (GSU06) for generous assistance in procuring secondary data sets from the Bangladesh Bureau of Statistics, government of Bangladesh (GoB).

David Warren (Practice Manager, GSU06) provided managerial guidance and support. Qimiao Fan (Country Director, Bangladesh, Bhutan, and Nepal), Martin Rama (Chief Economist, South Asia Region), Rajashree Paralkar, (Manager, Operations, SACBD), Sereen Juma (Country Program Coordinator, South Asia Country Management Unit for Bangladesh, Bhutan, and Nepal, SACBN), and Sanjay Srivastava (Program Leader, SACBN) provided overall guidance. Special thanks go to Maitreyi Das (Practice Manager, Social, Urban, Rural, and Resilience Global Practice-Global Programs - GSUGL) and Iffath Sharif (Practice Manager, Social Protection and Labor Global Practice - Africa South and West - GSP08) for their insightful comments and advice on the study's focus, overall content, and organizational structure.

The book peer reviewers were Zahid Hussain (Lead Economist, Macroeconomic Trade and Investment Global Practice, South Asia - GMTSA), Helle Buchhave (Senior Social Development Specialist, East Asia Social Development Unit, Social, Urban, Rural, and Resilience Global Practice - GSU02), Michael O'Sullivan (Senior Economist, GTGDR), and Maheen Sultan (Visiting Fellow, Centre for Gender and Social Transformation, Bangladesh Rural Advancement Committee [BRAC] Institute of Governance and Development). Gladys Lopez-Acevedo (Lead Economist, Poverty Global Practice, South Asia Region - GPV06) also provided helpful comments.

Discussions on framing the issues have benefited greatly from the views and feedback of Khander Sadia Arabin (Secretary, Cabinet Division, GoB), Naila Ahmed (Ministry of Disaster Management and Relief, GoB), Md. Azizul Haque (Ministry of Youth and Sports, GoB), Kazi Mohammad Salim (Information and Communication Technology Division, GoB), Shirina Khatum (Information and Communication Technology Division, GoB), Asma-ul-Husna (Ministry of Labour and Employment, GoB), Sayeda Nayem Jahan (Ministry of Social Welfare, GoB), Kamun Nahar Sumi (Medical Education and Family Welfare Division, Ministry of Health and Welfare, GoB), Sabah Moyeen (GSU06), Alicia Hammond (GTGDR), George Joseph (GWA09), A. T. M. Khaleduzzaman (GWA09), Hiska Reyes (GSU06), Maria Beatriz Orlando (GSU06), Selina Ahmed (Acid Survivors Foundation), Anwar Hossain (WAVE Foundation), Murshed Iqbal (Sabalamby Unnayan Samity Netrakona), Shohel Chandra Hajang (Bangladesh Indigenous People's Forum), Md. Ali Hossain (Brotee), Zakir Hossain (Nagorik Uddyog), Md. Abdul Hakim (Dushtha Shasthya Kendra - DSK) Afshan Choudhury (CED, BRAC University), Mahmudur Rahman Chowdhury (SNV Netherlands Development Organization), Eshrat Naris (BRAC), Khalida Khanom (BRAC), Md. Rafiqul Islam (BRAC), and Salma Akhter (Dhaka University).

This book has been made possible by Bank Budget from the Bangladesh Country Management Unit (SACBD); by Trust Fund support from a Department of Foreign Affairs and Trade (DFAT), government of Australia grant through the South Asia Regional Trade Facilitation Program (SARTFP); and by the South Asia Gender Innovation Lab, which received a grant from the World Bank Group's Umbrella Facility for Gender Equality (UFGE), a multidonor trust fund.

About the Authors

Snigdha Ali is a researcher and development practitioner with more than 10 years of experience in gender, research, qualitative methods, and management. She has worked on crosscutting issues affecting women and nutrition, climate change, infrastructure, economic engagement, and gender and social norms. Prior to co-authoring this book, she worked at the Bangladesh Rural Advancement Committee (BRAC) in Bangladesh as Program Head for two departments, and managed two teams and six projects. She has also worked for the International Food Policy Research Institute (IFPRI). She has experience in evaluating gender inclusion in World Bank operations, organizational gender mainstreaming at BRAC, and grassroots advocacy, project operations, stakeholder engagement, and policy advocacy at the national level. Ali has a master's of social science in economics from the University of Dhaka, and a master's of social science in development sociology from Cornell University.

Ferdous Jahan is an academic who blends teaching, research, evaluation, and practice in her work. She currently works at the University of Pennsylvania. Since 2007, she has been working with the World Bank as a consultant to provide support in project design, implementation, and evaluations in areas of social safeguards, gender, and citizens' engagement. Her projects at the Bank include education, energy, health, and transportation. She has also conducted numerous evaluations for the Asian Development Bank (ADB), UKAID, European Union, UN Systems (International Labour Organization, United Nations Development Programme, and World Food Programme), Save the Children, and CARE International. Jahan's work experience covers the regions of East Africa, South Asia, South East Asia, United Kingdom, and the United States. She has a doctorate in political science from the University of Pennsylvania.

Aphichoke (Andy) Kotikula is a Senior Economist with the Gender Group of the World Bank, where he works on research to promote more and better jobs for women, and greater gender equality in property ownership. Before that, he worked in the World Bank South Asia Region on projects and reports related to poverty reduction and gender equality in Afghanistan, Bangladesh, and Bhutan. He is the lead author of the book, *Interwoven: How the Better Work Program Improves Job and Life Quality in the Apparel Sector* (2015). He holds a doctorate and master's degree in economics from Johns Hopkins University, and a bachelor's degree in economics from Chulalongkorn University.

Tara Lonnberg is a Development Practitioner with more than 10 years of experience in social and urban development at the World Bank. Her work has focused on women's economic empowerment, gender-based violence, financial inclusion, local governance and accountability, and urban regeneration. Prior to this book, she co-authored the book, *Leveraging the Potential of Argentine Cities* and managed a pilot project in Bangladesh on women's economic empowerment and violence against women. She has undertaken operational work and conducted research in South Asia, Latin America, and East Africa. Lonnberg holds a master's degree from the London School of Economics, and a bachelor's degree from Barnard College, Columbia University.

Rohini Prabha Pande has more than 20 years of research and program experience in gender and development. Prior to this book, she co-authored a book on violence against women and girls in South Asia. Before coming to the World Bank, she worked at the International Center for Research on Women (ICRW) for over eight years, leading intervention research programs in South Asia that focused on adolescent reproductive health and empowerment. She has worked, also, with the Rockefeller and Ford foundations, CARE International, and other nongovernmental organizations in South Asia and West Africa on female education, women's income generation, and women's empowerment. Pande has a doctorate from the Johns Hopkins Bloomberg School of Public Health, and an MPA from Princeton University's Woodrow Wilson School of Public and International Affairs.

Jennifer Lynn Solotaroff is the Team Leader for this book, and a Senior Social Development Specialist with the Gender Group of the World Bank. Previously, she worked in the World Bank South Asia Region's Social Development unit on tasks related to gender and social inclusion, women's economic empowerment, and microenterprise in South Asian countries, with particular attention to Afghanistan, Bangladesh, Pakistan, and Sri Lanka. Recently, she led the South Asia Gender Innovation Lab and the South Asia Regional Gender Action Plan FY16–21. She is the lead author of the book, *Violence against Women and Girls: Lessons from South Asia* (2014) and the forthcoming *Getting to Work: Unlocking Women's Potential in Sri Lanka's Labor Force*. Her research interests include gender and labor markets, gender-based violence, and social stratification in South Asia and East Asia. Solotaroff has a doctorate in sociology and masters' degrees in economics and East Asian studies from Stanford University. She completed her bachelor's degree at Oberlin College in Ohio.

Executive Summary

Over the past decade, Bangladesh not only has maintained steady overall macroeconomic growth, but has considerably improved many of the gender gaps that have prevented this growth from being inclusive. The nation added a reduced gender gap in tertiary education enrollments to its achievement of gender parity in primary and secondary enrollments in the previous decade. The rate of child marriage (marrying before the legal age of 18) among girls declined from around 65 percent to 59 percent (as of 2014). The under-5-mortality rate ratio (the number of female deaths for every hundred male deaths among children aged zero to five years) dropped below 90, while the sex ratio at birth—which has been used as an indicator of sex discrimination—improved from 1.06 in 2001 to 1.04 in 2018, indicating minimal excess mortality of girls. Labor force participation (LFP) rates among women age 15 and above rose—from 26 percent in 2003 to 36 percent in 2016—in contrast to most other South Asian countries, where these rates fell. Additionally, the share of women in national parliament increased and remained slightly above the regional average (19.4 percent in 2016). Girls' and women's greater participation in the public spheres of school, labor markets, and political systems signals the increasing presence and power of their voices in these arenas. Does enhanced voice necessarily translate into greater choice, however? Do women and girls have a broader range of life choices—in terms of their education, their work lives, their ability to earn income and control assets, for instance—that they can pursue without concern for negative consequences meted out by family, community, and other institutions of society? Do they manage to attain the higher aspirations that spring from their augmented voice, status, and exposure to public life?

This book attempts to answer these questions by exploring different domains of women's economic empowerment, defined as succeeding and advancing economically, with "the power and agency to benefit from economic activities" (Golla et al. 2011). It focuses in particular on the decade since the release of *Whispers to Voices: Gender and Social Transformation in Bangladesh* (World Bank 2008)—a comprehensive analysis of the social, economic, and political developments in gender equality—and analyzes how women's lives have changed, specifically in the sphere of economic empowerment and related characteristics and dynamics. It examines both women's engagement (the extent to which they are represented and participate) and economic empowerment (as defined above) in four domains, namely: (1) labor force participation and other labor market outcomes, (2) women's ownership and control of household assets, (3) their use and control of financial assets, and (4) their opportunities for entrepreneurship. It gives attention to whether and what shifts have occurred since 2008 in some of the more "sticky" factors that might hamper women's economic engagement and empowerment, and which *Whispers to Voices* identified as continuing challenges for Bangladesh, such as child marriage and violence against women and girls inside and outside of the home. The book situates this analysis within an examination of the roles of these structural, normative, and other constraints and opportunities. It also places a spotlight on ethnic and religious minorities to examine the extent and characteristics of the "double" discrimination that might arise from being a woman as well as a member of an ethnic and/or religious minority. For each domain of economic empowerment, this book offers recommendations and good practice examples for further improvement in gender gaps in that domain.

This book employs mixed methods, comprising analysis of secondary quantitative data and primary qualitative data collected in 2016 and 2017 in Bangladesh. Secondary data include multiple rounds of the Bangladesh Labour Force Survey (Bangladesh Bureau of Statistics, BBS), three rounds of the World Bank's Global Financial Inclusion Data, or "Findex," one round of the Bangladesh Enterprise Survey (2013), BBS's 2012 Time Use Pilot Survey, multiple rounds of the Demographic and Health Surveys (DHS), and two rounds of the International Food Policy Research Institute's (IFPRI's) Bangladesh Integrated Household Survey in Rural Bangladesh (BIHS). Qualitative data were collected via a range of methods in a random sampling of upazilas—and from each upazila, a random sampling of a union parishad—in urban and rural communities in Dhaka, Chittagong, Sylhet, Rajshahi, and Barisal divisions.

Each domain of economic empowerment (labor force participation, asset control, financial inclusion, and entrepreneurship) is examined in a separate chapter, followed by a chapter focusing on ethnic and minority women's disadvantage across all four domains. Each chapter is organized as follows:

a. *The relevant outcomes for the pertinent domain of economic empowerment:* Each chapter starts by defining the domain of economic empowerment on which it focuses and identifying the related outcomes that will be analyzed.

b. *Descriptive data on women's economic engagement, empowerment, gender gaps, and changes over time:* Each chapter then presents descriptive findings on the extent to which women are represented or engaged in the outcomes defined for that domain; the extent to which women are economically empowered in that domain; gender gaps; and changes over time, where data are available, in all these patterns.

c. *Determinants of women's economic engagement and empowerment—enablers and barriers:* Multivariate analyses of secondary quantitative data, complemented by primary qualitative data, provide a detailed analysis of determinants of economic engagement and/or empowerment. This analysis distinguishes, where possible, between enabling factors and barriers.

d. *Recommendations supported by evaluated good practices to address barriers and close gender gaps:* Following analysis results, each chapter offers examples of evaluated, global good practices for addressing the range of gender gaps in its respective domain of economic empowerment, with some discussion of the possible roles for government, the World Bank Group (WBG), and other stakeholders in adapting and testing good practices in the Bangladeshi context.

The book's concluding chapter summarizes findings and discusses in detail the roles of government and other stakeholders in implementing recommendations and good practices from these chapters. This analysis aims to provide government, the private sector, researchers, development practitioners, the World Bank Group (through its country portfolio), and other stakeholders with guidance to collaborate on implementing recommended policy and programmatic interventions on the ground.

LABOR FORCE PARTICIPATION AND OTHER LABOR MARKET OUTCOMES

Bangladesh's female labor force participation (FLFP) rate has risen substantially—a full 10 percentage points between 2003 and 2016 (figure ES.1). Yet, women's participation still is only 44 percent that of men. Among Bangladeshi women ages 15–65, urban women, women over age 50, women living in Sylhet, those who complete a 10th grade education, and women from the wealthiest 20 percent of households are least likely to be in the labor force, with their odds of being in the labor force continuing to fall over time. Women ages 15-34 and rural women have the highest unemployment rates. Women who drop out of school after grade 10 face a double penalty: they have the lowest odds of participating in labor markets, but the highest odds of unemployment if they do participate, compared to women at all other levels of education, including those with no schooling at all.

Although married women are in Bangladesh's labor force at much greater rates than they were a decade ago, the persistence of child marriage continues to be a significant barrier. It is indeed a positive trend that married women are participating in the labor force more than in the past. Many still need permission—if not active support—from husbands or parents-in-law to work outside the home after marriage, however, according to our qualitative research.

FIGURE ES.1

Trends of labor force participation in Bangladesh, by sex and year, 2003–16

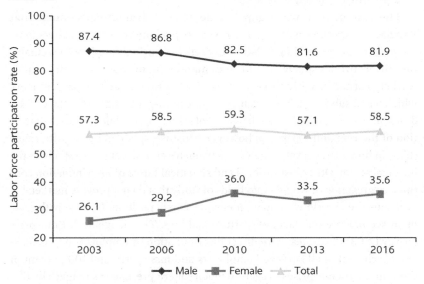

Sources: World Bank calculations based on LFS 2003, 2006, 2010, 2013, and 2016 data.

Obtaining marital family support to continue education after marriage is even more difficult and rare. This has dire implications for women's work choices: only 7 percent of women who complete their educations at grade 10—and 3 percent or less of those who leave school earlier—work in the formal sector. The earlier the age of marriage, the more a woman's education is truncated to the point where, even if she receives family support, her work choices will be limited to low-skill and low-pay jobs in workplaces with few (if any) women-friendly benefits and facilities. Lower age of marriage also implies the earlier absorption of young women into the responsibilities of housework and childcare, which are associated with a penalty for labor force participation. Although marriage of girls under age 18 dropped by six percentage points between 2004 and 2014 (the most recent year of measure-ment), it remains very high at 59 percent. This suggests that for more than half of adolescent and younger girls, their educations—and ultimately, their chances of decent and well-paying jobs—are cut short early in their lives. The fact that more than one-fourth of Bangladeshi girls are married before age 15 speaks volumes about the remaining strictures on more and better jobs for women in Bangladesh.

Women appear still to have very limited choices with regards to work options across broad sectors, although many industries have seen a decline in sex segregation. Labour Force Survey (LFS) data show that between 2003 and 2016, the share of women in industries employing balanced proportions of men and women quadrupled, while the share of women in female-dominated indus-tries decreased by more than two-thirds. Women's opportunities in industry and services—that is, outside of agriculture, where women have little chance of occu-pying positions with decision-making authority—have not increased as much as men's, however. In fact, a smaller proportion of women in 2016 work in both the industry and service sectors than in 2003. The degree of occupational sex-segregation in Bangladesh remains high, due in part to sex-based streaming into different education fields: boys gravitate toward STEM (science, technology, engi-neering, and math) fields (which build marketable skills for job markets), while girls overwhelmingly do not. Qualitative data reveal that girls who express inter-est in male-dominated fields in education and employment may be steered away from them. Sex-segregated occupational choice that is driven by gender norms appears to be more common in rural than in urban areas; urban women from the middle class, in particular, are able to choose from a broader set of occupations than are urban poor and rural women.

The raw gender wage gap has decreased dramatically—such that Bangladesh has the smallest gender wage gap of any country in the region—but gender norms and bias in labor markets increasingly explain the remain-ing differential, especially on the demand side of labor. In 2016, female workers earned roughly three-fourths of what men did (a 24-percent gap), which was a substantial improvement over the 43-percent gap of 2013. Gender differences in endowments, such as level of schooling, explain only a small frac-tion of the remaining pay gap, however. Most is explained by the difference (bias) in how markets value men's and women's endowments, especially in the informal sector. Other institutional and statistical forms of discrimination con-tinue. Segregation of women into fields of study that do not provide marketable skills, and then into lower-paying, nonmanagement positions (such as in the gar-ment sector), are one facet of institutional bias. The Bangladesh Enterprise Survey (2013) illustrates more direct discrimination by employers and manag-ers: nearly half of all surveyed employers and managers—and 100 percent of those in microenterprises—regard women's mere presence as potentially dis-ruptive to the work environment.

The fact remains that more than a third of women in Bangladesh's labor force are unpaid contributing family helpers. Further closure of gender gaps in labor markets requires practical interventions that address constraints on women's LFP and employment, while also improving working conditions for those who secure jobs in informal as well as formal enterprises. The latter creates a virtuous cycle of attracting more women into the labor force. The main categories of recommended interventions, for which details and good practice examples are given in chapter 2, include the following:

- Continue to lower rates of child marriage and address other barriers to girls' education beyond grade 10
- Improve women's technical (especially STEM) opportunities and skills to prepare them for jobs in higher-paying industries and occupations
- Address the very high rates of sexual harassment in workplaces and on transport, and improve working conditions and female-friendly benefits to draw more women into sustained private sector employment

OWNERSHIP AND CONTROL OF PRODUCTIVE ASSETS

Women own land, one of the four most valuable household assets, at much lower rates than do men in rural Bangladesh. Although qualitative findings suggest that women—both rural and urban—own more land than they did a decade ago, women still rarely own land. Among rural women, 12 percent solely or jointly own agricultural land and 7 percent own nonagricultural land, compared to 69 percent and 86 percent of rural men, respectively. Survey data also indicate that 96 percent of household land in rural areas still is owned by husbands alone (Quisumbing, Kumar, and Behrman 2017). The gender gap in land ownership is primarily attributable to male-biased practices in inheritance, the main channel through which land is acquired. The more devoutly religious a family is—among the vast majority of households, which are Muslim—the more likely it is to allow daughters to inherit their share of natal family assets, as dictated by the Quran or religious prescription, or inheritance as per respective religious laws. Focus group discussions and interviews with imams conducted for the primary qualitative research suggest, however, that it is far more common for daughters not to receive and claim their share, due to prevalent customary norms around men's role as breadwinners and household wealth owners. This holds true for non-Muslim as well as Muslim women. Household wealth is positively associated with women's inheritance; there is "more to go around," and families can afford to bypass strict gender norms.

Our qualitative research provides further insight into women's land inheritance. Rural women inherit land much less frequently (one in five rural female respondents in our qualitative research inherited) than do urban women, especially middle-class urban women. Even when women do inherit land, they face more obstacles than men in registering and legally owning their inheritance, such as high fees for registering land, for which they have to ask husbands; procedural obstacles; and limited mobility to travel to government offices. Natal families also worry about losing land if given to daughters who could register the land in names of husbands or children, which reflects the strength of clan-based, patrilineal customary practices as opposed to religious law that supports women's inheritance and ownership.

Multivariate analysis shows that agricultural land ownership is not positively associated with greater economic empowerment of women; rather, it finds a more robust relationship between women's economic activity and accumulation of assets other than agricultural land. Qualitative data help explain this finding: women's agricultural land ownership appears to be more determined by their relationships with men (fathers, brothers, husbands) than their ownership of other assets that might contribute to their economic empowerment.

Although most women may not own land and major productive assets, many exert more economic control over agricultural land and the three other valuable assets (cattle, house, and nonagricultural land) than ownership patterns suggest. Few meet the full criteria of direct ownership of land (that is, having the full range of economic rights over assets: the right to sell, mortgage, rent, and retain the revenue the asset generates), yet many possess some of these rights, though less so than do men. Among rural women whose households own any assets, 43 percent have rights to sell, give, rent or buy agricultural land (compared to 88 percent of men with household assets). Considering all four assets, 38 percent of rural women from households with any assets have full or joint ownership (compared to 96 percent of rural men), but 58 percent have economic rights (compared to 97 percent of rural men).

The only assets that women are more likely to own than are men comprise a few small, lower-value household assets—namely, poultry (chickens, ducks, and turkeys) and small consumer durables. More than two-thirds of women (70 percent) own small livestock compared to 59 percent of men. One drawback to owning small assets, however, is their higher likelihood of being sold off during economic shocks, thus making women asset-owners more economically vulnerable than men who own assets.

There is marked improvement in society's attitude toward women's asset ownership, which bodes well for women going forward. Women are claiming their inheritance at increasing rates over time, due in part to a change in attitudes. Qualitative data suggest that brothers are more supportive, compared to 10 years ago, of sisters claiming their inheritance. Married women have more of their own money thanks to rising FLFP and employment rates, and asset ownership is positively correlated with FLFP. Although still rare, women also are more likely than before to register and own land that they purchase with their own funds, as owning land through this channel is more acceptable than through inheritance.

Further closure of gender gaps in land and other household asset ownership requires policy change and practical interventions that institute legal reform for women's land inheritance, address social norms against such inheritance and registration of ownership, and improve women's land rights overall. Specific actions and examples of evaluated good practices are provided in chapter 3.

OWNERSHIP AND CONTROL OF NONLAND FINANCIAL ASSETS

Women's ownership, control, and use of financial assets all are increasing over time, but gender gaps persist. Bangladesh performs better than lower-middle-income countries as a group with regards to women's borrowing from formal financial institutions (figure ES.2). Between 2014 and 2017, however, Bangladeshi men's account ownership grew by 30 percentage points to reach 65 percent, whereas women's grew by only 10 percentage points to 36 percent. Bangladesh has lower rates of formal borrowing—by both women and men—than do comparator countries like Vietnam and Indonesia. Equally worrying, women,

FIGURE ES.2

Gender differences in borrowing from a financial institution, 2017

Source: World Bank calculations based on Findex 2017 data.

as well as men, have shifted away from borrowing and saving in a formal financial institution toward greater reliance on nonfinancial sources of savings and loans.

Women in Bangladesh appear to have less diversity—in other words, fewer choices—than men in *where* they save and borrow money, and in *which types* of financial products they typically use. In rural areas, for instance, nearly three-quarters of women borrow from or save with NGOs. Rural men's sources of savings and borrowing are much more diverse, and are spread almost equally among formal and several informal sources of lending and savings, such as friends, store credit, leasing land or informal lenders. Most women financial clients use credit, typically provided by MFIs through group loans that do not require traditional forms of collateral (which women lack due to their low ownership rates of high-value household assets). The next most commonly used product is savings, which is increasing among women due to mobilization by MFIs, though not as much as for men. Less common is insurance: women traditionally have been excluded from insurance markets, although MFIs have started offering life and health insurance to their female savers and borrowers (although use rates among the poorest women are extremely low).

Loans to women continue to be of lower value and shorter duration, and have stricter terms, than loans to men, despite financial institutions' incipient efforts to become more flexible toward female clients. Historically, the narrow terms of women's credit are related—in part—to their lack of collateral and low financial literacy, as well as to gender norms that deem men more responsible and better suited than women to controlling finances. As women have become more educated, exposed to work environments, engaged in household decisions, and confident, MFIs are increasingly unable to meet women's demand for loans.

The evidence on whether microcredit economically empowers women in Bangladesh is mixed. Loans are more likely to economically empower women if they are larger and of longer duration than the typical microloan. In contrast, microloans to women often end up under the control of husbands or other male household members, reinforcing women's minimal decision-making power in the household. In these cases, when loans are used for productive purposes (i.e., to start, operate, or expand a farm or business), they increase the capital of existing household business rather than promote women's entrepreneurship.

Few women are the sole decision makers on household financial issues (12–16 percent) or their own use of financial services (14 percent). Their spouses continue to make the majority of these decisions, and joint decision making is the next most common. Even parents or guardians have greater decision-making power than women alone over household assets and financial services. There is evidence that for rural women, however, sole decision making is slightly increasing over time (accompanied by a decrease in joint decision making), though men's rates of sole decision making are increasing even more. The 2015 BIHS finds that 70 percent or less of rural women control income spent on their own needs (for their own medicines, clothes, toiletries, and food), up from 50 percent or less in 2011–12.

Constraints on women's access to and control over finances emanate from inside and outside the family. Familial constraints on women's mobility—and other patriarchal norms that frown on women's control of finances or that generate household demands and leave women little time to seek finance—are key household and social barriers. Limited geographical coverage of financial institutions, especially in rural areas; minimum account balances and charge fees in banks (and high interest fees in MFIs); onerous paperwork and documentary requirements; and collateral requirements all are more likely to derail women's than men's efforts to access or use financial services such as bank accounts. Mobile banking and other digital technologies for accessing financial institutions have the potential to greatly ease many of these constraints on women; however, women comprise a minority of users of mobile or digital banking.

Chapter 4 discusses the following recommendations supported by evaluated good practices to close gender gaps in ownership and control of financial assets:

- Tackle patriarchal norms that undermine women's ability to use and control financial services
- Expand the types and flexibility of financial services available for women
- Improve the ease of documentation and other procedural barriers
- Raise women's rates of financial literacy
- Address high financial and transaction costs, and increase flexibility, by addressing multiple constraints simultaneously
- Address women's low use of mobile and digital technologies for finance

ENTREPRENEURSHIP

In spite of the government of Bangladesh's and Bangladesh Bank's laudable efforts to promote women entrepreneurs, Bangladesh has among the world's smallest shares of female-majority ownership of formal enterprises—a mere 1.7 percent, compared to the South Asian and global averages of 9.6 percent and 14.5 percent, respectively. When considering formal and informal firms together, women's ownership rate is higher and increasing over time, from more than 7 percent in 2013 to 10 percent in 2017. The relegation of women entrepreneurs primarily to the informal sector is due, in part, to barriers women face in registering enterprises (which is required for enterprises to be in the formal sector). In 2015, Bangladesh ranked 75 out of 77 countries in providing an environment that encourages development and growth of women-owned firms. This is despite tremendous growth in both the number of women's enterprises since the 1970s, and the rates of women's graduation from owning small-to-medium and medium-to-large enterprises. Not only do women comprise only one-tenth of all business owners; their firms are smaller, have lower survival rates, and are concentrated in fewer sectors (primarily wholesale and retail trade of textiles) than firms owned by male entrepreneurs. Although women entrepreneurs' access to credit has risen over time, the total value of credit disbursed to them annually from 2010 to 2017, was only 3 percent of the value disbursed to men entrepreneurs.

Differences between female and male entrepreneurs' demand for credit and aspirations to expand businesses *do not* explain this gender gap in disbursement amounts. Women business owners aspire to have larger-value loans and to expand their businesses more quickly than their circumstances allow. The heavy time burden of household responsibilities, lack of education and financial literacy, and onerous procedural requirements all hamper female entrepreneurs' aspirations more than they hamper men's.

In addition to these barriers, many other obstacles to women's use and control of finance hinder women's entrepreneurship. Aspiring entrepreneurs face patriarchal norms that constrain women's mobility; hinder access to markets, networks, and financial institutions; underlie family and community disapproval of women being entrepreneurs; and constrain opportunities beyond fulfilling family roles of wife and mother. These norms keep even women who manage to start businesses closely tied to the household, with enterprises often confined to home-based and informal activities associated with low value and low returns.

Improving rates of female entrepreneurship, as well as growth and survival rates of women-owned firms, will require expanding the range of choices available to women who aspire to create and grow businesses. As detailed in chapter 5, improving women's rates of starting and sustaining enterprises will require interventions that fall under the main recommendation areas listed below.

- Enforce policies and schemes that support women entrepreneurs and customize interventions
- Maximize success of business development training with complementary training that is of sufficient duration and is appropriately timed to accommodate women's schedules
- Address constraints arising from patriarchal norms that are binding for entrepreneurs
- Ensure that credit meets the demand of women entrepreneurs
- Address women entrepreneurs' poor access to networks and markets
- Reach more women by providing a women-friendly financial environment

ECONOMIC VULNERABILITIES OF MINORITY WOMEN

The economic vulnerabilities of ethnic and religious minority women are affected not just by the factors—social and institutional—that influence women's economic engagement overall, but also by the marginalization of minorities as a whole. These minority groups (as detailed in chapter 6) in Bangladesh are largely at the fringes of society, still struggling to achieve greater voice: the very existence of some of these groups remains unrecognized by the state, and the size of identified minority groups is believed to be significantly undercounted. For all ethnic minorities, these and other modes of social exclusion impede their agency in all domains of their lives. For ethnic minorities in the Chittagong Hill Tracts (CHT) region, geographical remoteness creates an additional barrier. Nonetheless, the government and development partners are attempting to address some of this exclusion, for instance by their initiative of introducing primary education using five indigenous languages. This and other policy interventions may open possibilities to introduce more inclusionary practices in the future.

The scant available data suggest that ethnic minority women are doubly marginalized in select domains. The dearth of gender-disaggregated economic data on ethnic and religious minorities—itself a sign of their marginalization from labor and other markets in Bangladesh—makes analysis of women's economic empowerment in these groups exceedingly difficult. Still, available data show that ethnic minority women have lower literacy rates compared to women in the total population and compared to ethnic minority men, although the gender gap in minority literacy rates is narrowing over time. Given ethnic minorities' low rates of land and other household asset ownership, financial access, and entrepreneurship, minority women's levels of ownership and control in these areas likely are lower than those for majority women. Our qualitative data indicate that minority women who come into any property—inheriting or even buying it with their own funds—hand it over to husbands to register in men's names and keep in the male line. Minority women have very limited control over household finances. In rural areas, average monthly wages for minority groups are one-fifth of those for the total rural population, and gender wage gaps favoring men are wider than among the total rural population. The large majority of ethnic minorities—especially minority women—work in the informal sector. Unlike other women who participated in the qualitative research, minority women did not express a sense of their economic empowerment improving over time.

Minority women in rural areas have higher rates of LFP—and in some cases, of educational attainment—than women in other groups. As discussed in chapter 6, existing data show higher LFP rates among ethnic minority households (men and women) than among nonminority households. Poverty may partly explain this pattern, as it does among some religious minority groups. Data from the Labour Force Survey reveal a considerable difference between the poorest and wealthiest women from the Buddhist and Christian minority groups, whose LFP rates roughly double as income falls (see table 6.2). No such pattern is discernible for Muslim or Hindu women, however. Ethnic minority women thus appear to be more responsive to economic factors than women from the ethnic majority, suggesting that the former may be less hampered by social restrictions on women's mobility and their confinement to family roles. Our primary qualitative research finds that the studied minority women may have greater flexibility and independence to work outside the household, compared to urban and rural women in majority groups, even after marriage and childbirth. Poverty also does not explain the higher relative education levels of women in some minority religious groups compared to majority women.

The dearth of documented interventions for minorities, coupled with the lack of relevant data, make it difficult to design policies and programs that would help enable minorities' advancement and economic empowerment. Still, chapter 6 uses the available evidence to discuss policy and practice recommendations to close gender gaps for minority women's economic engagement across domains in the following areas:

- Use more inclusive approaches to data collection to improve understanding of all ethnic minorities residing throughout Bangladesh
- Strengthen the national framework to address minority issues
- Develop a set of policies to protect and empower minorities
- Remove barriers to minority education and asset accumulation, with special attention to minority girls and women

SUMMARY OF MAIN FINDINGS

The main findings, facilitating factors, barriers, and recommendations from each chapter are presented in table ES.1 and discussed in detail in chapters 2 through 5.

TABLE ES.1 Select gender gaps, determinants, and recommendations for improvement, by domain of economic empowerment in Bangladesh

GENDER-GAP DOMAIN	MAIN FINDINGS	FACILITATING FACTORS	BARRIERS	GOOD PRACTICES AND OTHER RECOMMENDATIONS
Gender gaps in all domains			• Lack of money to save • Women's limited control of finance • Limited mobility of women	
Labor Force Participation (LFP)	FLFP increased over time, but remains low, while gender gap persists	• Tertiary schooling • Marriage[a] • Elderly in household • Professional networks	• Children under age 5 • Women's chore burden • Educational subject sex segregation • Occupational sex segregation • Employer discrimination • Lack of female-friendly benefits and facilities • Sexual harassment at work	• Childcare services • Girls' tech education • Women's acquisition of market-driven tech skills • Safe, affordable transport, informed by the Hazme el Paro example from Mexico City • Workplace women's facilities • Zero-tolerance harassment policy
Wages	Gender wage gaps narrowed	• Rising female education • Women's shift from agriculture to manufacturing • Rural-urban migration	• Unpaid family work • Gender-biased employers & markets	• Awareness of private sector employment options • Women's acquisition of marketable skills
Land ownership[a]	Inheritance is main route to own land and heavily favors men	• Familial adherence to Muslim Personal Law • Family wealth • Higher age of women • Women's natal assets as bargaining power	• Exogamy • Land registration • Low awareness of legal right to own, register land • Large household size	• Amend law with "cooling-off period"[c] • Land grants to landless[c] • Engaging community and religious leaders • Discounted registration fees
Economic rights over land	Persistent gender gap, with some rights for women	• Higher age of women	• Rights derived from men • Gender-biased marital property regime	• Awareness campaigns[c]
Nonagricultural land and smaller asset ownership	Minimal gender gap	• Labor force participation • Access to finance • Assets brought by brides • Higher education of HH head	• Small assets often spent to absorb economic shocks • Larger HH size	• Change attitudes about women's asset ownership[c]
Accounts in financial institutions	Gender gap has increased over time and is bigger than LMIC average	• Women's work • Women's inheritance • Mobile banking • Lowering transaction costs	• Lack of trust in banks • Cumbersome procedures • Women's limited mobility • Lack of documentation • Limited geographic access	• Engage men to help women's mobility and control of finance[c] • Women-only "commitment" savings accounts[c] • TV dramas and theater for awareness and behavior change[c] • Women-staffed banks[c]
Loans and savings in formal financial institutions	Decreased for all, but gender gap persists	• Land ownership (for loans) • Expansion of mobile/digital financial services • Offering liquid no-fee savings accounts	• Lack of collateral (loans) • High fees • Complex bank procedures • Bank discrimination • Lack of documentation • Poor geo/transport access • Unfair loan conditions • Women's low financial literacy • Men control wives' loans	• Increase women's use of mobile tech for finance[c] • Secure national ID system[c] • Agent banking[c] • Alternate testing for credit worthiness[c]

continued

TABLE ES.1, *continued*

GENDER GAP DOMAIN	MAIN FINDINGS	FACILITATING FACTORS	BARRIERS	GOOD PRACTICES AND OTHER RECOMMENDATIONS
Credit access/ use through MFIs	Women have greater access, but smaller loan size than men	• Increased income • Joining MF full program • Participation in networks • Women control use of funds • Women's economic mobility • Increased credit flexibility • More collateral-free credit	• Inability to meet initial payment • Difficulty in "graduating" to higher loan amounts • "Overlapping" loans • Indebtedness • Men control wives' loans	• Successful financial literacy programs[c] • Collateral-free, flexible credit through group lending[c] • Flexible loan sizes and repayment schedules
Enterprise ownership, growth and management[b]	• Large gender gaps • Women's enterprises concentrated in "female dominated" sectors	• Increased access to finance • Loans at below-market interest rates • Improved access to markets • Professional networks • Female education in nontraditional and technical fields	• Difficult loan application processes, paperwork • Women's lack of business development training • Inadequate credit • Lack of role models, mentors • Household care roles • Limited market access • Sexual harassment • Occupational segregation • Poor implementation of existing government schemes	• Offer childcare • Safe transport • Intensive business development training[c] • Networking opportunities[c] • Microfranchising for very poor women entrepreneurs

Notes: FLFP = female labor force participation; HH = household; LMIC = lower middle income country; MFI = microfinance institution; LFP = labor force participation.
a. For rural areas only.
b. All facilitators, barriers, recommendations and good practices summarized for all financial inclusion domains are also relevant to gender gaps in entrepreneurship. This row includes additional information that is specific only to women borrowers or savers who are also entrepreneurs.
c. Evaluated good practice.

ACTIONS TO INCREASE WOMEN'S ECONOMIC EMPOWERMENT IN BANGLADESH

There are multiple examples of good practices by government, civil society organizations, and the private sector, from Bangladesh and other countries, which could be tested, adapted, and implemented for Bangladeshi women. These are summarized in table ES.2 below and in table 7.1 of chapter 7, and analyzed in detail in chapter 7, with special attention to the role of government and other stakeholders in taking action. Table ES.2 first presents priority actions for all stakeholders, with the most urgent listed first, and then summarizes interventions that each type of stakeholder can take in closing select gender gaps in economic empowerment. "Low-hanging fruit"—that is, priority interventions that can be implemented within the next 1–2 years to see near- and medium-term results—are identified by an asterisk (*). In the arena of improving FLFP, interventions fall into two broad buckets: efforts to remove constraints on women's meaningful employment, and programs to improve workplace conditions for working women—particularly in the informal sector, which employs the lion's share of these women. Efforts to improve women's ability to own and control their rightful share of inherited and other land include legal reform and attention to proper enforcement; addressing social norms that prevent women from claiming their inheritance; and a range of other interventions. Organizations seeking to increase women's financial inclusion have tested interventions to expand the type and flexibility of financial services for women; address procedural barriers to accessing formal finance; and reach more women with a

(text continued on p. xxx)

TABLE ES.2 Stakeholder roles in reducing gender gaps in Bangladesh, by area/outcome of economic empowerment

GENDER GAP	KEY RECOMMENDATIONS	ACTIONS AND ROLES FOR SPECIFIC STAKEHOLDERS (BASED ON EVIDENCE FROM BANGLADESHI AND GLOBAL GOOD PRACTICES)		
		GOVERNMENT OF BANGLADESH	PRIVATE SECTOR	OTHER STAKEHOLDERS
Priority actions for all stakeholders to adopt in addressing gender gaps in all domains of economic engagement and empowerment				

1. Launch multimedia awareness campaigns about benefits of women's economic participation and costs of women's low economic empowerment
2. Lower procedural costs of women's ownership of land, formal financial accounts, and enterprises
3. Collect gender-disaggregated data that can be compared over time and covers all aspects of economic engagement and empowerment
4. Address sexual harassment and other safety concerns in workplaces, public spaces, and transportation
5. Provide childcare through public-private partnerships (PPPs) and private sector firms
6. Address social norms that underlie and perpetuate gender gaps in economic opportunity and control

GENDER GAP	KEY RECOMMENDATIONS	GOVERNMENT OF BANGLADESH	PRIVATE SECTOR	OTHER STAKEHOLDERS
Key gender gaps in labor market outcomes • Female labor force participation • Gender wage gap	1. Address barriers to girls' education beyond 10th grade 2. Improve women's access to technical education and other marketable skills* 3. Improve women's working conditions* 4. Provide female-friendly benefits like childcare* 5. Address gender norms to expand choices beyond traditional household roles 6. Further lower rates of child marriage	• Better enforce existing supportive laws • Review and improve policy and practice on quotas for women's employment in public sector* • Scale up tested education-related conditional cash transfers aimed at keeping girls and minorities in school beyond grade 10, and encouraging their acquisition of STEM skills* • Scale up CCTs and other established methods to further raise age at marriage • Better align TVET and other curricula to skills demanded by the market • Explore PPP options for childcare* • Consider extending school day to minimize need for childcare[b] • Improve gender-disaggregated economic data collection*	• Pilot employer-provided childcare good practices* • Proactively partner with Ministry of Labor and Employment, Ministry of Education, Ministry of Primary Education, and TVET providers to ensure their training curricula are imparting high-level technical skills that private sector employers are seeking, following enactment of the National Skills Development Act*	**NGOs** • Increase awareness of barriers to women's labor force participation and equal wages* • Engage men and community leaders in efforts to change gender norms around women in the workplace • Increase awareness of and experiment with programs to increase age at marriage **WB operations** • Transforming Secondary Education for Results* • Safety Net Systems for the Poorest (AF)* • Bangladesh Jobs Programmatic DPC*
		• Provide safe, accessible and affordable transportation for women between home and workplace (* for private sector only)		**WB operations** • Dhaka Public Transport Improvement Project
		• Address risks of sexual harassment and other gender-based violence in the workplace and provide redressal mechanisms		
		• Provide clean, functional, and separate sanitation facilities for women and men		
		• Share costs through PPPs to provide high-quality, affordable, accessible childcare either in addition to or as alternatives to private childcare		
				WB operations • Dhaka City Neighborhood Upgrading Project*

* Indicates a "quick win"; that is, an intervention to undertake in the next 1–2 years to yield near- and medium-term results.

continued

TABLE ES.2, *continued*

GENDER GAP	KEY RECOMMENDATIONS	ACTIONS AND ROLES FOR SPECIFIC STAKEHOLDERS (BASED ON EVIDENCE FROM BANGLADESHI AND GLOBAL GOOD PRACTICES)		
		GOVERNMENT OF BANGLADESH	PRIVATE SECTOR	OTHER STAKEHOLDERS
				• Dhaka Sanitation Improvement Project • Bangladesh Municipal Water Supply and Sanitation Project*
Gender gaps in ownership and control of household assets • Land ownership • Economic rights over land • Nonagricultural land and smaller household assets	1. Institute legal reform for women's inheritance of land 2. Address social norms against women's land ownership and registration	• Bring women's land inheritance and ownership rights into national dialogue about development • Offer discounted land registration fees for women[b] • Streamline property registration procedures* • Establish legal protection of marital property • Promote joint titling of land and property • Institute automatic mechanisms that register inheritance in daughters' names • Amend law with "cooling-off period" after division of land as per laws[a] • Land grants to landless[b]		**Legal aid associations** • Provide legal (including pro bono) services for women to use their inheritance rights • Provide dispute-resolution training* **Other NGOs** • Work with women advocates, including locally elected women, to raise issues of women's land rights **WB operations** • Integrated Digital Government Project • Livestock and Dairy Development Project* • Bangladesh Sustainable Coastal and Marine Fisheries* • Sustainable Forests and Livelihood Project*
		• Engage community and religious leaders in addressing social norms against women's asset ownership and inheritance by daughters per Muslim Personal Law		
Gender gaps in financial inclusion • Accounts in financial institutions • Loans & savings in formal financial institutions • Use and control of credit	1. Tackle patriarchal norms that undermine women's ability to use and control financial services 2. Expand the types and flexibility of financial services available for women* 3. Improve the ease of documentation and other procedural barriers 4. Raise women's rates of financial literacy	• Provide financial products (accounts, savings, loans, credit, wages, etc.) solely in women's names to enable women's control[b]* • Address the inflexibility of financial services that lead to high monetary and transaction costs for women • Experiment with alternate forms of evaluating creditworthiness since women often do not own land or other assets necessary for traditional credit rating[b] • Invest in secure national biometric identification to reduce the burden of documentation-related barriers • Train bank staff in how to work with women clients and engage more women bank staff to create women-friendly environments in financial institutions[b]* • Experiment with tested methods, such as agent banking, to increase access to banking and other financial services*		**Media** • Use television and other popular media to spread awareness of financial products and services, for example, through TV drama and theater[b]* **MFIs** • Provide collateral-free credit with more flexible repayment options[b]* • Bundle programs for skills training and market diversification along with microcredit **WB operations** • Cash Transfer Modernization Project • Integrated Digital Government Project

* Indicates a "quick win"; that is, an intervention to undertake in the next 1–2 years to yield near- and medium-term results.

continued

TABLE ES.2, *continued*

GENDER GAP	KEY RECOMMENDATIONS	ACTIONS AND ROLES FOR SPECIFIC STAKEHOLDERS (BASED ON EVIDENCE FROM BANGLADESHI AND GLOBAL GOOD PRACTICES)		
		GOVERNMENT OF BANGLADESH	PRIVATE SECTOR	OTHER STAKEHOLDERS
	5. Address high financial and transaction costs, and increase flexibility, by addressing multiple constraints simultaneously 6. Address women's low use of mobile and digital technologies for finance	• Engage with men and other community leaders to address patriarchal constraints, such as mobility and women's control of finance • Collaborate to create multifaceted programs to address financial illiteracy that combine financial education with financial services and community awareness-raising • Government, private sector and MFIs can collaborate to systematically increase women's use of mobile and digital technologies informed by good practices in other countries and in Bangladesh[b]		
Gender gaps in entrepreneurship • Enterprise ownership, growth and management	1. Enforce policies and schemes that support women entrepreneurs, customize interventions 2. Maximize success of business development training with complementary training, timing 3. Address constraints arising from patriarchal norms that are binding for entrepreneurs 4. Ensure that credit meets the demand of women entrepreneurs 5. Address women entrepreneurs' poor access to networks and markets 6. Reach more women by providing a women-friendly financial environment		• Provide high-quality training in business practices, such as formal accounting practices, registration practices, and managerial skills[b] • Business development training has to be intensive and of long duration to be effective[b] • Provide microfranchising opportunities (with NGOs)[b*]	**WB operations** • Sustainable Enterprise Project • Livestock and Dairy Development Project* • Bangladesh Sustainable Coastal and Marine Fisheries* • Sustainable Forests and Livelihood Project*
		• Address risks of sexual harassment and other forms of gender-based violence and provide redressal mechanisms • Provide credit that aligns with women entrepreneurs' needs, that is: flexible credit which accommodates women's lack of credit history and is bundled with other financial services to improve business performance and earnings[b*] • All other actions by the governmental and private financial sectors to improve financial inclusion would also improve women's entrepreneurship opportunities and growth		
		• There is no one-size-fits all approach. • Design interventions keeping in mind participating women's skills, constraints, motivations for entrepreneurship and other characteristics • Experiment with and evaluate a range of childcare provision interventions and scale up successful efforts • Combine microcredit with other services, such as skills training and market diversification • Create, encourage and increase awareness of women's professional networks[b] • Provide high-quality, affordable, accessible childcare either in addition to or as alternatives to private childcare		

* Indicates a "quick win"; that is, an intervention to undertake in the next 1–2 years to yield near- and medium-term results.

continued

TABLE ES.2, *continued*

GENDER GAP	KEY RECOMMENDATIONS	ACTIONS AND ROLES FOR SPECIFIC STAKEHOLDERS (BASED ON EVIDENCE FROM BANGLADESHI AND GLOBAL GOOD PRACTICES)		
		GOVERNMENT OF BANGLADESH	PRIVATE SECTOR	OTHER STAKEHOLDERS
Exclusion of minority ethnic women • Labor market outcomes • Land and household assets • Financial inclusion • Entrepreneurship	1. Improve understanding of all ethnic minorities residing throughout Bangladesh* 2. Strengthen the national framework to address minority issues 3. Remove barriers to minority education and asset accumulation	• Address lack of official recognition of several minority groups • Regularize ethnic minorities' customary land titles and/or provide alternative nationally recognized property rights • Disaggregate all national data by ethnicity* • Consider affirmative action and incentive programs, such as CCTs (e.g., for education) • Create programs to specifically expand employment opportunities for minority women • Collaborate to better orient minorities' job and skills to specific, local labor market needs		**WB operations** • Safety Net Systems for the Poorest (AF)* • Transforming Secondary Education for Results Operation*

Notes: CCT = conditional cash transfer; TVET = Technical and Vocational Education and Training; NGO = nongovernmental organization; MFI = microfinance institution; STEM = science, technology, engineering, and mathematics.
a. For rural areas only.
b. Evaluated good practice.
* Indicates a "quick win"; that is, an intervention to undertake in the next 1–2 years to yield near- and medium-term results.

women-friendly environment in financial institutions, to name a few. Across the board, however, rigorous evaluations are rare and urgently needed. Still, formal and informal assessments suggest that political will (by governments and the private sector) and engagement of women and their communities are essential elements in the success of any endeavor to improve women's economic empowerment.

REFERENCES

Golla, Anne Marie, Anju Malhotra, Priya Nanda, and Rekha Mehra. 2011. *Understanding and Measuring Women's Economic Empowerment: Definition, Framework and Indicators.* Washington, DC: International Center for Research on Women.

Quisumbing, Agnes R., Neha Kumar, and Julia A. Behrman. 2018. "Do Shocks Affect Men's and Women's Assets Differently? Evidence from Bangladesh and Uganda." *Development Policy Review.* 36:3–34. https://onlinelibrary.wiley.com/doi/epdf/10.1111/dpr.12235.

World Bank. 2008. *Whispers to Voices: Gender and Social Transformation in Bangladesh.* Bangladesh Development Series 22. Dhaka: World Bank.

Abbreviations

ASA	Association for Social Advancement
ATM	automated teller machine
BBS	Bangladesh Bureau of Statistics
BDT	Bangladeshi Taka
BIDS	Bangladesh Institute of Development Studies
BIHS	Bangladesh Integrated Household Survey
BISP	Benazir Income Support Programme
BRAC	Bangladesh Rural Advancement Committee
CDI	composite deprivation index
CFPR-TUP	BRAC's Challenging the Frontiers of Poverty Reduction—Targeting the Ultra Poor Program
CGAB	country gender action brief
CHT	Chittagong Hill Tracts
CNIC	Computerized National Identity Card
CPF	Country Partnership Framework
CS	case study
DCI	direct calorie intake
DHS	demographic and health surveys
EDGE	Evidence and Data for Gender Equality initiative (United Nations)
EPB	Export Promotion Bureau
EPR	employment-to-population ratio
EPZ	export processing zones
FAO	Food and Agriculture Organization
FGD	focus group discussion
FLFP	female labor force participation
FLFPR	female labor force participation rate
GDP	gross domestic product
GoB	government of Bangladesh
GPI	gender parity index
GQAL	Gender Quality Action Learning (BRAC)
GSN	gender and social norms
HIES	Household Income and Expenditure Survey
HSC	higher secondary school

IFC	International Finance Corporation
IFPRI	International Food Policy Research Institute
IPV	intimate partner violence
IT	information technology
KII	key informant interview
LFP	labor force participation
LFS	Labour Force Survey
LFPR	labor force participation rate
LMIC	lower-middle-income country
LTR	land tenure regularization
LUC	land use certificate
MDGs	Millennium Development Goals
MFI	microfinance institution
MIC	middle-income country
MLFP	male labor force participation
NBFI	nonbank financial institution
NGO	nongovernmental organization
NGO-MFI	nongovernmental microfinance institution
OECD	Organisation for Economic Co-operation and Development
OIZ	organized industrial zone
PKSF	Palli Karma-Sahayak Foundation
RMG	readymade garments
ROSCA	rotating savings and credit associations
SCD	Systematic Country Diagnostic
SDG	sustainable development goal
SES	socioeconomic status
SEWA	Self Employed Women's Association
SEZ	special economic zones
SMEs	small and medium enterprises
SSC	secondary school certificate
STEM	science, technology, engineering, and math
TFR	total fertility rate
TIN	tax identification number
TMSS	Thengamara Mohila Sabuj Sangha
TVET	technical and vocational education and training
UP	Union Parishad
VAT	value-added tax
WASH	water, sanitation, and hygiene
WBG	World Bank Group
WEE	women's economic empowerment

1 Introduction

Bangladesh has made remarkable strides in enhancing women's voices, choices, and lives in many domains. There has been notably less progress on closing gender gaps in several economic outcomes, however. These include labor force participation (LFP), meaningful employment, and ownership and control over physical and financial assets. Women's engagement in, and empowerment from, these economic outcomes are critical for continued prosperity and inclusive growth in Bangladesh. The World Bank Group (WBG) also considers such economic engagement and empowerment of women essential, and it is key to the Bangladesh Country Partnership Framework (CPF) (World Bank 2016a), the Bank's South Asia Regional Gender Action Plan for FY16–21 (World Bank 2016c), and the Bangladesh Country Gender Action Brief, which is required by the RGAP. This book seeks to contribute to these and other discussions among researchers, policy makers, NGOs, and civil society organizations in Bangladesh that seek to improve women's economic empowerment, and ultimately to directly influence relevant policy and programming in the country.

RATIONALE

Ten years ago, the World Bank released *Whispers to Voices: Gender and Social Transformation in Bangladesh,* a comprehensive analysis of the social, economic, and political developments in gender equality and women's empowerment in Bangladesh over the previous decade (World Bank 2008). This book focuses on the decade since *Whispers to Voices,* analyzing how women's lives have changed in terms of economic empowerment and including factors that facilitate or hinder such empowerment.

According to *Whispers to Voices,* Bangladesh had achieved enormous progress in enhancing women's voice and status, well beyond what might have been expected given the country's level of economic development. In part, this success has been attributed to government policy and program interventions in the realms of female education, contraception and fertility control, and basic health care. The microcredit "revolution" also has undoubtedly played an important role, as has the women's movement and other civil society. Yet, as *Whispers to Voices* notes, many challenges remain. Among these are persistent gender gaps in economic empowerment, characterized by low rates of women's employment and labor force participation (LFP), continued gendered segmentation of the labor market with women typically relegated to lower-skilled and lower-paying occupations, wage and hiring discrimination against women, and women's exclusion from ownership of property and other natal and marital household assets.

This book extends the analysis from *Whispers to Voices* by examining in-depth the changes over the last decade in all the above-mentioned aspects of women's economic empowerment, as well as in associated characteristics and dynamics. We choose this focus for several reasons. Increasing women's economic engagement is critical to poverty reduction. In addition to generating income and wealth, women's ability to monetarily contribute to their household likely augments the well-being of all family members, especially children. Finally, and at least as importantly, it also improves women's opportunities, choices, and engagement with society, in the process enhancing also their own sense of well-being and empowerment in other domains of their lives. We pay attention to whether and what shifts have occurred since 2008 in some of the more "sticky" factors that might hamper women's economic empowerment, and that *Whispers to Voices* identified as continuing challenges for Bangladesh, such as child marriage and violence against women and girls inside and outside of the home. Finally, we add a spotlight on ethnic and religious minorities to examine the extent and characteristics of the "double" discrimination that might arise from being a woman as well as a member of an ethnic and/or religious minority. Although the country certainly has other important minority groups to consider—such as the physically and mentally disabled populations, as well as lesbian, gay, bisexual, trans, and queer (LGBTQ) individuals—the lack of economic data on these groups unfortunately makes related analysis extremely difficult and thus beyond the scope of this book.

MAIN OBJECTIVES

The central questions guiding this study are the following:

1. What are key shifts over the last 10 years in different aspects of urban and rural Bangladeshi women's economic engagement and empowerment, including LFP and employment, ownership and control of land and other household assets, use and control of financial assets, and entrepreneurship?

2. What are key barriers and facilitating factors influencing women's economic empowerment in Bangladesh?

To help address identified barriers and bolster facilitators, the book analyzes good practice examples to make recommendations tailored to specific stakeholder groups in Bangladesh. This book aims to add knowledge to ongoing efforts to reduce these gaps in Bangladesh and in South Asia more broadly. From a policy and programmatic perspective, findings are intended for practical use by the many governmental, multilateral, donor, and civil society organizations in Bangladesh engaged in addressing barriers to women's employment and other aspects of economic empowerment. Findings also are intended to directly inform the design, implementation, and evaluation of relevant upcoming and future WBG-supported operations in Bangladesh, as well as additional programs supported by the government of Bangladesh (GoB) and other in-country stakeholders.

OVERVIEW OF THE COUNTRY AND THE MACROECONOMIC CONTEXT

Bangladesh has seen marked economic development since the 1990s, performing well on the Millennium Development Goal (MDG) of halving the incidence of extreme poverty between 1990 and 2015. In fact, Bangladesh is one of the few developing countries to experience a continuous decline in poverty since 2000. Data from the 2010 Household Income and Expenditure Survey (HIES) show that the pace of poverty reduction accelerated during 2000–10 compared to 1990–2000 (Government of Bangladesh 2015). Overlapping with this progress, the rate of women's participation in the labor force rose from 26 to 36 percent between 2003 and 2016, for women age 15 and above.

Bangladesh also has shown great progress in reducing gender gaps in certain human development indicators. Life expectancy at birth is higher for women (72.9) than for men (70.4) and higher than the average for South Asian women (69.9) (UNDP 2015). Bangladesh has had the highest Gender Parity Index (GPI) in South Asia since 1998.[1] The total fertility rate dropped from 3.6 to 2.1 per woman between 1996 and 2015,[2] while estimated contraceptive rates rose from 50.1 percent in 1997 to 63.4 percent in 2016.[3] Campaigns for sanitation, clean drinking water, immunization and oral rehydration therapy have dramatically reduced child morbidity and mortality relative to other South Asian countries. Bangladesh's maternal mortality rate—while still higher than acceptable (176 per 100,000 live births in 2015)—is lower than the regional average (182 per 100,000 in 2015).[4] Bangladesh's share of women-held seats in national parliament also tends to be higher than the regional average share. For more gender-relevant statistical information, please see appendix A.

Despite achieving MDG Target 1 to halve poverty between 1990 and 2015 (Bangladesh Planning Commission 2016), Bangladesh remains one of the poorer countries in the world. This strongly suggests the need to rethink the next stage of transformation in terms of women's roles in the economy; policy makers, researchers, and practitioners across sectors will need to consider carefully how to create more and better jobs for women—particularly disadvantaged women—and how to harness women's economic engagement to grow the Bangladeshi economy (box 1.1) and maintain progress in poverty reduction and inclusive development.

The GoB explicitly recognizes in its Seventh Five Year Plan (FY2016–FY2020) the importance of employment generation to grow the economy, and also a "…broad-based strategy of inclusiveness with a view to empowering every citizen to participate full and benefit from the

BOX 1.1

Female labor force participation and growth

A vast theoretical and empirical literature has confirmed the contribution of gender equality to economic growth. Gender parity in education and the labor market increase growth through better allocative efficiency (Aguirre et al. 2012; Cuberes and Teigner 2014; Dollar and Gatti 1999; Klasen 1999). An IMF paper presents evidence of macroeconomic gains from higher levels of women's involvement in labor markets. Cuberes and Teignier (2012) estimate that GDP per capita losses attributable to gender gaps in the labor market could be up to 27 percent in certain regions. Aguirre et al. (2012) suggest that raising the female labor force participation rate to country-specific male levels would raise GDP in, for instance, the United States by 5 percent, Japan by 9 percent, the United Arab Emirates by 12 percent, and the Arab Republic of Egypt by 34 percent.

Source: Elborgh-Woytek et al. 2013.

development process..." that includes efforts to foster meaningful employment for women (Government of the People's Republic of Bangladesh 2015, xxxvi). The Plan singles out low female labor force participation (FLFP) and continuing wage discrimination against women as policy issues that remain to be resolved. It also follows several prior schemes and policies that recognize and seek to further women's economic participation more broadly.

In its support to GoB, the World Bank Group (WBG) explicitly recognizes both the importance of women's role in the economy, as well as Bangladesh's progress toward enhancing FLFP and other aspects of women's economic empowerment. Its 2015 Bangladesh Systematic Country Diagnostic (SCD) notes that between 2002–03 and 2013, half of the net increase in employment was due to increases in women's employment (World Bank 2015a). Further, the gender gap in wages has decreased. The SCD also notes, however, that women continue to be under-represented in nonagricultural industry and services sectors; women still earn less than men; the gender gap in LFP remains large; and women entrepreneurs still face greater hurdles than do men in accessing appropriate and timely finance (World Bank 2015a).

Importantly, the SCD highlights that FLFP alone does not automatically improve women's economic empowerment; further research is needed to fully understand and address continuing foundational barriers to improving women's employment, job quality and occupational choice. Such barriers include the persistence of patriarchal norms that hamper women's economic choices and participation through—for example—early marriage, mobility constraints and care responsibilities, and working women's double burden of simultaneous productive and reproductive work (World Bank 2015a). Similarly, the World Bank's CPF emphasizes the WBG's continued role in improving Bangladeshi women's financial inclusion and formal employment, and women's economic empowerment is a specific outcome to be addressed (World Bank Group 2016a).

SOCIAL NORMS AND GENDER RELATIONS

Throughout the 20th century and nearly two decades since then in Bangladesh, laws that guarantee equality between men and women—and boys and girls— have been passed in the public spheres of education, employment, politics, and select areas of family law. Discourse on equality has had far less impact in the domestic (private) sphere, however. In the household, the core unit of society, the belief in the superiority of male household members—particularly the male household head—to female household members has proven resistant to change, even with improvements in the gender balance of intra-household deci- sion-making afforded by women's increased access to credit (Amin and Pebley 1994; Kabeer 2000; Kapur 2013). As in other South Asian countries, gender relations in Bangladesh are typified by patriarchy, according to Kandiyoti's (1988, 278) definition of *classic patriarchy*, under which "girls are given away in marriage at a very young age into households headed by their husband's father. There, they are subordinate not only to all the men, but also to the more senior women, especially their mother-in-law. The extent to which this represents a total break with their own kin group varies in relation to the degree of endog- amy in marriage practices and different conceptions of honor." Classic patriar- chy produces a system in which men and boys claim superiority to women and girls in nearly all aspects of life, exercising control over women and girls across the life cycle: girls are first subordinate to boys as sisters and to men as daugh- ters, and later, after marrying, as wives or daughters-in-law. Some scholars argue that such subordination gives power to the perception of women and girls as private property—and specifically commodities that can be sold, bought, or exchanged by men—who are wholly deprived of the rights and dignity enjoyed by men and boys (Kirti, Kumar, and Yadav 2011; Mahmud 2004). Patriarchal systems offer men and boys incentives to devalue women and girls. In South Asia, societies and family systems that assign men the role of providers for women and enforcers of their obedience, also reward women who comply with patriarchal norms and punish those who transgress (Kandiyoti 1988).

Son preference, male preference, and female roles

A historical preference for sons in Bangladesh—as in other South Asian countries—has dramatic and deleterious effects on society. In perhaps its most visible manifestations, elevated rates of malnutrition, illness, and mortality among girls because of familial preference and allocation of resources to boys, along with the practice of sex-selective abortions, have led to skewed sex ratios and the problem identified by Sen (1990) as "missing women" (Chowdhury and Biragi 1990; Self and Grabowski 2012). Although Bangladesh has made tremen- dous progress in closing gender gaps in primary and secondary education, recent data suggest that girls are on the losing end of growing gender disparities in ter- tiary enrollments and secondary school drop-out rates (Bangladesh Bureau of Educational Information and Statistics 2017; Camfield, Rashid, and Sultan 2017). Yet, in several ways son preference is weakening in Bangladesh: since the early 2000s—if not before—gender discrimination in treatment of children has been steadily declining, which has allowed Bangladesh to rebalance its sex ratio (Kabeer, Huq, and Mahmud 2014). Still, son preference continues to manifest in other household decisions, such as inheritance and asset ownership practices (explored in chapter 3).

Son preference springs primarily from circumstances in which the clan is the basic form of social organization, with marriage strictly exogamous: men from one clan may wed only women from outside the clan. Clan lineage and membership is imperative to the social order. With the exception of the Garos and Khasis minorities in Bangladesh (see chapter 6), lineage passes through men, and women shift from fathers' to husbands' lineage upon moving from natal to marital homes. Exogamy has negative implications for a woman's inheritance of land (see chapter 3), a key asset for her original clan. The rigidity of marital norms that define exogamy traditionally has devalued girls to their natal households, which raise them, spend money to get them married (in particular, through the practice of dowry, in which parental resources are transferred to the marital family), and thereafter have little to no contact with them. Das Gupta et al. (2003) identify this lack of perceived value of a daughter to the household as the key incentive for persistent son preference, aversion to daughters, and the consequential pervasive and systematic discrimination against daughters as they enter schooling age and, later, almost invariably become married women with children.

Perceptions of masculinity, femininity, and honor

The social dynamics associated with son preference, prescribed roles for males and females, and the regulation of honor all shape constructions of what Bangladeshi society considers feminine and masculine. Women and men alike are designated specific attributes that are directly linked to masculine and feminine social identities. Not only men (in private and public spaces) impose and enforce these prescribed distinctions; women also reinforce them—as mothers and mothers-in-law who "update the norms of acceptable and unacceptable behavior towards women" (Faizal and Rajagopalan 2005, 44).

Women in Bangladesh historically have functioned as caretakers of children and the household, meeting the requirements of the daughter, wife, and mother roles. These roles facilitate the control and discipline of female behavior; in addition, women and girls are required to adhere to specific modesty norms (Camfield, Rashid, and Sultan 2017; Jayawardena and De Alwis 1996). Numerous expectations are imposed upon young women, especially as soon they are married: they are expected to bear children and are likely to face disapproval if they express independent desires, goals, or choices (Camfield, Rashid, and Sultan 2017; Kabeer 1983, 2000; Schuler et al. 1996; Stark 1993).

Men encounter constructions of what is masculine, as well, such as being the family breadwinners, maintaining control over family resources, and appearing strong (Moore 1994; Nanda et al. 2013; Rashid and Akram 2014). Studies have established a correlation between expressions of masculinity and control of women in the household—particularly in terms of ensuring that they fulfill their designated roles (International Center for Research on Women 2002). Normative behaviors for men and women are reinforced by a range of venues, from religious institutions and the state to popular media and entertainment, especially television and movies (Banerjee 2005). Bangladeshi women, who watch primarily Bangladeshi and Indian channels, are bombarded with narratives that depict good women as devoted wives and mothers with little ambition. A bad woman, on the other hand, "is aggressive in the pursuit of her interests and dominating over her family" (Priyadarshani and Rahim 2014, 117). In the broadly distributed Tamil and Hindi movies from India, women often are courted by male protagonists through harassment and even more aggressive acts, including kissing and grabbing (Faizal and Rajagopalan 2005).

In both the private and public spheres, men are responsible for regulating girls' and women's behavior to protect familial or community honor, which is deeply connected to perceptions of femininity and masculinity and is upheld through conforming to socially sanctioned gender norms. In Bangladesh, as in most of South Asia, transgressing these norms not only undermines an individual's reputation; it sullies the reputation of the individual's family and even her community, particularly when the individual is female. Traditionally, even men's personal honor is tethered to a woman's behavior and public presence (Mandelbaum 1988), which provides men with the incentive to regulate the mobility of girls and women in multiple ways, including *purdah* (conservative dress or seclusion), segregation of the sexes, and even violence. The all-encompassing need for families to safeguard their daughters' honor has negative consequences for girls' and women's access to education and employment, along with other facets of economic empowerment.

Mobility constraints and purdah

Gender norms related to religious and other cultural factors continue to constrain women's mobility and use of transport, particularly in rural areas, according to studies from around the globe (Babinard 2011). Women's travel patterns traditionally have been deeply rooted in their mostly home-based domestic and family-oriented activities. Yet, increased connectivity has improved access to better educational options for children; health services for children, women, and the elderly; and a broader range of opportunities for women's engagement in economic activities. Greater opportunities, services, and household financial pressures have created new incentives for women's travel beyond their immediate communities (Priyadarshani and Rahim 2010). Their expanded presence and mobility in public spaces—particularly when unaccompanied by male relatives—challenges traditional gender roles and, in many cases, enhances their voice, control, and independence.

Socio-cultural restrictions persist in many communities, however, and women's practice of *purdah* continues, with women's movement confined largely to the household and immediate surroundings. Purdah is an ancient custom, said to have evolved in Persia and then adopted by various Islamic societies, that involves secluding women from public view—particularly from un-related men—by means of covering women's faces (and sometimes the entire body) with a veil or concealing clothing. It can include physical segregation of the sexes within buildings and restricting women's ability to travel unless accompanied by a male family member, typically limiting their movement to within villages (World Bank 2012).[5] Where purdah is observed, it serves to limit women's participation in public life (Blunch and Das 2007), including traveling to banks or engaging in any public setting with men (Sultana 2012), as explored in later chapters.

Complicated links between violence and women's economic empowerment

Alongside the rise in women's employment in Bangladesh is a high prevalence of violence against women. Prevalence rates are difficult to estimate due to under-reporting, yet, among 12,530 women interviewed for the 2011 Bangladesh Bureau of Statistics (BBS) Survey on Violence against Women, 65 percent reported having ever experienced physical violence perpetrated by their current husband and 33 percent reported having experienced such violence in the previous 12 months. More than 80 percent reported ever experiencing psychological violence perpetrated by husbands (72 percent in the last year). Three of every five Bangladeshi women experience physical or sexual violence, according to Naved and Amin (2013), cited in the Bangladesh Demographic and Health Survey 2014 (National Institute of Population Research and Training (2016). Such violence is prevalent across all social and economic groups in Bangladesh's rural and urban areas (Centre for Policy Dialogue 2009). On a more positive note, the most recent BBS Survey on Violence against Women (Bangladesh Bureau of Statistics 2016) estimates the percentage of women who have ever experienced physical abuse to have declined to 50 percent—down about 15 percentage points since the 2011 survey. Still, these levels of violence remain unacceptably high.

Male and female qualitative research respondents from Dhaka interviewed for this study concur about the persistence of intimate partner violence (IPV) and other kinds of violence against women in their neighborhoods (box 1.2). Dhaka participants frequently mentioned alcohol and drug abuse (which are strong risk factors for IPV) when referring to IPV. More broadly, the extent of IPV and other forms of gender-based violence (GBV) varied little between the rural areas and urban slums in which qualitative research was conducted; it is part of women's everyday lives, surfacing in almost all issues discussed (figure 1.1). The ethnic minority communities studied were exceptions, reporting little to no such violence. Female and male university students from Dhaka and Chittagong did not report as high a GBV prevalence as did participants in urban slums and rural areas.

Evidence is mixed as to whether employed women are at a higher risk of experiencing spousal violence than unemployed women. Research from around the world finds that rapid shifts in gender roles—such as improvements in women's employment and other economic empowerment forms—can trigger a backlash against women perceived as challenging engrained norms in the household and broader society (Babinard et al. 2010; Krishnan et al. 2010). However, other research suggests that employment, through reduced financial dependence on husbands, enhances women's power within households and reduces vulnerability to domestic violence (Krishnan et al. 2010). Women's contribution to household income is also associated with lower financial stress, a risk factor for domestic violence.

Sexual harassment in public spaces, workplaces, and schools

In addition to experiencing violence in their homes, women may be facing public violence at increasing rates at least partly because of their enhanced mobility and public presence over time. Research suggests the high incidence of public acts of violence against women in Bangladesh, including acid attacks, is linked to insufficient institutional preparation for women's entrance into the public sphere (Khan 2005). Working Bangladeshi women likely face multiple risks of

BOX 1.2

Selected quotes from female participants in Dhaka focus group discussions

"Women facing violence is a regular incidence. You can't find a day when husbands don't beat their wives" (nonworking adolescent boy in urban Dhaka, age 17).

"If wife stays like wife, and obeys me, then she will not outrage me... Wife will stay in home. She will not be asked to do outdoor work" (working adolescent boy in urban Dhaka, age 16).

One female focus group discussion (FGD) participant in urban Dhaka said that when women collect their payments at night, the gate keepers offer indecent proposals, saying "'Why are you coming here? I will give money if you come to my room.' Sometimes police attack, too. Sometimes if we are coming back late at night, people think we are prostitutes and then strike the rickshaw with bamboo sticks." Another said, "We also get hurt. We cannot move easily on the roads. They tease women." According to a third woman, "He keeps beating and takes his wife to the rail line, hitting with the handle of a dau (machete), with sticks."

A woman from rural Dhaka reported that three months ago her pregnant niece's head was fractured by her husband. "She stayed in the hospital for many days. Then she returned to her parents. The husband also beat her parents. But because she was pregnant, her parents sent her back to her husband's house. They thought that her husband would change after the birth of his child. But still he is on the wrong path."

FIGURE 1.1

Frequency of mentions of gender-based violence among women's FGDs, by issue

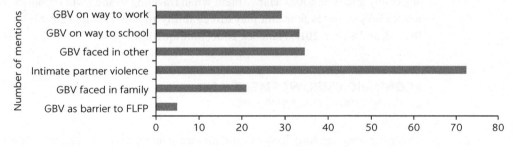

Source: World Bank calculations based on primary qualitative data collected in 2016.
Note: FLFP = female labor force participation.

harassment—traveling to and from work as well as at the workplace itself—with alarmingly high rates of harassment reported by women in the garment sector in particular, as discussed in chapter 2 (*Dhaka Tribune* 2018; Hancock 2006; Hossain and Ahmed 2017; Siddiqi 2003).

According to the 2015 Violence Against Women Survey, about a third (32.8 percent) of Bangladeshi women interviewed perceived sexual violence as likely to occur at their place of work (Bangladesh Bureau of Statistics 2016). The only location that was perceived as a more likely site for sexual violence (45.5 percent of women surveyed) was their husbands' home. The third most likely location (18.3 percent) was vehicles/roads/streets, with slightly more urban women (20.9 percent) than rural women (17.5 percent) reporting this perception.

Violence against women in public and at work can be interpreted as an extended manifestation of control over these women and a signal that society in general may regard them as a threat. Abiding by patriarchal norms, men may perceive women in the public sphere as deviating from appropriate roles and thus deserving of abuse and humiliation. Working women also are at risk of public violence that includes sexual abuse or eve-teasing.[6] Research from select areas of Bangladesh finds that as much as 80–90 percent of girls are affected by eve-teasing (Camfield, Rashid, and Sultan 2017). Poor women may be at a particularly high risk of sexual harassment related to travel for work; they are more likely to walk or use public transportation than professional women, who can afford private transport (Hancock 2006; Siddiqi 2003).

Sexual harassment can negatively affect young girls' schooling and women's productivity at work. Female children and adolescents in Bangladesh report sexual violence and abuse in schools. For adolescent girls, nonconsensual sexual experiences at school are one of the most common types of harassment (Jejeebhoy and Bott 2003); among surveyed Bangladeshi women, 14 percent perceived educational institutions to be locations at which sexual violence is likely to occur (Bangladesh Bureau of Statistics 2016). The persistence of sexual abuse of girls in schools may reflect recent trends, such as an increasing number of young girls continuing education beyond primary school or increased mingling of boys and girls in schools. Alternatively, it also could reflect how adults who occupy positions of authority over children and adolescents may take advantage of these positions (Jejeebhoy and Bott 2003). Regardless, sexual harassment—or the fear of it—is a key reason why parents in Bangladesh may withdraw girls from school at puberty,[7] which severely limits their lifetime opportunities for education and careers (Bott et al. 2003; Jejeebhoy and Bott 2003). Harassment when traveling to and from school or work also generates fear and may affect ability to concentrate (Camfield, Rashid, and Sultan 2017; Hancock 2006; Siddiqi 2003).

ECONOMIC EMPOWERMENT AND ORGANIZING FRAMEWORK

There is a longstanding debate in the literature on what comprises women's economic empowerment. At perhaps one end of the spectrum is the idea that LFP in and of itself—that is, merely entering the labor force—can economically empower women. A more nuanced viewpoint argues that the extent to which LFP is empowering for a woman will vary according to how empowerment is defined, the cultural and social acceptability of women working, and the kind of jobs available to and entered into by women in a particular context (Kabeer 2008). Others note that economic empowerment must be related to the broader concept of women's economic opportunities, which includes not just LFP and employment, but also women's ownership, access to, and control of household and financial assets (World Bank 2016b). Similar definitions include, for example, the conceptualization of women's economic empowerment by Golla et al. (2011, 4) who note, "A woman is economically empowered when she has both the ability to succeed and advance economically and the power to make and act on economic decisions." Kabeer (2012, 9) additionally emphasizes ideas of "recognition, dignity and transformative agency" that have to accompany economic engagement and advancement to be considered economic empowerment. In Kabeer's framework, enhancing economic empowerment necessitates not only policies to increase women's access, use and control of land, labor and financial assets and investments, but also investments in social protection, basic social services, and the other aspects of women's lives that constrain their economic engagement from being truly empowering for them (2012). These include aspects of broader, structural gender inequality, with outcomes such as domestic violence, political participation, and status in the community. Thus, as Kabeer, Mahmud, and Tasneem (2018, 249) observe, "Paid work, in other words, can act as a pathway to change beyond the economic domain."

This book examines economic empowerment using the definition suggested by Golla et al. (2011). *The World Bank Group Gender Strategy FY16–23: Gender Equality, Poverty Reduction and Inclusive Growth* (World Bank 2015b) analyzes the concept of economic empowerment in the same vein. The following chapters analyze patterns over the last 10–15 years in women's ability to "succeed and advance economically" and to "have the power and agency to benefit from economic activities" (Golla et al. 2011, 4). In addition to analyzing shifts over time in different domains of women's economic empowerment—which in most cases present as changes in gender gaps within these domains—the book identifies the determinants of various gaps. It pays particular attention to factors that act as constraints or facilitators toward reducing the gender gaps in these domains:

- *LFP and employment in formal and informal sectors,* with attention to gendered patterns of occupation and employment, wage inequality, and time use related to household roles.
- *Asset ownership and control of assets*: the ability to own and control assets such as land (often acquired through inheritance) and other family assets in a patriarchal society; and the extent of women's rights over land that they theoretically inherit and own.
- *Access to, use of, and control over nonhousehold financial assets,* such as savings, loans, and other sources of finance: patterns of use, as well as access to and control of different types of financial assets; gender gaps in financial inclusion.
- *Opportunities for entrepreneurship and growing owned enterprises.*

Structural and normative constraints and opportunities can influence all these different domains of women's economic empowerment, just as do endowments, such as education and skills. As explored in the previous section, other constraints and opportunities arise from the societal context and norms that influence women's and girls' ability to explore, access, and take advantage of existing opportunities for education, jobs or asset ownership, as well as to have a voice in enjoying the economic advantages that accrue from access to and use of economic opportunities. Such norms deeply influence women's and men's attitudes toward women gaining knowledge, experience, and control of economic matters.

This book thus aims to more fully analyze the roles of these structural, normative, and other factors in women's economic empowerment, using the following organizing framework for each main chapter:

a. **Category of economic empowerment:** Each of the four chapters following this one focuses on a particular domain of economic empowerment, as listed above.

b. **Descriptive data on gender gaps and changes over time:** Each chapter presents descriptive findings of gender gaps in each domain—and changes over time in these gaps, where data are available.

c. **Determinants of women's economic empowerment—enablers and barriers:** Findings about the determinants of these gaps are then discussed, drawing from multivariate analyses of secondary quantitative data and complemented by references to relevant primary qualitative research and select published and unpublished literature. Analytical findings about determinants distinguish between enabling factors and barriers.

d. **Recommendations and good practices to address barriers and close gender gaps:** Following the discussion of analysis results, each chapter offers related good practices and recommendations for addressing the range of gender gaps in its respective domain of economic empowerment.

e. **Role of government, WBG, and other stakeholders in implementing recommendations:** Each chapter briefly mentions these roles, while chapter 7 describes them in more detail.

DATA AND METHODS

We use a mixed-methods approach with secondary quantitative and primary qualitative data to measure and analyze the relationships described above. A literature review drawing from economics, sociology, demography, and gender studies supplements analysis findings.

Secondary quantitative data

Secondary data include multiple rounds of the Bangladesh Labour Force Survey, three rounds of the World Bank's Global Financial Inclusion Data (Findex), one round of the Time Use Pilot Survey, one round of the Enterprise Survey, multiple rounds of Demographic and Health Surveys (DHS), and two rounds of the International Food Policy Research Institute's (IFPRI's) Bangladesh Integrated Household Survey (BIHS). Multiple versions of Stata were used to analyze quantitative data.

The Labour Force Survey (LFS)[8] is conducted across several countries globally every year or every other year. We analyze multiple rounds (from 2003 to 2016) of the Bangladesh LFS conducted by the BBS. The latest survey round was conducted between July 2015 and June 2016. The survey provides relevant sex- and age-specific labor market information related to economic and noneconomic activities of the population age 15 or older in the labor force. The survey covers a sample of 126,000 households from all 64 districts of the country.

The Time Use Pilot Survey (Bangladesh Bureau of Statistics 2013) was first conducted in Bangladesh by the BBS between April 12th and 13th, 2012, to estimate the amount of time persons age 15 years and over spend on various activities. These data shed light on the different roles and activities that men and women perform.

The Enterprise Survey[9] is implemented by The World Bank Group (WBG) in 139 countries across the world, using standardized, comparable questionnaires. The Enterprise Surveys interview formal-sector firms in the manufacturing and service sectors to collect data on firm performance, firm structure, business perceptions of obstacles to enterprise growth, and the business environment in general. The Survey used in this study was implemented in Bangladesh between April and September of 2013.[10] The survey included 1,422 firms with five or more employees, stratified into 7 manufacturing industries (food, apparel, leather, chemicals, transport, furniture, and other manufacturing), and 2 service industries (retail and other services). We use specifically the data related to firms' attitudes towards hiring women in managerial and non-managerial positions.

The Global Findex,[11] implemented by WBG in partnership with Gallup World Poll and funded by the Bill & Melinda Gates Foundation, is the world's largest database on financial inclusion. This book analyzes Findex data collected from 1,000 firms in Bangladesh in 2011, 2014, and 2017 to examine levels and change in men's and women's use of accounts, savings, and borrowing.

The BIHS[12] is a panel survey implemented by IFPRI in Bangladesh in 2011–12 and then again among the same households in 2015. The survey is focused on rural areas only, however, with no urban data. The BIHS covers 6,500 households and is representative of rural Bangladesh nationally, and representative of rural areas in each of the country's seven administrative divisions. Data are collected for a range of agricultural and poverty-related outcomes. Of interest for this book is the survey's extensive list of variables on men and women's ownership and rights over key household and financial assets; a range of socioeconomic and demographic variables for men, women and their households; and a section on women's economic empowerment-related variables.

The DHS[13] is a multipartner global program funded by USAID. Implemented in developing countries since 1984, the surveys are conducted with a large, nationally representative cross-section of each country's population and collect data on a range of socioeconomic, fertility and reproductive health, child and adult mortality and morbidity, HIV and other health and population indicators. We use DHS data to analyze Bangladesh's trends in child marriage and factors associated with marriage of girls under age 15 and under age 18 over time.

Primary qualitative data

To ensure wide geographical coverage in our qualitative data, we conducted qualitative research in both rural and urban areas of Dhaka, Chittagong, Rajshahi, Sylhet, and Barisal divisions. In urban areas, participants were selected from the City Corporations of each urban area. For rural sites, from each division an *upazila*[14] was selected randomly, and from the selected *upazila*, a *union parishad*[15] was selected randomly. Two sites for two ethnic communities from different parts of the country—one from Chittagong and one from Rajshahi District—were selected as well. Table 1.1 details the study sites. Participants were selected from different population groups by gender, age, ethnicity, and occupational status, yielding male and female participants, adolescent boys and girls, working and nonworking women, and ethnic minority groups from urban and rural areas.

Data were collected using focus group discussions (FGD), key informant interviews (KII), case studies (CS), problem rankings, and a few sessions of institutional mapping and listening posts. KIIs included individuals of particular interest to this report's topics of study, such as local imams (religious leaders), government officials, women entrepreneurs, a management official at a garment factory, and a teacher at a Vocational Training Center. The CS selected women

TABLE 1.1 **Study sites for qualitative data collection, 2016**

DIVISION	URBAN AREA	RURAL/ETHNIC AREA
Dhaka	Dhaka North City Corporation	Dhamrai
Chittagong	Chittagong City Corporation	Rangamati (Asambosti)
Sylhet	Sylhet City Corporation	Zakiganj
Rajshahi	Santal community (Godagari upazilla)	Bagha
Barisal	Barisal City Corporation	Bakergonj

TABLE 1.2 **Number of data points, by method and location, qualitative data collection, 2016**

	DIVISION										
	DHAKA		CHITTAGONG		SYLHET		RAJSHAHI		BARISAL		
TOOLS	URBAN	RURAL	URBAN	ETHNIC	URBAN	RURAL	RURAL	ETHNIC	URBAN	RURAL	TOTAL
FGD	8	5	7	5	4	5	5	5	5	5	54
KII	7	1	3	3	3	2	4	2	3	3	31
Problem ranking	2	1	2	2	1	2	2	2	2	2	18
Case study	3	0	3	3	3	3	3	4	3	3	28
Institutional mapping	1	1	2	2	1	2	0	0	2	2	13
Listening post	0	0	1	0	1	1	0	0	1	1	5
Others	—	—	—	—	1	—	1	1	—	—	3
											152

Note: FGD = focus group discussion; KII = key informant interviews.

who inherited land or other assets, as well as examples of successful and unsuccessful women employees and entrepreneurs. Table 1.2 details the numbers of data points for each method in urban and rural areas of each of the five divisions from which data were collected. Qualitative data were analyzed using NVivo version 10. Two of the team's researchers created a codebook and then coded two transcripts to check inter-coder reliability. The codebook was subsequently revised and finalized before remaining transcripts were coded.

BOOK ROADMAP

Chapter 2 focuses on LFP and employment. It starts with a trend analysis of FLFP over the last decade, including changes in sectoral patterns and gender wage differentials. It then analyzes the key demand and supply factors that may constrain further growth in FLFP, as well as the barriers and facilitators associated with moving women out of low-paying and into higher-paying jobs and sectors. We examine how time use differs between women who are and women who are not in the labor force to get an idea of the extent of the double burden that working women may face. The chapter ends with an exploration of good practices to enhance FLFP.

Chapter 3 analyzes women's ownership and control over household assets, starting with gender differentials in control of land and inheritance rules in traditional, religious, and national laws. Using BIHS data, it explores factors associated with rural women's ownership and rights over land. The chapter then examines good practices from several parts of the world that can be adapted to Bangladesh and that have addressed women's inheritance and increased women's ownership and control over land.

Chapter 4 focuses on women's use and control of financial assets. It analyzes shifts over time in gender-differentiated use of formal and informal financial institutions and services; women's control over the financial services they use and the extent to which financial use and control can be empowering for them; barriers to women's use and control of savings, loans, bank accounts, and other sources of finance; recent efforts by microfinance institutions and GoB to address some of these barriers; and examples of evaluated good practices with potential for implementation in Bangladesh.

Chapter 5 addresses a subset of finance users: women entrepreneurs. As such, issues discussed in chapter 4 are relevant in this chapter, which analyzes additional concerns and dynamics specific to women's entrepreneurship, including patterns and trends in women's entrepreneurship; links between finance and entrepreneurship; barriers women face in starting, owning, and growing enterprises; global, evaluated good practices to address barriers; and data gaps.

Chapter 6 addresses patterns of women's economic empowerment among socially and economically excluded minority groups in Bangladesh. Gender and social inclusion are closely interlinked, and women from poor households, of religious minorities, and/or from indigenous groups may face double exclusion—because of their gender *and* their social identity. Research on these issues in Bangladesh is very limited, but small-scale studies illustrate such disadvantage among indigenous women, including those concentrated in the Chittagong Hill Tracts. Our primary qualitative data from some ethnic minorities supplements the scant existing literature.

Chapter 7 brings together the entire book, summarizing key findings about women's economic empowerment in various spheres of such empowerment. The chapter ends with recommendations for each key stakeholder in Bangladesh, including government, donors, the World Bank, NGOs, and civil society organizations engaged in improving women's LFP, employment, asset ownership and rights, and financial inclusion and entrepreneurship.

NOTES

1. https://data.worldbank.org/indicator/SE.ENR.SECO.FM.ZS.
2. https://data.worldbank.org/indicator/SP.DYN.TFRT.IN/.
3. 2015 update from http://www.un.org/en/development/desa/population/theme/family-planning/cp_model.shtml.
4. https://data.worldbank.org/indicator/SH.STA.MMRT.
5. Definition from *Encyclopedia Brittanica*: https://www.britannica.com/topic/purdah.
6. *Eve-teasing* is public sexual harassment or molestation of women by men. *Sexual harassment* is "Any unwelcome sexual advance, request for sexual favor, verbal or physical conduct or gesture of a sexual nature, or any other behavior of a sexual nature that might reasonably be expected or perceived to cause offence or humiliation to another" and occurs in public (UNHCR 2005).
7. Once girls enter adolescence, they begin their transition from childhood to adulthood. Because girls also enter their reproductive years at this life stage, societies universally associate it with the inception of female sexuality. The taboo around premarital sex in most South Asian countries places adolescent girls there at risk of sexual harassment (Solotaroff and Pande 2014).

8. http://www.ilo.org/dyn/lfsurvey/lfsurvey.list?p_lang=en.
9. http://www.enterprisesurveys.org/.
10. http://www.enterprisesurveys.org/data/exploreeconomies/2013/bangladesh.
11. http://www.worldbank.org/en/programs/globalfindex.
12. http://bangladesh.ifpri.info/our-work/bihs/.
13. https://dhsprogram.com/What-We-Do/Survey-Types/DHS.cfm.
14. The term *upazila* refers to subdistricts in Bangladesh.
15. The term *union parishad* refers to the smallest rural administrative and local government unit in Bangladesh.

REFERENCES

Aguirre, DeAnne, Leila Hoteit, Christine Rupp, and Karim Sabbagh. 2012. *Empowering the Third Billion: Women and the World of Work in 2012*. Booz and Company.

Amin, S, and Anne R. Pebley. 1994. "Gender Inequality within Households: The Impact of a Women's Development Programme in 36 Bangladeshi Villages." *The Bangladesh Development Studies 22, Vol. 22*, No. 2/3: 121–54.

Babinard, Julie. 2011. "World Bank Gender Transport Surveys: An Overview." Transport Note Series, No. TRN 43, World Bank, Washington, DC.

Babinard, Julie, John Hine, Simon Ellis, and Satoshi Ishihara. 2010. *Mainstreaming Gender in Road Transport: Operational Guidance for World Bank Staff.* Transport paper series TP-28, Washington, DC: World Bank.

Banerjee, Sikata. *Make Me a Man! Masculinity, Hinduism, and Nationalism in India.* Albany, NY: SUNY Press, 2005.

Bangladesh Bureau of Educational Information and Statistics. 2017. *Bangladesh Education Statistics 2016*. Dhaka: BANBEIS Ministry of Education, Government of Bangladesh.

Bangladesh Bureau of Statistics. 2012. *Report on Violence Against Women (VAW) Survey 2011*. Dhaka: Bangladesh Bureau of Statistics (BBS), Statistics and Informatics Division (SID), Ministry of Planning, Government of the People's Republic of Bangladesh.

——. 2016. *Report on Violence Against Women (VAW) Survey 2015*. Dhaka: Bangladesh Bureau of Statistics (BBS), Statistics and Informatics Division (SID), Ministry of Planning, Government of the People's Republic of Bangladesh.

Bangladesh Planning Commission. 2016. *Millennium Development Goals: End-Period Stocktaking and Final Evaluation Report (2000-2015)*. Dhaka: General Economics Division, Government of the People's Republic of Bangladesh.

Blunch, Niels-Hugo, and Maitreyi Bordia Das. 2007. "Changing Norms about Gender Inequality in Education: Evidence from Bangladesh." Policy Research Working Paper 4044, World Bank, Washington, DC.

Camfield, Laura, Sabina Faiz Rashid, and Maheen Sultan. 2017. "Exploring Bangladeshi Adolescents' Gendered Experiences and Perspectives." GAGE Research Brief, Gender & Adolescence Global Evidence (GAGE), London.

Centre for Policy Dialogue (CPD). 2009. "Domestic Violence in Bangladesh: Cost Estimates and Measures to Address the Attendant Problems," Report 97, CPD, Dhaka.

Chowdhury, Mridul K., and Radheshyam Bairagi. 1990. "Son Preference and Fertility in Bangladesh." *Population and Development Review* 16 (4): 749-757.

Cuberes, David, and Marc Teignier. 2012. "Gender Gaps in the Labor Market and Aggregate Productivity." Sheffield Economic Research Paper SERP 2012017, Department of Economics, The University of Sheffield, Sheffield, UK.

Cuberes, David, and Marc Teignier. 2014. "Aggregate Costs of Gender Gaps in the Labor Market: A Quantitative Estimate." UB Economics Working Papers 2014/308, Facultat d'Economia i Empresa, UB Economics, Universitat de Barcelona, Barcelona.

Das Gupta, Monica, Zhenghua Jiang, Bohua Li, Zhenming Xie, Woojin Chung, and Hwa-ok Bae. 2003. "Why Is Son Preference So Persistent in East and South Asia? A Cross-Country Study of China, India and the Republic of Korea." *Journal of Development Studies* 40 (2): 153–87.

Dhaka Tribune. "Study: Rights of Bangladesh's Female RMG Workers Still Unmet." February 27, 2018. https://www.dhakatribune.com/business/2018/02/27/study-rights-bangladeshs-female-rmg-workers-still-unmet.

Dollar, David, and Roberta Gatti. 1999. *Gender Inequality, Income, and Growth. Are Good Times Good for Women?* World Bank Gender and Development Working Paper 1, World Bank, Washington, DC.

Elborgh-Woytek, Katrin, Monique Newiak, Kalpana Kochhar, Stefania Fabrizio, Kangni R. Kpodar, Philippe Wingender, Benedict J. Clements, and Gerd Schwartz. 2013. "Women, Work, and the Economy: Macroeconomic Gains from Gender Equity." IMF Staff Discussion Note SDN/13/10, Washington, DC: International Monetary Fund.

Faizal, Farah, and Swarna Rajagopalan. 2005. *Women, Security, South Asia: A Clearing in the Thicket.* New Delhi: Sage.

Golla, Anne Marie, Anju Malhotra, Priya Nanda, and Rekha Mehra. 2011. *Understanding and Measuring Women's Economic Empowerment: Definition, Framework and Indicators.* Washington, DC: International Center for Research on Women.

Government of Bangladesh. 2015. *Millennium Development Goals—Bangladesh Progress Report 2015.* Dhaka: General Economics Division (GED), Bangladesh Planning Commission.

Government of the People's Republic of Bangladesh. 2015. *Seventh Five Year Plan FY2016–FY2020: Accelerating Growth, Empowering Citizens.* Dhaka: General Economics Division (GED), Planning Commission.

Hancock, P. 2006. "Violence, Women, Work and Empowerment: Narratives from Factory Women in Sri Lanka's Export Processing Zones." *Gender, Technology and Development.* Vol. 10, Issue 2, 211–228.

Hossain, Jakir, and Mostafiz Ahmed. 2017. "Watch Report: Promoting Women Ready-Made Garment Workers' Rights through Labour Regulation." Karmojibi Nari, Dhaka, Bangladesh.

International Center for Research on Women. 2002. *Men, Masculinity and Domestic Violence in India: Summary Report of 4 Studies.* ICRW.

Jayawardena, Kumari, and Malathi De Alwis. 1996. *Embodied Violence: Communalising Women's Sexuality in South Asia.* London and New Jersey: Zed Books.

Jejeebhoy, S. J., and S Bott. 2003. *Non-Consensual Sexual Experiences of Young People: A Review of the Evidence from Developing Countries.* Regional Working Papers, Population Council.

Kabeer, Naila. 1983. *Minus Lives: Women of Bangladesh.* Change International Reports: Women and Society, No. 10. London: CHANGE International Reports..

———. 2000. *The Power to Choose: Bangladeshi Women and Labour Market Decisions in London and Dhaka.* London: Verso Press.

———. 2008. "Paid Work, Women's Empowerment and Gender Justice: Critical Pathways of Social Change." Pathways Working Paper 3, Institute of Development Studies (IDS), Brighton.

———. 2012. "Women's Economic Empowerment and Inclusive Growth: Labour Markets and Enterprise Development." Discussion Paper 29/12, School of Oriental and African Studies, University of London, London.

Kabeer, Naila, Lopita Huq, and Simeen Mahmud. 2014. "Diverging Stories of 'Missing Women.'" *Feminist Economics* 20 (4): 138–63.

Kabeer, Naila, Simeen Mahmud, and Sabika Tasneem. 2018. "The Contested Relationship between Paid Work and Women's Empowerment: Empirical Analysis from Bangladesh." *The European Journal of Development Research* 30 (2): 235–251.

Kandiyoti, Deniz. 1988. "Bargaining With Patriarchy." *Gender and Society* 2 (3): 274–90.

Kapur, Ratna. 2013. "Violence against Women in South Asia and the Limits of Law." Background paper for Solotaroff, Jennifer L., and Rohini Prabha Pande. 2014. *Violence against Women and Girls: Lessons from South Asia.* South Asia Development Forum, Washington, DC: World Bank.

Khan, Farida. 2005. *Gender Violence and Development Discourse in Bangladesh.* UNESCO.

Kirti, Anand, Prateek Kumar, and Rachana Yadav. 2011. "The Face of Honour Based Crimes: Global Concerns and Solutions." *International Journal of Criminal Justice Sciences* 6 (1 & 2): 343–57.

Klasen, Stephan. 1999. "Does Gender Inequality Reduce Growth and Development? Evidence from Cross-Country Regressions." World Bank Policy Research Report, Engendering Development Working Paper 7, World Bank, Washington, DC.

Krishnan, Suneeta, Corinne H. Rocca, Alan E. Hubbard, Kalyani Subbiah, Jeffrey Edmeades, and Nancy S. Padian. 2010. "Do Changes in Spousal Employment Status Lead to Domestic Violence? Insights from a Prospective Study in Bangalore, India." *Social Science & Medicine* 70 (1): 136–43.

Mahmud, S. 2004. "Microcredit and Women's Empowerment in Bangladesh." In *Attacking Poverty with Microcredit*, edited by S. Ahmed and S. Hakim. Dhaka: The University Press Limited.

Mandelbaum, David G. 1988. *Women's Seclusion and Men's Honor: Sex Roles in North India, Bangladesh, and Pakistan.* Tucson, AZ: University of Arizona Press.

Moore, Henrietta. 1994. "The Problem of Explaining Violence in the Social Sciences." In *Sex and Violence: Issues in Representation and Experience*, edited by Penelope Harvey and Peter Gow, 139–55. London: Routledge.

Nanda, P., A. Gautam, R. Verma, S. Kumar, and D. Brahme. 2013. "Masculinity, Son Preference and Intimate Partner Violence." A Study Conducted by ICRW in Partnership with UNFPA.

National Institute of Population Research and Training (NIPORT), Mitra and Associates, and ICF International. 2016. *Bangladesh Demographic and Health Survey 2014.* Dhaka, Bangladesh: NIPORT, Mitra and Associates, and ICF International.

Naved, Ruchira, and Sajeda Amin. 2013. *From Evidence to Policy: Addressing Gender-Based Violence against Women and Girls in Bangladesh.* Dhaka: ICDDR B, UKAID, and Population Council.

Priyadarshini, A., and S. Rahim. 2010. "Women Watching Television: Surfing between Fantasy and Reality." *IDS Bulletin* 41(2): 116–24.

Rashid, Sabina Faiz, and Owasim Akram. 2014. "Pornography, Pleasure, Gender, and Sex Education in Bangladesh." Institute of Development Studies (IDS) Sexuality and Development Programme, IDS, University of Sussex, England.

Schuler, S. R., S. M. Hashemi, A. P. Riley, and S. Akhter. "Credit Programs, Patriarchy and Men's Violence against Women in Rural Bangladesh." *Social Science & Medicine* 43 (12): 1729–42.

Self, Sharmistha, and Richard Grabowski. 2012. "Son Preference, Autonomy and Maternal Health in Rural India." *Oxford Development Studies* 40 (3): 305–23.

Sen, Amartya. 1990. "More Than 100 Million Women Are Missing." *New York Review of Books* 37 (20).

Siddiqi, Dina M. 2003. "The Sexual Harassment of Industrial Workers: Strategies for Intervention in the Workplace and Beyond." CPD-UNFPA Paper 26 (40).

Solotaroff, Jennifer L., and Rohini Prabha Pande. 2014. *Violence against Women and Girls: Lessons from South Asia.* South Asia Development Forum, Washington, DC: World Bank.

Stark, N. 1993. "Gender and Therapy Management: Reproductive Decision Making in Rural Bangladesh." Dissertation, Southern Methodist University, Dallas, TX.

Sultana, Afiya. 2012. "Promoting Women's Entrepreneurship through SME: Growth and Development in the Context of Bangladesh." *Journal of Business and Management* 4 (1): 18–29.

UNDP. 2015. *Human Development Report 2015: Work for Human Development.* New York: UNDP.

UNHCR. 2005. *UNHCR's Policy on Harassment, Sexual Harassment, and Abuse of Authority.* UNHCR.

World Bank. 2008. *Whispers to Voices: Gender and Social Transformation in Bangladesh.* Bangladesh Development Series 22. Dhaka: World Bank.

———. 2012. *World Development Report (WDR) 2012: Gender Equality and Development.* Washington, DC: World Bank.

———. 2015a. "Bangladesh—More and Better Jobs to Accelerate Shared Growth and End Extreme Poverty: A Systematic Country Diagnostic." (accessed June 7, 2017), http://documents .worldbank.org/curated/en/158801468180258840/Bangladesh-More-and-better-jobs-to -accelerate-shared-growth-and-end-extreme-poverty-a-systematic-country-diagnostic.

———. 2015b. "World Bank Group Gender Strategy (FY16–23): Gender Equality, Poverty Reduction and Inclusive Growth." Working Paper 102114, World Bank, Washington, DC.

———. 2016a. "Country Partnership Framework for Bangladesh for the Period FY16–20." World Bank, Washington, DC.

———. 2016b. *Identification for Development: Strategic Framework.* ID4D, Washington, DC: World Bank.

———. 2016c. "South Asia Regional Gender Action Plan, FY16–21." World Bank, Washington, DC.

2 Gender Gaps in Bangladesh's Labor Market Outcomes

ABSTRACT *Over the past decade, Bangladesh has been moving toward greater gender equality in most labor market outcomes. Women—including those who are married—have been entering the labor force in increasing numbers, and the female labor force participation (FLFP) rate increased from 26 percent in 2003 to 36 percent in 2016. Still, the rate of FLFP is low, less than half of the male rate. More than one-third of the female labor force works as unpaid contributing family helpers. Even when women are in paid work, they earn less than men. The gender wage gap has narrowed so much over time that Bangladesh now has the smallest gender wage gap of any country in the region; however, the gender wage gap remains after controlling for education and employment sectors. Removing barriers to FLFP will help the country meet its challenges to create new jobs and enhance its economic competitiveness. Although declining fertility is a boon to female employment, household responsibilities still limit women's labor market opportunities. Restricted mobility due to cultural norms undermines women's access to higher-skill and higher-paying jobs in factories and offices, consigning many to jobs at home or no paid work at all. Girls' enrollment rates are on par with boys' in primary and secondary school, yet a gender gap persists at the tertiary level, which further disadvantages women in LFP and securing well-paid jobs. Finally, many employers are biased against hiring and promoting women, maintaining that doing so disrupts the work environment.*

PATTERNS OF LABOR FORCE PARTICIPATION AND EMPLOYMENT STATUS OVER TIME: DESCRIPTIVE STATISTICS

Gender gaps have shrunk over time, but remain very wide

The Bangladeshi labor force rapidly expanded at a rate of 2.3 percent per year between 2003 and 2016. At the same time, the country's economy has undergone a structural shift with a gradual decline in the share of agricultural employment

FIGURE 2.1

Trends of labor force participation in Bangladesh, by sex and year, 2003–16

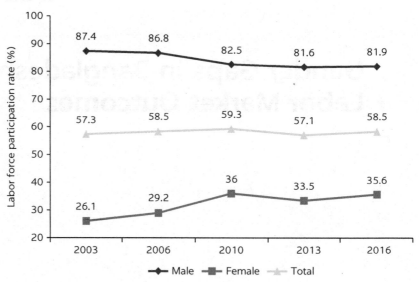

Sources: World Bank calculations based on LFS 2003, 2006, 2010, 2013, and 2016 data.

and strong employment growth in urban areas. About three-quarters of new jobs added over this period were in nonagricultural sectors. As of 2016, however, over 40 percent of Bangladesh's working-age population remained outside the labor force, mainly due to the lack of women participating. Only 36 percent of working-age women are in the labor force, compared to 82 percent of working-age men. Bangladesh's FLFP is lower than that of other lower middle-income countries in Asia such as Nepal, Vietnam and Indonesia (80 percent, 77 percent and 51 percent, respectively).[1]

The female labor force has grown at a much faster rate than the male labor force in Bangladesh (ADB 2016), however (figure 2.1). The World Bank's 2015 Bangladesh Systematic Country Diagnostic (SCD) notes that between 2002–03 and 2013, half of the net increase in employment was due to increases in women's employment (World Bank 2015). In fact, Bangladesh is one of the few countries in South Asia that in recent years has experienced a rapid increase in women's employment, largely due to growth in the readymade garment (RMG) industry and a rise in livestock rearing (Rahman and Islam 2013).

Gender gaps by urban-rural residence and division

The labor force participation (LFP) gender gap has narrowed over the last decade in both rural and urban areas. Whereas men's urban and rural LFP rates have both decreased and coalesced at the same rate of 82 percent in 2016, women's LFP rates have diverged. The rural FLFP rate recovered to almost 38 percent in 2016 after a decline between 2010 and 2013. Urban FLFP, however, continued to decline after 2013 to under 31 percent.

Farole and Cho (2017) explain that declining urban FLFP may be due to lower demand for female labor, associated with the rapid slowdown in job creation in the RMG and textile sectors—the largest source of urban female employment—since 2010 (see box 2.1 for further discussion of the RMG sector). On the other hand, the higher FLFP in rural areas as compared to urban areas may not suggest

BOX 2.1

Balancing act of the RMG sector: Slowdown, working conditions, and competitiveness

The Export Promotion Bureau (EPB) reports a fall in global demand for Bangladesh's garment industry, which has caused a slowing in the export earnings growth rate in the last fiscal year (Ovi 2017). Broadly publicized safety incidents and labor unrest have contributed to slowing growth of the ready-made garment (RMG) sector, as some companies move their manufacturing elsewhere and the sector faces increased scrutiny (World Bank 2017). In particular, the massive 2012 fire in the Tazreen Fashions factory and the 2013 collapse of the Rana Plaza building—which housed five garment factories—highlighted the poor working conditions of garment workers, as well as an array of occupational safety issues at their job sites. Difficult working conditions and the absence of worker rights and benefits have led to labor unrest in the sector, with protesting and rioting common over the last few years (Blumer 2015). This has caused huge losses in terms of property, lives, and the reputation of the garment industry (Salam and McLean 2014).

Conditions for women RMG workers are especially poor, characterized by pressure to work overtime more than men; disproportionately low odds of promotion to supervisor and management positions (even though they operate 85 percent of machines in the industry); inconsistent provision of government-guaranteed maternity leave; inadequate arrangements for childcare and breastfeeding; and frequent abuse (Hossain and Ahmed 2017). A forthcoming study commissioned by Karmojibi Nari, an NGO based in Dhaka that organizes and mobilizes women workers in support of their rights, finds alarmingly high rates of harassment among garment factory workers in particular, with 84.7 percent of women workers reporting experience of verbal harassment, 71.3 percent reporting mental harassment, 20 percent physical harassment, and 12.7 percent sexual harassment (*Dhaka Tribune* 2018). More than half (52 percent) reported experiencing harassment by supervisors. Women workers in the RMG industry in Chittagong who participated in this book's primary qualitative research reported experiencing frequent sexual harassment and other violence in the workplace, including incidents of inappropriate touching and rape. Female participants in general reported experiencing sexual harassment while commuting to and from their places of work. Even policemen on the streets or guards of the factory make illicit proposals, with the connotation that "working women" are not "good women." To lower the risk of such violence, women form groups to travel to and from work. Also for safety reasons, a woman often will try to work in the same factory as her female friend or relative or acquaintance. The harassment women face at work directly impairs productivity, as women fake illness or intentionally slow their work to avoid the harassment; the harassment faced by one woman affects all the others, as other young women tend to become resentful or anxious.

Although women comprise 55 percent of RMG workers—and government policy, *de jure*, recognizes their rights—RMG firms' uptake and enforcement of policy has been slow at best. In response to garment workers' discontent over low pay, the government increased the minimum wage for RMG work in 2013 (Yardley 2013). Two 2013 agreements—the Alliance for Bangladesh Worker Safety and the Bangladesh Accord on Fire and Building Safety—created clear standards for garment factories to improve safety, whereby any factory failing to meet standards would risk losing its relationship with the western brands that are signatories (White 2017). The requirements of these international agreements, as well as increasing demands for improved working conditions and accountability—from both RMG workers and the brands manufacturing their goods in Bangladesh—have led to a number of initiatives and improvements in the sector.

Still, Bangladesh continues to have the world's lowest wages in the garment sector (Yardley 2013). Its losses can possibly be offset by picking up business from China, which has started to cede some ground as a dominant producer due to higher wages (Lopez-Acevedo and Robertson 2016). McKinsey (Berg et al. 2011) believes Bangladesh capable of filling the space left by China's market exit, with its research determining that the country has "what it takes to be the next sourcing hot spot."

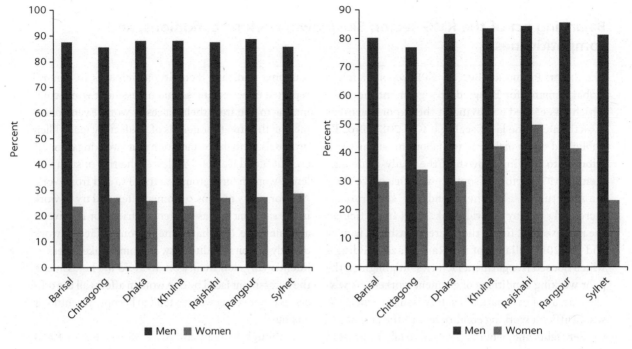

FIGURE 2.2

Labor force participation by sex and division, 2003

Source: World Bank calculations based on Bangladesh LFS 2003 data.

FIGURE 2.3

Labor force participation by sex and division, 2016

Source: World Bank calculations based on Bangladesh LFS 2016 data.

greater economic empowerment, as 2016 Labour Force Survey (LFS) data suggest that many rural women end up working as unpaid family workers. The percentage of women working in paid employment is quite similar between rural and urban areas (22 percent and 26 percent, respectively) despite the almost seven-percent difference in overall female urban and rural LFP.

Between 2003 and 2016, there was an overall improvement in FLFP across divisions, with the exception of Sylhet (figures 2.2 and 2.3). Increasingly so over time, there is distinct variation in women's LFP, whereas men's LFP hovers around 80 percent in all divisions. The northern divisions of Rajshahi and Rangpur tend to have higher FLFP than other divisions, and Sylhet the lowest. Such variation suggests that local and community-specific gender norms, as well as local variations in demand for female labor—and for labor more generally— may dictate FLFP rates.

Gender gaps by education level

Women are increasingly joining the labor force regardless of their educational attainment (figures 2.4 and 2.5)—except for women with tertiary education, who participate in the labor force at slightly lower rates (42 percent in 2016) than before (46 percent in 2003). FLFP rates by education level follow the U-shaped pattern typically found in developing countries: women with low (no or only primary) and high (Diploma or university) levels of education participate more than do women with moderate (secondary) educational attainment (figure 2.5). LFP has decreased for men at most education levels.

FIGURE 2.4

Labor force participation by sex and education level, 2003

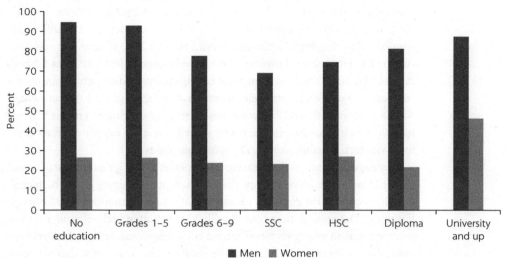

Source: World Bank calculations based on Bangladesh LFS 2003 data.
Notes: The education system of Bangladesh is divided into three tiers: primary, secondary, and tertiary. Primary education includes grades 1–5; secondary includes grades 6–10. There is a distinction between students who have completed 10th grade and those with the secondary school certificates (SSC), who have taken and passed the exam. Higher secondary school (HSC) comprises grades 11 and 12, and the tertiary level includes university level and post-graduate education. After grade 10, students can choose to continue to higher secondary school (and then perhaps on to college) or opt for a diploma track for vocational training.

FIGURE 2.5

Labor force participation by sex and education level, 2016

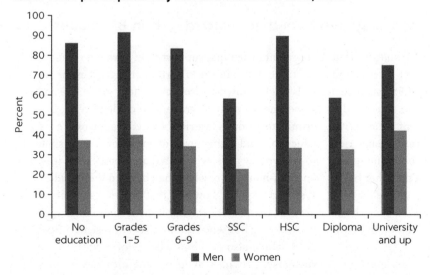

Source: World Bank calculations based on Bangladesh LFS 2016 data.
Notes: The education system of Bangladesh is divided into three tiers: primary, secondary, and tertiary. Primary education includes grades 1–5; secondary includes grades 6–10. There is a distinction between students who have completed 10th grade and those with the secondary school certificates (SSC), who have taken and passed the exam. Higher secondary school (HSC) comprises grades 11 and 12, and the tertiary level includes university level and post-graduate education. After grade 10, students can choose to continue to higher secondary school (and then perhaps on to college) or opt for a diploma track for vocational training. SSC = secondary school certificates.

For all education levels, women's LFP in 2016 is 20–40 percentage points lower than men's. The gender gaps are narrowest among those with education above the higher secondary level, which was also the case in 2003. Promisingly, the gender gap in LFP among those with technical or vocational qualifications (presented as "Diploma") also narrowed between 2003 (figure 2.4) and 2016 (figure 2.5). Of concern, however, is the drop in already-low LFP rates for both males and females (by more than 10 percentage points and 0.5 percentage points, respectively) who complete their education at the SSC (grade 10) level. Of particular concern is that LFP of women with tertiary education remains low and has declined by four percentage points since 2003; it has fallen even further for men with tertiary education, by 12 percentage points.

Marriage is the most common reason (28 percent) why girls drop out of school (box 2.2), which negatively affects their odds of later obtaining jobs of high quality. The second-most common reason is that school is unaffordable. Although fewer girls (1.2 million) than boys (2 million) never attend school at all, the most common reason why girls never attend is the requirement that they perform domestic chores instead. For boys, the most common reason is that school is unaffordable. This has not changed much over time: reasons for never attending school provided by today's youth—and by elderly about their situations 40 years ago—are roughly the same. Among elderly (over age 65) women, the most common reason they did not attend is that "parents did not want" (31 percent) and "to do domestic chores" (30 percent). FLFP rates of married teenagers in 2016 are roughly the same across household income levels, which challenges the hypothesis that child brides tend to work more than unmarried girls because they are poorer and cannot afford to attend school.

BOX 2.2

Married boys are more likely to stay in school than married girls in Bangladesh

Policy makers and practitioners alike suggest that teenagers should remain in school after marriage to keep girls from dropping out, but 2016 LFS data reveal that few married female teenagers do so. Among adolescent girls age 15–19, about 31 percent are married and not in school, while only 3.7 percent are married but enrolled. In other words, only about one in ten married teenage girls is in school. On the other hand, few boys are married at this age, accounting for only about 2.7 percent of all 15-to-19-year-old teenage boys. Even among boys who are married, about one-fifth remain in school.

In their study of Bangladeshi adolescents' gendered experiences and perspectives in one urban and one rural community in Gangachara, Rangpur district, Camfield, Rashid, and Sultan (2017) find that although aspirations of girls and boys alike center on education, girls who prefer to continue their studies are less confident of familial support than boys who want to continue. In addition to early marriage, reasons for girls' higher rates of drop-out before grade 10—and sometimes as early as grade 6—include poverty, discriminatory norms favoring boys' education over girls' education, and higher levels of household responsibilities borne by girls, who spend an average of at least one half-hour per day less than boys on their studies. It should be noted, however, that gender disparities in drop-out rates were smaller in poor households than in wealthier households. More recent research from 2018, which also develops a behavioral intervention response, provides deep insight into the various factors—such as trenchant patriarchal attitudes that value education for boys, but marriage for girls—that serve as incentives and disincentives for parents to marry off daughters at an early age (Jahan, Moyeen, and DRI, forthcoming).

FIGURE 2.6

Labor force participation by sex and wealth quintile, 2016

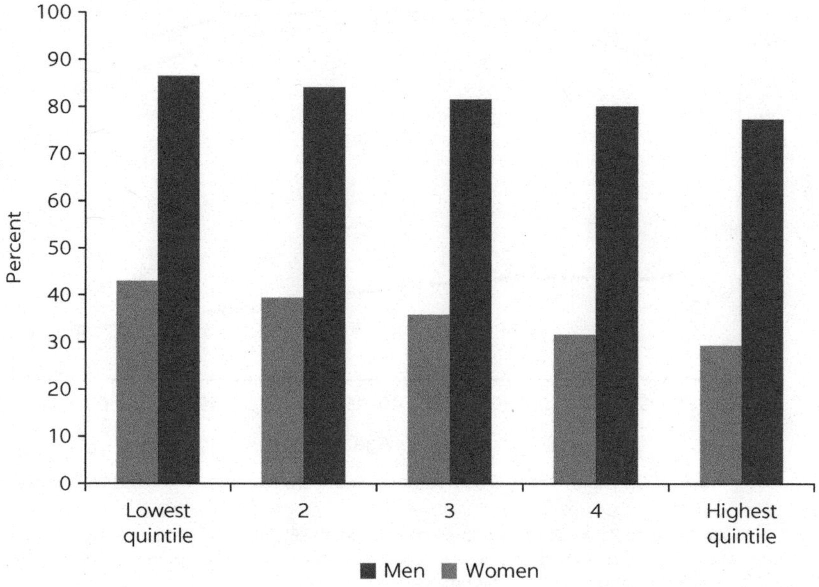

■ Men ■ Women

Source: World Bank calculations based on Bangladesh LFS 2016 data.

Gender gaps by household wealth and income

Rising family wealth is associated with greater reductions in women's labor force participation than men's. Data on LFP of men and women by quintiles of wealth[2] show that while female LFP is much lower than that of males in every quintile of wealth, there is a small and consistent decline of LFP for both men and women as household wealth increases (figure 2.6). FLFP appears to drop at a steeper rate than does men's LFP however—on average by 3.4 percent for women and 2.3 percent for men—with each step up in household quintile of wealth. Similarly, there is a clear and gradual decrease in female LFP as the income of the head of household increases, regardless of who is the household head.

Gender gaps by age group

Over the past 13 years, the age-LFP profile of women has shifted. As a general rule in labor markets around the world, LFP tends to be low among youth, many of whom are still in school. LFP rates are highest among workers of "prime age"—around 25–54 years old[3]—and then taper off as workers approach retirement. By 2016, LFP for both men and women peaks around age 30–39 (figure 2.7), but there is an interesting evolution for women's participation by age between 2003 and 2016; whereas, the labor market profile for men remains roughly the same, the profile for women shifts upward across all age groups.

EMPLOYMENT BY SECTOR

Formal versus informal employment

Female workers are much more likely to be employed in the informal sector[4] than their male counterparts. In 2016, only 4.6 percent of women workers held

FIGURE 2.7

Trends of labor force participation by age group and sex, 2003 and 2016

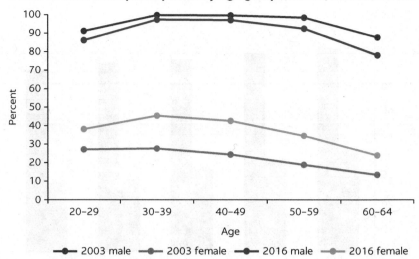

Sources: World Bank calculations based on Bangladesh LFS 2003 and 2016 data. Age groups under 20 years are excluded to allow for comparability between years given expanding education in Bangladesh over this time period.

FIGURE 2.8

Formal employment by sex and education, 2016

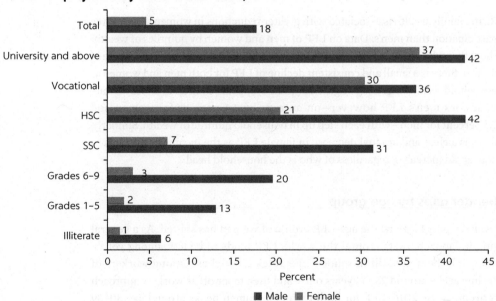

Source: World Bank calculations based on Bangladesh LFS 2016 data.
Note: HSC = higher secondary school; SSC = secondary school certificates.

formal-sector jobs, compared to 17.7 percent of working men; most of Bangladesh's 17.8 million women employed in the informal sector reside in the country's rural areas (13.3 million workers) (Bangladesh Bureau of Statistics 2016).

Formal employment is associated with higher levels of education for both men and women (figure 2.8). Whereas only 10 percent of employed persons with only primary education are in formal employment, this number increases with each additional level of educational attainment, reaching an overall rate of 41 percent formal sector employment for those with tertiary education (42 percent and 37 percent for men and women, respectively). Men have higher rates of formal employment than women at all education levels, but the gap is greatest at the secondary level and below (figure 2.8).

Structural and industry-specific gender gaps

Bangladesh's economy has undergone considerable structural change since it achieved independence in 1971, increasingly moving from agriculture toward industry and services. Whereas the majority of all jobs in 2003 were in agriculture, around 84 percent of all new jobs created between 2003 and 2016 were outside of agriculture (Farole and Cho 2017). This is largely due to the reduction of agriculture and expansion of industry in urban areas, with industry jobs accounting for 74 percent of the change in employment share over this period. The structural shift shows a gendered pattern (figure 2.9), given the occupational sex-segregation of Bangladesh's labor market (discussed later in this chapter). Women have not been able to move into higher-paid industry and service jobs as much as men; the 63 percent of employed women working in agriculture is nearly double that of men in agriculture. Men dominate the service sector at 43.7 percent of all male employment, compared to 20.8 percent of female employment. There is less of a gender gap in the industry sector, which accounts for 16.1 percent of female and 22.3 percent of male employment. Rural female agricultural workers constitute the largest share of Bangladesh's unpaid employment: female rural employment makes up about 70 percent of all unpaid employment, and 87 percent of these unpaid jobs for rural women are in agriculture (Farole and Cho 2017).

FIGURE 2.9

Sector composition of employment by gender, 2003–16

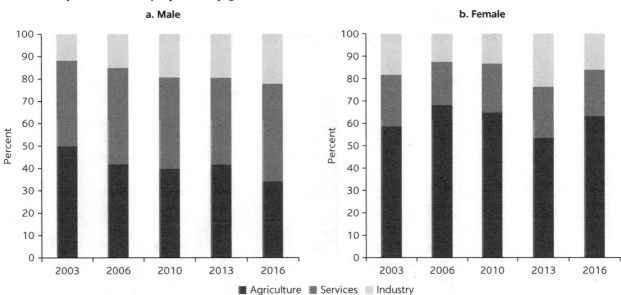

Sources: World Bank calculations based on Bangladesh LFS 2003, 2006, 2010, 2013, and 2016 data.
Note: Employment of persons age 15 and older.

UNEMPLOYMENT AND EMPLOYMENT STATUS

Successive LFSs indicate that unemployment rates for women are higher than those for men; moreover, they have been higher and have fluctuated more than men's over the past two decades. The gender gap persists in both urban and rural areas, where female unemployment (7.7 percent and 6.5 percent, respectively) is higher than male unemployment (3.2 percent and 2.9 percent, respectively). Unemployment is highest (10.2 percent) among those age 15–24 years, followed by those age 25–34 (5.1 percent), and is higher for women than men in these age groups (figure 2.10).

Unemployment also is higher among those with greater educational attainment and varies by sex and location (figure 2.11). The rate is lowest for those with no school, gradually increasing with each education level and peaking at the tertiary level (9 percent). Rates are highest for women with tertiary education (16.8 percent, compared to 6.9 percent for university-educated men)—especially rural women, who have a whopping 24 percent unemployment rate (Bangladesh Bureau of Statistics 2016). Urban female and male rates are 13.1 and 4.9, respectively (figure 2.11).

Farole and Cho (2017) note that youth unemployment rates have spiked in recent years, whereas those for older workers have remained stable. The large gender gap among post-secondary youth makes school-to-work transitions an important challenge, especially given slowing job growth (Farole and Cho 2017).

Employment status continues to be a major challenge for most women who do work. Much more so than men, women continue to be relegated to jobs in the informal sector and jobs with lower wages, receive lower salaries than men who occupy the same job, and generally have less decision-making authority and status—and thus likely lower job quality—than do men.

More than one-third of the female labor force works as unpaid contributing family helpers. People participating in the labor market can be grouped into four categories: employers, employees, own-account workers, and contributing family helpers (figure 2.12). Compared to men, women who work are disproportionately

FIGURE 2.10

Rate of unemployment by age group, sex, and residence, 2016

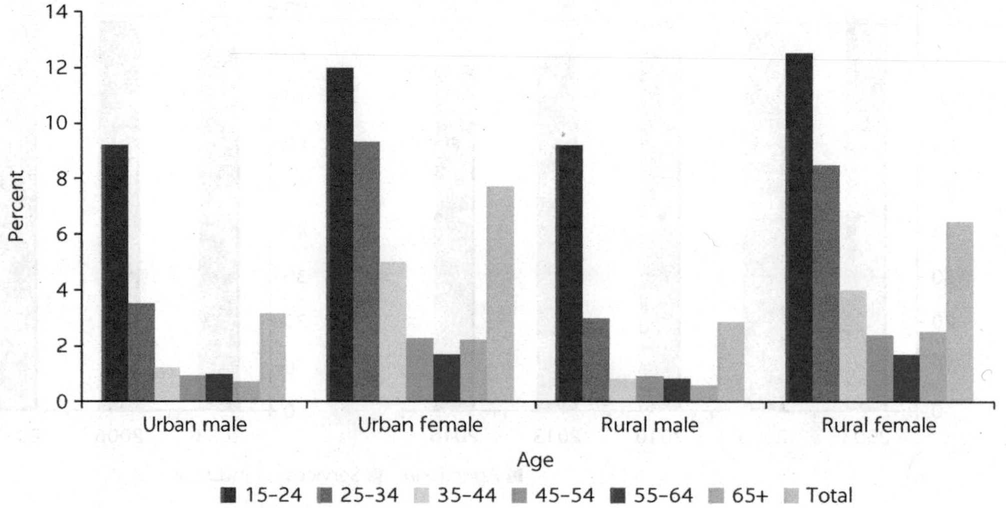

Source: World Bank calculations based on LFS 2016 data.

not directly earning income on their own, but instead work as "contributing family helpers" (box 2.3), especially in rural areas. Such work is likely less economically empowering than paid work, as women work as helpers on household enterprises (for example, family farms), instead of managing and making decisions about them. More importantly, contributing family helpers are neither paid nor do they handle proceeds from household enterprises or control money in any other way.

FIGURE 2.11

Unemployment rate (age 15+), by education level, sex, and area, 2016

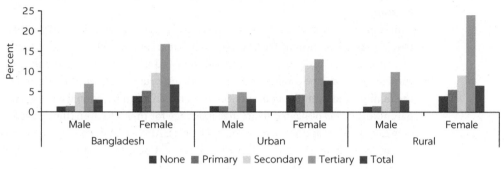

Source: World Bank calculations based on LFS 2016 data.

FIGURE 2.12

Employment status by sex and residential area, 2016

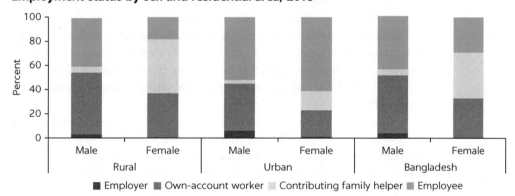

Source: World Bank calculations based on LFS 2016 data.

Definition of contributing family helpers

According to the Bangladesh Bureau of Statistics, "contributing family workers" or "helpers" are those who hold a self-employment job in a market-oriented establishment operated by a related person living in the same household, and who cannot be regarded as partners. Thus, they are usually unpaid and sometimes are categorized as unpaid family workers. On the other hand, own-account workers (who typically earn income) work on their own or with one or more partners as self-employed workers and do not engage any employees on a continuous basis to work for them. The partners may or may not be members of the same family or household.

Source: Bangladesh Bureau of Statistics 2016.

RELATIVE IMPORTANCE OF DIFFERENT BARRIERS AND ENABLERS TO WOMEN'S LFP AND EMPLOYMENT

Multivariate analysis of LFS data sheds light on the relative importance of different societal, human capital and other barriers to women's LFP, employment, and odds of securing paid work.

Family and household roles and responsibilities

Marriage

Unlike in most other South Asian countries, marriage penalizes only urban women's participation in Bangladesh's labor markets, whereas it is associated with higher LFP probabilities for urban men and for both women and men in rural areas. Marriage often is regarded as an important socio-cultural event for the family—and even the community—rather than as an individual choice, and parents often feel obligated to arrange marriage for their children (though rates of arranged marriage are decreasing over time). Almost all women are married by age 25. In 2016, the probability of LFP was 6.4 percentage points lower for urban married women than for urban unmarried women, whereas marriage was associated with a 14-percentage-point premium for urban men (see table B.1 in appendix B for regression results). In rural areas, women's LFP probabilities appear to benefit from marriage by 2.2 percentage points; those of men benefit by 13 percentage points. There may be more—or stronger—barriers for married women to work in urban areas than in rural ones. A very large share of rural women's work is performed close to the household and within the local community, as much of it is agricultural. Urban women's work may more often require leaving the community, which is more likely to face familial disapproval. Arranging childcare may also be easier in rural settings. These hypotheses are explored below.

This relationship between marriage and work reflects several shifts in married women's work patterns over time. First, over the past 15 years, FLFP has increased across the board, but the most pronounced shift is among married women. FLFP for married women over 20 years old was higher in 2016 than in 2003 (figure 2.13). Whereas only unmarried women's LFP by age group had a convex or "hump" shape in 2003 and married women's LFP rates conveyed a downward slope by age group, the shape of the FLFP-age profile for married women had also assumed the convex shape by 2016.

Second, more married women who did not work formerly have entered the labor market. Unmarried prime-age (25–54-year-old) women, who comprise a small minority of women, have higher LFP rates than their married peers. This "single premium" has not changed over time. Gains for married women have been substantial, however. The LFP rate of married women in the cohort born between 1968 and 1977 (who were thus 26–35 years old in 2003, and 39–48 years old in 2016) increased from 26 percent in 2003 to 42 percent in 2016. This is a remarkable shift in the labor market behavior of Bangladeshi women, given its departure from the past negative association between marriage and FLFP. Life cycle changes may partly explain the finding that older married women (in their 30s and 40s) have higher LFP rates than younger married women (20s and under). As women become older, they have fewer childcare responsibilities; more recently, they also may have more freedom and agency to join labor markets.

FIGURE 2.13

Age profile of female labor force participation by marital status and marriage rate

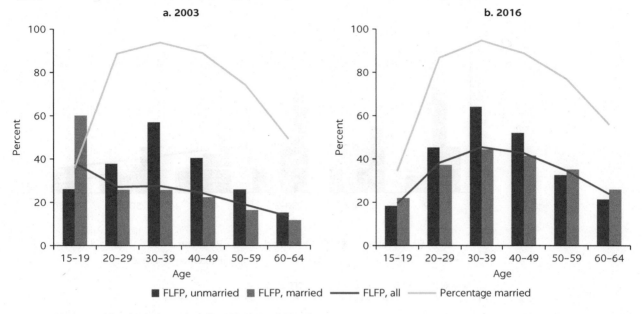

Sources: World Bank calculations based on LFS 2003 and 2016 data.
Note: FLFP = female labor force participation.

FIGURE 2.14

LFP and paid employment of women, by age range and marital status, 2016

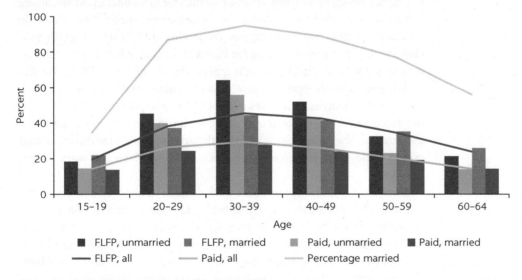

Source: World Bank calculations based on LFS 2016 data.
Note: LFP = labor force participation; FLFP = female labor force participation.

Third, although more married women enter labor markets as they become older, many still enter as unpaid workers. Figure 2.14 shows the age profile of both LFP and paid employment for women in 2016. A large portion of married women in the labor force are unpaid family workers. Although 44 percent of married women age 30–39 are in the labor force, about one-third are unpaid, whereas almost 90 percent of unmarried women are paid employees. Unlike overall FLFP, for which the age profile's shape has shifted, age profiles for paid employment are concave for 2003 and 2016 (figures 2.14 and 2.15).

FIGURE 2.15

LFP and paid employment of women, by age range and marital status, 2003

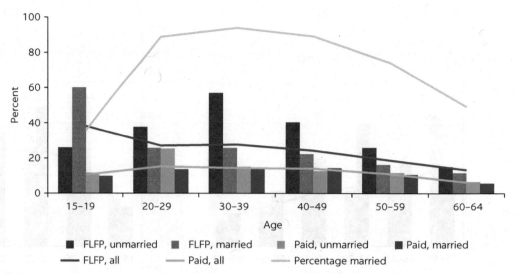

Source: World Bank calculations based on LFS 2003 data.
Note: LFP = labor force participation; FLFP = female labor force participation.

Fourth, whereas in 2003, LFP rates among female youth who marry early were high, this rate has dropped over time. The LFP of women age 15–19 in 2016 was higher among those who were married than for those unmarried; yet, among women ages 20–29, LFP was lower for those married (figure 2.14). Given the association of child marriage with poverty, this high LFP in 2003 might be associated with higher poverty among families with early marriage. Comparing LFS data from 2003 and 2016, however, it appears that the higher FLFP among married teenagers has dropped drastically. As LFS data do not allow for analysis of whether child marriage increases odds of FLFP or of paid work (LFS does not record age at first marriage; it only collects data on current marital status), we use data from the Demographic and Health Surveys (DHS)[5] in multivariate analysis to explore the relationship between child marriage and work for pay (box 2.4).

Marriage may influence women's work through its effect on education. This is true for child brides, as well as adult brides. Like the quantitative findings presented in box 2.4, qualitative findings from women's focus group discussions (FGDs) suggest that continuing education after marriage is extremely difficult and almost nonexistent, especially among working-class communities. Almost all participants of all ages, male and female, and in urban and rural areas, reported that women could only continue studying if their husbands and/or in-laws allowed them to do so. This perception contrasted starkly with the aspirations of girls and young women, many of whom wished to eventually work as doctors, journalists and other professionals, and even policewomen. Husbands and in-laws appear to regulate married women's desire for jobs that require considerable education and training, even when resources or infrastructure are not obstacles.

Wives and daughters-in-law are permitted to work when necessary, on the other hand, especially in circumstances of financial need (box 2.5). As a mother-in-law from a Dhaka slum said, "A son brings a daughter-in-law to the family by

Child marriage and women's work for pay in Bangladesh over time—a multivariate analysis

Child marriage can negatively influence women's odds of working for pay through at least two channels: (1) its impact on education, as girls who marry early are typically forced to end their education at lower levels than girls who marry later; and (2) a higher lifetime fertility and more time spent in childbearing and childrearing, which detract from time available to seek work or work for pay (Parsons et al. 2015). A recent cross-country analysis by Wodon et al. (2017) finds, however, that the direct effect of child marriage on women's work for pay may not be statistically significant or consistent across countries, after accounting for education and other pathways by which child marriage may influence work for pay.

Our analysis of multiple DHS rounds for Bangladesh from 2004 to 2014 is consistent with these findings (figure B2.4.1; see appendix C for full regression tables). Child marriage does not have a direct or consistent relationship with women working for pay across survey years, after accounting for other factors such as a woman's own education, spousal education, urban-rural and divisional residence, and household

wealth. In fact, other variables are more likely to have consistent, statistically significant effects over time on women's work for pay. Urban women are significantly more likely to work for pay than rural women, in all survey years. Women whose partners are educated or who come from higher socioeconomic households are less likely to work for pay, across survey years, than women from poorer households or with less-educated spouses: this relationship is consistent with other findings of lower labor force participation at higher levels of household wealth as families who can afford to do so withdraw women from the labor force (for instance, see Klasen and Pieters (2015)).

On the other hand, our analysis across multiple DHS rounds of the relationship between child marriage and years of schooling shows notably different patterns. As found by Wodon et al. (2017) and in Bangladesh by Field and Ambrus (2008), child marriage has a notable dampening effect on girls' educational attainment (figure B2.4.2). Women and girls married as children have significantly fewer years of schooling than those married later, after controlling

FIGURE B2.4.1

Marginal effect of child marriage on women's probability of working for pay

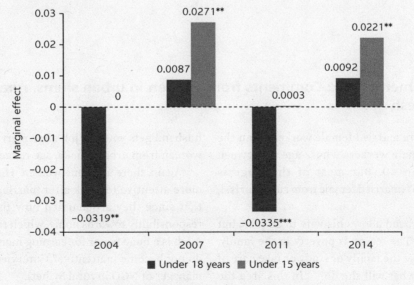

Source: World Bank analysis based on data from multiple DHS.
Note: ** signify $p < 0.05$; *** signify $p < 0.001$.

continued

Box 2.4, *continued*

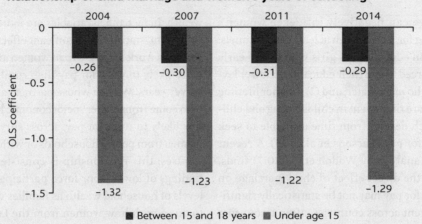

FIGURE B2.4.2
Relationship of child marriage and women's years of schooling

Source: World Bank analysis based on data from multiple DHS.

for a range of other factors (all coefficients are statistically significant with $p < 0.001$); this effect was as strong in 2014, as 10 years before. Notably, and not surprisingly, marriage under age 15 has a much stronger negative effect than marriage between 15 and 18 years, compared to marriage after 18, across all survey years. It is important to note that concerns of endogeneity (for a discussion and references see, for example, Solotaroff and Pande [2014]) suggest tempering the interpretation of these results. Instrumental variables

can be used to overcome some of the endogeneity. Field and Ambrus (2008) use age at menarche as an instrument for child marriage, on the assumption that most marriage in Bangladesh occurs after it. Nguyen and Wodon (2017) use age at marriage in the past and contemporaneous with survey year in the area where a girl lives as their instrument. Both sets of analyses also find that child marriage has a significant negative impact on schooling for girls, particularly at secondary levels.

BOX 2.5

Married women's work: Comments from women in urban slums, rural areas of Bangladesh

"There are more married female workers than the unmarried female workers whose age is between 20–35 or even 40. But most of their age is between 20–35" (married female from rural Barisal, age 35).

"A good husband allows his wife to do jobs, but not to study." "The reason is poverty in the family. Will she manage the family or study or take care of her husband...what will she do?" "In this area the

husband gets you in a job after marrying." (FGD of women from urban Dhaka, age range 25–45)

"Again, there are some women who become even more attentive to work after marriage. They think that since they are married now they have more responsibility towards home, which requires money. A job is a huge factor for earning money and so they do not become inattentive" (interview with female manager of NGO in rural Sylhet).

Source: Primary qualitative data collected in 2016.

his own choice, but a daughter-in law does not bring any resources or wealth with her. She should work and earn an income to support her living costs. Otherwise, who will bear her expenses?" Women also often work when husbands migrate to other areas or when their household requires additional income. Even when husbands and in-laws permit them to work, however, women must constantly be mindful of adhering to gender norms, returning home from work in time to cook dinner, not interacting with male colleagues, and not moving out of the locality for work. In other words, the traditional norm that relegates married women to the household can be relaxed to the extent that women are allowed to access work opportunities in cases of household economic need, but some aspects of the norm remain firmly in place.

Household composition

Providing care—for domestic tasks, children and the elderly—has intrinsic economic value. It helps others have time to pursue work if they want to. Unfortunately, in most countries women perform a disproportionate share of care work compared to men, and the economic value of this care work is not considered. This lopsided burden within the household constrains women from engaging in paid employment; although husbands increasingly share this burden with their wives (particularly in urban Bangladesh), women still bear the lion's share of it.

Having children in the household is significantly related to LFP probabilities of both men and women, though the relationship varies by the child's age. Women with children age 0–5 years in the household are significantly less likely to join the labor force than women without young children (for men the relationship is not significant), but if there are children age 6–10 years in the household, both women and men are more likely to be in labor markets (compared to women and men without children this age). The negative association between LFP probabilities and children age 0–5 is nearly three times the magnitude for urban women as for rural women (see table B.1 in appendix B for full regression results). This finding suggests that provision of childcare services for young children could help women—particularly in urban areas—enter labor markets. Oaxaca decomposition models that help explain which factors contribute to the increase in FLFP rates between 2003 and 2016 also emphasize the role of young children (see table B.3 in appendix B): declining fertility has had the greatest positive association with the rise in FLFP in this period. On average, households have fewer young children (five years old or less) in 2016 than in 2003. The relationship between child rearing and FLFP also has changed; whereas taking care of young children is more of a constraint in 2016 (that is, has a larger significant, negative association with FLFP) compared to 2003, taking care of older children (age 6–14) interferes less with women's LFP than before.

The presence of elderly in the household is positively associated with LFP, unlike before, which suggests an increase in support from elder family members. The presence of elderly household members is associated with slightly higher FLFP rates for both men and women than of those who do not live with elders in 2016. The decomposition analysis confirms this observation. In 2003, however, the presence of elderly women had a significant positive association only with men's LFP probabilities (see table B.2 in appendix B). These findings suggest two important, complementary developments over the past decade. First, Bangladeshi women may be shifting their priorities away from providing care for elderly family members (fulfilling expectations of women's traditional roles) toward depending on the elderly to provide care for children or other household responsibilities so these women can work. Second, attitudes of in-laws toward women's employment may have shifted over the past decade in a more supportive direction.

Female heads of household are 12 percentage points more likely to be in the labor force than other women. The need for financial resources is likely a prime motivation, since female household headship indicates a lack of male earners in such households. These odds are even higher in urban areas (by 16 percentage points), which could reflect urban female heads' relative lack of support networks—or perhaps their greater relative agency to choose work—compared to rural female household heads.

Household constraints and women's time use

Bangladeshi women's disproportionate burden of household and care work makes them time-poor. To examine gender differences in time use, we analyze data from the 2013 LFS,[6] focusing on the married population because it is most relevant to the discussion of time allocation within households. Married women spend more than 22 hours per week on care work, while married men spend about 6 hours per week (figure 2.16). These results are similar to those from a more geographically focused research of rural men and women in Lalmonirhat and Gaibandha districts in Rangpur, carried out from November 2013 to October 2014 (Mahmud and Mustafa 2015). In this study, surveyed men spent much less time (1 hour) in mean hours per day on care work, and much more time in productive work (8 hours) than women (7 and 5 mean hours per day, respectively). Moreover, most of men's work for the household takes them outside the home; compared to women's 22 hours inside the home, men spend less than two hours per week there. That men often take sole responsibility for shopping for households is likely related to the gender norms of purdah and women's lack of mobility and control over household finances.

Bangladesh's Time Use Survey data from 2012 also convey married women's heavier burden: women spend more than six hours per day on household domestic services and unpaid care work—four times what men spend on these

FIGURE 2.16

Time use in care work among married men and women, 2013

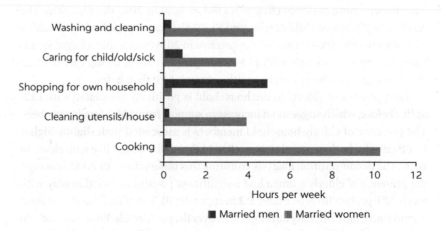

Source: World Bank calculations based on Bangladesh LFS 2013 data.

activities (table 2.1). Time allocated for personal care is roughly the same for men and women. Nonworking urban women spend more time on caregiving than nonworking rural women, but there is no difference between employed rural and urban women. This reinforces the multivariate analysis finding that care work may present an even greater obstacle to urban women's work than to rural women's, suggesting that access to child care services may be most urgently needed to bringing more urban women into the workforce.

Such care work hampers female employment. Data on reasons for respondents' absence from the labor force (urban and rural residents pooled) reveals that housework and care of family is perceived as a far more critical constraint on women's LFP than on men's: close to 80 percent of women but only about 15 percent of men report these as major constraints. The greatest constraint on men's LFP is schooling or training for future work. The finding that housework is the main constraint on women's LFP is also corroborated by BIHS 2015 data on Bangladesh's rural population (box 2.6).

Mobility constraints

Mobility constraints substantially hinder women's ability to work for pay and contribute to lower salaries for them than men. When women work, they still tend to work at or near home (figure 2.17). Sixty-nine percent of working rural

TABLE 2.1 Time spent on various activities (hours), by sex and residential area, 2012

| | RURAL | | | | | | URBAN | | | | | |
| | FEMALE | | | MALE | | | FEMALE | | | MALE | | |
EMPLOYED (ACTIVITY)	NO	YES	TOTAL	NO	YES	TOTAL	NO	YES	TOTAL	NO	YES	TOTAL
Work	0.0	5.3	1.4	0.0	7.4	6.4	0.0	7.0	2.0	0.0	8.6	7.5
Care—children, elderly	0.9	0.7	0.9	0.1	0.1	0.1	1.2	0.7	1.1	0.1	0.1	0.1
Domestic—cook, clean	6.2	3.1	5.4	2.2	1.3	1.4	5.6	2.2	4.7	1.7	0.8	0.9
Leisure/others	2.3	1.4	2.1	3.4	1.9	2.1	3.1	1.8	2.7	4.0	2.1	2.4
Personal maintenance	14.5	13.5	14.2	18.2	13.3	14.0	14.1	12.3	13.6	18.1	12.4	13.1

Source: World Bank calculations based on Bangladesh Time Use Survey 2012 data.

BOX 2.6

Reasons for not working among rural women in Bangladesh

Bangladesh Integrated Household Survey (BIHS) 2015 data confirm that, among household chores, taking care of children is the biggest constraint on rural women's LFP (for about 50 percent of those who do not work). The second most important reported reason—for about 17 percent who do not work—is household wealth. Somewhat surprisingly, lack of demand for female labor does not appear to be a problem in rural areas; it was not among the reasons women reported for not working.

Interestingly, familial support appears to be a minimal constraint. Less than five percent of rural women report unsupportive husbands, in-laws, or society as a constraint. Among women who work, when asked "At first did your husband or other household member want to prevent you from working to earn money?," the vast majority (96 percent) reported "no." Moreover, about 50 percent reported that they themselves made the decision to join the labor force.

FIGURE 2.17

Location of work, by sex and residential area, 2016

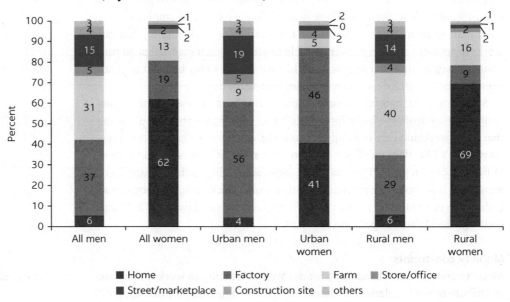

Source: World Bank calculations based on Bangladesh LFS 2016 data.

FIGURE 2.18

Location of work, by sex and residential area, 2003

Source: World Bank calculations based on Bangladesh LFS 2003 data.

females work inside their home (or right outside of it). In urban areas, this share is smaller, around 42 percent. On the other hand, almost all men work outside their homes. The share of urban workers working in factories has increased more than threefold for both men and women. However, while the share of men working at home remains small, the share of women working at home has increased notably, as well (figure 2.18). LFS data also show that though women earn less than men in all locations, the wage gap is largest among those working at home, with women earning 6,000 Bangladeshi Taka (BDT) less per month on average compared to men. The gender-based earnings differential is less than 3,000 BDT (or about 23 percent) for workers in factories.

Mobility restrictions also limit women's ability to migrate for work. The 2016 LFS data reveal that far fewer women migrated to seek new employment opportunities than men. As it is customary for brides to move to grooms' houses after marriage, women migrate more than men and overwhelmingly for marriage and other family reasons. To consider this factor judiciously, we exclude those whose reason for migration is marriage (figure 2.19). Far fewer women cite job search as their primary reason for moving (21 percent of women compared to 57 percent of men). At the same time, those women who do migrate in search of work are able to find work: the same dataset shows that close to 83 percent of women who migrate for job opportunities find a job.

Women may gain power in the household when men migrate. Qualitative research suggests that in the absence of a male head of household, women exercise greater (in some cases full) control over the income husbands send home, greater decision making, more mobility, and improved family status. In particular, both men and women opined that women's mobility is likely to increase substantially when the male head of household migrates. To some extent this is unsurprising; women must take on several of their (absent) husband's household and external responsibilities and go outside the household as needed. Women also feel their status in the family increases along with decision-making ability and control over money.

Skills mismatch and occupational segregation

Achieving gender equality in education levels alone will not help close gender gaps in LFP. Bangladeshi women's poor labor market outcomes are especially confounding given the tremendous improvements in girls' education in the past two decades, with educational outcomes of female youth now on par with those of male youth, if not slightly better: in 2016, more female than male youth

FIGURE 2.19
Reasons to migrate (excluding marriage), 2016

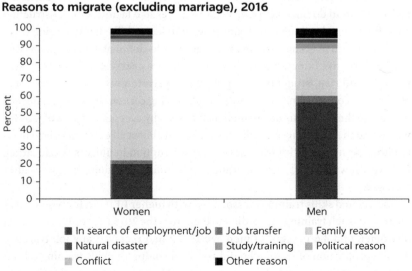

Source: World Bank calculations based on Bangladesh LFS 2016 data.

completed secondary education (10.5 percent versus 7.5 percent), but their LFP rate was still much lower than that of men. Given Bangladeshi women's current educational attainments, they should be participating in the labor market at higher rates. Compared to those who are illiterate, however, both men and women with more education have a lower propensity to join the labor force (see table B.1 in appendix B). This holds true for men and women in urban areas, as well as for rural men. Only rural women with at least some college-level education have a higher probability of working than rural women with no education.

Does a skills mismatch explain the phenomenon of gender parity in education but not in employment? Sex segregation in choice of educational stream likely contributes to women pursuing skills that are not marketable, thus lowering their opportunities for employment even when highly educated. Data from UNESCO illustrate that female students are disproportionately sorted into humanities and social sciences in most countries; across 106 countries (where data are available), engineering is considered "male-dominated" in 98 percent of countries (Das, Carranza, and Kotikula, forthcoming). On the other hand, education and health are considered "female-dominated" in 81 percent and 85 percent of countries, respectively. Such sex segregation across subject areas at the tertiary level also appears to be true for Bangladesh. Yet, the same UNESCO data show that Bangladesh has roughly the same share (about 44 percent) of female students enrolled in humanities and science, with a smaller percent (about 35 percent) enrolled in the field of education.

The qualitative data suggest that these patterns vary by urban/rural residence. Interviews with trainers at government vocational training centers in urban areas and trainers at livelihoods training centers in rural areas reveal that in urban areas, female students prefer studying architecture or computer science rather than subjects like civil engineering that would require site visits or construction supervision. Whereas boys in rural areas tend to learn computer skills, rural girls take up stitching, sewing, tailoring, and similar work associated with traditional women's activities. Although social norms also are at play in urban areas, urban middle-class women may choose from a greater range of socially acceptable professions. Overall, however, both urban and rural female students appear to make "safe" choices: urban female students across income levels tend to choose subjects that will lead to employment and at the same time will not require them to do internships or work in places like factories or construction sites. Rural female students or trainees want to learn skills that will bring them income but will not require them to engage in male-dominated occupations that involve extensive interaction with male colleagues or traveling to distant locations. In addition, students from public and private universities report that teachers discourage female students from studying certain subjects and instead encourage them to focus on areas aligned to socially acceptable types of jobs for women, such as teaching and administration. In almost all cases, marriage leads to either permanent withdrawal or serious disruption in university education. Only very few female students continue their studies or training programs after marriage.

Job-related skills training is associated with higher LFP, but few young people receive such training. According to data from the 2016 LFS, only 2.3 percent of women and 4.6 percent of men age 15–30 had received any job training. A large proportion of those who did received computer skills training (about 40 percent of women and 55 percent of men). Most people received training in private institutes (about 75 percent of trainees), followed by government and nongovernmental organization (NGO) locations (Bangladesh Bureau of Statistics 2016).

Young men and women who received training had substantially higher LFP rates—especially young women, who saw a 40 percentage-point increase. Our qualitative data are consistent with this pattern. Both male and female respondents, irrespective of their age and across urban and rural areas, report that training and skills-building helped in obtaining employment or making progress in their careers when already employed. Women strongly voice the importance of skills, even more so than education; however, participants remark on the lack of nearby skills training centers. Even when a center is geographically accessible, it may be difficult for women to travel on local transportation because of mobility constraints, including fear of sexual harassment; others lack resources to pay for training. Female respondents recognize the value of skills training, which not only equips them a better bargaining position and higher odds of vertical professional mobility but builds confidence and self-esteem, as well.

Qualitative study respondents also highlight the importance of training and education for meaningful work in the RMG sector, a major employer for women. A majority of respondents reported that obtaining entry-level employment does not require experience; however, those who already possess skills—such as sewing or stitching in the case of RMG workers—are able to bargain for a higher salary than other workers. Interviewees from the RMG sector also mention the importance of leadership and management training for higher-skill and higher-status jobs. Having some level of education reportedly is almost always required by RMG and other formal sector employment. According to a married working woman from Dhaka, "Before it did not matter and garment factories would hire workers without expertise. But now they want workers who have at least completed secondary school [received their secondary school certificate (SSC)] to be employed at the garment factory. They do not want to give work to women who are without an education. If workers have a long working experience, garment factory supervisors will take them as a worker and do not factor in the level of education." Another married woman from Dhaka who works as a helper at a garment factory said, "A helper's salary in the garments factory is 5,000 BDT. Supervisors do not want to pay such an amount to young girls by hiring them as helpers, so operators also perform the responsibility of a helper. In this area girls sometimes get work as per their choices, but sometimes they have to accept work that they dislike due to their lack of education and expertise." FGDs with male participants echoed these findings. An adult man from urban Chittagong said, "Females are able to do a good job when they complete their education. Not only that—those who are educated are able to do jobs in garment factories with more salary. Females are supervisors in many garment factories."

In the absence of preferred skills and education, networking and gendered beliefs about women workers may explain the strong female presence in the garment sector, our qualitative respondents note. Female RMG employees most often obtain jobs through referrals from someone they know already working at the factory. Male FGD participants from Dhaka's urban slums believe that garment factories prefer hiring women for their perceived docile, compliant nature, and because they can be paid less than their male colleagues for the same work performed.

Occupational sex segregation is another constraint on women's access to higher-paying jobs. In labor markets across the world, a phenomenon observed across the board is the imbalance in the types of employment in which men and women engage, and the consequent existence of male-dominated and female-dominated sectors or jobs. We refer to such a phenomenon as "gender-based employment segregation." Reducing employment segregation is central to women's economic empowerment in three ways: (1) improving job quality and earnings for women and further reducing the gender wage gap; (2) increasing skill acquisition and overall economic productivity; and (3) improving household welfare and intergenerational social mobility (Das, Carranza, and Kotikula, forthcoming).

In Bangladesh, what are "women's jobs"? The labor market in Bangladesh exhibits occupational sex-segregation. Using the Duncan Index,[7] occupational segregation is at about 0.50—more than Asian comparator countries like Indonesia (0.18) but less than Algeria (0.67) and El Salvador (0.64). Most Bangladeshi men (60 percent) work in male-dominated industries[8] but, since men account for about 70 percent of all employment in Bangladesh, most industries are male-dominated. About 21 percent of women work in female-dominated occupations, and three-quarters in "mixed gender" industries. These sectors tend to offer lower wages than male-dominated occupations. Notably, a significant number of male workers (almost 40 percent) also work in mixed occupations.

What precisely defines a job as a "woman's" job in Bangladesh? Gender norms often relegate women to certain types of jobs, and people form related perceptions about which are most appropriate for men and which for women. Market forces may also drive these differences. Using LFS data, we examine which jobs in Bangladesh are most likely to be women's jobs, defined as occupations where the proportion of female workers is higher than 30 percent (roughly the national average of women among the working population). These are thus jobs that women occupy at the same or a greater rate than the overall participation of women in the labor force nationally (figures 2.20 and 2.21).

FIGURE 2.20

Occupations with high shares of female workers, 2003

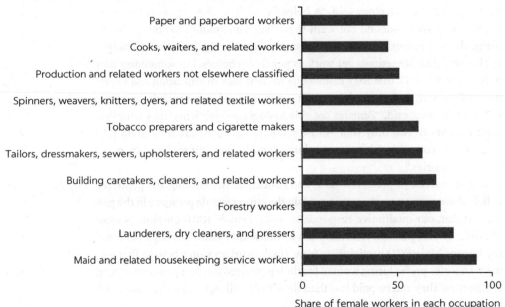

Source: World Bank calculations based on Bangladesh LFS 2003 data.

FIGURE 2.21

Occupations with high shares of female workers, 2016

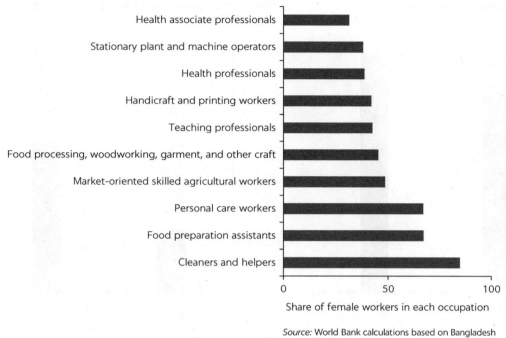

Source: World Bank calculations based on Bangladesh
LFS 2003 data.

The data reveal that agriculture has roughly equal shares of male and female
workers and that women comprise nearly half of workers in skilled agriculture.
Whereas traditional low-pay workers such as cleaners and maids are predominantly female, the share of female workers in human services sectors such as
health and education is less than 50 percent. On the other hand, many manufacturing and higher-skill service occupations show a high share of female workers
in 2016, an encouraging trend. Our qualitative data provide further nuance.
In the formal sector, employed women participants work in garment factories,
PVC tape factories, small manufacturing factories, dyeing factories, and baker-
ies. In the informal sector, female participants mainly work as housemaids, day
laborers, hawkers, community cleaners, and tailors. Across all FGDs, women
emphasize the lack of opportunities to work in the formal sector in rural areas.
Instead, rural educated and otherwise qualified women work as school teachers
or upazila government officials, or in clinics and factories. The main informal
sector work opportunities in rural areas are in cattle rearing, poultry farming,
day labor, handicrafts, handlooms, and tailoring.

Encouragingly, Bangladesh's labor market shows a distinct evolution in occupational sex segregation between 2003 and 2016 (figures 2.22 and 2.23). Overall,
many more workers are in mixed gender industries in 2016 than in 2003; either
those industries moved from being male- or female-dominated to mixed-gender,
or mixed gender industries have expanded. The percentage of women working
in female-dominated industries also has fallen, from 15 percent of female workers in 2003 to only 4 percent in 2016. The expanded presence of mixed-gender
employment could be a positive sign that Bangladesh's labor market is malleable
enough to accept women into a wide variety of occupations. Most importantly,
the surge of women in mixed-gender industries (from 16 percent in 2003 to
75 percent in 2016) suggests an increased acceptability of women working
with men.

FIGURE 2.22

Proportion of men and women in male-dominated, female-dominated, and mixed industries, 2003

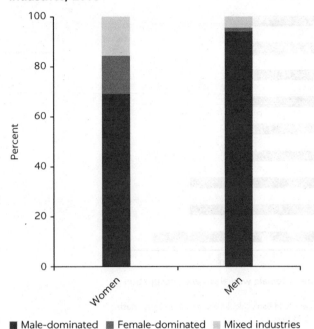

Source: World Bank calculations based on Bangladesh LFS 2003 data.
Note: Male-dominated denotes when the share of men is greater than 60 percent, mixed when between 40 percent and 60 percent, and female-dominated when less than 40 percent.

FIGURE 2.23

Proportion of men and women in male-dominated, female-dominated, and mixed industries, 2016

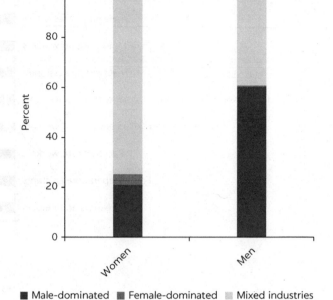

Source: World Bank calculations based on Bangladesh LFS 2003 data.
Note: Male-dominated denotes when the share of men is greater than 60 percent, mixed when between 40 percent, and 60 percent and female-dominated when less than 40 percent.

TABLE 2.2 Employers' views on employing women

CHALLENGES	% AGREE
Challenges of working with women due to their family commitments	33
Challenges of hiring women given government regulations, such as working hours and maternity leave	35
Hiring women could cause disruption in the working environment	45
Required benefits and other expenses, such as providing separate workplace facilities for women, make them more expensive employees	43

Source: World Bank calculations based on Bangladesh Enterprise Survey 2013 data.

Gender-based bias and discrimination in labor demand

Many employers actively and openly discriminate by gender in hiring and promotion processes, both quantitative and qualitative data suggest. Up to 45 percent of respondents[9] in Bangladesh's Enterprise Survey believe that hiring women nonmanagerial employees disrupts the work environment (table 2.2). Thus, the most prominent reason for not wanting to hire women reflects employers' prejudice that "women disrupt the work environment," rather than a decision made on the basis of costs or skills.

TABLE 2.3 **Percentage of firms agreeing with the statement "hiring women could cause disruption in the working environment"**

SIZE OF ESTABLISHMENT	% AGREE
Micro <5	100
Small ≥5 and ≤19	57
Medium ≥20 and ≤99	42
Large ≥100	29
Total	45

Source: World Bank calculations based on Bangladesh Enterprise Survey 2013 data.

This biased attitude toward working with women appears to be more pronounced among employers of smaller firms (table 2.3). Some employers interviewed in our qualitative study are very open about their gender bias in hiring and promoting employees. A female garment factory manager[10] in urban Dhaka explained, "Females can't do some of the work, like operating the machines. That requires much strength. This is not for the female.... Supervisor is a responsible position, which can't be filled by a female. Not everyone can provide leadership. A supervisor has to control 15–20 workers, which are impossible for the female. We have more male staffs in our factory. That's why supervisors are also male."

GENDER DIFFERENTIALS IN EARNINGS

Earnings gaps[11] persist in Bangladesh but have narrowed dramatically between 2003 and 2016. In 2003, working women earned 3,763 BDT per month; men's earnings were 43 percent higher at 6,653 BDT. By 2016, working women's earnings were about 76 percent that of men, at about 7,000 BDT per month compared to men's earnings of above 9,200 BDT. According to the Global Wage Report 2018 (ILO 2018), Bangladesh now has the smallest gender wage gap of any country in the region, yet a gender differential remains.

The persistence of an earnings gap reflects a combination of factors influencing women's and men's employment. As discussed earlier, occupational sex-segregation determines the types of jobs that men and women perform. As these jobs pay differently, women are disadvantaged by taking home less than men in monthly earnings. Men's tendency to work more hours than women do (as time to work is determined largely by women's traditional roles in household responsibilities), exacerbates the gender pay gap. Employers' bias in giving promotions also could be limiting women to low-paying positions.

Improvements in women's education could be one explanation for the gender wage gap's decline. Whereas both men's and women's educational attainment has improved over time, women's progress has been faster than that of men (Farole and Cho 2017). RMG sector expansion also could be responsible for the narrowing gap, particularly in the manufacturing sector (figures 2.24 and 2.25). The piece rate pay and production quota practice in this sector may constrain RMG employers' wage discrimination. Studies of Cambodian and Vietnamese workers indicate little reported gender wage discrimination: workers reason that they are paid on a per-piece basis, which applies to everyone working in a certain occupation within their factory (Kotikula, Robertson, and Pournik 2015). International buyers' scrutiny of the industry might mitigate employers' tendency to discriminate, moreover. Gender segregation by job level in the RMG

FIGURE 2.24

Monthly earnings from main activity by industry and sex, 2003

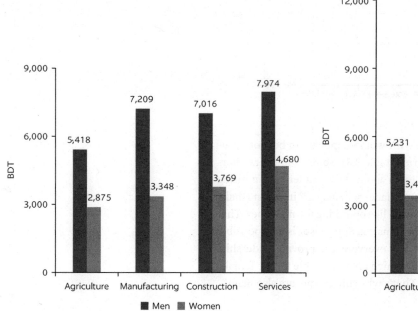

Source: World Bank calculations based on Bangladesh
LFS 2003 data.
Notes: Monthly income in BDT, but only from the primary
source; unpaid family helpers and those with zero income are
excluded. The 2003 values were converted to 2015 values
using the consumer price index (CPI) from the World
Development Indicators (WDI) database.

FIGURE 2.25

Monthly earnings from main activity by industry and sex, 2016

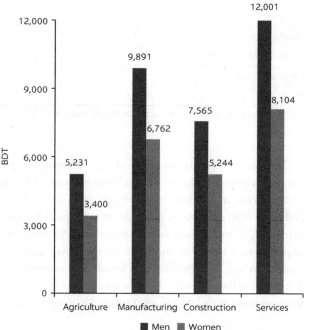

Source: World Bank calculations based on Bangladesh
LFS 2003 data.
Notes: Monthly income in BDT, but only from the primary
source; unpaid family helpers and those with zero income are
excluded. The 2003 values were converted to 2015 values
using the CPI from the WDI database.

sector (for example, men are more likely than women to be supervisors, for instance), however, could explain the overall persistence of gender wage gaps.

The gender wage gap has significantly decreased over time for paid employees even when controlling for worker characteristics and sector of employment. Multivariate regression analysis of male and female formal workers' earnings by level of schooling suggests that, for the most part, individuals with higher levels of schooling tend to earn more than those with no schooling. For women with education between grades 6–9, however, wages are not statistically significantly different from those who are illiterate. In terms of sectors, workers in agricultural sectors earn the least. Women in the service sector tend to have significantly higher incomes than women in other sectors. The pattern is different for men, in which earnings in manufacturing and construction sectors tend to be higher than in the service sector. Spatial variables also explain earning differences. Urban residency is correlated with higher earnings: more men and women work in paid jobs in urban areas; moreover, their wages are higher when compared to those of their rural counterparts (see table B.4 in appendix B).

Oaxaca-Blinder decomposition models help explain the difference in earnings between men and women in the formal sectors of Bangladesh (see table B.5 in appendix B). The decomposition results show that very little, if any, of the difference in earnings is attributable to differences in endowments (such as level of education) of men and women. Almost all of it is due to how labor markets value endowments of men and women differently (that is, the coefficients). It is worth noting, however, that men who work in the formal sector do have higher levels of endowments than women in this sector; reducing this disparity between men and women would help lower the wage gap to a small extent.

GOOD PRACTICES AND RECOMMENDATIONS

Governments, civil society organizations and the private sector across the globe—including in the developing world—increasingly recognize the barriers to women seeking to join labor markets and attempt to mitigate these barriers. A detailed analysis of all types of efforts undertaken to-date is beyond the scope of this book; instead, below we highlight select, appropriate examples for raising FLFP in Bangladesh. These can be grouped under two broad categories: addressing constraints that prevent women from entering the labor force to begin with, and improving working conditions for working women. Clearly, underlying patriarchal norms (see chapter 1) are critical to address, as well.

Help girls stay in school past grade 10; study science, technology, engineering, and math; and avoid child marriage

Bangladesh needs to keep girls in school past grade 10 by supporting them to graduate from higher-secondary school. The multivariate analysis makes clear that girls who complete their educations at grade 10 have the lowest odds of LFP—even lower than odds of girls with fewer years of schooling or no schooling at all. Government programs can incentivize girls and their families—especially in ethnic minority or other poor communities—using conditional cash transfer programs that require girls to stay in school for at least two additional years beyond grade 10. Such programs can offset the potential loss of income due to increased time spent in school. Indeed, government of Bangladesh (GoB) already has experienced tremendous success with its Female Secondary School Assistance Program (FSSAP) launched in 1994, with its significant impact on retaining girls in secondary school (ultimately closing and even reversing the gender gap in Bangladesh's secondary school enrollments) and keeping them from marrying early. Cash transfers that provided tuition fees and monthly stipends for rural girls through grade 10 were conditional upon maintaining a 75 percent school attendance rate, some level of measured academic proficiency, and unmarried status. Not only did the program increase enrollment of girls age 11–18 by 12 percentage points, it also was associated with a 1.4–2.3-year increase in the average female age of marriage (Khandker et al. 2003). Punjab, Pakistan saw similar success with its Female School Stipend Program on Public School Enrollment. Girls were given stipends upon meeting similar conditions to those of the Bangladesh program, eventually making them more likely to complete middle school, transition to high school, and ultimately to delay marriage and have an average of 0.3 fewer children (Alam et al. 2011).

To help girls avoid early marriage and complete secondary school, education interventions could consider more focused partnerships with the GoB's Multi-Sectoral Programme on Violence Against Women. Implemented under the Ministry of Women and Children Affairs, the program has been a pioneering force in government efforts to address violence against women and girls. Among its many important services is the National Helpline Centre for Violence Against Women and Children (NHCVAWC), dedicated to violence treatment and prevention. NHCVAWC helps raise awareness and encourages reporting—and possibly prevention—of incidents of violence, including child marriage. It is important to sustain and, as needed, scale up the Helpline Centre and other components of the program, with concerted efforts to map, harmonize, and coordinate with the many NGO initiatives in Bangladesh that aim to prevent child marriage.[12] Now in its fourth phase (2016–21), the multisectoral program is implemented jointly by the respective governments of Bangladesh and Denmark through the Ministry of Women and Children Affairs and in collaboration with a range of other ministries, including the Ministry of Education (Ministry of Women and Children Affairs 2018). The NHCVAWC and broader Multi-Sectoral Programme on Violence Against Women also could have a stronger presence on the ground by strengthening its partnerships with locally operating NGOs and civil society organizations in Bangladesh that work tirelessly to prevent child marriage and have helped bring down its incidence in recent decades. Ideally, these organizations could be mapped and their efforts harmonized (see appendix E and appendix S in Solotaroff and Pande (2014), for a review of evaluated interventions to prevent child marriage and a list of select organizations in Bangladesh working on child marriage, respectively).

To keep girls not only in school, but also to ensure that they are learning marketable skills, Bangladesh needs to target messaging to parents and use female role models, public information campaigns, and (though less so) in-school counselors to fight stereotypes and encourage girls and young women into science, technology, engineering, and math (STEM) fields of study. Parental influence on girls' and women's decisions about education and school-to-work transition is significantly stronger than that of other influences, such as in-school guidance counselors (see Babin et al. 2010; Ferriman et al. 2009; Leaper et al. 2012). Training school counselors to encourage girls in STEM should thus be accompanied by outreach efforts to improve parental perceptions and support. Role models can significantly influence girls' learning and career aspirations: reserving leadership positions for women in randomly selected village councils in India was linked to a 20-percent closure of the gender gap in parental aspirations and a 32 percent closure among adolescents (Beaman et al. 2012).

As noted by Priyadarshini and Rahim (2010), television and other popular entertainment media are powerful modes through which Bangladeshi women can be engaged and influenced, such as to encourage daughters to pursue STEM education and careers for jobs in the private, rather than public, sector. Finally, following the passage of the government of Bangladesh's National Skills Development Authority Act (NSDA)—which was submitted to Parliament in September 2018—multiple stakeholders can coordinate to establish a sustainable institutional mechanism to promote harmonization and relevance of Bangladesh's fragmented network of programs for STEM and other skills development of young women and men. For example, this would involve coordination between the private sector, the Ministry of Labour and Employment, the Ministry of Education, and even the Ministry of Primary and Mass Education.

School-based peer support groups and role models have proven quite effective at retaining female students—especially those who belong to ethnic minority groups—once they already are enrolled in STEM courses (Asian

Development Bank 2012; Espinosa 2011; Hermann et al. 2016). A short and scalable online intervention in introductory chemistry and psychology courses found that, compared to those in the control group, intervention group members, who received a letter from a female role model among instructors and teaching assistants that normalized concerns about belonging in STEM, emphasized its worth as an investment, and exemplified persistence and overcoming challenges, received higher grades and had lower rates of failing and withdrawal (Hermann et al. 2016).

Bangladesh needs to provide STEM-Pathway focused programs and mandatory universal computer training. Research suggests these as effective ways of preparing girls, as well as boys, for job markets (Lyon et al. 2012; Ruel et al. 2002). Universally requiring (for boys, as well as girls) computer training in secondary school or even earlier—or variations thereof, as implemented by several countries—appears to reach more girls than do interventions that target only girls to take computer training courses countries (Passey 2017).

Address constraints on women's gainful employment

Bangladesh needs to improve women's technical skills. GoB's Technical and Vocational Education and Training (TVET) program, in collaboration with the EU, is an ongoing effort that deserves closer scrutiny and evaluation (European Commission n.d.). The skills development sector in Bangladesh is characterized by gender inequalities and stereotyping in many sectors, leading to gender divisions in many roles. The EU is working with the Bangladeshi government to remove many gendered barriers to women's training in a range of unconventional sectors for women, including the fast-growing leather industry. The program also seeks to tap into the private sector and encourage more public-private collaboration. This and a range of other programs in Bangladesh need to be carefully monitored and evaluated to learn from their experiences.

TVET programs need to ensure that their curricula—for male and female students alike—are directly informed by potential employers in ICT, engineering, and other growth sectors and occupation types in an increasingly modern economy. The Republic of Korea's successful experience with transforming its TVET system involved concentrating more on training for skills needed in capital-intensive and eventually knowledge-based industries and less on those needed for labor-intensive industries. To create more technicians for capital-intensive industries, the country expanded its junior college system (especially technical colleagues) and required workplace training for firms emphasizing skills upgrading. To enlarge the pool of engineers and scientists needed in knowledge-based industries, the industries actively cooperated with universities to ensure tertiary education's focus on engineering and school-industry research and an emphasis on long-term development of competencies within enterprises.

Bangladesh needs to increase women's employment in the private sector. The garment sector has greatly contributed to increases thus far. As detailed in box 2.1, however, women continue to face sexual harassment, poor working conditions and other problems in this sector, which undermine women's well-being and other potential benefits of employment. Efforts to improve such conditions are underway and can be studied, adapted and expanded to be more effective. For instance, the formation of the Accord, the Alliance, and other initiatives has compelled greater compliance by garment factories to ensure a safer working environment for women (box 2.1). The BEPZA Counselors Program focuses on labor and social compliance—including gender, as well as occupational health and safety issues—and provides informal dispute mediation (Simavi 2012). Efforts to improve mandated childcare centers need to be better documented, evaluated and modified accordingly; for example, most of the centers operate during normal factory hours but not when women need to work overtime (Sebastio 2014; UNICEF 2015).

Bangladesh needs to evaluate and improve existing quotas for women in government jobs. It is important to recognize that women in Bangladesh do flock to the public sector. Until social norms change, this may be among the most acceptable work options for women, which suggests the value of efforts to make the public sector more accessible and welcoming to them. GoB has experimented since 1976 with women's quotas for civil services jobs. Currently, the government ensures a 15-percent quota for nongazetted posts and 10- quota percent for gazetted posts for women (Ferdous 2014). The extent to which these quotas have helped increase women's participation in, and experience working at, civil service jobs is unclear, however. The government needs to undertake careful evaluation of its quota programs and address deficiencies therein.

India's experience of government job quotas for women in India appears to be generally positive. Pande and Ford (2011) note that mandated quotas reserving one-third of local government leadership positions levels have increased female leadership in India, improved voice and decision-making, and influenced policy outcomes. Beaman et al. (2010) find that women are 25 percent more likely to speak at village meetings when the local political leader position is reserved for a woman. Well-implemented programs of women's quotas appear to not only increase the voice of the female leader, but also the voices of other women in her community. Female legislators also introduce policies that are more beneficial to females. Chattopadhyay and Duflo (2004) find that reserved leadership positions for women in India have led to increased local investments in particular goods favored by women in their districts.

Improve incentives and conditions for working women

Women in the workplace face a series of hurdles, including lack of childcare, unavailability of adequate water and sanitation facilities, insufficient workplace safety, and sexual harassment.

As shown in this study and by numerous other studies around the world, providing women who have young children with childcare services significantly increases their probabilities of LFP and employment (Blau and Hagy 1998; Chevalier and Viitanen 2002; Diaz and Rodriguez-Chamussy 2013; Jaumotte 2003; Gelbach 2002; Pettit and Hook 2005). According to the Bangladesh Labour Act 2006, all factories and other workplaces with 40 or more workers are required to have a daycare center for workers' children under the age of six. Although select firms in the garment sector have been diligent in abiding by this law by providing on-site childcare, use of such centers more broadly remains very limited, in part because workers are unsure of the quality of care (UNICEF 2015). Community-based childcare centers may be better options. Typically run by civil society organizations, they have greater funding and numbers of staff, and staff are well-trained and motivated; however, these are not currently viable alternatives for working parents, as they typically accept only children under age 2 years (UNICEF 2015). Given the number of large and well-run NGOs in

Bangladesh, such as BRAC, and their improving relationship with government, the network of centers has the potential to expand.

Given the enormous cost of childcare provision, public-private partnerships (PPP) should always be considered as a means of funding these efforts. Below is one example of such a public-private partnership in Turkey, followed by two examples of strictly private sector employer-provided childcare, from the IFC's report, *Tacking Childcare: The Business Case for Employer-Supported Childcare* (2017).

- Borusan in Turkey: In 2012, the Borusan Group launched the "My Mom's Job Is My Future" (*Annemin İşi Benim Geleceğim*) project, which offers childcare in industrial areas with the objective of improving FLFP. Although men predominate in the heavy manufacturing industry in these areas, the project is one among many of Borusan's efforts to foster a gender-diverse workforce. The project is implemented through PPP between the Borusan Group; the Ministry of Science, Industry, and Technology; and the Ministry of Families and Social Policy. The project will establish daycare centers in 10 organized industrial zones (OIZs). These centers are open to children up to age six whose mothers are employed in the OIZs.

- Mindtree in India: Providing childcare helps Mindtree, an information technology firm, to recruit and retain highly-trained and qualified male and female software engineers in a competitive market. Mindtree offers a large range of child care options including childcare subsidies for employees, flex-work opportunities for parents, extended childcare hours, on-site daycare, reserving spaces at daycare centers, explicit inclusion of fathers in childcare options, and reintegration of mothers into the workplace. These childcare solutions have yielded measurable results: more than 90 percent of women employees return after completing maternity leave, and more than 87 percent of mothers are still working at Mindtree 12 months after their return. Mindtree continues to support women's empowerment in the workplace once they are mothers by encouraging them to aspire to leadership positions and providing training and mentoring for 100 women with high potential to acquire middle-management positions. To combat the social stigma against childcare and general distrust of providers, Mindtree conducts outreach to families of female employees considering placing their children in the high-quality on-site daycare.

- MAS Kreeda Al Safi-Madaba in Jordan: This garment factory of the Sri Lanka-based MAS holdings also has seen improvements from providing childcare: in just nine months after opening its on-site crèche, employee absences from sick leave declined by nine percent, and mothers with children at the daycare were given employer-paid daily nursing breaks. Offering childcare allows MAS Kreeda Al Safi-Madaba to comply with related laws and is a critical part of its strategy to recruit and retain women in a region where women—especially mothers—tend not to work outside the home. Its investments in childcare also have helped strengthen "relationships with high-value, international buyers, hence ensuring greater and more long-term market access and growth opportunities" (Niethammer et al. 2017, 9).

The government of Bangladesh also should consider education-focused alternatives to private childcare services, such as early childhood education programs or extending the school day. For more than half a century, the Head Start preschool program in the United States has provided early childhood education to disadvantaged (predominantly poor) children ages 3 to 4 to improve their skills and increase their odds of succeeding in primary school and beyond. A review of evaluations of Head Start finds that it brings participating children (especially more disadvantaged children) significant near- and medium-term benefits and that smaller "model" versions of the program have helped improve educational attainment and earnings. A cost-benefit analysis, moreover, indicates that "Head Start would pay for itself in cost-savings to the government if it produced even a quarter of the long-term gains of model programs" (Curie 2001, 214).

In the mid-1990's, Chile undertook a nation-wide reform that extended the length of the school day from a half-day to a full day (by about 35 percent), without increasing the length of the yearly school calendar. Even though childcare was not an explicit goal of the policy, by increasing the time that children spend in school and the number of hours for which they receive adult care, the reform was able to affect the employment decisions of their mothers. Berthelon, Kruger, and Oyarzun (2015) found that the program significantly increased mothers' LFP by about 45 percentage points. In addition, the probability of being in the labor force for at least six months rose by 19 percentage points.

Bangladesh needs to improve work and factory safety compliance. Bangladesh offers several good practices for improving working conditions and safety for women, such as those attempted in its Special Economic Zones (SEZ). These include the BEPZA Counselors Program, which assesses company compliance with labor standards, and programs in Chittagong's SEZ to provide on-site health facilities for women workers. The BEPZA program significantly improved safety and security, as well as the processes to record grievances, while the on-site health facilities improved women's personal health and contributed to fewer days off for illness. A key contributor to the success of these programs important to keep in mind for replication is the commitment of senior management in instituting these reforms (World Bank and IFC 2011).

The public, private, and NGO sectors together need to address risks of sexual harassment related to the workplace, including in public spaces and on transport women use to travel to work. A strong policy framework already exists in Bangladesh, but enabling laws are not sufficient: rates of sexual harassment and other forms of sexual violence in workplaces and on public transport remain far too high; an estimated 33 percent of Bangladeshi women perceive workplaces as likely locations for the occurrence of sexual violence, 16 percent perceive vehicles/roads and streets to be likely, and nearly 10 percent perceive stations for buses, launches, and trains to be likely locations (Bangladesh Bureau of Statistics 2016). Hossain and Ahmed (2017, 17), moreover, suggest that even aspects of the legal framework could be changed to better protect women before focusing on implementation: "The law must clarify 'indecent behavior' in order to make it effective for prevention of harassment, especially sexual harassment. Moreover, specific provision [sic] on protection against sexual harassment must be incorporated in the law."

Rigorously evaluated, successful examples of implementing policies to protect against violence include AASHA in Pakistan, Safe Cities Intervention in Delhi, Gender Equity Movement in Schools (GEMS) Program, and Jagori's "safety audits" in India. For instance, the AASHA movement in Pakistan was instrumental in ensuring the passage of Pakistan's Protection against

Harassment of Women at the Workplace Act, 2010, and the Criminal Law Amendment Act, 2009. Equally worth emulating is the fact that the movement did not stop at legislation. Rather, AASHA focused on setting up and institutionalizing the structure needed to implement the program; working alongside a range of stakeholders including the government, private sector and civil society organizations to increase awareness and acceptability of the law; and showed flexibility in engaging different points of view (Khaliq 2012; Solotaroff and Pande 2014). The Safe Cities and "safety audit" programs address this issue from yet another perspective: that of ensuring women's safety in public spaces on the way to and from work, another major barrier in women's gainful employment. An important element of this program for replication is its active engagement of the police and the citizenry in making streets and transport safer for women through ensuring adequate street lighting, sensitizing police to women's safety issues, improving safety features on public transportation, and more (Jagori and Multiple Action Research Group [MARG] 2013; Jagori and UN Women 2011). Bangladesh could dramatically scale up its use of Safetipin (the map-based mobile phone application for the safety audit program), which it began implementing in 2015, primarily in Dhaka (Asian Development Bank 2017).

Piloted in 2015 in Mexico City, the Hazme el Paro project undertook a broad range of measures to address the city's very high rates of sexual harassment on public transport. These measures addressed three important intervention areas: training, reporting, and campaign and involved multiple partnerships between the government and other sectors. First, a local NGO trained bus drivers on nonconfrontational strategies to intervene in instances of sexual harassment and had drivers create their own protocol through an empowering, participatory process. The local Ministry of Women facilitated training of policy on gender-informed response mechanisms. Second, the project used technology to equip buses with Wi-fi and develop a mechanism to make reporting easy and reliable. The mobile application enables reporting of harassment occurring to others, queries to drivers and friends for help, and receipt of orientation and response from policy. Third, the efficacy and broad reach of the information campaign can be credited, in part, to the use of a colloquial slogan that encouraged bystanders to intervene (*Hazme el Paro*, which translates as "have my back"), the use of tested nonconfrontational strategies of intervention (such as offering to help the victim and report the crime), and efforts to change attitudes based on cultural misconceptions (for example, "Women are asking to be harassed" (Gonzalez and Alvez 2016). An evaluation of the pilot intervention finds that it had several significant impacts on the treatment group, including increased intention to intervene upon witnessing an act of harassment (George Washington University 2017).

Finally, the GEMS program, replicated in several Asian and Latin American countries, has sought to target this issue at its root by changing understandings of masculinity, femininity and violence among boys and girls in childhood and early adolescence. Evaluations of this innovative in-school program show significant changes in the attitudes of young boys and girls towards gender roles and gender-based violence (Achyut et al. 2011).

Bangladesh needs to provide adequate, women-friendly water and sanitation (WASH) facilities. There is limited research on WASH facilities for women in the workplace, especially facilities that support menstrual hygiene (Sommer et al. 2016). Trade unions have pushed for better WASH facilities in countries as disparate as the Philippines, Indonesia and some in southern Africa; other programs showcasing government and private sector collaboration in Africa and Asia (Sommer et al. 2016) merit further consideration for Bangladesh.

DATA GAPS

Sex-disaggregated data are essential to understand gender gaps in labor market outcomes. The Bangladesh LFS is an important tool for monitoring these gender gaps, yet data about constraints and enabling factors are still scarce; moreover, some data are collected only at the household level, preventing estimation of intra-household gender gaps in outcomes. Data related to gendered constraints such as time use, mobility, and perceptions of safety also are missing from many household surveys.

Better measurement of economic activities, particularly those often carried out by women, is also urgent. For instance, in Bangladesh, although 92 percent of women from households with any assets own poultry (compared to only 38 percent of men), labor and economic data may not fully capture their poultry rearing activities. Indeed, whether owning poultry is considered an economic activity appears to explain the difference in the estimate of the rural FLFP in the LFS (where ownership of poultry appears not to have been explicitly measured and included) and rural FLFP in the BIHS (which explicitly asked about ownership of poultry). Moreover, the LFS's current definition of employment does not capture services produced for own final use (such as child and elder care, food preparation and other household chores), which are often performed by women and which have economic value. Bangladesh could benefit from implementing the 19th International Conference of Labor Statisticians (ICLS) resolution concerning statistics of work, employment and labor underutilization. An important contribution of the new ICLS standards is to narrow the definition of *employment* (as work performed for pay or profit) and introduce the new definition of *work* (including all productive activities, paid and unpaid). Multitopic surveys, such as the Household Income and Expenditure Survey, provide an important opportunity to gather data on certain aspects of the new definitions that the LFS cannot gather, such as income or consumption data.

CONCLUSION

Over the past decade, growth in female employment has far outpaced growth in male employment. Women have entered labor markets in larger numbers, including married women and women who had never previously participated, and the FLFP rate increased from 26 to 36 percent between 2003 and 2016. Still, it trails behind those of peer economies. Disaggregating the upward trend in FLFP reveals a few worrying signs: FLFP in urban areas has declined due to the RMG sector's decelerating growth, and much of FLFP's rise is from unpaid agricultural work in rural areas, which is not associated with women's economic empowerment.

Removing the main barriers to women's work will help bring more Bangladeshi women into the labor force:

- Household duties and related gender roles are a key reason for low FLFP, particularly for women with small children; however, women now return to labor markets after marriage. Having elderly women in the household no longer is negatively associated with FLFP.
- Restricted mobility tends to compel women to work from home. Providing home-based work may seem like a solution to narrowing gender gaps in LFP, but it undermines women financially as it is associated with lower earnings than those received when working in factories, offices or shops.
- Achieving gender parity in different education levels alone will not help close gender gaps in LFP. Women with higher education face higher unemployment than do men with higher education. Women still trail behind men in tertiary enrollments, the only education level associated with increased odds of women's LFP and of getting jobs on par with men. In university, women are less likely to choose STEM fields than humanities and biological sciences due to social pressures.
- Occupational sex segregation restricts women from securing higher-paying jobs. Although such segregation remains strong in Bangladesh, it has improved over time. Far fewer workers are now employed in female-dominated jobs compared to a decade ago.
- Many employers actively and openly discriminate by gender in hiring and promotion processes. Many believe that hiring women disrupts the work environment.
- Gender earnings gaps persist—overall and within different sectors—even when controlling for education. The bulk of gaps are determined by the different value that labor markets give to men's versus women's qualifications, rather than on qualifications themselves. The smallest pay gaps are among university graduates and the largest among people with secondary education.

Despite a narrowing of the gender gap in LFP, much work remains to provide women with better quality jobs, better work environments, and wages that are commensurate with those received by men. Efforts made in Bangladesh and elsewhere provide examples of how to address these persistent gender discriminatory issues in the labor market.

NOTES

1. Figures presented are International Labour Organization (ILO) estimates of FLFP for 15 and over population. We use ILO estimates to ensure cross-country comparison as country statistics may use slightly differently definitions and are not available every year. National statistics' FLFP rates for Vietnam and Indonesia in 2015 are 73 percent and 49 percent and for Nepal in 2014 is 78 percent. All figures are obtained from the World Bank's World Development Indicator database.
2. The metric for wealth in this analysis was constructed by the authors using household assets, such as land holding and ownership of durable goods. It indicates relative wealth of households in which men and women reside.
3. "Prime age" of workers is between 25 and 54 years of age, as defined by the U.S. Department of Labor (1999).

4. Persons can be defined as working in the informal sector in terms of their main activity. For this analysis, we use the Bangladesh Bureau of Statistics (BBS) definition, which is a combination of both the informal character of the individual job, as well as employment in the informal sector: (1) All individual job-based informal employment—operationally comprises all employed persons in the nonagriculture sector, both wage and salaried workers (employees) with no pension or no contribution to a retirement fund; (2) All contributing family workers; (3) All employers and own-account workers in the informal sector enterprises (operationally defined in Bangladesh as all private unincorporated enterprises engaged in nonagriculture work that do not have any registration); (4) All own-account workers employed in a private household.

5. The DHS surveys ask a series of questions related to women's work. For women who report they have done a job for which they are paid in cash of kind, either currently, in the last seven days or ever in the 12 months prior to the survey, the DHS asks if the work was compensated in cash. We use the subsequent "working for pay" variable in the DHS analysis presented here.

6. Bangladesh LFS 2013 collected data from all individuals age 15 and older on noneconomic activities during the seven days prior to the survey). The Bangladesh LFS 2015–16 does not record the time each person spends a week doing household chores; instead, it collects only binary data ("yes" or "no" answers) to the question asking if the person spends at least one hour per week doing the chore.

7. The Duncan Index is defined as the difference between the proportion of males (among the entire male population) and the proportion of females (among the female population) in a given employment type. Used by Das, Carranza, and Kotikula (forthcoming), this index is a description of the percentage of employees who would need to switch jobs to obtain an equal distribution of men and women in each job type. The Duncan Index can range from 0, which represents perfectly equal distributions of men and women across employment categories, to a value of 1, which represents perfect inequality.

8. Gender-based segregation is calculated at the 2-digit industry level.

9. As the survey targets firms, survey respondents could be owners, staff managers, etc.

10. Note that factory managers usually manage the operation of the entire factory, while (line) supervisors are directly overseeing a small team of workers (generally are promoted from workers).

11. This analysis uses earnings from the workers' main activity only.

12. For a review of evaluated child marriage prevention initiatives in Bangladesh and elsewhere up to 2014, see Solotaroff and Pande 2014, appendix E. Appendix S of the same publication displays a list of select organizations working to prevent child marriage in South Asian countries. An in-depth understanding of the determinants of child marriage in Bangladesh and related recommendations to effectively address these determinants is beyond the scope of this book; however, for one such study, see the forthcoming publication (Jahan, Moyeen, and DRI), "Addressing Child Marriage in Bangladesh: Developing a Behaviour Change Intervention in Bangladesh."

REFERENCES

Achyut, P., N. Bhatla, S. Khandekar, S. Maitra, and R. K. Verma. 2011. *Building Support for Gender Equality among Young Adolescents in School: Findings from Mumbai, India*. New Delhi: International Center for Research on Women.

Asian Development Bank. 2012. *Innovative Strategies in Technical and Vocational Education and Training for Accelerated Human Resource Development in South Asia*. Manila: ADB.

——. 2016. "Employment and the Labor Market in Bangladesh: Overview of Trends and Challenges." ADB Briefs, No. 62, ADB.

——. 2017. *Bangladesh Gender Equality Diagnostic of Selected Sectors*. Manila: ADB.

Babinard, Julie, John Hine, Simon Ellis, and Satoshi Ishihara. 2010. "Mainstreaming Gender in Road Transport: Operational Guidance for World Bank Staff." Transport paper series no. TP-28, Washington, DC: World Bank.

Bangladesh Bureau of Statistics. 2016. *Bangladesh Quarterly Labour Force Survey (LFS) 2015–16*. Statistics and Informatics Division, Ministry of Planning, Dhaka: Bangladesh Bureau of Statistics, 2016.

Beaman, Lori, Esther Duflo, Rohini Pande, and Petia Topalova. 2010. *Political Reservation and Substantive Representation: Evidence from Indian Village Councils.* Washington, DC: India Policy Forum, Brookings, and NCAER.

———. 2012. "Female Leadership Raises Aspirations and Educational Attainment for Girls: A Policy Experiment in India." *Science* 335 (6068): 582–586.

Berthelon, Matias, Diana I. Kruger, and Melanie Alejandra Oyarzún. 2015. "The Effects of Longer School Days on Mothers' Labor Force Participation." IZA Discussion Paper 9212, IZA, Bonn, Germany.

Blau, David, and Alison Hagy. 1998. "The Demand for Quality in Child Care." *Journal of Political Economy:* 106 (1): 104–139.

Blumer, Helene. 2015. *Internal Communication in Bangladeshi Ready-Made Garment Factories: Illustration of the Internal Communication System and Its Connection to Labor Unrest.* Berlin: Springer Gabler.

Chattopadhyay, Raghabendra, and Esther Duflo. 2004. "The Impact of Reservation in the Panchayati Raj: Evidence from a Nationwide Randomized Experiment." *Economic and Political Weekly* 39 (9): 979–86.

Chevalier, Arnaud, and Tarja Viitanen. 2002. "The Causality Between Female Labour Force Participation and the Availability of Childcare." *Applied Economics Letters:* 9 (14): 915–18.

Currie, Janet. 2001. "Early Childhood Education Programs." *Journal of Economic Perspectives* 15 (2): 213-38.

Das, Smita, Eliana Carranza, and Aphichoke Kotikula. Forthcoming. "Addressing Gender-Based Employment Segregation." Jobs Working Paper, World Bank, Washington, DC.

Dhaka Tribune. "Study: Rights of Bangladesh's Female RMG Workers Still Unmet." February 27, 2018. https://www.dhakatribune.com/business/2018/02/27/study-rights-bangladeshs -female-rmg-workers-still-unmet.

Diaz, Mercedes Mateo, and Lourdes Rodriguez-Chamussy. "Childcare and Women's Labor Participation: Evidence for Latin America and the Caribbean." Technical Note No. IDB-TN-586. IDB, Washington, DC.

Espinosa, Lorelle. 2011. "Pipelines and Pathways: Women of Color in Undergraduate STEM Majors and the College Experiences that Contribute to Persistence." *Harvard Educational Review* 81 (2): 209–241.

Farole, Thomas, and Yoonyoung Cho. 2017. *Jobs Diagnostic Bangladesh.* Job Series Issue 9, Washington, DC: World Bank.

Ferdous, Jannatul. 2014. "Women in Bangladesh Civil Service: Stumbling Blocks towards the Way of Participation." *Social Sciences* 3 (5): 177–82.

Ferriman, Kimberley, David Lubinski, and Camilla P. Benbow. 2009. "Work Preferences, Life Values, and Personal Views of Top Math/Science Graduate Students and the Profoundly Gifted: Developmental Changes and Gender Differences during Emerging Adulthood and Parenthood." *Journal of Personality and Social Psychology* 97 (3): 517–532.

Field, Erica, and Attila Ambrus. 2008. "Early Marriage, Age of Menarche, and Female Schooling Attainment in Bangladesh." *Journal of Political Economy* 116 (5).

Gelbach, Jonah B. 2002. "Public Schooling for Young Children and Maternal Labor Supply." *American Economic Review* 92 (1): 307–322.

George Washington University. "Reducing Violence against Women in Public Transportation Systems in Mexico City: Results from a Pilot Study." [Unpublished]. Paper presented at the "Personal Security for Women in Public Transport" seminar, World Bank Group, June 1 2017.

Gonzalez, Karla Dominguez, and Bianca Bianchi Alves, "'No One Helps...nadie me hace el paro;' Preventing Violence Against Women in Public Transport," Transport for Development Blog, The World Bank Group, March 8, 2016, http://blogs.worldbank.org/transport/no-one-helps -nadie-me-hace-el-paro-preventing-violence-against-women-public-transport.

Hermann, S. D., R. M Adelman, J. E. Bodford, O. Graudejus, M. A. Okin, and V. S. Y. Kwan. "The Effects of a Female Role Model on Academic Performance and Persistence of Women in STEM Courses." *Basic and Applied Psychology* 38 (5): 258–68.

Hossain, Jakir, and Mostafiz Ahmed. 2017. *Watch Report: Promoting Women Ready-Made Garment Workers' Rights through Labour Regulation.* Karmojibi Nari: Dhaka, Bangladesh.

International Labour Organization. 2018 (ILO). *Global Wage Report 2018/19: What Lies Behind Gender Pay Gaps.* Geneva: ILO.

Jahan, Ferdous, Sabah Moyeen, and Development Research Initiative (DRI). Forthcoming. "Addressing Child Marriage in Bangladesh: Developing a Behaviour Change Intervention in Bangladesh." SARTFP Working Paper, Washington, DC: World Bank.

Jaumotte, Florence. 2003. "Labour Force Participation of Women: Empirical Evidence on The Role of Policy and Other Determinants in OECD Countries." OECD *Economic Studies,* No. 37, 2003/2.

Khaliq, B. 2012. *External Assessment of the Implementation of Anti-Sexual Harassment Legislation.* Lahore and Islamabad: WISE and AASHA.

Klasen, S., and J. Pieters. 2015. "What Explains the Stagnation of Female Labor Force Participation in Urban India?" *The World Bank Economic Review* 29 (3): 449–78.

Leaper, Campbell, Timea Farkas, Christia Spears Brown. 2012. "Adolescent Girls' Experiences and Gender-Related Beliefs in Relation to Their Motivation in Math/Science and English." *Journal of Youth and Adolescence* 41 (3): 268–82.

Lopez-Acevedo, Gladys, and Raymond Robertson. 2016. *Stitches to Riches? Apparel Employment, Trade, and Economic Development in South Asia.* Washington, DC: World Bank.

Lyon, Gabrielle H., Jameela Jafri, and Kathleen St. Louis. 2012. "Beyond the Pipeline: STEM Pathways for Youth Development." *Afterschool Matters* 16: 48–57.

Mahmud, Simeen, and Sadia Mustafa. "Pattern of Time Use of Adult Women and Men in Rural North Bangladesh in 2013-2014." Centre for Gender and Social Transformation (CGST), BIGD, BRAC University. Unpublished. Submitted to ActionAid Bangladesh on January 31, 2015.

Ministry of Women and Children Affairs. *Multi-Sectoral Programme on Violence against Women.* Ministry of Women and Children Affairs Multi-Sectoral Programme on Violence against Women. 2018, (accessed September 10, 2018), http://www.mspvaw.gov.bd/.

Nguyen, M. C., and Q. Wodon. 2017. *Impact of Child Marriage on Literacy and Educational Attainment in Sub-Saharan Africa.* Education Global Practice, Washington, DC: The World Bank.

Niethammer, Carmen, Rudaba Zehra Nasir, Bénédicte de la Brière, Michelle Caitlin Davis, Amanda Epstein Devercelli, Gharam Alkastalani Dexter, Tazeen Hasan, Nathalie Hoffmann, and Anna Kalashyan. *Tackling Childcare: The Business Case for Employer-Supported Childcare.* Washington, DC: World Bank.

Ovi, Ibrahim Hossain. 2017. "Fears for Bangladesh GDP as RMG Growth Slows." *Dhaka Tribune,* June 7.

Pande, Rohini, and Deanna Ford. 2011. "Gender Quotas and Female Leadership: A Review Background Paper for the World Development Report on Gender." Background paper, World Bank.

Parsons, Jennifer, Jeffrey Edmeades, Aslihan Kes, Suzanne Petroni, Maggie Sexton, and Quentin Wodon. 2015. "Economic Impacts of Child Marriage: A Review of the Literature." *The Review of Faith & International Affairs* 13 (3): 12–22.

Passey, Don. 2017. "Computer Science (CS) in the Compulsory Education Curriculum: Implications for Future Research." *Education and Information Technologies* 22 (2): 421–43.

Pettit, Becky, and Jennifer Hook. 2005. "The Structure of Women's Employment in Comparative Perspective." *Social Forces* 84 (2): 779–801.

Priyadarshini, A., and S. Rahim. 2010. "Women Watching Television: Surfing between Fantasy and Reality." *IDS Bulletin* 41 (2): 116–24.

Rahman, R. I., and R. Islam. 2013. "Female Labour Force Participation in Bangladesh: Trends, Drivers and Barriers." ILO Asia-Pacific Working Paper, ILO.

Ruel, M. T., B. de la Briere, K. Hallman, A. Quisumbing, and N. Coj. 2002. "Does Subsidized Childcare Help Poor Working Women in Urban Areas? An Evaluation of a Government-Sponsored Program in Guatemala City." FCND Discussion Paper 131, IFPRI: Washington, DC.

Salam, Md. Abdus, and Gary N. McLean. 2014. "Minimum Wage in Bangladesh's Ready-Made Garment Sector: Impact of Imbalanced Rates on Employee and Organization Development." DOI: 10.13140/RG.2.1.4839.3361.

Sebastio, Filippo. 2014. "Female Empowerment in the Bangladeshi Garment Industry." November 18. (accessed February 15, 2018), https://www.theigc.org/blog/female-empowerment-in-the-bangladeshi-garment-industry/.

Siddiqi, Dina M. 2003. "The Sexual Harassment of Industrial Workers: Strategies for Intervention in the Workplace and Beyond." CPD-UNFPA Paper 26 (40). Dhaka: Centre for Policy Dialogue.

Simavi, Sevi. *Fostering Women's Economic Empowerment through Special Economic Zones: The Case of Bangladesh*. Washington, DC: The World Bank and the International Finance Corporation, 2012.

Solotaroff, Jennifer L., and Rohini Prabha Pande. 2014. *Violence against Women and Girls: Lessons from South Asia*. South Asia Development Forum, Washington, DC: World Bank.

Sommer, M., S. Chandraratna, S. Cavill, T. Mahon, and P. Phillips-Howard. 2016. "Managing Menstruation in the Workplace: An Overlooked Issue in Low- and Middle-Income Countries." *International Journal for Equity in Health* 15 (1): 86.

UNICEF (United Nations International Children's Emergency Fund). 2015. "The Ready-Made Garment Sector and Children in Bangladesh." New York: UNICEF.

White, Gillian B. 2017. "What's Changed since More than 1,110 People Died in Bangladesh's Factory Collapse?" *The Atlantic*, May 3.

Wodon, Quentin T., Chata Male, Kolobadia Ada Nayihouba, Adenike Opeoluwa Onagoruwa, Aboudrahyme Savadogo, Ali Yedan, Jeff Edmeades, Aslihan Kes, Neetu John, Lydia Murithi, Mara Steinhaus, and Suzanne Petroni. 2017. *Economic Impacts of Child Marriage: Global Synthesis Report*. Washington, DC: World Bank.

World Bank. 2015. "Bangladesh—More and Better Jobs to Accelerate Shared Growth and End Extreme Poverty: A Systematic Country Diagnostic." World Bank, Washington, DC. https://openknowledge.worldbank.org/handle/10986/23101.

———. 2017. *Nepal Poverty Alleviation Fund Project*. Project Performance Assessment Report, Independent Evaluation Group, Washington, DC: World Bank.

World Bank and IFC. 2011. *Fostering Women's Economic Empowerment through Special Economic Zones: The Case of Bangladesh*. Washington, DC: World Bank and IFC.

Yardley, Jim. 2013. "Bangladesh Takes Step to Increase Lowest Pay." *New York Times*, November 4.

3 Ownership and Control over Productive Assets

ABSTRACT *Ownership and rights over productive assets, such as land, housing, and livestock are closely related to economic empowerment of women. Rural women who report in the primary qualitative research having rights over productive assets tend to hold jobs, have access to financial services, and control income. In general, however, women lag behind men in terms of asset control and ownership in Bangladesh; only 13 percent of rural women report owning, solely or jointly, agricultural land. Compared to men, women often own assets of smaller value, such as livestock, making them more vulnerable than men. Whereas inheritance is the main channel through which people acquire land in Bangladesh, few women receive their fair share according to their religious personal laws. Families and local communities continue to pressure women to give up their inheritance. Religiosity of family members is an enabling factor for women's land ownership. Women still benefit from economic rights even when they lack ownership, but women's property rights are often derived from their relationships with men.*

Women's control and ownership of productive assets[1] are important to their economic empowerment: assets "generate income and facilitate access to capital and credit; strengthen individuals' and households' ability to cope with, and respond to, shocks by enhancing [women's] ability to diversify their income; and serve as a store of wealth that can be sold to generate income" (World Bank 2015a, 52). Ownership of productive assets can facilitate livelihoods activities, such as agricultural production and animal rearing; ownership of household durable assets can promote households' mobility and working capability (Rahman and Matsui 2009). Productive assets are significant indicators of household wellbeing; they can both generate income and serve as collateral to access credit (Doss et al. 2014). The Food and Agriculture Organization (FAO) (2011) estimates that if women globally were to use the same amount of resources as men on the same land farmed, they would fully close the current 20–30 percent yield gap to lift 100–150 million people out of food insecurity. Several impact evaluations demonstrate that formal legal titles or documentation securing women's land rights (along with access to agricultural inputs and technology) increase female farmers' agricultural productivity, crop yields, sales and income (Buvinić and O'Donnell 2016).

In addition to land, housing is a key asset for women as a store of wealth as well as a means of generating income—for example, home production of goods and services—as women's enterprises tend to be home-based. Yet globally women generally access land through male relatives (Klugman et al. 2014) and exercise only subordinate rights, making them vulnerable in the event of breakdowns in relationships, divorce, and male landowners' changing priorities (UN-HABITAT 2008). Even where women do have equal rights to land, religious and social or customary restrictions often prevent them from claiming or controlling the land.

In addition to productivity and economic benefits, women's ownership and control over assets boosts their empowerment. Women's property ownership is associated with power over intra-household decision making and greater expenditures toward children and families (UN-HABITAT 2008; Villa 2017). In Nepal, female landowners have more power over household decisions than women who own no land, and their ownership is associated with better child nutrition (Allendorf 2007). Bangladeshi women who own livestock report increased levels of confidence and social capital (Das et al. 2013).

In order to address the differences in control and ownership of productive assets between men and women in Bangladesh, we use a common analytical framework for this study, starting with the description of gender gaps and followed by results of our qualitative research and quantitative analysis pinpointing causes of such gaps. Finally, we discuss potential interventions that are logically linked to each determinant of gender gaps, prioritizing interventions with strong track records according to rigorous impact evaluation (though interventions with mixed results are also noted). Although some factors may contribute to more than one gender gap and some interventions could address many causes of gender gaps, we adhere to the theory of change by clearly linking each intervention to the gender gaps it can address, as indicated in figure 3.1.

GENDER GAPS IN PRODUCTIVE ASSETS

As agricultural land is the most valuable asset that households possess, we distinguish between agricultural and nonagricultural land. Agriculture is the most important source of employment for women in many countries; a larger share of employed women than employed men work in agriculture in South Asia, East Asia, North Africa, sub-Saharan Africa, and the Middle East (Team and Doss 2011). We examine differences in control and ownership of a broader set of productive assets, such as housing and livestock, finding that not only do women own fewer assets than men, but the assets they control are more vulnerable than those of men. Most data on land ownership, housing, and other assets are available only at the household level; however, most assets are owned by individuals—either solely or jointly. Such a paucity of data on individual ownership hinders gender analysis, as women and men may not have the same access to assets in the household. Not all household members may equally benefit from household assets; women and men use, acquire, and dispose of assets differently (UN Women 2013). Fortunately, the Bangladesh Integrated Household Survey Data (BIHS)—a rural survey conducted by International Food Policy Research Institute (IFPRI)—includes a great deal of information on male and female ownership of productive assets and economic empowerment. This chapter uses these data extensively (box 3.1).

FIGURE 3.1

Process diagram of gender asset gaps in Bangladesh, causes, and interventions

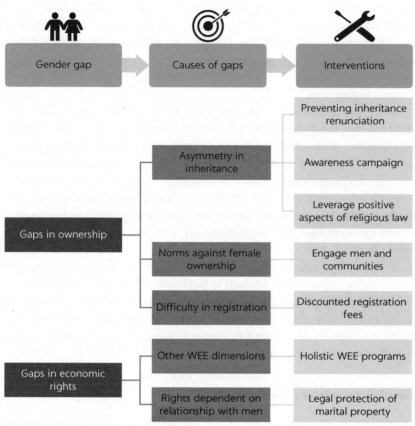

Note: WEE = Women's economic empowerment.

BOX 3.1

Bangladesh Integrated Household Survey data (BIHS)

The Bangladesh Integrated Household Survey (BIHS) is a representative rural household survey, covering all topics related to rural households in the country along with indicators of women's empowerment. The International Food Policy Research Institute (IFPRI) conducted the first round in 2011/12 and the second round in 2015. The survey was administered to the same sample of households in both rounds, creating a panel dataset. By tracking households over time, BIHS has uncovered some of the underlying dynamics of poverty, food security, and agricultural development in rural Bangladesh.

Most importantly, the survey collects detailed data on women's empowerment through an instrument on men and women's ownership and rights over key assets, decision making, and voice. A community survey supplements the BIHS data to provide information on area-specific contextual factors. The BIHS covers 6,500 rural households, and the sample is statistically representative at two levels: (a) nationally representative of rural Bangladesh; and (b) representative at the division level of rural areas, comprising seven divisions in 2015: Barisal, Chittagong, Dhaka, Khulna, Rajshahi, Rangpur, and Sylhet. Mymensingh—a recently created eighth division—was part of Dhaka division in this analysis.

The analysis carried out in this chapter primarily examines disparities in asset ownership between husbands and wives. All analyses, therefore, involve only married women.

Source: Ahmed, Tauseef, and Ghostlaw 2016.

Gender gaps in land ownership

Land in Bangladesh remains largely owned and/or controlled by men, which constrains women's decision making and productivity, as well as their access to extension services and credit, as discussed in later sections. The 2015 BIHS data show that only 12.1 percent of rural females have sole or joint ownership of agricultural land, and 6.9 percent own nonagricultural land; in comparison, rural men own agriculture land (69.3 percent) and nonagricultural land (86.5 percent) at much higher rates.[2]

The FAO's gender and land rights database shows that women own only 10.1 percent of Bangladesh's agricultural land in terms of area (FAO n.d.). A study by Rakib and Matz (2016) finds women to have less ownership than men of any kind of high-value asset other than jewelry. The most significant difference is in land holdings, with husbands owning 96 percent of total household land. According to Quisumbing et al. (2017), husbands exclusively own much larger amounts of land than wives exclusively own, and than husbands and wives own jointly. Quisumbing (2011) finds husbands to exclusively own much higher values of land as well.

In all divisions men own vastly more agricultural land than women. Among land-owning households (in which at least one member owned agricultural land) in rural Bangladesh, about 70 percent of male respondents reported sole or joint ownership of agricultural land compared to just 10 percent of women in the same households (figure 3.2). Across divisions, the gender gap is smallest in Sylhet and widest in Barisal.

Gender gaps in economic rights

In addition to ownership, rights to assets is another important gender gap to consider. Such rights include the right to sell, mortgage, rent, and keep the revenue generated by the asset, revealing the role of assets in reducing vulnerability

FIGURE 3.2

Agricultural land ownership (self or joint) by men and women, by division, 2015

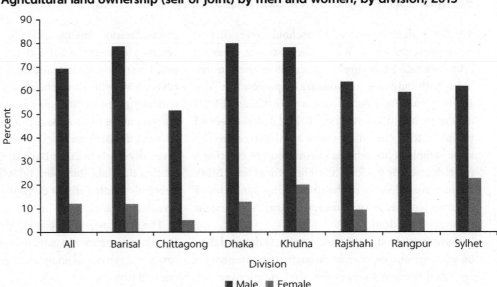

Source: World Bank calculations based on BIHS 2015 data.

and poverty. Ownership of an asset denotes possession of a "bundle of rights" over that asset (Johnson et al. 2016). Ownership implies holding *all* rights within a bundle that typically includes the right to make improvements on, rent out, and decide how to use land. Some people may have only some of the rights in this bundle. This concept is even more important in defining (whole or partial) ownership when land cannot be sold, due to laws or social norms (Doss et al. 2015).

To measure rights, Doss (2016) emphasizes two dimensions of data on women's land rights: the bundle of relevant land rights and security of these rights. Although there are no standard definitions for the bundle of rights, access to land usually involves the right to farm land and obtain economic gains. Control over land covers more rights, including rights to make decisions regarding use (what to plant, what inputs to use, when and how much to harvest, and how to dispose of the crops) (Doss, Grown, and Deere 2008; Doss et al. 2015). As a woman often acquires use rights through her relationship to a man—usually a husband or father—those rights are subject to continuation of that relationship (Sarwar et al. 2007; USAID 2010).

Many rural women who do not own assets actually report having economic rights over them. Using the metrics available in the BIHS dataset, we analyze men's and women's ownership, as well as rights over key assets (box 3.1), including data on rights to sell, to give, to rent, or to buy. The data underscore the importance of understanding gender gaps in rights (in addition to ownership). Many more rural women who do not have direct ownership over land report that they have some economic rights—that is, they jointly with their husband and other family members decide whether to sell, rent out, bequeath, or buy agricultural land (table 3.1). We hypothesize that some women, due to tradition, may not outright admit (to the survey interviewers) that they are part-owners of the land and defer the ownership to their husbands, but they may in fact be part-decision makers about the land.

In the Bangladeshi context, studying gender gaps in economic rights is doubly important, because norms may prevent women from directly owning agricultural land. Participants in the focus group discussion (FGD) with women in rural Rajshahi mentioned that "the society is not really comfortable" if a woman registers land under her name. An indication of this social unacceptability is the large difference between the percentage of women who report ownership and the percentage of women who report having rights over agricultural land.

TABLE 3.1 **Self or joint ownership and right over household assets, 2015**

TYPES OF OWNERSHIP AND CONTROL OF ASSETS	MALES	FEMALES
Own any of the assets	100	98
Has right over any of the assets[a]	100	98
Own any of the 4 valuable assets (ag land, cattle, house, or non-ag land)	96	38
Has right over any of the 4 valuable assets (ag land, cattle, house, or non-ag land)	97	58
Own agricultural land	70	13
Has right over agricultural land	88	43

Source: World Bank calculations based on BIHS 2015 data.
Note: Assets considered in this analysis include agricultural land; large livestock; small livestock; poultry; fish pond or fishing equipment; farm equipment (nonmechanized); farm equipment (mechanized); nonfarm business equipment; houses (or other structures); large consumer durables; small consumer durables; cell phones; nonagricultural land; and means of transportation.
a. Includes rights to sell, give, rent, or buy. Denominators are those whose households own relevant assets.

The data show that while few women own agricultural land (13 percent), many more report rights to sell, to give, to rent or to buy over such assets (43 percent). While it is also true that more men report rights than ownership, the gap between rights and ownership is much bigger for women. This suggests that many women in rural Bangladesh face gender constraints in formally owning agricultural land, as land likely has stronger ties to local customs than do other assets.

Gender gaps across asset portfolio

Gender gaps persist but vary across types of assets. Rural women have very low ownership rates of the four valuable assets (agricultural land, cattle, house, and nonagricultural land), compared to men (figure 3.3). Few exclusively or jointly own houses, large livestock, farm and nonfarm business equipment, large consumer durables, and any means of transportation. Women have higher rates than men of exclusive or joint ownership of lower-value assets, however, such as poultry (chicken, turkeys, and ducks) and small consumer durables. The largest gender gaps (favoring men) are in ownership of high-value items, such as land, mechanized farm equipment, houses, and vehicles. The difference in asset values highlights women's disadvantage in a broader context, and the gender disparity in patterns of asset portfolios contributes to greater vulnerability among women (box 3.2).

FIGURE 3.3

Ownership of different types of assets, 2015

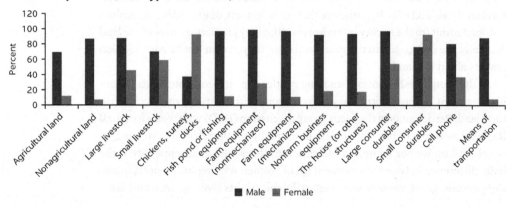

Source: World Bank calculations based on BIHS 2015 data.

BOX 3.2

Types of assets that women own increases their relative vulnerability

Earlier studies on asset accumulation (Davis 2011; IFPRI 2016; Quisumbing and Maluccio 2003; Rakib and Matz 2016) find similar results as those revealed by analysis of BIHS data (figure 3.3). Jewelry is a notable small durable good that women tend to own in larger quantities than men do (Quisumbing and Maluccio 2003), but research by Rakib and Matz (2016) finds that the share owned jointly is higher than the share owned by wives. Quisumbing, Kumar, and Behrman (2017) find that

continued

Box 3.2, *continued*

whereas women own more jewelry than men, most jewelry in the household is jointly owned, and reductions in nonland assets to cope with economic shocks come largely from selling jointly held jewelry. As women's assets are generally smaller and more easily sold off in times of need, shocks can increase intra-household gender asset inequality. These gendered patterns of asset ownership in Bangladesh leave women vulnerable.

Assets of husbands and wives are used differently to absorb sudden losses. Women's asset ownership in Bangladesh is vulnerable also because it is tied to a number of life-cycle and climate-related events. Generally, events such as dowry receipts, inheritance, and remittances increase asset accumulation in Bangladesh. On the other hand, *shocks* have complicated and occasionally counter-intuitive effects on asset accumulation (Quisumbing and Baulch 2013). Households often cope with shocks by selling assets to pay for medical care, business losses, or dowries (Davis 2011). Risk is not shared equally among members of a household, however, with assets owned by men and women used differently to cope with different types of shocks (Quisumbing 2011).

Idiosyncratic shocks—such as illness, death, dowry payments, and wedding expenses—affect only a few individuals or households at a given time. Land and cattle are important protective assets sold to fund dowries and medical care, and to meet other urgent life-cycle needs (Davis 2011). Quisumbing et al. (2017) finds illness, dowry, and wedding expenses to significantly reduce only wives' landholdings. The fact that shocks do not affect husbands' assets may suggest attempts to dispose of wives' exclusively owned land to cope with shocks.

Covariate shocks—such as floods, drought, and cyclones—affect many individuals in a given locality at the same time. Jointly owned assets generally are not sold in response to shocks, either because they are actively protected or due to the difficulty of agreeing on a coping strategy (Rakib and Matz 2016). Floods reduce the size of only husbands' owned land while increasing joint land accumulation, perhaps due to effective flood assistance or households rebuilding landholdings (Quisumbing et al. 2017). In contrast, crop loss from drought reduces the size of wives' owned land; perhaps it is disposed of first to pay for supplemental irrigation if the wife's land is of lower quality than the husband's.

CAUSES OF GENDER GAPS IN ASSET OWNERSHIP

This section lists factors associated with the gender gaps noted in the previous section. Factors are listed in no particular order; however, certain gender gaps are clearly mapped to specific factors, as displayed in figure 3.1. We begin with gender bias in inheritance, the most salient factor of gender disparities in land ownership in the country, followed by social norms about whether women can own land as men do. Difficulty in registering land with the government is also explored as a factor in gender-unequal land ownership. Finally, intra-household bargaining and the fact that women's economic rights over property tend to be derived from their relationships with men exacerbate gender gaps in the rights sphere.

Gender bias in inheritance

Inheritance is the main channel through which one gains access to land in Bangladesh. Whereas statutory laws on land rights and ownership are gender-neutral in the country, customary laws and cultural norms guide ownership in ways that favor men's ownership and control over land. Although inheritance is the main source of households' land acquisition in rural Bangladesh (table 3.2), differences in how much land women versus men have the right to inherit, and in the extent to which women feel they can accept and use the inheritance, are key contributors to gender gaps. The vast majority of inherited land is from the husband's family, exceeding inheritance from the wife's family by a factor of ten. *Khas* land is public land owned by the government, often allocated to poor or landless households. The data suggest that women in rural Bangladesh rarely receive and retain inheritance in the form of land.

Given the overwhelming Muslim majority in Bangladesh, inheritance is generally guided by Muslim Personal Law.[3] Despite females having these rights to inheritance according to personal law, they are not necessarily receiving their rightful property shares. Imams interviewed for this study agreed that women receive less inheritance than their rightful share (box 3.3).

TABLE 3.2 **Households' agricultural land, by means of acquisition**

METHOD OF LAND ACQUISITION	PERCENTAGE OF LAND ACQUIRED BY EACH METHOD
Purchase	14
Inherited from wife's family	5
Inherited from husband's family	54
Rent	24
Khas land	3

Source: World Bank calculations based on BIHS 2015 data.

BOX 3.3

Interviews with imams on women's inheritance rights in Bangladesh

Key informant interviews conducted with eight imams (local Islamic religious leaders) in rural and urban areas indicate that these imams support women's inheritance rights according to Islamic law. "The provision in Islam is that the girl will get one portion from three, and the brother will get two portions from their father because women also inherit property from their husbands," according to an imam from rural Dhaka. An imam from rural Barisal said, "Women should inherit their rightful shares and men should support it, because women have the right to claim their shares of inheritance according to Islamic law, and men abide by Islamic law by helping women receive their shares."

Regarding women's inheritance and land acquisition, imams said that Islam entitles women to inherit; however, very few receive their inheritance. Five out of eight imams interviewed recognized that women receive less than their rightful share of inheritance as per Sharia law. "The distribution rule of family property is clearly mentioned in the *Quran*, but women in our country are usually deprived of it," said an imam from urban Dhaka. As the imam from rural Barisal described,

"Some women get their portion of the inheritance, but some do not, and about 70 percent of the women do not receive their inheritable properties." In some regions, when it comes time to divide up the father's land, daughters are overlooked in favor of sons. As an imam from urban Chittagong explained, "Most of the time, brothers provide some money to sisters in exchange for their written statements surrendering the inheritance rights; however, the cash payments are not commensurate to the market value of the inheritance."

Imams' ability to influence inheritance practices may be limited. None of those interviewed had actively tried to intervene and apply Islamic law related to women's inheritance. A couple of the imams noted that property disputes are settled by *Shalish* (local community councils which make critical decisions for their communities and arbitrate disputes). In addition, an imam in urban Chittagong mentioned that decisions to give money to divorced women (*mahr*— the amount to be paid to the bride, decided by both families during the wedding) did not come to him because they were decided by the Shalish.

FIGURE 3.4

Layers of constraints on women's inheritance

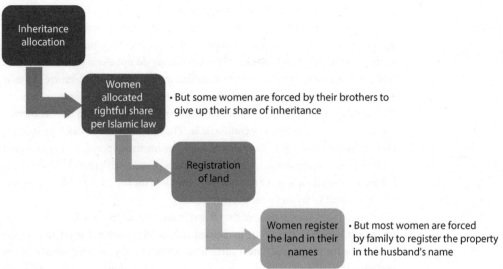

Gender gaps in inheritance vary by location and economic class. FGDs with women and men across Bangladesh shed light on constraints and enabling factors affecting women's inheritance. Among high- and low-income women's FGDs, rural women mentioned inheriting land disproportionately less frequently than urban women did. The gap between the incidence of women mentioning inheriting vs. not inheriting land from parents was widest in rural FGDs (one inheriting for every four not inheriting), followed by urban low-income FGDs, and smallest among the urban middle class (roughly a one-to-one ratio).

Multiple layers of constraints curtail women's inheritance. The qualitative data, together with a review of existing literature, help inform a model of the process—and its constraints and enabling factors—that characterizes women's inheritance in Bangladesh (figure 3.4). The first step is for the woman's natal family to allocate inheritance to her. The best-case scenario is that the woman receives her rightful share according to the *Quran* without being undermined by her brothers or others in the natal family. The second hurdle for the Bangladeshi woman is to register the land or property in her own name.

Positive and negative factors that influence the first step (bias in inheritance allocation) are discussed below, and gender constraints related to land registration are discussed in the following section.

a. Family and society pressure sisters to give up their shares of inheritance to brothers. Forfeiting their inheritance is traditionally considered proper and respectable behavior for women in Bangladesh. *Naior* denotes the practice of women's visitation to their natal home after they are married. The customary practice that has evolved around *naior*—and is now common—is that in order to preserve their right to uphold *naior* and ensure future protection in case of conflict or other calamity in the marital home, women forfeit their legal rights to property in their natal home (Sourav 2015). Activists in Bangladesh call this "the good-sister syndrome," but more often than not, brothers do not reciprocate in the way the good sister anticipates (*The Economist* 2013).

b. Fear of losing good relationships with natal families and societal pressure to relinquish their shares to brothers are among the top reasons women give up their share of inheritance. A male respondent in the rural Dhaka FGD mentioned that "when the time comes to distribute the property, the brothers appeal to the sisters to accept an arbitrary amount of money in exchange for the sisters' shares of property. The brothers claim that they are unable to pay more and that the sisters should legally give up their claims in return for the money received. The sisters are asked to allow the land to be registered in the brothers' names. Usually the sisters cannot refuse." He added, "Women usually do not claim their inheritance from their parents, unless they are compelled to. Those who do claim are not usually welcome at their brothers' houses." An urban middle-class women in Chittagong stated, "Women do not claim their inheritance from the brothers if their husbands are financially comfortable. They do not want to risk jeopardizing their relationships with their brothers. But if the husbands pressure them to claim their shares, women will do so even if it creates tension with their brothers. This is because they do not want to create any problem for their marital lives and prioritize husbands' wishes over other things."

Interestingly, almost none of the interviewed imams reported that women give up their inheritance rights due to familial and social pressure. The narrative used to describe the practice of sisters surrendering their inheritance rights to brothers includes the woman's "love for her brother" and "it's her own will." Only one imam mentioned the fear of losing relationships with the natal family as a reason that women waive their inheritance rights.

c. Limited awareness of the utility and importance of property for women is another barrier to women's inheritance. Given the traditional perception that women are not involved in economic activities, many rural families believe that female heirs would not fully utilize their inherited property. According to an imam from rural Barisal, these families say things like, "What is the use of property for women?" Many people also believe that women do not "need" the property, as men are traditionally responsible for providing *nafaqah*—money for sustenance—to their wives and children (Khan et al. 2016) and caring for their parents. The perception and practice that women will not be able to register the land under their own names provides justification for natal families not to allocate inheritance to women. An imam from rural Barisal explained, "The natal family feels that giving women their share of the inheritance would mean giving away part of the family's assets to another family, as the women would register the asset under their husbands' or children's names." Attitudes such as this reflect the prevailing nature of traditional, clan-based customs that help a natal family retain land in a society with exogamous marital practices, thereby bypassing Muslim Personal Law and civil laws that guarantee women's right to inherit.

Some families resort to equivocating that wedding expenses and dowry are substitutions for women's share of inheritance to justify not allocating the rightful share to daughters. Because dowry is paid by the bride's family to the groom's family in marriage, and the son's family traditionally is responsible for the care of parents, parents are reluctant to give land to daughters after they marry. Such marital customs disadvantage women by depriving them of owning property (Parveen 2007). An imam in rural Barisal said, "Families think that they have expended a great deal in family resources on a daughter's upbringing and her wedding." Some argue that daughters "belong" to their natal families only until they are married and that parents should not live with their married daughters or accept financial help from them (Das 2008).

d. Religiosity is an enabling factor. Religious fathers insist on giving land to women, according to FGD participants. A woman from urban Barisal said that her father transferred assets to her verbally because he was religious-minded.

Interviews with imams indicate that when consulted, they always guide families to allocate land to daughters and sisters according to Muslim Personal Law; however, imams also admit to not knowing if families are following their recommendations. Both imams from Sylhet were very articulate about women's land rights per Muslim Personal Law and cited the religiosity of the local population as a factor in women's receipt of their inheritance. Incidentally, the BIHS 2015 data suggest that Sylhet has the smallest gender gap in land ownership.

e. The data also show that limited property of natal families poses difficulty in dividing such property, particularly when final recipients of property lack money to compensate female heirs for their shares. An FGD participant from rural Dhaka mentioned that she and her sister will inherit a portion of the house along with their brother, but they are reluctant to claim their shares since he is living in their parents' house. A woman from rural Rajshahi said, "Since the land we get is a negligible amount, we do not mind giving it up for our brothers." The scenario is similar in rural and urban slum areas, but not in urban middle-class areas, according to the FGDs.

Women are more likely to receive inheritance when their natal families are affluent. Women from urban middle-class FGDs reported both claiming their inheritance and giving up their inherited portions to brothers, but the majority have inherited land or other property (apartment or money equivalent to the land). Their rural and low-income urban counterparts, however, are less likely to receive any inheritance; moreover, urban middle-class women did not report the need to register land under husbands' or children's names. An imam from urban Sylhet estimated that women from wealthy households are more likely than other women to receive their fathers' properties after the death of their fathers. Comments from FGD participants are consistent with findings from quantitative analysis of BIHS data, which suggest that women's land ownership is determined by the conditions of their natal families (proxied by the value of assets that women bring to marriage).

The mere presence of an equitable inheritance law has shown mixed results, as it may not be sufficient to effect change. One example is the modification of India's Hindu inheritance law that had discriminated against daughters inheriting land. The Hindu Succession (Amendment) Act 2005 modified the original law to provide women with the same rights to inherit as their brothers. An assessment of its effect on women cultivators in rural areas of three Indian states finds that a significant gap remains between women's legal right of ownership and their actual ownership, as well as between their ownership and actual control over land. Merely changing the law has not addressed the underlying barriers that women face in inheriting land (Sircar and Pal 2014).

Gender norms against women owning property

Traditional masculine and feminine roles (discussed in chapter 1) underlie the disapproval of communities and families toward women's control and ownership of productive assets, as these are traditionally men's roles. Recent trends reveal improving gender equality in land inheritance practices, however. Women are increasingly claiming their inheritance, compared to a decade ago, especially in urban areas. According to a female FGD participant from rural Barisal, "People's attitudes have changed over the last ten years. Previously, brothers did not want to give any portion of property to their sisters, but now they are a bit more supportive. In cases where brothers do not offer sisters their rightful shares, they at least offer some portion or an amount of money in exchange.

Women also used to give up their portions to brothers voluntarily. They did that to maintain a good relationship with brothers and the parental families, but now women want their shares even at the risk of straining their relationships with the brothers. Now at least 95 percent of women take their share. They are even ready to take legal steps if needed. Women are more aware now that they have the right to inherit and own property." A participant from a women's FGD in urban Chittagong remarked, "Many men nowadays register properties under their wives' names. They think that, after their death if the sons do not take care of their mothers, the wives will be in trouble, so they want to ensure some security for their wives." A respondent from the woman's FGD in rural Sylhet said that, "Some women register property under their names if they have bought the assets with money they earned. They may not register the property under their children's names, as the children may disappoint parents in the future; they may waste the asset or not take care of the parents when needed." She further mentioned, "Women will not register property in their husbands' names either, even if the husbands want to register the inherited property under their names. But the wives do not want that. They fear that the husbands may leave them after owning the property; however, if the husbands force it, women let their husbands register the property under their [husbands'] names."

Difficulty registering land under women's names

Land registration remains highly gendered, with land purchased by families generally registered only in the name of the male heads of households (USAID 2010). The 2006 World Bank Gender Norms Survey finds that less than 10 percent of all women in Bangladesh and less than three percent of young women between the ages of 15 and 25 have their names on marital property papers, such as rental agreements or ownership papers for land or homesteads (World Bank 2006). Although rural women often provide the primary labor on household land, they usually cannot receive compensation for any crop loss due to regular flooding and erosion, because the land tends not to be registered in their names (ADB 2004). Women rarely purchase land themselves, due to lack of control over household finances (oftentimes even their own earnings) and sociocultural pressure to stay confined to their traditional roles.

Almost all women participating in the qualitative study mentioned that, even in cases when they do inherit and acquire possession of family land, they register it under the husbands' and—in some cases—the children's (that is, sons') names. Registering land under women's names often creates a sense of threat for men that women will become "out of control" and that gender norms within the family will be upended, and women do not want to challenge these norms. Some husbands pressure their wives to register wives' property in husbands' names. As reported by a participant in a woman's FGD in rural Rajshahi, "Husbands of this area are very keen in registering their wives' land in their own [husbands'] names." Women and men alike mentioned that if a woman buys land with her own income, she can register it under her name, even though very few cases were reported where women did buy and register land with their income and under their names. Gender constraints related to land registration are discussed below.

a. Land registration fees are high, which disadvantages women who do not work for pay and lack control over income. Even women who have been allocated land as part of their inheritance report that their inability to pay the registration fee prevents them from registering the land under their own names. Many women do not have their own income; if they need money to pay land registration fees, they have to ask for it from their husbands. In such cases, they are left with no choice but to register land in their husbands' names. It should be noted that land registration fees in Bangladesh are relatively high by global standards (World Bank Group 2017).

b. Procedural obstacles also limit female land ownership in Bangladesh. Bangladesh's land titling and registration system is inefficient, expensive, and prone to corruption (USAID 2010). In its 2018 *Doing Business* report, the International Finance Corporation ranks Bangladesh 185th out of 190 countries in terms of registering property (World Bank Group 2017). Among the challenges to registering a property are the large amount of time it takes to do so (244 days, more than double the South Asian average of 112 days), the high number of procedures legally required to register a property (8 procedures), and the very poor score on the "quality of the land administration" index. Moreover, cost of registration is relatively high—about 6.4 percent of property value, compared to the OECD high-income countries' average of 4.2 percent.

    While the high fees and cumbersome procedures may appear to affect both men and women, these constraints disproportionately hinder women's ability to register the land. The FGDs show that, contrary to popular perceptions, women are aware of their rights to inherited land, but they face numerous social and procedural constraints in claiming and registering it. As indicated in chapter 2, women tend to have fewer resources of their own due to lower rates of labor force participation, compared to men's rates, and gender wage gaps. Many women thus may find it difficult to come up with the registration fee when their family (particularly their husband) is not supportive. *Purdah* (as discussed in chapter 1)—specifically in the form of enforced female seclusion—further constrains women from registering land. In addition to limiting women's mobility (Blunch and Das 2007) and their ability to travel to government offices, the concept of purdah also prevents many women from engaging in any public setting with men (Sultana 2012), which is further complicated by the fact that most land office officials are male and are not always sensitive to women-specific challenges (Sourav 2015).

c. Gender norms against women owning property, as discussed in the above section, also prevent women from registering land under their names. These norms are encouraged by (a) women's perceptions that their husbands' assets are also their assets, and (b) the relative ease of transaction if property is registered under a male name. Some female participants from rural Rajshahi remarked that husbands' assets essentially are their assets as well due to marriage; moreover, it is convenient if husbands are legally responsible because any land transactions require permission from the legal owner. In Bangladesh's patriarchal society, men are not comfortable obtaining permission from women.

Other dimensions of women's economic empowerment

Women's economic rights over major assets are associated with other dimensions of women's economic empowerment, such as labor force participation and control over income. Our multivariate analysis of the BIHS 2015 data reveals that productive assets, broadly defined—that is, including ownership and rights over any of the four major assets (agricultural land, cattle, houses or nonagricultural land)—are significantly and positively correlated with women's participation in the labor force. The multivariate analysis of control over income reveals similar results (see appendix D for regression tables). To explain this finding, one may allude to the fact that as women have independent sources of income from employment, they have greater opportunity to accumulate assets.

Ownership or rights over *agricultural land* are not significant explanators of women's economic empowerment, however. Qualitative data on social norms against women's agricultural land ownership suggest fewer constraints on ownership of other productive assets, such as large livestock and other property, which could explain the multivariate analysis finding of a more robust relationship between women's economic activities and accumulation of assets other than agricultural land. The qualitative analysis suggests that agricultural land ownership is determined by factors related to women's natal families and marriages—not situations that current interventions can influence.

Access to credit helps women accumulate assets. Analysis of BIHS 2015 data shows a significant and positive relationship between women's ability to make decisions about credit and ownership of other assets. Ownership and control over assets other than agricultural land are determined not only by inheritance, but also by the ability to purchase assets. Access to financial services—credit in particular— is a critical factor in women's ability to own and control assets. According to Quisumbing and Baulch (2013), greater numbers of nonNGO credit suppliers in a village are associated with increased nonland asset growth for households that own land. This relationship does not hold for functionally landless households (with no or very small areas of land), likely because financial providers require land as collateral. The International Labour Organization (ILO) suggests that Bangladeshi women's access to microcredit is the single most important factor contributing not only to their access to income-generating activities, but also to their empowerment (Rahman and Islam 2013).

In addition to mere asset ownership, greater resource control by women is found to increase household investments in women's and children's education, health, and nutrition, as well as increase household savings (for instance, see Blunch & Das 2007; Bhagowalia et al. 2010; Hussein & Hussain 2003; Khandker 1998; Roomi 2005). Research by Quisumbing and Maluccio (2003) suggests that the positive association between female control of household resources and share of expenditures on education may not indicate greater female altruism, as it also has a strategic benefit. As women in Bangladesh are overwhelmingly younger than their husbands and have greater life expectancy, women may make greater investments than their husbands in the children's education since they are more likely to rely on them in old age. Of course, greater investments in children's education could also pay financial dividends in terms of increasing the long-term earning potential of children.

Rights over assets depend on relationships with male family members

Addressing gender gaps in economic rights over productive assets is further complicated by the fact that such rights usually are determined by women's relationships with male family members. To understand gender gaps in rights over assets, it thus is essential to examine intra-household bargaining patterns—in particular, how women negotiate balance of power within the household.

Increasing age is a key factor in improving women's intra-household bargaining power. As women become older, their likelihood of owning land increases (figure 3.5), given that the cumulative probability of receiving inheritance rises

FIGURE 3.5

Women's ownership of key assets, by age, 2015

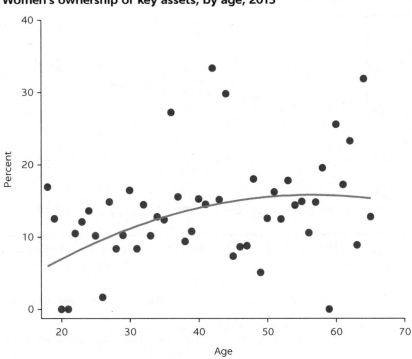

Source: World Bank calculations based on BIHS 2015 data.

as people grow older, and most land is acquired through inheritance. Moreover, women's power and agency may grow as they become older. A positive relationship between age and land ownership exists for both men and women. Household size (or number of household members), on the other hand, is negatively correlated with ownership; women may face less competition to control resources in smaller households.

Conditions related to women's marriage are also important; in particular, assets women bring to their marriages are positively correlated with women's land ownership.[4] The result is consistent with literature that depicts assets brought to marriage as a proxy for women's bargaining power within the household (Quisumbing and de la Brière 2000). The multivariate regression analysis confirms that assets women bring to their marriages are significantly and positively correlated with women's ownership of agricultural land in Bangladesh. This suggests that women's bargaining power, as proxied by assets they bring into marriage, enhances their economic empowerment. Findings from the FGDs corroborate these regression results: as inheritance is the main source of land ownership for people in rural Bangladesh, women's inheritance is determined by factors related to women's natal families.

Higher levels of education are not positively associated with women's odds of asset ownership. Analysis of the 2015 BIHS data shows diverging patterns between men's and women's ownership and rights over agricultural land. For men, the data indicate a clear positive correlation between higher levels of education and higher levels of ownership and rights over agricultural land (figure 3.6; note that the percentages shown are for people who report that someone in their households owns agricultural land). For women, however, level of

FIGURE 3.6

Ownership and rights over agricultural land, by sex and level of education, 2015

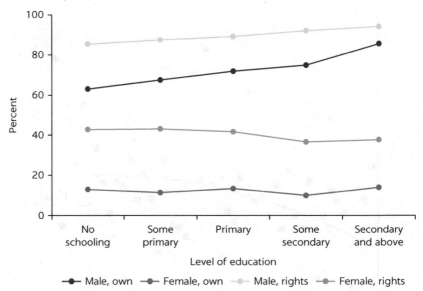

Source: World Bank calculations based on BIHS 2015 data.
Note: The sample includes only individuals living in households with any agricultural land ownership.

education does not appear to be correlated with ownership or rights—even when controlling for household income. Gender gaps in asset ownership therefore grow with higher levels of education.[5] These findings indicate women's relative lack of ability to expand their agency along with their educational attainments, especially when compared to men's expansion of agency by improving their education. Other household characteristics appear to be determinants of nonland asset growth. Demographic attributes, such as women's age and education, do not explain their ownership of productive assets like large livestock. Household size, on the other hand, is negatively correlated with ownership, which suggests that women face less competition to control resources in smaller households. Similar to other models of determinants of land, the value of assets women bring to marriage is positively correlated with ownership of large livestock. This result alludes to the bargaining power of women in households that assets at marriage bolster. In addition, research by Quisumbing and Baulch (2013) the number of years of schooling of the household head is positively associated with nonland asset growth, while households with higher proportions of women older than 55 again experience slower asset growth. Older husbands also experience higher nonland asset growth and accumulate nonland assets faster than their wives (Quisumbing, Kumar, and Behrman 2017). Older wives are associated with husbands' slower asset accumulation, but unchanged own asset accumulation. Finally, similar to land, larger household size is associated with increased joint-asset accumulation.

GOOD PRACTICES AND RECOMMENDATIONS

This section reviews efforts to address gender gaps in women's ownership and control over productive assets, both in Bangladesh and in other countries with similar profiles. These include active program interventions, such as asset transfers and community engagement to change social norms, as well as legal interventions. Lastly, we discuss efforts to generate more asset data that can be sex-disaggregated.

Prevent inheritance renunciation

The social pressure on women to renounce their inheritance shares and give property to male relatives is pervasive across South Asia and the Middle East. This tradition lingers despite Islamic teaching and modern family codes. To ensure women's inheritance rights as per Islamic and civil laws, Jordan has developed an innovative policy instituting an automatic mechanism that registers inheritance in daughters' names.

Jordan has arguably one of the most efficient and effective land administration systems in the region. In Jordan, the law grants women the right to register land both as individuals and jointly through marriage. As in many Muslim countries, shares of inheritance are determined by the Personal Status Code, which is based on Islamic principles of inheritance. Percentages of female land-owners and the amount of land owned by women remain low, however (World Bank 2013a). The practice of female heirs renouncing their inheritance rights to male relatives—a process known in Jordan as *takharoj*—is common. Media reports indicate that "one out of five women concedes her rights to inheritance"; while 74 percent of women in the second-biggest governorate in Jordan "do not receive their full share of inheritance" (Alazzeh 2017).

To challenge this practice, Jordan has introduced measures to protect women's inheritance rights. Amendments to the Personal Status Code in 2010 led the Islamic courts to issue an instruction to offer protection to women's inheritance rights, particularly to address the social pressure faced by women to renounce rights. "The instruction provides a three month 'cooling off' period after the division of inheritance rights during which heirs cannot renounce rights, except in special circumstances permitted by the Islamic courts. If a woman would like to renounce her inheritance rights after the cooling-off period is completed, the court must first explain the impacts of the renunciation and, in the case of immovable property, such as land, the property must first be registered in the name of the heirs before it can be renounced and transferred." This policy's efficacy is not yet evaluated, but anecdotal evidence suggests it is now more difficult to renounce rights, especially outside of major urban centers (World Bank 2013, 66).

Conduct awareness campaigns

As demonstrated above, bias in inheritance allocation may stem from lack of awareness about women's legal rights, as well as community perceptions about women's rights to property. In Bangladesh and other countries, a number of interventions aim to engage women and their communities to raise awareness about women's rights over land and productive assets.

The Tanzania Community Based Legal Aid program trains paralegals from program villages, focusing on women's land rights. Professional legal staff from the implementing NGO support the paralegals (who receive a small stipend but are otherwise volunteers), who conduct outreach and community education on legal rights and procedures; help with dispute mediation, lawyer referral, advocacy in case of disputes; and help people write wills. They also organize general legal awareness programs in the community. One of a few rigorous evaluations of awareness raising for women's land rights, a randomized control trial of the one-year Tanzania Community Based Legal Aid program reveals the benefits and also constraints of a short intervention using this approach to improve women's knowledge, attitudes, and practice of land-related issues, as well as their perceptions of gender equity in rights to land (Mueller et al. 2017). The evaluation finds an increase in the level of land-related regulations on women's land rights but no change in attitudes or practice. The authors hypothesize that perhaps a one-year program is sufficient only to change knowledge, but that to change attitudes and behavior requires a longer time period. This is an important lesson for Bangladeshi community-based programs going forward.

India and Nepal also offer examples of social mobilization programs to promote women's rights to land. Though not focused specifically on women's land rights, some of the programs still provide instructive lessons that could be adapted to address women's land ownership. In India's state of Odisha, the state government partnered with CSOs to engage community members as intermediaries to assist local land administration officials to identify those without land and grant them land. These Community Resource Persons were trained in various arenas, including how to identify those without land, and engaged the wider community in their endeavors. The program, scaled up to cover the entire state, is considered a model in "people-centric land governance" (Choudhury and Nanda 2014).

Media campaigns by the USAID-supported Property Rights Program in Kosovo have been successful in raising awareness of women's property rights and increasing rates of female inheritance and property registration. Although the country has a gender-equal legal framework, in which the constitution guarantees rights to property for women and men, society is considered patriarchal and patrilineal; women's rate of owning property is relatively low. The program uses a Social Behavior Change Communications (SBCC) approach though a media campaign, creating positive and authentic content with targeted messages. The campaign is delivered through media, such as TV, radio, billboards, Facebook, and grassroots events for children, which include drawing events, forum theater, and puppet theater. From the roll-out of the program in 2015, until the mid-line evaluation in 2017, affirmative attitudes among men toward equal property rights increased from 64 percent to 73 percent, while the share of women inheriting property nearly doubled (from 3.8 percent to 7.5 percent). Moreover, the number of women filing inheritance claims in the courts increased by 10 times (Limani, Cuizon, and Zeqiri 2018).

In Bangladesh, a few community mobilization programs have been implemented to raise awareness of women's property rights.[6] A program by the NGO, Centre for Development Services (CDS), identifies discriminatory laws and customary practices that create barriers for women to claim property. CDS conducts interactive media campaigns on women's rights to raise awareness among women of their property and inheritance rights. Importantly, CDS selects women from the community and trains them to mobilize their communities to redress violations of property rights through advocacy (USAID 2003). The "mobilizers" incorporate messages pertaining to women's property and inheritance rights into street theater and folk songs. They also engage with mediation committees and local leaders, sharing with them information on personal laws and productive ways to handle local land disputes.

Similarly, the Madaripur Legal Aid Association (MLAA) is developing a network of Muslim women leaders drawn from grassroots women's groups to address gender equity, property, and inheritance rights through a combination of awareness raising and engaging and training women to advocate for their own land rights (USAID 2003). The network provides these women with information on their rights, logistical support to exercise them, and related training for engaging other women in their communities. The Khan Foundation funds a Women's Lawyers Network that provides free legal resources at the local level and information and skills training to locally elected women, enabling them to raise awareness and engage on issues and laws pertaining to property and inheritance rights (USAID 2003). Unfortunately, we find no rigorous evaluations of these programs; still, evaluated examples from other countries suggest that it is essential to engage women and their communities to ensure women's land ownership.

Leverage religious leaders

Muslim Personal Law is clear on women's property rights through inheritance, but enforcement of such laws is lacking. As discussed in the last section, women's natal families often are either unaware of Muslim Personal Law's provisions for women's inheritance or are so embedded within customary practice that they pressure women to relinquish their share to their brothers or other male relatives. Engaging religious leaders to educate the public and advocate for women's inheritance rights could be another approach to addressing gender gaps in asset ownership.

A promising example shows that leveraging religious leaders can be effective. In Niger, women in the Zinder region face similar challenges as Bangladeshi women with regard to property rights because of the way the *Quran* is interpreted by local religious authorities (*marabouts*) to influence customary regulations on inheritance. In this regard, an aid agency, SNV Niger, helped collect testimonies from women. Based on this information, religious and customary leaders worked with the district land commission and women's organizations to better understand the relevant passage in the *Quran* and concluded that women can inherit a part of family land. As a result, women were better able to exercise their rights with full control of the crops grown on their own land, which has contributed to improved food security and household savings (SNV Netherlands Development Organisation 2012).

Engage men and communities

As discussed above, women face pressure from their families, husbands, and immediate communities to cede property ownership. Programs aiming to change gender norms need to work with all stakeholders—not only with women, but also with men and community leaders. Below are examples of programs aiming to promote gender equality, some of which target men and others whole communities.

An example of a program targeting men, Program H was first launched in 2002 by the NGO Promundo and its partners and is now used in more than 22 countries. The program primarily targets young men to encourage critical reflection on rigid norms related to manhood and generate more gender-equitable attitudes. The program's methodology promotes group education sessions combined with youth-led campaigns and activism to transform stereotypical roles associated with gender (such as contraceptive use or distribution of household responsibilities). Partners usually implement 10–16 activities, once a week, over a period of several months in conjunction with community awareness campaigns created by youth themselves (Promundo n.d.). Replicated in several Asian and Latin American countries, the program has sought to target this issue at its root by challenging ideas of masculinity, femininity, and violence among boys and girls in childhood and early adolescence. Evaluations of this innovative in-school program reveal significant changes in the attitudes of young boys and girls towards gender roles and gender-based violence (Achyut et al. 2011).

Although this program is being implemented in many settings, the Rwandan program has been rigorously evaluated with randomized control trial method. The program, called Bandebereho (local language for "role model") consists of a 15-session curriculum adapted from Program H. Bandebereho targets new and soon-to-be fathers, as well as their partners/spouses in Rwanda. Sessions are organized as guided group discussions on gender and power; fatherhood; couple's communication and decision making; violence; caregiving; child development; and engaging men in reproductive and maternal health. The study conducted a multisite randomized controlled trial in four Rwandan districts with expectant and current fathers and their partners, who were randomly placed in the intervention (n = 575 couples) or control group (n = 624 couples). The impact evaluation reveals that the program resulted in greater gender equality in the households, where men spent almost one hour more a day doing unpaid care work and women had increased power over financial decision making (Doyle et al. 2018).

Another group of interventions uses a community mobilization approach to engage with communities and their leaders. In Rwanda, community mobilization improved land registration processes. The government had discussions with communities before setting up land registration processes to implement its very gender-egalitarian inheritance law: communities wanted land registration to have not just the name of the owner(s), but also the names of those who had "interests" in the land. This meant that women who were not officially owners could still be formally registered as having an "interest." Evaluation of the Rwanda approach finds increases in registration of inheritance rights without gender bias (Lastarria-Cornhiel et al. 2014). Other countries—such as the Lao People's Democratic Republic—have used radio and other popular media to educate local land functionaries on women's rights to land (Lastarria-Cornhiel et al. 2014). Interventions elsewhere have focused on increasing the participation of women in land registration departments by training women as land administrators. A program that did so in Ethiopia finds that this practice encourages female-headed households to register their land; Lastarria-Cornhiel et al. (2014) suggests that a key aspect of enforcing this law is extensive awareness raising and community consultation prior to the passing of the law. Resistance and reluctance among women to claim land did continue to some extent, but daughters were found to increasingly inherit.

BRAC's Gender Quality Action Learning (GQAL) in Bangladesh, while still seeking to engage communities and raise awareness, has also emphasized changing gender norms (Jahan et al. 2016). The training program was originally created for BRAC employees, but was expanded to community members in 2001. Working with men and women, the program engaged religious leaders and local elites as agents of change, and emphasized cooperation over conflict. According to available program data and independent studies, the program has successfully changed local people's traditional views about women's asset ownership. In the past, women living within program areas rarely owned assets or inherited property; it was commonly believed that if a woman took her father's property, her husband would become poor. A woman did not get *dower* (the mandatory payment at time of marriage by the husband or his family to the wife, especially to support her in the event of his death) or any property from her husband; most women did not know of their right to dower even though Muslim Personal Law requires payment of dower to a wife, as it is a mandatory element of the marriage contract. Women had very little access or control over resources and could not engage in any income-generating activity, as it was viewed as a sin.

These customary practices changed through the GQAL program as women and men became increasingly aware of women's rights to assets and property. Newly bought land is now being registered in the name of both husband and wife, and joint decision making in financial and other household aspects is becoming common. Women continue to face problems in realizing their parental inheritance, however, with little having been achieved in this regard (Jahan et al. 2016); this may be due to the fact that the program was not implemented in women's natal villages. Still, the findings suggest that programs with an explicit aim to change gender norms may be more effective than those merely focusing on awareness raising.

Discounted land registration fees for women

Recognizing land registration fees as one obstacle to women registering land in their own name, many countries have enacted policies that waive such fees or provide discounts for women who register property in their name. The government of Nepal has in recent years made provisions to waive registration fees while transferring entitlement to women undertaking land registration fee reforms to promote women's land and property ownership, including a 25–50 percent discount (depending on the geographical location) on registration fees for land owned by women and a 35-percent tax discount for single women (Financial Bill 2072, Ministry of Finance). Joint registration of land in the names of husbands and wives incurs a fee of only NPR 100 (or less than USD $1) (IOM 2016).

In India, many states (such as Uttar Pradesh, Delhi, Punjab, and Haryana) offer discounts on property registration fees to female buyers. More moderated discounts are also offered to couples who register property jointly. For example, in Delhi, a woman pays a 4-percent stamp duty compared with 6 percent for a man and 5 percent for joint registration between husband and wife (Shanbaug 2012; The Logical Buyer 2015). In Jharkhand state, the government went further in 2017 and waived registration fees for property registered in a woman's name. Specifically, women can register real estate property worth up to INR 5 million by paying only a token sum of INR 1 as a stamp fee, with no court fee (IANS 2017); however, there has not been a rigorous evaluation of whether the policy has resulted in greater female land ownership and whether women exercise economic rights over such properties.

In addition to reducing property registration fees, streamlining property registration procedures could narrow the gender gap in property registration, as cumbersome bureaucratic processes are more problematic for women than men due to women's relative lack of agency, purdah practices, and mobility constraints that make it harder for women to complete transactions requiring travel. Property registration reform also will benefit the Bangladeshi economy as a whole, since the reform will improve the country's investment climate and directly impact Bangladesh's Doing Business ranking.

Comprehensive programs for all aspects of women's economic empowerment

Analysis in the previous section underscores the importance of holistic approaches to women's economic empowerment. Rights over a broad class of productive assets (not only agricultural land, but also housing and livestock) are associated with multiple dimensions of this empowerment—namely employment, access to finance, and control over income. Policy interventions to improve women's ownership must recognize the existing economic power distribution and dynamics in the household and the need to change the balance of power to achieve sustainable results. A group of interventions can address this need by offering combined (or "bundled") provision of large (often in-kind) capital transfers, asset-specific training and technical assistance, cash stipends and access to savings, and often health information and life skills coaching. In their review of evidence from impact evaluations on women's economic empowerment, Buvinić and O'Donnell (2016) notes that such bundled interventions are effective among the very poor. An evaluation of a bundled program in Burkina Faso demonstrates that women's ownership and control over assets improved and community perceptions about who can own and control certain assets also shifted, suggesting that changing social norms is indeed possible (van den Bold et al. 2013).

BRAC's Challenging the Frontiers of Poverty Reduction—Targeting the Ultra Poor (CFPR-TUP) Program provides livestock and training to rural women in "ultra-poor" households, identified through a wealth ranking exercise using several inclusion and exclusion criteria.[7] Targeted women appear to retain ownership over transferred livestock but with limited control of assets (Das et al. 2013). A study by Roy et al. (2015) finds an increase in women's ownership and control over the livestock (along with increased "intangible" benefits, such as more social capital), but ownership of new agricultural investments mobilized by the project going to men. This suggests that empowerment effects may be short-lived (Buvinić and O'Donnell 2016), with cultural norms about what is acceptable for men and women unchanged.

These asset transfers also appeared to decrease women's mobility outside the homestead, likely due to the increased workload as well as to maintenance of the transferred livestock being home-based, thus shifting work to the homestead. Finally, women's voice was reduced in decisions related to control over their own income, purchases for themselves, and decision making for household budgeting. A long-term impact evaluation of the program, however, shows that while female participants are less likely than other women to be in vulnerable occupations and more in self-employment, the long-term effect is much smaller for most outcomes when compared to short- and medium-run impacts (Asadullah and Ara 2016). Bandiera et al. (2017) also finds substantial increases in women's labor supply and earnings—women who receive livestock tend to spend more time taking care of livestock and working as maids—but they find no significant long-term impacts on metrics of women's economic empowerment. Unfortunately, the study does not examine women's asset ownership over the long term.

Legal protection of marital property

Because women's property rights are often derived from their relationships with men, women are vulnerable to losing legal rights to property when their relationship status changes due to death of husbands or divorce. Several countries have implemented legal solutions to strengthen women's legal claim of marital property (property accrued during marriage). These solutions can be categorized into three groups: promoting joint ownership of property, remedying the marital property regime, and instituting gender equal property rights in higher laws.

Bangladesh needs to promote joint ownership of property. A range of legal and policy reforms to promote joint ownership have been undertaken to enable women to gain access, rights and control over assets (Aluko 2015). In the Philippines, joint ownership laws ensure that married women have legal claim to property along with their husbands, thus enabling women to protect their rights in property ownership. In the early 1990s, Vietnam launched a reform program that broke the pre-existing communal land structure and reorganized the communal farming models to redistribute land to individual households. Initially the Land Use Certificate (LUC) issued by the government had only the husband's name as the head of the household, but with support from the World Bank, the government changed this practice by issuing LUCs that require the names of both husband and wife (Zakout 2016). In India, the municipal government of Chandigarh town introduced joint titling in 2000 to prevent property sales by husbands alone. As part of this effort, the government started allotting houses in both the husband's and wife's names, replacing the pre-existing practice of allotting in the name of the head of the household, who in most cases was male. This reform towards joint property rights contributed to women's increased decision making and bargaining power, heightened sense of security, improved self-esteem and higher status within the family (Datta 2006). Bangladesh's efforts to distribute public or khas land have evolved to register publicly distributed lands in both the husband's and wife's names; however, significant gaps remain between women's legal land rights and actual ownership, as well as between ownership and control (Agarwal 1994).

Some evidence suggests that land formalization programs requiring joint registration between both spouses may promote female land ownership. A quasi-experimental study of Rwanda's pilot land tenure regularization (LTR) program—in which married female spouses were registered as co-owners of land by default—shows significant impacts of the LTR on women's land rights (among married couple households) (Ali et al. 2015). Women are more likely to be registered owners (either alone or jointly with spouses), with the size of effects ranging between 19 and 34 percentage points. Women's economic rights also increase considerably, including their access to mortgage (between 9 and 13 percentage points), as well as to lease out land (between 8 and 10 percentage points). The increase in women's rights to bequeath or sell land (alone or jointly with their spouses) is similar (Ali et al. 2015). Another experiment from urban

Tanzania, where women's documented land ownership is low, shows that a small conditional subsidy can induce households to adopt joint land titles without dampening demand for the title (O'Sullivan 2017).

Legal reforms can remedy the martial property regime. Default marital property laws—typically indicated in the civil code—greatly influence women's ability to claim marital properties; they are especially crucial in situations where women's land rights tend to be dependent on their relationships with men. There are two main types of regimes that govern property owned prior to and during marriage: *community (of) property* and *separate property*. In *community property* regimes, all assets acquired during the marriage are considered the joint property of the couple. In contrast, in the *separation of property* regime, all property (irrespective of when or how it was acquired), is treated as individually-owned property; in the event the marriage is dissolved due to divorce or death, there is no community property to distribute. When women lack economic means to acquire assets, as in Bangladesh, the community of property regime may offer better protection of women's economic rights (Iqbal 2015). In the case of Bangladesh, where separation of property is the default marital property regime, women are vulnerable to losing economic rights, particularly when the relationship status with men changes due to death or divorce.

Legal protections of the marital home are provisions that can be enacted, regardless of the default marital property regime. Such laws comprise provisions related to administration of the marital home, such as requiring both spouses to agree to any major transaction involving the home, including selling or pledging it as collateral, or the court will intervene when spouses disagree. Several countries include provisions protecting women's marital homes, such as Burkina Faso, Cambodia, Turkey, Kenya, Tanzania, and Uganda. Currently, Bangladesh has no special provisions governing the marital home other than the Domestic Violence (Prevention and Protection) Act 2010, the implementation of which is far from satisfactory.

As switching the default marital property regime could be challenging, some countries amend the civil code to add legal protection for women. Morocco reformed its *Family Code* in 2004 to strengthen women's control over economic assets in marriage. The reform allows couples to sign a contract (separate from the marriage contract) establishing terms of managing assets acquired during marriage—effectively to opt into the community property regime. Implementation of reforms remains mixed, however. A 2006 study finds that a majority of Moroccans surveyed (68 percent of men and 62 percent of women) reported knowledge of the reforms (World Bank 2015b); however, in 2011 only 609 such contracts were concluded—representing only 0.002 percent of marriages registered that year—and in 2013 only 1,520 contracts. A number of factors could contribute to the low uptake, such as a lack of awareness, the lack of a model contract that could be used to assist couples entering marriage, and restrictive social norms (World Bank 2015b).

Data gaps

Bangladeshi women's level of decision making and control over jointly and exclusively owned assets remains largely unexplored in literature to date. A small number of studies have assessed women's control of assets in the context of specific development programs that have transferred assets to women. Broader, more systematic evaluation of intra-household resource allocation and women's control over assets would reveal which assets are more likely to be real-located to male relatives and which are more likely to remain in control of female owners. This may shed light on some of the varying resource control hurdles for different types of assets, as well as help identify particular opportunities for property-owning women to maximize their property for economic and social empowerment. Furthermore, given the regional differences in female asset ownership, collecting data on relative resource control over jointly and exclusively owned assets in households across Bangladesh's divisions would provide insight—and better help guide policy recommendations—for particular communities to support cooperation within households (see description of data collection efforts in box 3.4). Women's asset transfer programs could then be informed by different areas' particular reallocation patterns, if any, to focus on less diverted assets that tend to remain more under women's control.

The government of Bangladesh needs to collect individual-level asset data in its regular household survey. Currently, the Household Income and Expenditure Survey cannot enable policy makers to understand gender gaps; moreover, maintaining individual data on land ownership is essential to tracking Sustainable Development Goals (SDGs) indicators. SDGs comprise the ongoing paradigm for development, with an unprecedented emphasis on gender and asset ownership. Target 5.A aims to "undertake reforms to give women equal rights to economic resources, as well as access to ownership and control over land and other forms of property, financial services, inheritance and natural resources, in accordance with national laws." Tracking progress requires knowing the (a) proportion of the total agricultural population with ownership or secure rights over agricultural land, by sex; and (b) share of women among owners or rights-bearers of agricultural land, by type of tenure (5.A.1).

BOX 3.4

International efforts to collect sex-disaggregated data on assets

Traditional asset studies focus on the household level, but individual-level data is important because most assets are owned by individuals, either individually or jointly with others. Women and men may not have the same access to assets in the household; all members do not benefit equally from household assets; and women and men use, acquire, and dispose of assets differently. By measuring women's asset ownership at the individual level, we are better equipped to understand the state of women's empowerment and well-being; the status of women's fallback positions (in the case of separation, divorce, widowhood, or in the choice of whether to marry in the first place); and their bargaining power within the household (UNSD and UN Women 2013).

Since 2010, there have been efforts in different countries to collect such data, such as the Gender Asset Gap project, the World Bank Living Standards Measurement Study-Integrated Surveys on Agriculture, and the United Nations Evidence and Data for Gender Equality (UN EDGE) initiative. The methodology developed by EDGE has been pilot tested in many countries, including Fiji, Georgia, Maldives, Mexico, Mongolia, the Philippines, South Africa, and Uganda. A draft guideline was submitted to the 48th session of the United Nations Statistical Commission in March 2017, and is in the process of consultation with member countries. In Bangladesh, only IFPRI surveys can provide such data and only for rural areas.

Sources: UNSD and UN Women 2013, UNSD 2018.

CONCLUSION

Bangladeshi women lag behind men in terms of control and ownership of productive assets. Gender gaps are largest in high-value assets, such as land. On the other hand, women own more assets of smaller value, such as livestock. In addition to land ownership, women's economic rights and control over agricultural land are critical. While only 13 percent of women report owning agricultural land, 43 percent report having some economic rights over land belonging to the household. Our analysis shows strong, positive correlations between economic rights over productive assets and women's economic empowerment outcomes such as employment, access to finance, and control over money. This reflects the multidimensionality of women's economic empowerment: control over productive assets, paid employment, and control over income tend to move in the same direction. In terms of channels through which people acquire land, inheritance is the main source of land ownership in Bangladesh. Our qualitative research shows that cultural norms for women to give up inheritance remain strong, and pressure from brothers to do so is prevalent. Women who do not surrender their land find it difficult to register it under their own names. Imams and other religious leaders can play a positive role in enabling women's land ownership. This chapter recommends the following policies to address gender gaps in asset ownership and to further boost women's economic empowerment:

- Prevent the common practice of inheritance renunciation through automatic property transfer and impose a cooling-off period before women can transfer property
- Raise awareness of women's rights to assets and women's ability to use assets to generate economic gains, as a means of changing local gender norms
- Leverage Muslim Personal Law and engage religious leaders to ensure that women receive their rightful shares of inheritance without socio-cultural impediments
- Engage men and broader communities to generate support for women's right to asset ownership
- Offer reduced registration fees and taxes for female property owners and joint ownership of property between husband and wife
- Implement holistic interventions that address multiple dimensions of women's economic empowerment at the same time
- Introduce minor legal reforms to offer additional protection of marital property and the marital home
- Collect data on rights and ownership of assets at the individual level

NOTES

1. Productive assets are any assets that grow by things happening to them or being done with them on a nondestructive basis, to generate value or income to the owner. The many types of productive assets include businesses, land, real estate, livestock, poultry, fisheries, seeds, and all kinds of modern and traditional agricultural machinery. Land, housing, and livestock, however, are perhaps the most important productive assets, as they play key roles in rural areas (Bhatt and Bhargava 2006).
2. The survey question on individual ownership asks, "Does anyone in your household currently have any [ITEM]?" and thus is applicable only to those whose household owns that asset. Of the sample's 6,500 households, only 469 women responded that someone in the household owns nonagricultural land—among whom 6.9 percent reported having sole or joint ownership of it.

3. The Sunni Hanafi Law of Succession recognizes three classes of heirs, namely Ashabul faraiz, Asabah or Agnates, and Dhauil-arham. The distribution of property of a deceased Muslim person is determined by what class of heirs the deceased is survived by and their pre-determined degree of closeness. The inheritance shares of the Ashabul faraiz, considered the nearest family members, prescribe specific and differing shares for different categories of heirs. Generally speaking, female children inherit half the property inherited by male children. While the 1961 Muslim Family Laws Ordinance, 1985 Family Court Ordinance, and 1974 Muslim Marriage and Divorce Registration Act have provisions more favorable for women than traditional Islamic principles, Bangladeshi women have difficulty using the law to protect their land rights due to inadequate resources, lack of knowledge of the law and legal processes, and cultural norms (USAID 2010).

4. The BIHS does not collect information on assets that men brought to their marriages.

5. Quisumbing et al. (2017) find that husbands' schooling is associated with greater ability to build joint landholdings with their wives, while husbands' age is correlated with greater individual land accumulation and larger husband-wife disparities in land ownership. Wife's schooling increases both her husband's and her own ability to accumulate land, but it does not affect the husband-wife difference. In larger households, individual land accumulation by husbands is slower, and joint land acquisition is faster. As husbands age, they may be giving land to sons, reducing individual land in favor of jointly held land.

6. See, for example, the programs run by Community Legal Services, a five-year intervention from 2012 to 2017 in Bangladesh funded by DFID (http://communitylegalservice.org/).

7. Households were identified as being eligible for the program through a wealth ranking exercise assessing several inclusion and exclusion criteria. Households were deemed "ultra-poor" if they met at least three out of the following five inclusion criteria: (1) the household is dependent upon female domestic work, for example, begging; (2) the household owns less than 10 decimals of land; (3) there are no active male adult members in the household; (4) there are no productive assets in the household; (5) school-age children have to engage in paid work. Households also had to meet all of the following three exclusion criteria to be considered "ultra-poor:" (1) no adult woman in the household is able to work; (2) the household does not participate in microfinance; and (3) the household is not a beneficiary of a government or NGO development project.

REFERENCES

Achyut, P., N. Bhatla, S. Khandekar, S. Maitra, and R. K. Verma. 2011. "Building Support for Gender Equality among Young Adolescents in School: Findings from Mumbai, India." New Delhi: International Center for Research on Women.

Agarwal, Bina. 1994. "Gender and Command Over Property: A Critical Gap in Economic Analysis and Policy in South Asia." *World Development* 22 (10): 1455–78.

Ahmed, Akhter, Salauddin Tauseef, and Julie Ghostlaw. 2016. "IFPRI's Bangladesh Integrated Household Survey (BIHS) Second Round Dataset Now Available." *IFPRI Research Blog*, December 19. (accessed October 31, 2017), http://www.ifpri.org/blog/ifpris-bangladesh -integrated-household-survey-bihs-second-round-dataset-now-available.

Alazzeh, Muhannad. 2017. "Women's Right to Inheritance in Jordanian Law: Requirements and Prospects of Change." Research Paper. Arab Center for Research and Policy Studies, Doha.

Allendorf, Keera. 2007. "Do Women's Land Rights Promote Empowerment and Child Health in Nepal?" *World Development* 35 (11): 1975–88.

Ali, Daniel Ayalew, Klaus W. Deininger, Markus P. Goldstein, and Eliana La Ferrara. 2015. "Empowering Women through Land Tenure Regularization: Evidence from the Impact Evaluation of the National Program in Rwanda." Development Research Group Case Study. Washington, DC: World Bank.

Aluko, Yetunde A. 2015. "Patriarchy and Property Rights Among Yoruba Women in Nigeria." *Feminist Economics* 21 (3): 56–81.

Asadullah, M. Niaz, and Jinnat Ara. 2016. "Evaluating the Long-Run Impact of an Innovative Anti-Poverty Programme: Evidence Using Household Panel Data." *Applied Economics* 48 (2): 107–120.

Asian Development Bank. 2004. *Bangladesh: Gender, Poverty and the MDGs.* Bangladesh Resident Mission and Regional and Sustainable Development Department, Asian Development Bank.

Bandiera, Oriana, Robin Burgess, Narayan Das, Selim Gulesci, Imran Rasul, and Munshi Sulaiman. 2017. "Labor Markets and Poverty in Village Economies." *The Quarterly Journal of Economics* 132 (2): 811–70.

Bhagowalia, Priya, Purnima Menon, Agnes R. Quisumbing, and Vidhya Soundararajan. 2010. "Unpacking the Links Between Women's Empowerment and Child Nutrition: Evidence Using Nationally Representative Data From Bangladesh." Presented at the Agricultural & Applied Economics Association 2010 AAEA, CAES, & WAEA Joint Annual Meeting, Denver, Colorado, July 25–27, 2010, World Bank, Dhaka.

Blunch, Niels-Hugo, and Maitreyi Bordia Das. 2007. "Changing Norms about Gender Inequality in Education: Evidence from Bangladesh." Policy Research Working Paper 4044, World Bank, Washington, DC.

Buvinić, Mayra, and Megan O'Donnell. 2016. *Revisiting What Works: Women, Economic Empowerment and Smart Design.* Washington, DC: Center for Global Development.

Choudhury, Sibabrata, and Susanta Nanda. 2014. "Improving Land Governance through Community Participation in Odisha, India." Landesa Rural Development Institute.

Das, Maitreyi Bordia. 2008. "Whispers to Voices: Gender and Social Transformation in Bangladesh." Bangladesh development series, paper no. 22, World Bank, Washington, DC.

Das, Narayan, Rabeya Yasmin, Jinnat Ara, Md. Kamruzzaman, Peter Davis, Julia Behrman, Shalini Roy, and Agnes R. Quisumbing. 2013. "How Do Intrahousehold Dynamics Change When Assets Are Transferred to Women? Evidence from BRAC's Challenging the Frontiers of Poverty Reduction-Targeting the Ultra Poor Program in Bangladesh." IFPRI Discussion Paper 01317, International Food Policy Research Institute (IFPRI), Washington, DC.

Datta, N. 2006. "Joint Titling—A Win-Win Policy? Gender and Property Rights in Urban Informal Settlements in Chandigarh, India." *Feminist Economics* 12 (1–2): 271–98.

Davis, Peter. 2011. "The Trappings of Poverty: The Role of Assets and Liabilities in Socio-Economic Mobility in Rural Bangladesh." Working Paper 195, Chronic Poverty Research Centre, Chronic Poverty Research Centre, Bath.

Doss, Cheryl. 2016. "Strengthening Women's Land Rights: What Does Data Have to Do With It?" March 7 (accessed May 15, 2018), http://pim.cgiar.org/2016/03/07/strengthening-womens-land-rights-what-does-data-have-to-do-with-it/.

Doss, Cheryl, Caren Grown, and Carmen Diana Deere. 2008. "Gender and Asset Ownership: A Guide to Collecting Individual-Level Data." Policy Research Working Paper 4704, World Bank, Washington, DC.

Doss, Cheryl, Sung Mi Kim, Jemimah Njuki, Emily Hillenbrand, and Maureen Miruka. 2014. "Women's Individual and Joint Property Ownership: Effects on Household Decisionmaking." IFPRI Discussion Paper 01347, International Food Policy Research Institute (IFPRI), Washington, DC.

Doss, Cheryl, Chiara Kovarik, Amber Peterman, Agnes Quisumbing, and Mara van den Bold. 2015. "Gender Inequalities in Ownership and Control of Land in Africa: Myth and Reality." *Agricultural Economics* 46: 403–34.

Doyle, Kate, et al. 2018. "Gender-Transformative Bandebereho Couples' Intervention to Promote Male Engagement in Reproductive and Maternal Health and Violence Prevention in Rwanda: Findings from a Randomized Controlled Trial." *PLoS One* 13 (4).

The Economist. "Women and Property Rights: Who Owns Bangladesh?" August 21, 2013. https://www.economist.com/blogs/banyan/2013/08/women-and-property-rights.

FAO (Food and Agriculture Organization). 2013. *Gender and Land Rights Database.* Geneva: FAO.

———. 2011. *FAO at Work 2010–2011: Women—Key to Food Security.* Rome: FAO.

———. n.d. *Gender and Land Statistics.* http://www.fao.org/gender-landrights-database/data-map/statistics/en/?sta_id=1168&country=BD (accessed January 5, 2018).

Hussein, Maliha, and Shazreh Hussain. 2003. "The Impact of Microfinance on Poverty and Gender Equity—Approaches and Evidence From Pakistan." Pakistan Microfinance Network.

IANS (Indo-Asian News Service). 2017. "No Registry Fee on Property in Woman's Name in Jharkhand." May 3 (accessed May 13, 2018), http://www.business-standard.com/article /news-ians/no-registry-fee-on-property-in-woman-s-name-in-jharkhand-117050301036_1 .html.

International Food Policy Research Institute. 2016. *Bangladesh Integrated Household Survey (BIHS) 2015.* Washington, DC: International Food Policy Research Institute (IFPRI).

IOM (International Organization for Migration). 2016. "Securing Women's Land and Property Rights in Nepal." June 28, (accessed May 14, 2018), https://www.iom.int/news/securing -womens-land-and-property-rights-nepal.

Iqbal, Sarah. 2015. *Women, Business, and the Law 2016: Getting to Equal.* Washington, DC: World Bank.

Jahan, Ferdous, Asif M. Shahan, Shameem Reza Khan, Akter Uz-zaman, Shakila Sharmin, and Mishkat Jahan. 2016. "Gender Quality Action and Learning Program: Documenting the 'Transformations Achieved' and the 'Process of Achieving Them.'" Unpublished working paper.

Johnson, Nancy L., Chiara Kovarik, Ruth Meinzen-Dick, Jemimah Njuki, and Agnes Quisumbing. 2016. "Gender, Assets, and Agricultural Development: Lessons from Eight Projects." *World Development Volume* 83 (July): 295–311.

Khan, Issa, Md. Faruk Abdullah, Noor Naemah Abdul Rahman, Mohd Roslan Bin Mohd Nor, and Mohd Yakub Zulkifli Bin Mohd Yusoff. 2016. "The Right of Women in Property Sharing in Bangladesh: Can the Islamic Inheritance System Eliminate Discrimination?" *SpringerPlus* 5 (1).

Khandker, S. 1998. *Fighting Poverty with Microcredit: Experiences in Bangladesh.* New York: Oxford University Press for the World Bank.

Klugman, Jeni, Lucia Hanmer, Sarah Twigg, Tazeen Hasan, Jennifer McCleary-Sills, and Julieth Santamaria. 2014. *Voice and Agency: Empowering Women and Girls for Shared Prosperity.* Washington, DC: World Bank.

Lastarria-Cornhiel, Susana, Julia A. Behrman, Ruth Meinzen-Dick, and Agnes R. Quisumbing. 2014. "Gender Equity and Land: Toward Secure and Effective Access for Rural Women." In *Gender in Agriculture: Closing the Knowledge Gap*, edited by A. R. Quisumbing, R. Meinzen-Dick, T. L. Raney, A. Croppenstedt, J. A. Behrman, and A. Peterman. Springer Science & Business.

The Logical Buyer. 2015. "Advantages of Buying a Property in Woman's Name." October 12, (accessed May 13, 2018), http://www.thelogicalbuyer.com/blog/?p=1171.

Merlita Limani, Don Cuizon, and Driton Zeqiri. 2018. "The Effectiveness of Social Behavior Change Communications (SBCC) in Changing Social Attitudes on Equal Rights to Property for Women—The Case for Kosovo." Paper prepared for presentation at the "2018 World Bank Conference on Land and Poverty," Washington, DC, March 19–23, 2018.

Mueller, Valerie, Lucy Billings, Tewodaj Mogues, Amber Peterman, and Ayala Wineman. 2017. "Filling the Legal Void? Impacts of a Community-Based Legal Aid Program on Women's Land-Related Knowledge, Attitudes, and Practices." *Oxford Development Studies.*

O'Sullivan, Michael. 2017. "Gender and Property Rights in Sub-Saharan Africa: A Review of Constraints and Effective Interventions." Policy Research Working Paper 8250, World Bank, Washington, DC.

Parveen, Shahnaj. 2007. "Gender Awareness of Rural Women in Bangladesh." *Journal of International Women's Studies* 9 (1): 253–69.

Quisumbing, Agnes R. 2011. "Do Men and Women Accumulate Assets in Different Ways? Evidence from Rural Bangladesh." IFPRI Discussion Paper 01096, International Food Policy Research Institute (IFPRI), Washington, DC.

Quisumbing, Agnes R., and Bob Baulch. 2013. "Assets and Poverty Traps in Rural Bangladesh." *The Journal of Development Studies* 49 (7).

Quisumbing, Agnes, and Bénédicte de la Brière. 2000. "Women's Assets and Intrahousehold Allocation in Rural Bangladesh: Testing Measures of Bargaining Power." FCND Discussion Paper No. 86, International Food Policy Research Institute (IFPRI), Washington, DC.

Quisumbing, Agnes R., and John A. Maluccio. 2003. "Resources at Marriage and Intrahousehold Allocation: Evidence from Bangladesh, Ethiopia, Indonesia, and South Africa." *Oxford Bulletin of Economics and Statistics* 65 (3): 261–394.

Quisumbing, Agnes R., Neha Kumar, and Julia A. Behrman. 2017. "Do Shocks Affect Men's and Women's Assets Differently? Evidence from Bangladesh and Uganda." *Development Policy Review* 36 (1): 3–34.

Rahman, Rushidan I., and Rizwanul Islam. 2013. "Female Labour Force Participation in Bangladesh: Trends, Drivers and Barriers." ILO Asia-Pacific Working Paper Series, ILO DWT for South Asia and Country Office for India, New Delhi.

Rahman, Pk. Md. Motiur, and Noriatsu Matsui. 2009. *The Chronically Poor in Rural Bangladesh: Livelihood Constraints and Capabilities.* New York: Routledge.

Rakib, Muntaha, and Julia Anna Matz. 2016. "The Impact of Shocks on Gender-differentiated Asset Dynamics in Bangladesh." *The Journal of Development Studies* 52 (3).

Roomi, Muhammad Azam. 2005. "Women Entrepreneurs in Pakistan: Profile, Challenges and Practical Recommendations." University of London, School of Management.

Roy, Shalini, Jinnat Ara, Narayan Das, and Agnes R. Quisumbing. 2015. ""Flypaper Effects" in Transfers Targeted to Women: Evidence from BRAC's "Targeting the Ultra Poor" Program in Bangladesh." *Journal of Development Economics* 117: 1–19.

Sarwar, Md. Golam, Rezaul Islam, and Shahorin Monzoor. 2007. *Women's Rights to Land in Bangladesh: Roles, Limitations and Transformation.* Dhaka: Unnayan Onneshan.

Shanbaug, Amit. 2012. "Benefits of Buying a House in Your Wife's Name." *The Economic Times,* August 13.

Sircar, Ashok K., and Sohini Pal. 2014. "What Is Preventing Women from Inheriting Land? A Study of the Implementation of the Hindu Succession (Amendment) Act 2005 in Three States in India." Paper prepared for presentation at the 2014 World Bank Conference on Land and Poverty, Washington DC, March 24–27, Landesa.

SNV Netherlands Development Organisation. 2012. "Gender and Agriculture." SNV Practice Brief Issue 4, The Hague.

Sourav, Md. Raisul Islam. 2015. "Unjust Land Right of Women in Bangladesh." *International Research Journal of Interdisciplinary & Multidisciplinary Studies (IRJIMS)* 1 (3): 5–13.

Sultana, Afiya. 2012. "Promoting Women's Entrepreneurship through SME: Growth and Development in the Context of Bangladesh." *Journal of Business and Management* 4 (1): 18–29.

Team, SOFA, and Cheryl Doss. 2011. "Role of Women in Agriculture." ESA Working Paper No. 11–02, Geneva: FAO, pp. 2–17.

UN Women. 2013. *Realizing Women's Rights to Land and other Productive Resources.* New York and Geneva: United Nations.

UN-HABITAT. 2008. *Secure Land Rights for All.* Nairobi: UN-HABITAT.

UNSD. 2018. *Evidence and Data for Gender Equality (EDGE).* (accessed October 20, 2018), https://unstats.un.org/edge/methodology/asset/.

UNSD and UN Women. 2013. "Evidence and Data for Gender Equality (EDGE) Project Report of the Technical Meeting on Measuring Asset Ownership." New York.

USAID. 2003. *Women's Property and Inheritance Rights: Improving Lives in Changing Times.* Final Synthesis and Conference Proceedings Paper, USAID Office of Women in Development, Bureau for Global Programs, Field Support and Research. Washington, DC: USAID.

USAID. 2010. "Bangladesh—Property Rights and Resource Governance." USAID Country Profile.

van den Bold, Mara, Abdoulaye Pedehombga, Marcellin Ouedraogo, Agnes R. Quisumbing, and Deanna Olney. 2013. "Can Integrated Agriculture Nutrition Programs Change Gender Norms on Land and Asset Ownership? Evidence from Burkina Faso." IFPRI Discussion Paper 01315, International Food Policy Research Institute (IFPRI). Washington, DC.

Villa, Monica. 2017. "Women Own Less than 20% of the World's Land: It's Time to Give Them Equal Property Rights." *World Economic Forum.* January 11, (accessed November 2, 2017), https://www.weforum.org/agenda/2017/01/women-own-less-than-20-of-the-worlds-land-its-time-to-give-them-equal-property-rights/.

World Bank. 2006. *Survey of Gender Norms.* Dhaka: World Bank.

———. 2013a. *Jordan Country Gender Assessment: Economic Participation, Agency and Access to Justice in Jordan.* Washington, DC: World Bank.

———. 2013b. *Opening Doors: Gender Equality and Development in the Middle East and North Africa.* MENA Development Report, Washington, DC: World Bank.

———. 2015a. *Bangladesh—More and Better Jobs to Accelerate Shared Growth and End Extreme Poverty: A Systematic Country Diagnostic.* Washington, DC: World Bank.

———. 2015b. *Morocco: Mind the Gap—Empowering Women for a More Open, Inclusive and Prosperous Society.* Washington, DC: World Bank.

———. 2017. *Nepal Poverty Alleviation Fund Project.* Project Performance Assessment Report, Independent Evaluation Group, Washington, DC: World Bank.

Zakout, Wael. "How joint land titles help women's economic empowerment: the case of Vietnam." *Voices, Perspectives on Development, World Bank.* World Bank. January 20, 2016. http://blogs.worldbank.org/voices/how-joint-land-titles-help-women-s-economic -empowerment-case-vietnam (accessed February 14, 2018).

4 Use and Control of Financial Assets

ABSTRACT *Women's use of financial institutions—as well as the gender gap in such use—varies by type of financial asset, but as a whole, men tend to use most financial institutions more than do women, whether for savings, loans or accounts. Microfinance has played a key role in improving access for women; more than 80 percent of microfinance institutions' clients are poor, rural women. Significant barriers remain for women's full financial inclusion, however. Poverty is a key barrier for both men and women, but there exist a number of other, gendered constraints that particularly impact women. These include patriarchal norms that delegitimize women's control of finance and limit women's access to financial services; high procedural and financial costs; low levels of financial literacy; limited geographical access to sources of finance; and low use of mobile and digital technology. Efforts to address these barriers exist in Bangladesh and elsewhere. Though rigorous evaluations are limited, existing programs provide promising lessons for improving women's use and control of a range of financial assets in Bangladesh.*

This chapter examines women's use and control of financial assets and the barriers they face, as well as promising lessons to address women's financial exclusion in Bangladesh. We analyze the shifts over time in women's and men's use of formal and informal financial institutions and services; women's control over the financial services they use; the relationship between financial access, use, and control; key barriers that women face in using and controlling savings, loans, bank accounts and other sources of finance; recent efforts made by microfinance institutions and the Bangladesh government to address some of these barriers; and good practices from evaluated interventions in other parts of the world.

We combine an overview of select existing literature with our own qualitative and quantitative analysis, as an exhaustive review of the enormous literature on these issues in Bangladesh is beyond this study's scope. Our quantitative analysis uses data from the 2011, 2014, and 2017 rounds of World Bank's Global Financial Inclusion (Findex) database;[1] and the 2011–12 and 2015 rounds of the Bangladesh Integrated Household Survey (BIHS),[2] conducted by the International Food Policy Research Institute (IFPRI) among a representative sample of rural households. We also analyze our primary qualitative data, described in chapter 1.

GENDER DIFFERENCES IN ACCESS TO AND USE OF FINANCIAL SERVICES

The gender gap in the use of most financial services is equal to or larger than the poverty gap or the urban-rural gap. In 2016, 55 percent of the Bangladeshi population used some financial service; however, less than half of all women (46 percent) used any financial service. Women were also less likely than even poor or rural groups to use mobile money (46 percent of women versus 53 percent of the latter). The gender gap in use of banks and nonbank financial institutions (NBFIs) is similar to the poverty and urban-rural gaps (InterMedia 2017).

Accounts in banks and other financial institutions

The gender gap in accounts[3] in banks or other financial institutions[4] has increased in Bangladesh; Bangladesh also fares worse than several comparison countries on the gender gap in accounts. The gender gap in ownership of accounts increased in Bangladesh between 2014 and 2017. According to our analysis from Findex data, in 2017 about one-third of Bangladeshi women had an account, compared to 64.6 percent of men (figure 4.1). Men's account ownership almost doubled since 2014, when it stood at 35.4 percent, while women's ownership grew by 10 percentage points from about 26 percent in 2014, according to findings from Findex data. In 2017, the proportion of women with an account in Bangladesh was lower than the overall lower- and middle-income country average of 53 percent and also lower than in India and Indonesia. The gender gap in

FIGURE 4.1

Accounts by sex and comparator country, 2017

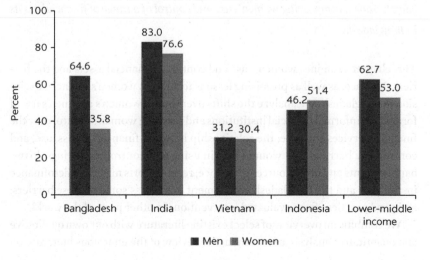

Source: World Bank calculations based on Findex 2017 data.

Bangladesh was larger than all three comparator countries and the overall lower- and middle-income country average for gender gaps.

Loans from formal, semi-formal, and informal sources

The extent of the gender gap in credit is small according to some data, but not according to other sources. According to the International Property Rights Index's Gender Equality (GE) measure (Levy Carciente 2016), Bangladesh was among the poorer-performing countries in women's access to credit and several other indicators of women's economic status (Singh, Asrani, and Ramaswamy 2016). Yet, Findex data show that in 2017 Bangladesh performed at par with lower-middle-income countries (LMICs) as a whole on the proportion of women borrowing[5] from a formal financial institution, both in terms of women's use of loans and the gender gap therein (figure 4.2).

More worrying is the over 50-percent decline in borrowing from financial institutions by both men and women between 2011 and 2014 that has persisted through 2017. This decline is likely a macrofiscal issue related to the banking sector's ongoing struggle with nonperforming loans. The World Bank's 2017 Bangladesh Development Update suggests that with a continuing high range of nonperforming loans, a poor legal framework and weak governance structures that make loan recovery difficult, and the absence of "good borrowers," the banking system may be increasingly risk averse in its lending (Hussain et al. 2017; p.14). A range of informal institutions, such as family and friends or store credit, has compensated: informal borrowing from family or friends doubled for men and increased more than threefold for women. Both men and women also seem to have switched to using store credit.[6] On the other hand, private sources (private lenders in 2011 and 2014, and savings clubs in 2017), remain a minor source of borrowing for men and women (figure 4.3).

Rural areas demonstrate large gender gaps in credit from formal lenders[7] and in access to informal sources of credit. There are no comparable data for urban areas. According to BIHS data, in 2015 18 percent of rural men but only

FIGURE 4.2

Gender differences in borrowing from a financial institution, 2017

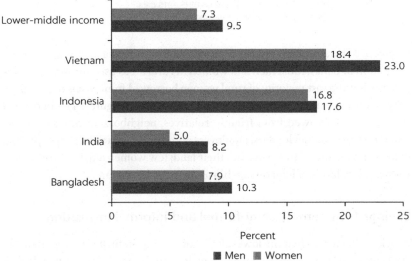

Source: World Bank calculations based on Findex 2017 data.

FIGURE 4.3

Shifts over time in sources of loans

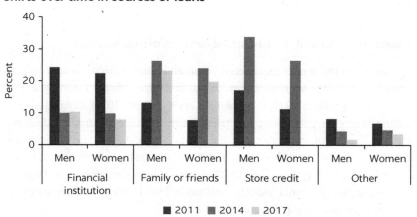

Sources: World Bank calculations based on Findex 2011, 2014, and 2017 data.

FIGURE 4.4

Sources of loans in rural areas, 2015

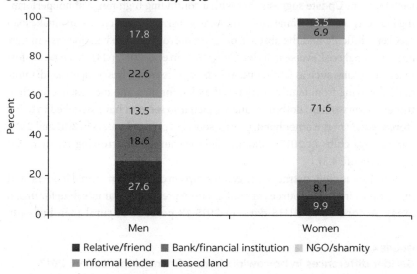

Source: World Bank calculations based on BIHS 2015 data.
Note: NGO = nongovernmental organization.

8 percent of rural women reported borrowing from a formal lender (a financial institution or bank). Most men and women in rural areas used informal sources of loans, but the vast majority of rural women borrowed from NGOs or shamitys[8] (72 percent), whereas men's sources were more diverse (figure 4.4). Almost half of rural men borrowed from friends, relatives, neighbors, or other informal lenders, such as moneylenders, employers and shops. A much larger proportion of men also borrowed by leasing out their land; few women did, likely reflecting women's low levels of land ownership as described in chapter 3.

Savings from formal, semi-formal and informal institutions

Bangladeshi women had the lowest levels of savings[9] in financial institutions in 2017 compared to women in similar countries, but the gender gap in Bangladesh was smaller. Just under 10 percent of Bangladeshi women saved in financial

FIGURE 4.5

Gender differences in savings at a financial institution, 2017

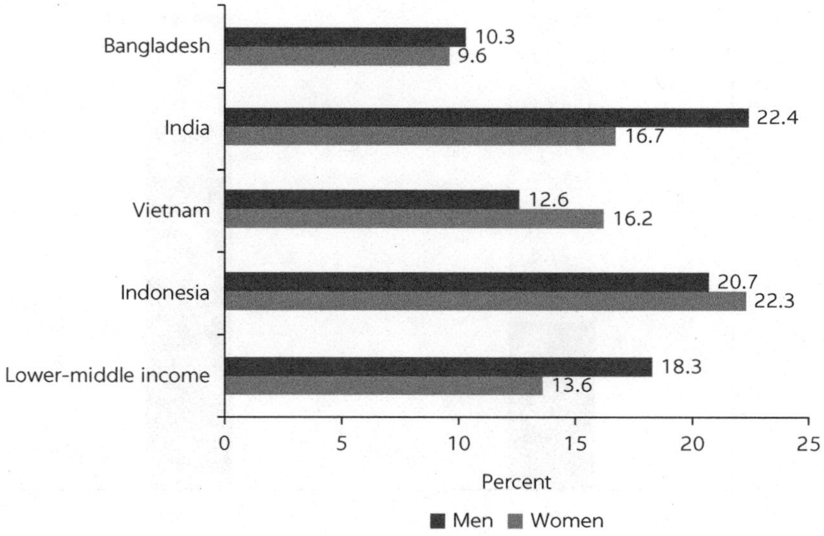

Source: World Bank calculations based on Findex 2017 data.

institutions in 2017, compared to the LMIC average of 13.6 percent (figure 4.5); however, the gender gap in use of a financial institution for savings was lower for Bangladesh than for LMIC and all comparison country averages.

Both men's and women's saving in financial institutions dropped between 2011 and 2014, but then rose again. According to the Findex data analysis (not shown here), the proportion of savings held at a financial institution more than halved between 2011 and 2014 for men and women, from 15.3 percent and 18.1 percent in 2011, respectively, to 6.5 percent and 8.3 percent, respectively, in 2014. By 2017, these trends rose again to the levels shown in figure 4.5. In none of the years were gender gaps statistically significant.

Qualitative data suggest that men tended to save more in financial institutions than did women. Most respondents who discussed savings noted that if women saved, they tended to do so with savings clubs, NGOs or other informal mechanisms, rather than in financial institutions and banks. As a respondent from an FGD with men in urban slums of Dhaka noted, "The women of the research area save money. Most of them save in clay pots, some save in the associations. They also keep their savings with a trusted person so that they can get their money in difficult times."

BIHS data suggest that Bangladeshi women in rural areas not only used formal institutions less than men did for savings; they also had less diversity in savings options overall. In 2015, 75.6 percent of rural women used NGOs or shamitys for savings (figure 4.6), while less than 20 percent saved in formal sources—that is, in banks or other financial institutions. In contrast, rural men used a diverse range of both formal and informal sources, saving almost equally across NGOs/shamitys, banks, and through investments in land.

Microfinance

Microfinance[10] (box 4.1) emerged in Bangladesh in the 1970s in response to the limitations of the financial market in reaching the poor, especially women. Since then, a range of institutions—including specialized MFIs, as well as NGOs, commercial banks and other financial institutions—have included the provision of

FIGURE 4.6

Where rural men and women save, 2015

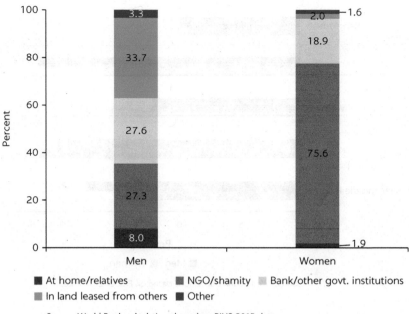

Source: World Bank calculations based on BIHS 2015 data.
Note: NGO = nongovernmental organization.

BOX 4.1

Definition of microfinance in Bangladesh

In Bangladesh, the term "microfinance" is understood as the provision of small-scale financial products and services (including loans, savings, insurance, and money transfer services) for the poor and marginalized—with a special focus on women—explicitly oriented to reducing their vulnerabilities (Mujeri 2015). Microcredit, which refers specifically to the small loans provided to these target populations, constitutes a significant portion of Bangladesh's total domestic credit. A recent World Bank study suggests that microcredit accounts for a 10-percent reduction in rural poverty over the last two decades, lifting around 2.5 million Bangladeshis out of poverty (Khandker, Khalily, and Samad 2016).

---

microcredit and other types of microfinance among their services (box 4.2). As of June 2015, MFIs had granted loans equaling about 9 percent of total private sector credit provided by the banking system; microfinance provides the majority of financial services to women, particularly the poorest women in rural areas.[11] Currently, the largest MFIs in the country are the Association for Social Advancement (ASA), the Bangladesh Rural Advancement Committee (BRAC), Buro Bangladesh, Grameen Bank, Proshika, and Thengamara Mohila Sabuj Sangha (TMSS) (Cubero et al. 2016). Three MFIs dominate the provision of microfinance to women and rural populations, namely, Grameen Bank, BRAC and ASA. These three organizations collectively accounted for more than 60 percent of the total amount disbursed by the microfinance sector in 2015–16 (Credit and Development Forum 2016).

One reason for turning to MFIs may be a lack of trust in the formal financial system. A 2010 study working with a sample of microenterprise owners in

Types of microfinance providers in Bangladesh

The Bangladeshi microfinance sector is a mix of formal, semi-formal and informal suppliers that are subject to varying degrees of regulation. As of 2015, there were less than 100 formal institutions involved with microcredit delivery in Bangladesh, all regulated by Bangladesh Bank (Mansur 2015). Public microfinance programs also exist under various ministries that provide women with microfinance loans and support female entrepreneurship development through credit programs, such as the Bangladesh Rural Development Board and the Bangladesh Small and Cottage Industries Corporation. Such formal providers do not lead in microfinance provision, however.

An enormous semi-formal sector is known for pioneering large-scale provision of tiny collateral-free loans to poor women (Nasher 2011). As of June 2014, there were a reported 676 NGOs providing a range of microfinance services; collectively, these NGOs reached 25 million clients, of which 20 million were borrowers (IMF 2016). Not all these NGOs are registered, however. Other semi-formal microfinance providers may be regulated, but do not fall under the jurisdiction of the central bank, insurance authority,

Securities and Exchange Commission, or any other enacted financial regulator (Asian Development Bank 2015). Ten large semi-formal institutions and Grameen Bank represent 87 percent of total savings and 81 percent of total outstanding loans of the sector (Asian Development Bank 2015). Most other MFIs have very small loan portfolios and/or number of borrowers. Microfinance institutions provide an equally large range of financial products as other, formal financial institutions, including credit, savings, insurance, and money transfers.

Finally, unregistered and unregulated informal suppliers—such as friends, relatives, neighbors, employers, or shopkeepers—provide an important, more flexible alternative for women without access to formal and semi-formal MFIs. Rotating savings and credit associations (ROSCAs) provide another source of informal finance and savings in both urban and rural Bangladesh. Centered on pooling resources with a group of friends and/or acquaintances, ROSCA members regularly contribute money to a common pot that is allocated to one member of the group in each period (Armendáriz and Morduch 2010).

Bangladesh finds that reasons for not using banking facilities were rooted in perceptions of hazardousness of interest payment, lack of trust in the bank, hazardousness in granting loans, lack of independence in operating businesses after taking loans, and an overall sense of increased risk (Ahmed 2010).

The Bangladeshi microfinance sector has less of a presence in urban areas; however, even here women comprise a majority of MFI borrowers. Urban members constitute only about 12 percent of total MFI borrowers, but in 2016 80 percent of urban disbursement went to female borrowers (Credit and Development Forum 2016). However, also between 2015 and 2016, the percent of active MFI account holders decreased from 17 percent to 8 percent, a change largely driven by declines in rural areas, among men, and among those below the poverty line (InterMedia 2016). These declines may be attributed to the surge in economic growth in these years, which resulted in lower demand for MFI loans that are typically used as insurance in poor economic times (InterMedia 2016). In recent years, the microfinance sector is increasingly seeking to provide products and services to the country's growing urban population, with microfinance membership estimated to be increasing at a faster pace in Bangladesh's cities than in its rural areas. Rural areas continue to dominate for now, however (figure 4.7). Yet, microcredit has been accessible to all districts in the country since 2006 (IFC and KfW Bankengruppe 2009).

FIGURE 4.7

Distribution of MFI loans disbursed by gender and residence, 2015–16

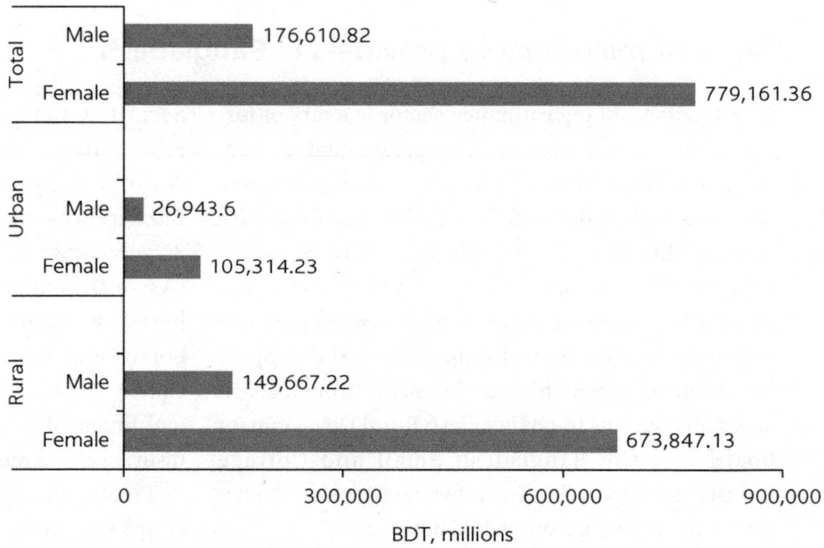

Source: World Bank calculations based on Credit and Development Forum 2016 data.

This plethora of Bangladeshi microfinance institutions provides a large range of financial products including credit, savings, insurance, and money transfers; the extent to which women use them varies. To date, women are most likely to use microcredit, and they increasingly use savings; however, the types and flexibility of services that women use, as well as control over funds, remain limited.

Credit is the most common financial product offered by MFIs in Bangladesh. It is typically provided to women through group loans and without demanding traditional collateral as security. This has been made possible largely through the application of group-based lending technologies introduced by Grameen Bank. Until recently the group lending model was quite rigid, with specified group sizes, formal guarantees and mandatory weekly meetings; however, research has suggested that this standard Grameen group lending model of fixed repayment schedules with standard floors and ceilings on loan sizes may be inappropriate for the extreme poor or the vulnerable nonpoor (Zaman 2004). Recently, Grameen and other organizations have started developing alternate programs to reach these sections of the population, including more flexible products that allow borrowers to select the length of loan they need (Rhyne 2012). The types of loans available include general loans, program loans, and housing loans, the first two of which are typically used for a range of income-generating activities.

Bangladesh's MFIs have also been successful in mobilizing savings as a crucial source of internal capital for women. Traditionally, Bangladeshi MFIs have focused on mandatory savings products, with compulsory weekly savings from their clients as part of the group lending process (Zaman 2004), though savings products have also diversified in recent years. Due to regulatory rules, however, MFIs are not permitted to offer long-term savings or to collect savings from the general public outside of their formal members, collecting only member savings that are generally tied to loans (Khalily, Khaleque, and Badruddoza 2014); these restrictions raise the cost of services provided for members (Bedson 2009), who are largely women. Most of the net savings mobilized are from rural areas (Credit and Development Forum & Institute of Microfinance 2010), and most savers are women. Our qualitative data are consistent with this pattern: both urban and rural respondents in FGDs noted that when women save in any institutions (as opposed to in the home) they are likely to save in local MFIs.

MFIs in Bangladesh are increasingly offering insurance products to women. Microinsurance has recently emerged as a new product area, particularly life and health insurance, due at least in part to growing recognition that illness can translate into a major income shock for resource-poor households and that women are particularly vulnerable (Fletschner and Kenney 2011). Different models demonstrate different abilities to access the poorest women, however. For instance, BRAC offers health insurance, yet a 2005 study found that poorer households were less likely to know about it and less likely to enroll than better-off households; some clients found it difficult to pay the annual premium; and 55 percent of clients who enrolled for the service did not renew after the first year (Matin, Imam, and Ahmed 2005). By 2009, the renewal rate had dropped further to 25 percent (Ashan et al. 2013). Adopting a different approach, SKS offers health insurance as a requirement for all new borrowers or renewing borrowers, with women between the ages of 16–30 found to be the heaviest users (Fletschner and Kenney 2011).

Despite women being MFIs' main customers, average loan sizes are smaller for women than for men and are insufficient for the demand. MFIs tend to make small initial loans to women (Alamgir 2009), typically granting them under a group-based lending model. Upon successful and timely repayment, women borrowers may progressively graduate to higher eligibility levels with larger, longer, and/or more flexible loans. Loans to women are increasingly smaller than those given to men, however, even by MFIs. A study using panel data of 126 NGO-MFIs between 2007 and 2010 (Credit and Development Forum & Institute of Microfinance 2010) finds a growing gender divide in loan size. In 2007 the size of MFI loans taken by women and men was about the same (21,475 and 21,853 Bangladeshi Taka (BDT), respectively). A gender disadvantage emerged between 2007 and 2010, when the average loan size for women increased by 32 percent, compared to 76 percent for men. Demand for capital is generally far greater than supply; one study finds that over 70 percent of borrowers demanded more funds than they managed to obtain (Bashar and Rashid 2012).

Because women's demand continues to outstrip the supply of microfinance, repeat borrowing and multiple borrowing—known as "overlapping"—are commonplace practices in Bangladesh, but the evidence is mixed regarding the extent and consequences of such borrowing. "Overlapping" typically arises from the inability to access the desired loan amount from any one source (Gan and Nartea 2017). Some estimate that over 30 percent of microfinance borrowers in Bangladesh have loans from more than one MFI (Khalily and Faruqee 2011; Chen and Rutherford 2013). Respondents in urban and rural areas where qualitative data were collected for this study noted also that women use savings to repay loans. Overlapping can increase women's indebtedness, such as in the case of women in households that experience negative shocks, like floods, which can destroy existing assets and exacerbate borrowers' inability to pay (Khalily, Faridi, and Saeed 2016). Some studies report that MFIs create an environment of fear and intimidation against such borrowers through, for example, the use of coercive tactics to collect installments on microcredit loans (Cons and Paprocki 2008; Melik 2010). Others note that overlapping does not necessarily indicate irresponsible borrowing, finding that overlapping and nonoverlapping borrowers have very similar loan use patterns, with either group using a small share of funds to repay existing debt (Osmani, Khalily, and Hasan 2016). Other research suggests that households borrowing in parallel from multiple lenders experience greater asset growth than they do liability over time, with higher net savings, net assets, income, food and nonfood expenditures, number of earning members, diversification of occupation structure, and employment creation (Khalily, Faridi, and Saeed 2016; Khandker, Faruqee, and Samad 2013; Khandker, Khalily, and Samad 2016).

As a whole, microfinance is not a "magic bullet" for women's lives (Kabeer 2005). Rather, the extent to which engagement with MFIs can be empowering for Bangladeshi women depends on a number of factors, and on how empowerment is defined. Key factors that determine the empowering potential of microfinance include the type of microfinance (loans, credit, insurance, etc.) and, for microcredit, the loan size, duration of involvement with the MFI, and involvement in income-generating activities (Nessa, Ali, and Abdul-Hakim 2012). In any determination of the extent to which microfinance can empower women borrowers, intrahousehold relations and power that determine who controls credit, and women's own views of their empowerment, also have to be taken into account (Kabeer 2001).

Some studies find microcredit to be associated with little to no empowerment, or even a reduction of empowerment for participating Bangladeshi women. Goetz and Sen Gupta (1996) report that 63 percent of women loan holders surveyed in a Bangladesh study of three microcredit programs had exercised "partial, very limited or no control" over their loans, granting them minimal household decision-making power. Using a household-level survey of 920 households randomly selected from female Grameen Bank, BRAC, and ASA borrowers, Chowdhury (2008) finds that participation in microfinance programs does not promote women's entrepreneurship at the household level, instead significantly increasing the capital of existing businesses of participating households. Research by Karim (2008) suggests that women's participation in microcredit programs works to disempower them, casting them into a cycle of debt while their husbands control the loan funds.

Other studies find that microfinance participation is associated with improved women's empowerment in Bangladesh. Nessa, Ali, and Abdul-Hakim (2012), for instance, find that loan size, duration of involvement with the MFI, and involvement in income-generating activities are significant determinants of women's empowerment. Alam (2012) reports that female microcredit borrowers are better able to allocate their income toward goods more valuable to them and make major household decisions when their income increases. Panel data from a nationally representative sample of households indicate that women's participation in microfinance programs is associated with increased intra-household decision making—singly or jointly—on matters such as livestock, fruit or vegetable production and sewing (Mahmud et al. 2017). In contrast, no such impact of microfinance borrowing has been observed for men's decision making about household production activities. Kumar, Hossain, and Gope (2013) find that rural female borrowers are more independent and can better engage in household decision making after participating in Grameen Bank's microfinance programs; however, such participation does not notably remove constraints on borrowers' abilities to effectively market their products. Other studies report more nuanced processes at play. Razzaque and Bidisha (2012) find a strong positive association between participating in microcredit programs and women's empowerment, but also note that women engaging in productive employment and contributing to household incomes are likely to be "empowered" regardless of their involvement in a credit program. This also suggests that several studies of this relationship between microcredit and empowerment likely suffer from endogeneity and other methodological issues.

The processes of microfinance in Bangladesh may be as empowering as the received financial products themselves, likely due to the social network gained through required female group formation, which allows microfinance partici-pants access to information from providers and support from other community women. Nessa, Ali, and Abdul-Hakim (2012) find that for 600 women in eight districts in Rajshahi Division, participation in microfinance programs positively affected not only women's economic decision making and ownership of prop-erty, but also household decision making, freedom of movement, and political and social awareness. According to Chowdhury and Chowdhury (2011), com-pared to women who take loans from other sources, women participating in microcredit or microfinance programs have better individual and household-level outcomes, including higher labor force participation, greater accumulation of nonland assets, such as livestock and poultry, and greater odds of sending children to school.

Uses of savings and loans

Women (and men) use savings and loans for a variety of purposes, with produc-tive or income-generating purposes being one among many. According to anal-ysis using the Findex 2014 data, a very small proportion of both men and women used savings and loans for the reasons asked about in the Findex for that year. Thus, only 16.5 percent of men and 17.1 percent of women used savings for old age, education expenses or to start, operate, or grow a business or farm. About one-fifth of men (20.3 percent) and women (21.2 percent) used loans for educa-tion or health expenses, to start, operate, or grow a business or farm, or to buy a home. Analysis of Findex data also shows that use of savings for productive pur-poses (defined as starting, operating, or expanding a farm or business) increased somewhat between 2014 and 2017 for both men and women, but remained min-imal at 9 and 7 percent for men and women, respectively.[12] Recent analysis by InterMedia (2017) echoes these themes: its nationally representative sample finds that while business-related uses of savings and loans in 2016 were among the top six uses for both men and women, less than 10 percent of men and women used savings or loans for these purposes. In contrast, about one-fifth of both women (21 percent) and men (23 percent) used savings for emergency pur-poses. The most common use of loans was routine purchases, such as groceries (10 percent of women and 12 percent of men).

Primary qualitative data suggest that women use their finances for the family. Across FGDs among rural, urban, and ethnic men and women, respondents noted that women who save "spend their savings for family betterment" (urban men, Sylhet). These family uses can include children's education, clothes, hous-ing repairs, emergency needs, medical needs or other consumption needs. A few respondents pointed to purchases of livestock, but this was much less prevalent than were family consumption needs.

In rural areas—for which the BIHS provides detailed quantitative data—men were more likely to spend savings on productive purposes or to buy land than were women. However, this usage still represented only a small share of savings

FIGURE 4.8

Use of savings in rural Bangladesh, 2015

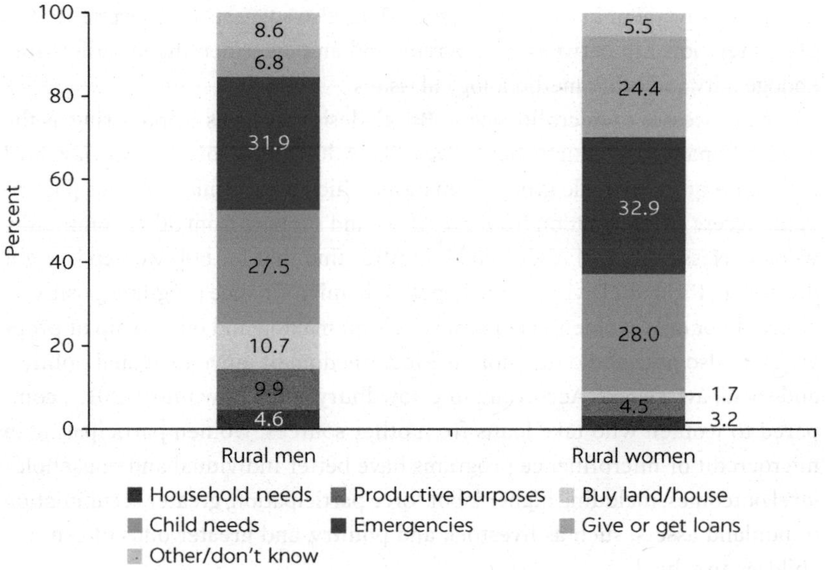

Source: World Bank calculations based on BIHS 2015 data.

even for men. Less than 5 percent of rural women and almost 10 percent of rural men used savings for productive purposes, such as starting a business or purchasing agricultural or other productive assets (figure 4.8). Men were much more likely to buy land or a house—a potentially productive use of savings—than were women. Women were notably more likely to use their savings to give or get loans (24.4 percent) than were men (less than 10 percent). Emergencies formed the largest use of savings, with about one-third of men's and women's savings used for medical or other emergencies, or against an uncertain future or "difficult times." Another quarter of all savings went towards children's needs, including marriage or dowry.

Rural men also were more likely than women to use loans for agricultural assets and enterprise, but both rural men and women spent the great majority of their borrowed money on consumption needs. Almost half of loans taken by both men (47 percent) and women (44 percent) went to consumption expenditures, including household consumption needs, marriages, funerals, etc. (figure 4.9). About one-fifth of men and women taking loans reported using this money for business enterprises or buying productive assets, or investing in land, livestock and housing. About 16 percent of women (compared to 10 percent of men) used loans to repay other loans.

Evidence is mixed regarding the extent to which women use MFI loans for income-generation or entrepreneurial activities, as opposed to consumption or emergency needs. MFI loans are used for a number of purposes, not all of which are related to income-generation (Islam 2011). The reported extent to which loans are used for income-generation versus consumption varies across studies, however. The 2010 study cited earlier, using panel data from 126 NGO-MFIs, finds that microfinance funds in 2010 typically were used for small businesses, crop production, and livestock (Credit and Development Forum and Institute of Microfinance 2010). In contrast, a 2012 study estimates that only about

FIGURE 4.9

Use of loans by gender in rural Bangladesh, 2015

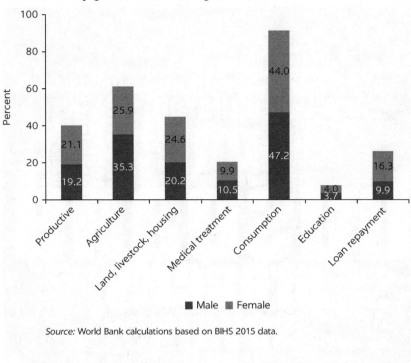

Source: World Bank calculations based on BIHS 2015 data.

30 percent of women MFI clients used loans for their self-initiated enterprises (Bashar and Rashid 2012).

WOMEN'S CONTROL OVER FINANCIAL ASSETS

An increasing *number* of female financial clients does not in itself indicate a corresponding increase in women's *control* over financial assets, and women face multiple hurdles in controlling the finance that they do manage to obtain. Even women's official ownership of the funds acquired does not necessarily translate into women's control over finances or expansion of their intra-household choices, decision-making power, or bargaining position (Kabeer 1999). For instance, the large majority of surveyed women (73 percent) in a study on rural women's empowerment reported not having money that they could spend as they wished (Mahmud, Shah, and Becker 2012). More recently, only one-third of women surveyed by Nawaz (2015) reported either partial or full control over loan utilization.

Our qualitative data show a range of degrees of control. Several respondents noted that even when women earn or have access to financial assets, they have little control over these assets or in household financial decision making. An adolescent girl from an FGD in Chittagong noted that although working women "...can make wealth, they cannot save...they have to hand over the whole salary to their husbands. If they refuse to give, husbands start beating them." Some need their husbands' permission or save in secret. In a word cloud (figure 4.10) on the theme of decision-making control over income, the terms "husband" and "family" are much more likely to occur in discussions on use and decision making of financial assets than are terms like "freedom" and "choice."

FIGURE 4.10

Decision making about financial assets

Source: Primary qualitative data collected for this book, 2017.

Recent survey data show that women are rarely primary decision makers on household financial decisions or even their own use of financial services. InterMedia and the Bill and Melinda Gates Foundation's nationally representative 2016 survey of over 3,000 women finds evidence of very limited financial control by women (InterMedia 2017). A minority of women (12–16 percent) reported being the sole decision makers about household finances or assets (figure 4.11). Only 14 percent said they could decide which financial services they used (figure 4.12). Men were undoubtedly the main decision makers regarding which financial services to use, with only four percent saying their wives were involved. Husbands also were the main decision makers about household finances.

Other qualitative research respondents, however, said that women do have control over how to use their own savings. Working women in an FGD in Dhaka said that they "can spend their savings as they wish." Ethnic minority women in rural Rajshahi also noted that women could decide how to use their money, including whether and how to save, but first discussed these decisions with their husbands.

Rural areas show a slightly different decision-making pattern than the country as a whole. Analysis of BIHS data indicates that among rural populations, the majority of women made financial decisions jointly with their husbands, though this was declining. More than three-quarters of responding women made

FIGURE 4.11
Women's household financial decision making

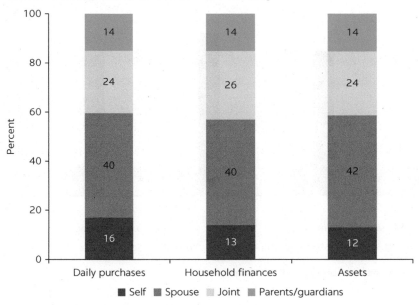

Source: InterMedia 2017.

FIGURE 4.12
Who decides women's use of financial services?

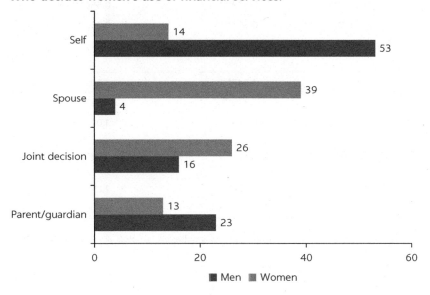

Source: InterMedia 2017.

decisions along with their husbands about use of loans (figure 4.13). Between 2011–12 and 2015, however, joint decision making declined. Instead, sole decision making rose for both men and women, though the extent of husbands' sole decision making rose to a greater degree than did sole decision making by women themselves. Whereas in 2011–12 less than 10 percent of husbands were the sole decision makers in their wives' access to NGO loans—and only five percent solely decided how money should be spent—by 2015, 16 percent of husbands were sole

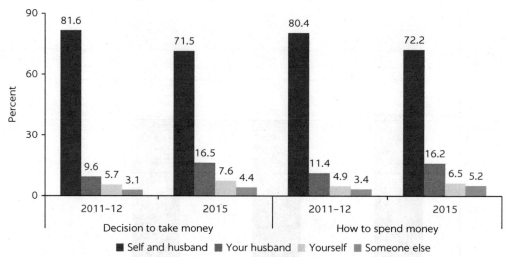

FIGURE 4.13

Control of credit among rural women who take loans, 2015

Source: World Bank calculations based on BIHS 2015 data.

TABLE 4.1 **Factors associated with decision making on loans among rural women, 2015**

	SELF DECIDED HOW TO USE ANY OF THE BORROWED MONEY	SELF DECIDED TO BORROW FROM ANY ONE OF THE SOURCES	SELF DECIDED TO BORROW FROM AT LEAST ONE SOURCE & SELF DECIDED WHAT TO DO WITH THE MONEY
Is not a member of any group	0.563***	0.572***	0.550***
Is not comfortable speaking in public in at least one context	0.73***	0.693***	0.703***
Who decides who can go to haat (ref: other)			
Self decides	1.332*	1.347*	1.309*
Self and husband decide	1.429***	1.370**	1.337**
Owns any of agricultural land, large livestock, house, and other land (baseline)	1.051	0.988	1.007
Right over any of agricultural land, large livestock, house, and other land (baseline)	1.219**	1.341**	1.285**
Works for pay (baseline)	1.142	1.154	1.155
Observations	3,209	3,209	3,209

Source: World Bank calculations based on BIHS 2015 data.
Notes: Controls for age, age at marriage, completed years of schooling, household expenditure (baseline) and division. Sample is all women between 20 and 73 years of age. *** $p <0.01$, ** $p <0.05$, * $p <0.1$.

decision makers about whether their wives should obtain loans and how loans were to be spent. Yet, multivariate analysis suggests that after controlling for other factors in decision making on loans, women were significantly more likely to make decisions (either alone or jointly with a spouse) on whether to access credit and how to use it than were others in the household (table 4.1).

At the same time, rural women's control over how money is used for items of personal and household use appears to be increasing. According to the BIHS, between 2011–12 and 2015 the proportion of rural women reporting that they themselves controlled the money used for a range of household and personal items, such as food, clothes for themselves, and their own medicines, toiletries or

FIGURE 4.14

Rural women's control over income for own use, 2015

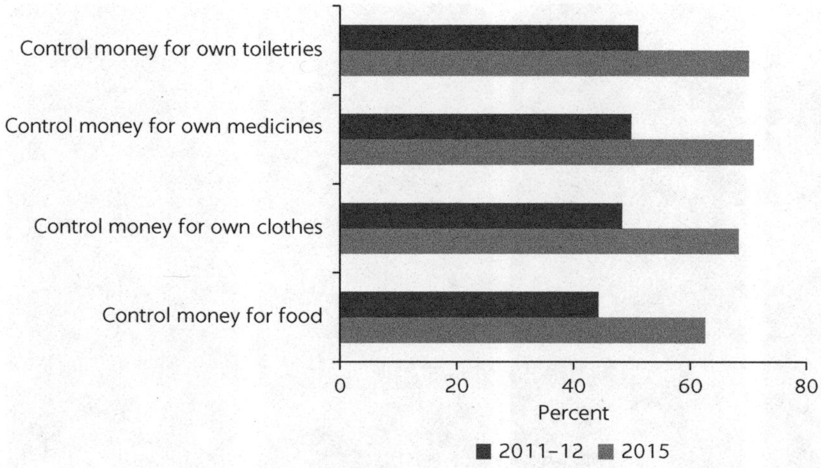

Source: World Bank calculations based on BIHS 2015 data.

cosmetics increased (figure 4.14). Although rural women surveyed were still far from playing a large role in decision making on purchases of larger, more valuable, items for the household, this is a promising development.

Women's control of financial assets is related to other aspects of women's empowerment, such as mobility and public participation. Multivariate analysis of 2015 BIHS data finds that, among rural women, those with greater decision making over their own economic mobility (measured by participating singly or jointly with husbands in decisions about whether or not they can go alone to a *haat*, or market) were significantly more likely to also have control over credit[13] than women with less decision making over mobility. At the other end of the spectrum, women who did not belong to NGOs or other groups, and women who reported discomfort speaking in public, were significantly less likely to control credit than women who engaged in these two aspects of public participation. It is possible that such public exposure gives women added confidence in their abilities, which then spills over into aspects of their financial lives as well, or that these different aspects of women's empowerment tend to cluster (table 4.1[14]).

BARRIERS TO WOMEN'S USE AND CONTROL OF FINANCES

Lack of money—poverty—is reportedly the main reason why both men and women in Bangladesh do not access a range of financial services. According to our analysis of 2014 Findex data, 71 percent of women and 84 percent of men without an account in a bank or other financial institution reported that the lack of money prevented them from opening an account. The issue of having no extra money to save after taking care of basic needs arose repeatedly across FGDs in rural areas and urban slums of Dhaka and Chittagong. Respondents remarked that although working women and those who inherit do tend to save, many women do not simply because not enough money remains to save after meeting household consumption needs. As one adolescent girl from rural Rajshahi noted, "We have no money to buy a biscuit, let alone be saving." Others pointed to the

FIGURE 4.15

Barriers to women's use and control of financial services

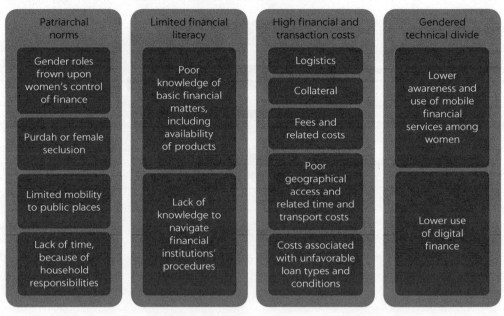

necessity of making choices between current consumption and savings, with a nonworking woman in Dhaka explaining, "Suppose I want to eat better food with my family—then I skip this desire and save the money."

There are several other gendered barriers to the use and control of financial services that disadvantage women. Barriers can be grouped into those arising from patriarchal norms; those women face due to their limited financial literacy and low awareness and knowledge of financial dynamics; a range of financial and transaction costs that arise from high fees, lack of collateral, complex bank procedures, poor geographic access, logistics, or even unfavorable loan conditions; and barriers arising from women's limited use of growing mobile and digital financial services. Figure 4.15 summarizes these barriers.

Patriarchal constraints: gender roles, mobility, and lack of time

The persistence of patriarchal roles for women and men that give men authority to lay claim *ex ante* to any financial resources that enter a household is a key barrier for women's financial inclusion. Clearly delineated acceptable social roles for men and women frown on women's engagement in financial matters (Kabeer 2005). Such a system clearly affects women's ability to use banks, choose sources for loans or destinations for savings (if men in the household allow women to have own savings), and to decide how to use money. For instance, patriarchal roles in the household mean that women do not have the power to make business investment decisions required for productive use of credit. Thus, even informal loans are likely to be used for small consumption expenses rather than larger, productive investment (Islam, Nguyen, and Smyth 2015). A large literature documents men's control over women's financial assets and their use of these assets as they see fit, rather than for productive enterprises of the woman's choice (see, for example, Goetz and Gupta 1996; InterMedia 2017; Karim and Law 2013).

A patriarchal insistence on the primacy of women's domestic roles leaves women little time to access financial institutions. Their primary responsibility is still regarded as household-based, whereas men's primary responsibility—as head of household—is to earn and control income and other household financial assets. Household responsibilities of cooking, cleaning and childcare limit women's time to travel to various institutions to obtain finance (Ahmed 2001) or to learn more about financial options.

The institution of *purdah*, or enforced female seclusion, raises an additional barrier by limiting women's mobility and thus access to a diverse range of financial services. In Bangladesh, the system of purdah that is followed in many areas creates at least two specific barriers for women to access and control finance. First, purdah serves to generally limit women's mobility and participation in public life (Blunch and Das 2007), including their ability to travel to banks or other financial institutions. Even where purdah is not observed, patriarchal norms that determine the suitability of women's public participation restrict women's mobility. Second, purdah prevents women from engaging in any public setting with men (Sultana 2012). Since less than 15 percent of staff at any level across financial institutions in Bangladesh are female (Bangladesh Bank 2014), these institutions are rendered relatively inaccessible to women.

Limited financial literacy, awareness, and knowledge of financial dynamics

Bangladeshi women have lower levels of financial literacy than do men. Though financial literacy[15] is low among both men and women, there is a notable gap between the two groups: a study from the Institute of Microfinance's 2014 national survey of Access to Financial Services covering 8,456 households over seven divisions and 63 districts finds an 18-percentage-point difference between men and women in bank-related knowledge (Khalily and Miah 2015). More recent data from the Financial Inclusion Insights (FII) program show a slight narrowing of the gap: 14 percent of surveyed men and 8 percent of surveyed women had some financial literacy.[16] Low financial literacy suggests that women have low awareness of financial products and processes they can access, such as banks, other formal sources of credit and savings, the range of informal choices for loans or savings, and other financial products, such as microinsurance. Limited financial literacy also likely affects investment decisions for finances that women do have.

Low levels of overall education combined with low financial literacy mean that women have limited awareness and understanding of the gamut of procedures that financial institutions necessitate. Obtaining finance in Bangladesh involves time consuming, cumbersome, and confusing paperwork and bureaucracies that can present particular challenges for women (Parvin, Jinrong, and Rahman 2012) because of their combination of low education levels, limited financial literacy, and mobility and control restrictions of patriarchy. Procedures to access formal sources of credit, such as paperwork like bank account records and guarantees required for bank loans are a huge barrier to women accessing credit and may be more of a barrier for women than men (Rabbani and Chowdhury 2013). In fact, complicated application procedures are cited as one of the top three reasons for not having loans (IFC and KfW Bankengruppe 2009).

Poor financial literacy increases financial institutions' reluctance to provide credit to women. In a study by Singh, Asrani, and Ramaswamy (2016), most bankers perceived women to have very poor financial literacy; this was not considered to be the case for men. Banks considered these gender differences to be associated with higher loan processing costs for loans to women, assuming that women would need more assistance in identifying appropriate financial products and completing documentation requirements.

Financial and transaction costs of financial services

Using financial services can come with fees and other costs that are likely to be more of a barrier for women than for men. For instance, many financial institutions in Bangladesh have a minimum account balance requirement or charge fees for opening a checking or savings account. As a result, people from lower-income households tend to exclude themselves from these financial services (Islam and Al Mamun 2011). These requirements inherently disadvantage women who, on average, earn lower wages than men. Banking with MFIs comes with costs in terms of interest rates and for loan repayment. Higher than those of commercial banks, MFI interest rates may discourage women's investment (The Financial Express 2012).

Additional transaction costs add to these financial costs. For instance, women do not have in their names much of the documentation that is required to access formal finance. Government or other official identification, proof of domicile, and reference letters are often required to open a checking or savings account in Bangladesh, yet many people lack such documentation (Islam 2016), especially women. Utility bills may be required as proof for loan applications, which is a problem when these are in men's names rather than in women's or both partners' names. Even accessing collateral-free loans requires a long list of documents that women may not have, such as a nationality certificate, voter ID card or Tax Identification Number (TIN) (Hughes and Jennings 2012). Further, these substantial documentary requirements for accessing finance in Bangladesh are oftentimes not made explicit by bankers (Choudhury and Raihan 2000). All these complexities increase women's transactions costs of accessing the formal financial sector.

Women are also less likely than men to have the collateral that many sources of credit demand. Formal finance in Bangladesh continues to go predominantly to men as women are less likely to own land or other major assets in their name, as detailed in chapter 3. This lack of collateral severely limits the types, size and conditions of loans that women can get (Ara and Hamid 2011; Singh, Asrani, and Ramaswamy 2016). For rural women, in particular, the lack of ownership of physical assets—including land—means they have little or nothing that can be used as collateral for loans (Fletschner & Kenney 2011; Singh, Asrani, and Ramaswamy 2016).

Even with the paperwork and required collateral, getting a loan takes a large amount of time, a factor which is likely to impact women more than men given women's typical extra responsibilities in the household and limits on mobility. According to Singh, Asrani, and Ramaswamy (2016), women SME entrepreneurs on average made nearly 13 visits to the bank to get a loan approved and drawn out application processes took almost 41 days to complete. Reasons included the requirement of male signatories and guarantors and the complexity of bank forms. A high 71 percent of these women entrepreneurs surveyed by Singh, Asrani, and Ramaswamy (2016) also reported indifference and unhelpfulness on the part of the bankers with whom they dealt. Finally, women entrepreneurs have cited issues of corruption (Rabbani and Chowdhury 2013), delays

(Parvin, Jinrong, and Rahman 2012), and dependency on middlemen (Sultana 2012) as other procedural bottlenecks.

A serious transaction cost arises from the limited geographical coverage of financial institutions. Given women's limited mobility and low levels of financial literacy, this is likely a greater obstacle for women than men. Bangladesh fares worse than comparator countries in access to banks: in 2015, Bangladesh had 6.79 ATMs and 8.4 commercial bank branches per 100,000 adults; Pakistan, India, Vietnam, and Indonesia all showed higher levels of access (International Monetary Fund 2015). Rural populations have particularly restricted or no access to banking services. Similarly, a significant number of highly poor districts—especially in the Northwest—have relatively few MFIs and consequently a lower number of poor borrowers, compared to relatively prosperous districts where a larger share of the population can more easily access microcredit.

Lower use of mobile and digital technologies by women

As mobile financial services grow, the gender technical divide increasingly disadvantages women in a range of financial services. Mobile banking and point-of-sale devices can enable transactions across a larger geographic area than is possible with physical banking—particularly important for increasing access for the rural poor and women. Yet, women are less likely to own mobile phones than men in Bangladesh (Parvez, Islam, and Woodard 2015), contributing to a notable gender gap in mobile banking. FII program data show that in 2016 only one in four women—compared to half of men—were aware of mobile money services or used mobile money services (figure 4.16), and three times as many men as women (19 percent versus 6 percent, respectively) had their own mobile money account.[17]

Women also are less digitally included than men—that is, less likely than men to access financial services via debit cards, credit cards, or mobile banking. Only 18 percent of digital finance users in Bangladesh are women; even fewer hold registered accounts (Shrader 2015). Most smartphone menus are in English, additionally disadvantaging the large number of women with limited English language skills (Sinha and Highet 2017).

FIGURE 4.16

Gender differences in mobile money

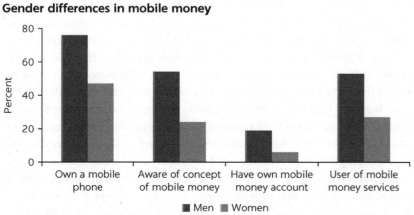

Source: http://finclusion.org/data_fiinder/.

Less trust in mobile services than in traditional financial institutions may also make women reluctant to use these services. In its 2013 FII Tracker Survey, InterMedia (2013) finds that 97 percent of Bangladeshi respondents either "fully" trusted or "somewhat" trusted state-owned banks, 79 percent trusted private banks, and 47 percent trusted MFIs; furthermore, 66 percent "fully" or "rather" trusted mobile money services, and 63 percent trusted mobile money agents.

GOOD PRACTICES AND RECOMMENDATIONS

The Bangladeshi government, civil society and MFIs have responded in varied, innovative ways to the gravity of women's continued exclusion from financial services relative to men. There are also evaluated good practices from across the global South that could be piloted and tested in the Bangladeshi context. In particular, there is a large and growing evaluation literature. Internationally known studies include those conducted by Bangladesh's Grameen Bank and SEWA in India. Reviewing the entire universe of such interventions and related literature is beyond the scope of this book. Rather, below we discuss a sub-sample of experimental and other evaluation results to highlight some potential lessons, good practices, and recommendations to address the barriers identified for Bangladeshi women.

Address patriarchal norms

Underlying patriarchal constraints need to be addressed to improve financial inclusion. The aspects of patriarchy that appear most damaging to Bangladeshi women's ability to use and control financial services are: norms that frown on women's control of finance, purdah resulting in women's seclusion or other mobility constraints, and women's limited time due to their household and other "feminine" responsibilities. Examples from across the global South provide insight into how these could be addressed.

A range of programs show that providing savings and other financial products solely in women's names can increase their control of financial resources. When women have financial assets in their own names—rather than in their husbands' names or jointly with their husbands—they are more likely to have control over these financial resources. Experiments across the world have used large-scale cash transfers to pull households out of poverty and also empower women; evaluations indicate that these programs, such as in Brazil and Mexico, increase women's bargaining power in the household (Ambler and De Brauw 2017).

A good South Asian example that Bangladesh could adapt and adopt is Pakistan's Benazir Income Support Program (BISP). Rigorous evaluations have shown that BISP has helped diminish two of the patriarchal norms that undermine women's financial inclusion: rejection of women's control over financial resources and restrictions on women's mobility. The final evaluation of BISP finds that 76 percent of women beneficiaries controlled the cash they received from the program; over time, men and boys acknowledged that the cash their families received through the program was because of the women and should thus be controlled by them. Similarly, mobility increased too, likely because of the necessity—in at least some cases—of women having to travel to collect their cash transfers (Cheema et al. 2016).

A randomized control trial linked to the Mahatma Gandhi National Rural Employment Guarantee Scheme (MGNREGS) of Madhya Pradesh state government in India also finds that a shift from depositing work payments into single household accounts to depositing in accounts in women's name increased women's mobility and engagement in other economic activities. Being the recipient of the money likely increased women's power to negotiate mobility and other gender norms (Field et al. 2016). A randomized control trial in the Philippines created "commitment" savings accounts solely in women's names. Women could choose their own goals for their savings and withdraw funds after a time period they themselves designated. Only women could make the deposit, set goals and withdraw funds. Econometric analysis shows an increase in women's decision making about the purchase of large items for the household, plus an increase in the purchase of household items (such as washing machines) that could ease women's burden of work, compared to the control group. Results were particularly significant among women who had been less-empowered at baseline than among women who already had some level of household empowerment on such decision making (Ashraf, Karlan, and Yin 2010). This suggests that such savings accounts, that were committed to a certain purpose *and* in women's names only, were likely to have a strong effect for women who were particularly disempowered by patriarchal norms.

Increasing the use of women's mobile technology for finance addresses other patriarchal barriers. A growing literature attests to the imperative to improve women's use of mobile and digital technology for financial transactions and services to decrease the financial inclusion gender gap (see, for example, Gammage et al.'s (2017) recent review of this research). The use of this technology can specifically undermine patriarchal barriers to women's financial inclusion by increasing women's ability to conduct financial transactions and decisions in private. In a qualitative study in Kenya, for instance, women said that using the available mobile financial options allowed them to own personal bank accounts without needing to get their husbands' permission (Wandibba, Nangendo, and Mulemi 2014). That privacy is an important precondition for higher savings and productive use of income among women is also borne out by other randomized control studies reviewed by Buvinić, Furst-Nichols, and Pryor (2013) that test the effect of privacy on women's investment decisions and use of cash transfers. The ability to manipulate their finances through mobile financial services rather than physically traveling to a bank branch also helped women negotiate mobility and time constraints, as explored in more detail later in this chapter.

Efforts within the banking system to create a women-friendly environment and women-staffed banks also show promise in addressing purdah and mobility constraints that arise from households' reluctance to let women interact publicly with men. Families of women who observe purdah typically do not permit them to interact with men. Men primarily staff most banks and other financial institutions. Recent efforts by formal banks in India and Pakistan provide examples of women-centered and women-only banks to address this problem. One example is the Habib Bank in Pakistan, with which the IFC has partnered since 2007 to increase gender equality among its staff and customers. In 2016, the Habib Bank launched a dedicated platform for women to access services, titled HBL Nisa. A recent evaluation of the Habib Bank's various endeavors to increase women's financial inclusion in Pakistan shows positive results of the bank's training programs on staff attitudes towards women clients and an increase in deposits from women clients (Hamm et al. 2017). Although the evaluation does not specifically measure the impact of women-sensitive bank practices on purdah or mobility, it likely is easier for women practicing purdah to go to a woman-operated or woman-friendly bank than to one that is not known as such. Another example—for which we could not find evaluations, yet which has potential for further study—is the Yes Bank in India, which collaborated with the World Bank/IFC to open three all-women operated bank branches in 2016 (Schnabel and McNally 2017).

Programs and policies that tackle the difficult issue of gender-unequal patriarchal norms need to be subject to scrutiny to guard against inadvertent negative consequences. Programs that ameliorate women's financial inclusion may have other negative impacts on their lives that need to be carefully considered when designing financial inclusion programs. For instance, in his qualitative analysis of BISP beneficiaries, Arshad (2011) found that though cash transfers increased women's control over household resources, they also increased women's household burden: because the cash was used primarily for household goods and childcare, husbands tended to transfer some of their household responsibilities (such as buying groceries) to wives without any concomitant decrease in wives' other responsibilities. In a study by Wandibba, Nangendo, and Mulemi (2014), Kenyan women noted that although mobile banking allowed them greater access and control over finances, the privacy inherent in mobile banking increased household tension and spousal suspicion, for example, of extra-marital affairs and the use of family resources; tension also arose because mobile banking allowed users to hide the "true" nature of family finances.

Programs addressing patriarchal norms may also need to be examined to assess the strength and longevity of apparent effects on such norms. For instance, Ambler and de Brauw (2017) in their analysis of BISP find that though women's mobility did increase, it did so selectively and not for mobility to public places, such as the local market or a shrine or mosque. In the Philippines, Ashraf, Karlan, and Yin (2010) find that the observed large, beneficial effect of their savings program on women's household financial decision making declined and became insignificant after the first year. They suggest that the program was perhaps able to break the pre-existing decision-making norms only for a short time and that greater, continued advocacy efforts may be needed to achieve longer-term, sustainable improvements in women's economic empowerment.

Address low financial literacy

Financial literacy programs need to be implemented keeping in mind that without other complementary interventions, financial literacy alone may not be enough to improve women's financial inclusion. Interventions across the world have addressed low financial literacy among women and other disadvantaged populations; however, evidence on the effectiveness of financial literacy education on improvements in financial knowledge and financial behavior is mixed.

Some intervention evaluations do not disaggregate findings by sex. For instance, a meta-analysis of 168 research papers covering 201 studies reports almost no effect of financial literacy programs on financial behaviors, though this analysis did not examine women separately (Fernandes, Lynch Jr., and Netemeyer 2014). In another review specifically focused on women, Buvinić and O'Donnell (2016) find financial literacy training on its own to be "unproven" in improving women's financial inclusion; rather, such training is effective only when combined with other initiatives, such as monetary incentives or financial counseling. In contrast, a recent meta-analysis of 128 evaluation studies of financial literacy education programs finds that financial education programs can, in fact, improve financial awareness and knowledge and thereby financial behavior. The authors caution, however, that "the field of financial education is not developed enough that established standards could be followed 'blindly'," in all contexts (Kaiser and Menkhoff 2017, 22).

Nonetheless good practices that can be emulated do exist. Evaluated examples from several countries illustrate how soap operas can be used to improve women's financial education together with financial behavior and use of financial services. Using an innovative randomizing design, Berg and Zia (2017) evaluated "Scandal," a soap opera in South Africa with a financial education storyline and a 70-percent-female viewership. Viewers were less likely than control viewers of an alternative show to engage in high-risk financial behaviors. Qualitative data suggest that the show owed its success to strong community involvement in its design and high levels of identification among viewers with the show's main characters.

Women's World Banking has experimented with such soap operas across several countries, specifically targeting women. Recognizing that financial education alone may not be enough to influence women's financial behavior or use of services, their programs have combined mass media with interactive materials, campaigns and staff outreach to clients. Evaluations of two programs to encourage women to save in formal financial institutions yield promising lessons (Women's World Banking and Credit Suisse 2013). In the Dominican Republic, a telenovela named "Contracorriente" was created specifically to encourage women to save and was accompanied by a widespread communications campaign and classroom-based financial education opportunities to build on the telenovela's messages. Episodes of an existing soap opera in Kenya, "Makutano Junction," that focused on financial literacy encouraged low-income, non-banked rural women to open formal bank accounts. Evaluations of both programs found a significant increase in viewers opening bank accounts compared to the control group; in qualitative interviews, women confirmed that their behavior had been influenced by the shows. The evaluations distilled the critical characteristics of these shows that likely contributed most heavily to their success (figure 4.17). In a country like Bangladesh, similar shows could be produced for television and/or radio.

FIGURE 4.17

Elements of a successful financial literacy program

Source: Based on information from Women's World Banking and Credit Suisse 2013.

Address high financial and transaction costs

MFIs in Bangladesh provide good practices on how to make available collateral-free, flexible credit to women to remove related transaction and financial costs women would otherwise have to incur. Microfinance loans are typically provided without demanding traditional collateral as security, made possible largely through the application of group-based lending technologies introduced by Grameen Bank. The group lending model in Bangladesh typically requires participants to belong to a five-member group of prospective borrowers, who act as guarantors of sorts for one another. However, this standard Grameen group lending model of fixed repayment schedules with standard floors and ceilings on loan sizes was found inappropriate for the extreme poor or the "vulnerable nonpoor" group, resulting in alternate programs being developed by other organizations to reach this section of the population (Zaman 2004). Recently, the Grameen Bank model has started to become more flexible, too, and formal guarantees and even, in some cases, weekly group meetings are increasingly being replaced by more flexible rules and products that allow borrowers to select the length of the loan they need (Rhyne 2012). The types of loans available also vary, including general loans, program loans, and housing loans, the first two of which are typically used for a range of income-generating activities.

Most MFIs thus simultaneously offer collateral-free finance and address other barriers to women's financial inclusion related to flexible loan sizes and repayment schedules, financial literacy, geographical access, and women-friendly environment, among others. Hence, it is difficult to ascertain the specific effect of the collateral-free nature or flexibility of the loan in increasing financial inclusion for women compared to these other aspects of credit. The larger literature reviewed here and elsewhere suggests, nonetheless, that a package of characteristics that simultaneously address multiple, often-related barriers to women's financial inclusion is likely necessary to notably increase their inclusion (Banerjee et al. 2015).

Addressing the lack of appropriate identification through biometric or other secure, national identification (NID) systems is a critical aspect of lowering high transaction costs for women seeking formal finance. Programs in Bangladesh, Pakistan and India illustrate how to do so. Through the *Identification System for Enhancing Access to Services project (IDEA)*, the government of Bangladesh and the World Bank Group have worked to create a secure, accurate, and reliable national ID system that provides more efficient and transparent delivery of various services, including financial ones (Population and Development Review 2017). Thirty-three agencies from Bangladesh's public and private sectors have thus far signed on to use the digital national IDs and biometrics-based ID cards—including Bangladesh Bank (Population and Development Review 2017). NIDs and related technology have eased the documentary demands by, for example, providing an online verification system that allows Bangladesh Bank's (BB) Credit Information Bureau to easily authenticate the identity of citizens seeking loans from financial institutions (World Bank 2016b).

Pakistan's Computerized National Identity Card or CNIC was not created in order to improve financial inclusion but it has had that effect because of being required for eligibility for benefits. In particular, linking the CNIC to the BISP program has substantially increased the number of women with this formal identification. Having these official identification documents, in turn, is increasing women's confidence, easing their access to other financial services and thus lowering transaction costs; it is also facilitating women's control over the finance they do access, including the BISP funds. Multiple evaluations of BISP also point to increased mobility and higher status for Pakistani women using the new CNIC cards.[18] Similarly, assessments of the Aadhar card—India's recently implemented biometric national identification card—note that women working on government programs are able to use their Aadhar cards to directly receive cash transfers into their bank accounts (Banerjee 2016). This then obviated the cost of physically accessing this cash, and also increased women's control over their finances.

Several other countries are testing the use of biometric identification, in some cases linked to financial services, especially for the poor and women. It is highly likely that women will benefit from formal identification that lowers transaction costs to access and control finance. Rigorous, continuous monitoring and evaluation will be necessary to gauge how to maintain effectiveness and coverage over time, ensure the security of financial data, and monitor and prevent government abuse of citizens' right to privacy.

Providing access to fully liquid, no-fee savings accounts to increase women's savings can also eliminate transaction costs. A randomized experiment in Nepal among poor, female-headed households revealed an unsatisfied demand for savings, perhaps because poor individuals tend to be unable to save in formal institutions due to prohibitive transaction costs. According to a randomized experiment's (Prina 2015) test of this hypothesis, providing free, simple, liquid savings accounts in a local bank increases participants' savings more than is saved by a control group with access only to traditional, informal sources of savings. The experiment findings also suggest the need to simultaneously address multiple transaction costs, such as the direct cost of fees (which can be addressed by providing a no-fee account), the logistical cost of access to a financial institution (addressed by making accounts available at a local bank branch), and information costs (addressed by publicizing the availability of these accounts).

Transaction costs also arise from poor geographic access. Several of the interventions cited above as evidence for other recommendations illustrate how to address transaction costs related to poor access. For example, the savings accounts experiment tested in Nepal made no-fee savings accounts accessible and available in local bank accounts in slum areas (Prina 2015). Mobile banking and linking bank accounts electronically to cash transfers from government programs also solves the problem of financial institutions being too far away for women to use for their finances. When biometric ID systems are further linked to mobile banking and government financial transfers, not only geographic access but also women's control over these more easily accessible finances is increased.

Agent banking can decrease a range of transaction costs for women, including those arising from limited geographic access to formal finance sources. "Agent banking" refers to the use of local retailers as less formal, low-cost conduits through which people can make deposits, withdrawals, money transfers and pay back loans. In a recent study in the Democratic Republic of Congo (DRC), Cull et al. (2017) analyze whether a cadre of agent bankers could make financial services more easily accessible to poor customers who cannot use formal channels to get finance due to geographic barriers. Their multivariate analysis of data from 2011 to 2015, on 190 agents of a large MFI named FINKA DRC finds that agents trained and deployed in neighborhoods to provide banking services door-to-door were able to successfully provide a range of such services in densely populated, low-income areas that lacked access to formal financial institutions.

The DRC study unfortunately did not examine the effect of agent bankers on women specifically; however, there is anecdotal and qualitative evidence that women agents can increase women's access to and use of finance (Thakur et al. 2016). Bangladesh has been using agent bankers since 2015. In 2017, Bangladesh Bank created guidelines for agent banking that recommended employing women agents specifically to access rural women clients (Bangladesh Bank 2017b). There are very few women agents relative to the need identified in this and other studies, however (Shrader 2015). Cull et al. (2017) provide useful lessons for expanding and improving the quality of a cadre of agent bankers, finding that frequent monitoring is a necessary input to improve agents' services. It also is important to test whether agent bankers are as effective in more sparsely populated areas where the volume of transactions would be lower, which has implications for engaging agent bankers in less-populated minority or indigenous areas.

Providing door-to-door financial services is yet another way to address poor geographic access, as MFIs in Bangladesh and elsewhere demonstrate. Several studies of SEWA's financial inclusion program examine the heightened access to finance via a model of door-to-door banking (among other loan characteristics), as well as the salubrious effect of such increased use of finance on a range of other outcomes (Field, Hollander, and Pande 2014). MFIs in Bangladesh also typically provide their financial services through field staff that go to women's homes or villages, thus removing geographic distance as a barrier.

Address women's low use of mobile and digital technologies for finance

There are few experimental evaluations of interventions on what works to expand use of mobile or digital technology for financial inclusion of women specifically; also, much of the research and findings on the use of mobile and digital money technologies are in reports and other gray literature, rather than in peer-reviewed journals. Further, there is limited work on how gender norms or women's empowerment and status can shape their adoption of mobile and other technologies in using and controlling finance, and influence barriers therein (Gammage et al. 2017).

Existing experiments and large-scale programs recommend first investing in feasibility research before introducing technological solutions for financial inclusion. Assessments of various large mobile money experiments note that one element of success is likely the time taken to first understand the financial and social situations, and needs and constraints, of potential users. The mobile technology program should then be built to fit user needs, as was done in the scaled up and replicated M-Pesa model in Kenya (Hughes and Lonie 2007). In fact, neighboring Sub-Saharan countries that attempted to "copy" the system of M-Pesa quickly learned that adoption rates are not guaranteed by just having a product and system; rather, the system needs to be modified for the local context (Yousif et al. 2013), which necessitates preparatory feasibility research. In an assessment of its mobile money financial inclusion program in India, the Grameen Bank notes that "[a]s the use of mobile phones to deliver products and services grows in popularity, it is prudent to ask who benefits and which products are in the most demand" (Grameen Foundation 2012, 29). Thus, patience, and investing time and money into feasibility and situational research are considered important to the success of a mobile money financial services venture. Given the additional gendered constraints women face makes this kind of initial investment even more critical.

Training is also absolutely critical. It needs to be in small groups, occur repeatedly, and have dedicated funds allocated in program budgets. Several studies of mobile financial services find that even if women own the phones, it is typically men or children that operate them and conduct the financial transactions (Yousif et al. 2013). This then does not offer women financial independence, empowerment or control. The M-Pesa model found in its pilot phase that training women in the use of mobile financial services was more effective if conducted in small groups and in surroundings comfortable for trainees. Importantly, the program realized that there would be a need for repeated trainings and visits to mobile financial agents, leading to the creation of a dedicated budget line item for training funds (Hughes and Lonie 2007). An assessment of Bangladesh's bKash system finds that it was important for women users to have a certain level of comfort with the m-banking technology and system (Hanouch and Rotman 2013), which they would acquire only from training on how to use the technology. It is also critical to monitor the quality and effectiveness of training: the Grameen Foundation's study of its program in India found that despite training by the provider, a large proportion of women participants did not know how to use the mobile money app (Yousif et al. 2013).

Given women's limited financial literacy and low access to phone and digital technology, keeping a financial technology product simple is important. In the M-Pesa project, the more complex product initially piloted was stripped down to a much simpler version when going to scale that had easy-to-follow instructions and provided a few basic services. This lessened the training burden and was easier for consumers to understand, adopt and use (Hughes and Lonie 2007). A multiyear household panel study of the M-Pesa program later carried out by Suri and Jack (2016) found that even the most basic financial services, such as the ability to have easy and safe access to money, and to be able to store, send, and receive funds, could have a significant impact on the poverty of female headed households and other poor women. In other words, mobile and digital financial products do not have to be complex to work.

Findings are inconclusive on whether or not to charge fees for the use of mobile money services. On the one hand, some programs that have charged fees report no negative effects. The M-Pesa program charges a transaction fee to the sender of funds, whose amount varies by the type of transaction and amount of funds being moved. The M-Pesa service itself is free, deposits are free, and there are no repercussions of mobile money use on overall airtime. Users were found to prefer M-Pesa to money transfer companies for transferring funds between individuals because M-Pesa fees were lower (Hughes and Lonie 2007; Omwansa 2009). In a modified adoption of the M-Pesa model in Tanzania, a similar fee structure did not depress the use of the service though women users did note that they would carry out more transactions were the fees lower (Helmore 2011). In contrast, experimental evidence from a mobile banking program in the Philippines finds that even though the mobile service decreased transportation costs of going to a physical financial institution, the more direct transaction fees for the mobile money service dissuaded users, resulting in a drop in deposits and savings through this program (Harigaya 2016).

Programmers and policy makers do, however, need to be aware of potential unintended negative social consequences of digitizing financial services for women. Morawczynski and Pickens (2009) find that once people in M-Pesa could transfer money or repay loans using mobile technology and e-money, urban migrants decreased their visits home to families. This was a concern and source of discomfort for rural women whose husbands had migrated to urban areas for work and started to see their spouses less frequently.

In particular, combining mobile banking with microfinance requires very careful planning and preparation to avoid unintended negative consequences. Costs to the organization are one such consequence, as modifying standard MFI savings and loan programs through the insertion of mobile banking may generate costs for MFIs even if users benefit. For instance, in both Kenya and the Philippines, when mobile banking was added to MFIs in a way that all transactions could be done on the phone, attendance at weekly meetings declined (Harigaya 2016; Hughes and Lonie 2007). Harigaya's (2016) experimental study observes a drop in deposit frequencies and savings balances, also. She posits (p. 9) that "[b]y removing cash handling from meetings, mobile banking makes savings and payment decisions less visible to peers and lowers the motivation to attend center meetings. These changes could disrupt the social architecture of group banking and weaken the peer effects, reducing deposit frequencies and savings balances."

A different study that reviews various MFIs' efforts to integrate mobile banking into their systems, however, finds no evidence of these dynamics (Hanouch and Rotman 2013). Still, MFIs integrating mobile banking into their systems have to bear the additional costs of modifying systems and all the procedures that go along with the change (Hughes and Lonie 2007), necessitating careful planning and preparation.

The Grameen Foundation's review of good practices in implementing mobile financial services in MFIs provides a roadmap. The review's central message (Yousif, et al. 2013) is that implementing mobile financial services may not be suitable for all MFIs as the financial resources and human capacity requirements are demanding. Thus, MFIs need to consider a range of factors and undertake a range of preparatory actions to determine whether and how to provide mobile financial services for their clients, as well as how to prevent some of the potential negative social consequences discussed above (box 4.3).

DATA GAPS

Despite the longstanding and widespread tradition of women's microfinance in Bangladesh, there remains a critical need to collect gender-disaggregated data on financial issues, such as portfolio statistics and quality of women's access to and use of various financial products and services. To use data to inform the reorientation of policies and design new programs and products that are better aligned with women entrepreneurs' needs requires the following: (a) maintaining gender-based data on credit disbursement and dissemination of information on credit opportunities; (b) conducting annual studies to ensure data are compared and progress is measured until specific targets for women-owned businesses are met; and, (c) strengthening the statistical basis for gender-related cross-country analyses and longitudinal studies of the impact of financial developments and relevant policies.

BOX 4.3

Recommended good practices to structure mobile microfinance

- Conduct a feasibility study of all aspects of the market, network coverage, and a cost-benefit analysis.
- Choose the right model: identify relevant partnerships and weigh the costs and benefits of creating a new model versus modifying an existing one. Copy an existing model only after testing feasibility and applicability to the context.
- When choosing which products to offer through mobile financial services, start small and simple and build as experience grows.
- Take the time to fully integrate new mobile financial services with pre-existing systems.
- Secure staff support from top to bottom, at all levels.
- Provide comprehensive training for own staff and current and potential users. The most effective training takes time, and is face-to-face or in small groups.
- Address potential decline in group meetings by creating larger goals for group meetings than cash

- collection and disbursement and lowering the frequency of these meetings.
- Design, conduct and rigorously evaluate a pilot before rolling out a new mobile money service.
- Ensure continuous communication both internally (across staff at different levels) and externally (with users in communities) to promote the mobile product, get feedback, and address problems effectively.
- Create a widespread network of agents to provide mobile money services, keeping in mind location, reputation, commitment and other features identified in the feasibility study. Train and incentivize agents appropriately.
- Establish good relationships with financial regulators.
- Consider the option of not implementing mobile financial services if research suggests that the MFI or the market is not ready for a viable program.

Source: Information adapted from Yousif et al. 2013.

Aside from the lack of data, there is also limited gender-disaggregated research overall on financial inclusion. Recent research is lacking on a range of financial issues, such as women's financial access, use of loans, control over borrowed finance, and access to and use of business development services. Consequently, some of the findings above are from years-old studies. Bangladesh's financial and economic scenario is rapidly changing, necessitating updated research on gender differences in financial inclusion.

CONCLUSION

The Bangladeshi government and various stakeholders, such as in the microfinance sector, have longstanding efforts in place to increase women's financial inclusion. Yet, inclusion alone does not guarantee control. Similarly, increasing numbers of women financial clients alone does not indicate a corresponding increase in their level of financial inclusion or economic empowerment. Research finds that a significant (albeit unknown) share of women's financial assets remain controlled by their male family members. Women continue to rely mostly on semi-formal and informal sources of finance, as formal financial products and services remain largely inaccessible. Many of these also are inappropriate given women's situations, constraints and needs.

Experience from across the world strongly suggests that an integrated approach that simultaneously addresses multiple constraints is needed to successfully address women's financial exclusion and that the more successful interventions are likely to be multifaceted. For women to be more actively engaged in financial markets, a range of market conditions must exist (figure 4.18). Several reviews of evaluated programs from several countries note that policies and programs need to address not just the obvious market failures related to banking structures or the range and type of financial instruments available to women, but also other constraints on women's access to even well-designed products and institutions, including social and patriarchal norms and related barriers (Banerjee et al. 2015; Karlan et al. 2016).

Finally, programmers and policy makers actions must avoid unintended negative consequences for women. Perhaps the most serious of these is the possibility of increasing women's risks of domestic abuse. Multiple studies find that increasing women's use of and control over financial assets threatens traditional patriarchal power structures and thus may trigger a spike in domestic or partner violence (as mentioned in chapter 1). Unforeseen shifts in social and spousal relationships or increases rather than declines in overall costs of finance discussed above are additional types of unintended effects. Good pre-intervention research to understand the norms and context of the

FIGURE 4.18

Integrated approach for women's financial inclusion

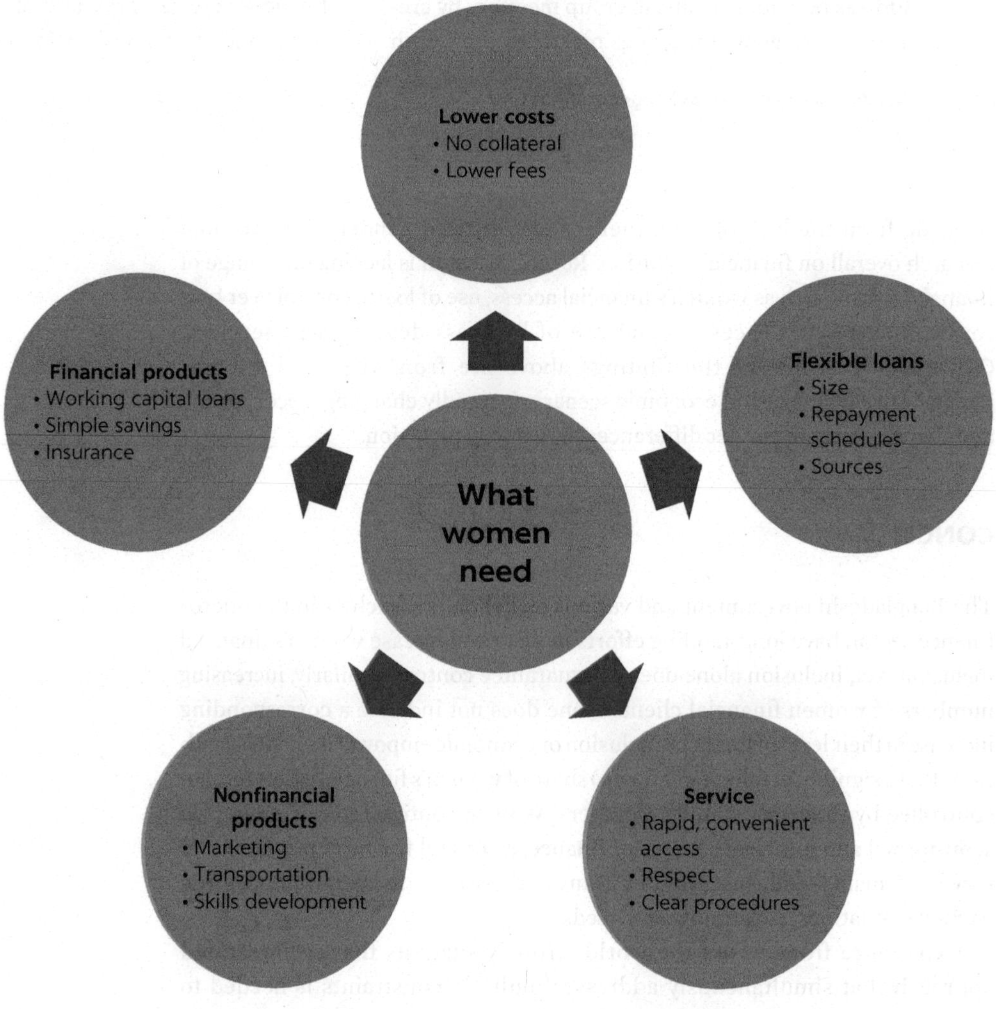

communities targeted for women's financial inclusion efforts, systematic monitoring as a policy or program is rolled out, and communication with communities and participants will be necessary to offset these unintended possibilities and ensure that women become financially empowered without risking other aspects of their lives.

NOTES

1. http://www.worldbank.org/en/programs/globalfindex.
2. http://www.ifpri.org/publication/bangladesh-integrated-household-survey-bihs-2015
3. Findex 2017 defines "account" as a way to "save money, to make or receive payments, or to receive wages or financial help" (https://globalfindex.worldbank.org/sites/globalfindex/files/databank/2014%20Findex%20Questionnaire.pdf) at a bank or other financial institution or using a mobile money service in the two months prior to the survey (https://globalfindex.worldbank.org/sites/globalfindex/files/databank/Glossary2017.pdf).
4. Findex defines a "financial institution" as a bank or another type of financial institution, such as a credit union, a microfinance institution, a cooperative, or the post office (if applicable).
5. The Findex 2017 defines "borrowing from a financial institution" as borrowing money—individually or with some-one else—for any reason from a bank or other financial institution in the 12 months preceding the survey.
6. Store credit is used in the Findex to include purchases at a retail store without paying at the time of purchase (Demirguc-Kunt et al. 2015). Data were not available for store credit in the 2017 Findex.
7. The BIHS defines "formal lenders" as "banks and financial institutions". Other lenders are grouped as per figure 4.4.
8. A "shamity" is the Bangladeshi term for a local association or cooperative. The BIHS considers shamitys separate from NGOs.
9. The Findex 2017 defines "savings in a financial institution" as personally saving or setting aside any money for any reason in a bank or other financial institution.
10. There is a large literature that debates the extent to which microfinance impacts a range of outcomes for women across the global South. It is beyond the scope of this chapter to discuss this literature. Rather, this section focuses on describing the MFI sector in Bangladesh as it specifically relates to women's use and control of finances.
11. There is a large and well-cited literature about microfinance in Bangladesh. Summarizing and analyzing this entire literature is beyond the scope of this book. Here we cover select points about microfinance dynamics and concerns among women.
12. Unfortunately the Findex data do not tell us the other purposes for which savings and loans might have been used.
13. We define 'control over credit' as decision making over at least one source of credit plus over at least one use of this credit.
14. Full regression results are available in appendix F.
15. The OECD (2005) defines financial literacy as the combination of understanding financial products and concepts plus the ability to realize financial risks and opportunities, so as to make informed choices, know where to go for help, and take further effective steps to improve one's own financial welfare.
16. http://finclusion.org/data_fiinder/.
17. http://finclusion.org/data_fiinder/.
18. See, for example, evaluations cited in World Bank (2016) at http://www.worldbank.org/en/news/feature/2016/02/04/pakistan-building-equality-for-women-on-a-foundation-of-identity.

REFERENCES

Ahmed, Nilufer Karim. 2001. "Jobs, Gender and Small Enterprises in Bangladesh: Factors Affecting Women Entrepreneurs in Small and Cottage Industries in Bangladesh." SEED Working Paper, No. 14, Series on Women's Entrepreneurship Development and Gender in Enterprises—WEDGE, ILO, Geneva and Dhaka: ILO.

Alam, S. 2012. "The Effect of Gender-Based Returns to Borrowing on Intra-Household Resource Allocation in Rural Bangladesh." *World Development* 40 (6): 1164–80.

Alamgir, Dewan A. H. 2009. "State of Microfinance in Bangladesh." Institute of Microfinance.

Ambler, Kate, and Alan De Brauw. 2017. "The Impacts of Cash Transfers on Women's Empowerment: Learning from Pakistan's BISP Program." Social Protection and Labor Discussion Paper 1702, Washington, DC: World Bank.

Ara, Jinnat, and Syed Abdul Hamid. 2011. "Against the Odds." D+C Development and Cooperation, German Federal Ministry for Economic Cooperation and Development Publication.

Armendáriz, Beatriz, and Jonathan Morduch. 2010. "The Economics of Microfinance." Massachusetts Institute of Technology.

Arshad, Muhammad. 2011. *Does Money Matter for Women's Empowerment? A Study of the Benazir Income Support Program (BISP) Pakistan.* The Hague: International Institute of Social Studies.

Ashan, Syed M., M. A. Baqui Khalily, Syed A. Hamid, Shubhasish Barua, and Suborna Barua. 2013. "The Microinsurance Market in Bangladesh: An Analytical Overview." *Bangladesh Development Studies* XXXVI (1).

Ashraf, Nava, Dean Karlan, and Wesley Yin. 2010. "Female Empowerment: Impact of a Commitment Savings Product in the Philippines." *World Development* 38 (3): 333–44.

Asian Development Bank. 2015. *Financial Soundness Indicators for Financial Sector Stability in Bangladesh.* Mandaluyong City: Asian Development Bank.

Banerjee, Shweta. 2016. "Aadhaar: Digital Inclusion and Public Services in India." World Development Report 2016 Digital Dividends Background Paper, World Bank, Washington, DC.

Banerjee, Abhijit, Esther Duflo, Nathanael Goldberg, Dean Karlan, Robert Osei, William Parienté, Jeremy Shapiro, Bram Thuysbaert, and Christopher Udry. 2015. "A Multifaceted Program Causes Lasting Progress for the Very Poor: Evidence from Six Countries." *Science* 348 (6236): 1260799.

Bangladesh Bank. 2014a. *A Primary Survey on Banks in Promoting Women Entrepreneurship in Bangladesh.* Special Research Work: 1501, Monetary Policy Department & Research Department, Dhaka: Bangladesh Bank.

———. 2014b. *Quarterly SME Loan Statement as on 31.12.2014.* Dhaka: Bangladesh Bank.

———. 2014c. *We Shall Overcome: Review of CSR Activities of Bangladesh Bank, Commercial Banks & Financial Institutions.* Dhaka: Bangladesh Bank.

———. 2017a. *Bank Categorywise Quarterly SME Loan Statement, as on 31.12.2017.* Dhaka: Bangladesh Bank.

———. 2017b. *Prudential Guidelines for Agent Banking Operation in Bangladesh.* Dhaka: Bangladesh Bank, 2017.

Bashar, Toriqul, and Salim Rashid. 2012. "Urban Microfinance and Urban Poverty in Bangladesh." *Journal of the Asia Pacific Economy* 17 (1): 151–70.

Bedson, Jamie, ed. 2009. "Microfinance in Asia: Trends, Challenges and Opportunities." The Banking with the Poor Network (BWTP) and SEEP Network.

Berg, Gunhild, and Bilal Zia. 2017. "Harnessing Emotional Connections to Improve Financial Decisions: Evaluating the Impact of Financial Education in Mainstream Media." *Journal of the European Economic Association* 15 (5): 1025–55.

Blunch, Niels-Hugo, and Maitreyi Bordia Das. 2007. "Changing Norms about Gender Inequality in Education: Evidence from Bangladesh." Policy Research Working Paper 4044, World Bank, Washington, DC.

Buvinić, M., R. Furst-Nichols, and E. C. Pryor. 2013. *A Roadmap for Promoting Women's Economic Empowerment.* United Nations Foundation and ExxonMobil Foundation.

Buvinić, Mayra, and Megan O'Donnell. 2016. *Revisiting What Works: Women, Economic Empowerment and Smart Design.* Washington, DC: Center for Global Development.

CDF (Credit and Development Forum). 2016. "Bangladesh Microfinance Statistics 2015–2016." Dhaka: CDF. http://www.cdfbd.org/new/page.php?scat_id=161.

Cheema, Iftikhar, Simon Hunt, Sarah Javeed, Tanya Lone, Sean O'Leary. "Benazir Income Support Programme: Final Impact Evaluation Report." Oxford: Oxford Policy Management Limited. https://www.opml.co.uk/files/Publications/7328-evaluating-pakistans-flagship-social-protection-programme-bisp/bisp-final-impact-evaluation-report.pdf?noredirect=1.

Chen, Greg, and Stuart Rutherford. 2013. "A Microcredit Crisis Averted: The Case of Bangladesh." CGAP Focus Note No. 87, Consultative Group to Assist the Poor, Washington, DC.

Choudhury, Toufic Ahmad, and Ananya Raihan. 2000. *Structural Adjustment Participatory Review Initiative Bangladesh, Study Theme 2(C): Implications of Financial Sector Reforms.* Dhaka: Government of Bangladesh and Civil Society.

Chowdhury, M. Jahangir Alam. 2008. "Does the Participation in the Microcredit Programs Contribute to the Development of Women Entrepreneurship at the Household Level? Experience from Bangladesh." CMD Working Paper 04, Center for Microfinance and Development, University of Dhaka, Dhaka.

Chowdhury, Sarahat Salma, and Sifat Adiya Chowdhury. 2011. "Microfinance and Women Empowerment: A Panel Data Analysis Using Evidence from Rural Bangladesh." *International Journal of Economics and Finance* 3 (5 2011): 86–96.

Cons, Jason, and Kasia Paprocki. 2008. "The Limits of Microcredit—A Bangladesh Case." *FoodFirst Backgrounder* 14 (4).

Credit and Development Forum & Institute of Microfinance. 2010. "Bangladesh Microfinance Statistics 2010—Trends and Growth of Microfinance Programs of MFI-NGOs in Bangladesh Using Panel Data." Credit and Development Forum, Dhaka.

Cubero, Rodrigo, Jayendu De, Souvik Gupta, and Stella Kaendera. 2016. *Bangladesh: Selected Issues.* IMF Country Report No. 16/28, Washington, DC: International Monetary Fund.

Cull, R., X. Gine, S. Harten, and A. B. Rusu. 2017. "Agent Banking in a Highly Under-Developed Financial Sector." Policy Research Working Paper 7984, World Bank Development Research Group, Finance and Private Sector Development Team, World Bank, Washington, DC.

Fernandes, Daniel, John G. Lynch Jr., and Richard G. Netemeyer. 2014. "Financial Literacy, Financial Education, and Downstream Financial Behaviors." *Management Science* 60 (8): 1861–83.

Field, Erica, Abraham J. Hollander, and Rohini Pande. 2014. "Microfinance: Points of Promise." HKS Working Paper RWP16-036, Harvard Kennedy School, Cambridge, MA.

Field, Erica, Rohini Pande, Natalia Rigol, Simone Schaner, and Charity Troyer Moore. 2016. "On Her Account: Can Strengthening Women's Financial Control Boost Female Labor Supply?" Working Paper, Harvard University, Cambridge, MA.

The Financial Express. "Financial Inclusions Scales New Peak—Farmers Figure Prominently in Opening Bank Accounts." August 12, 2012.

Fletschner, Diana, and Lisa Kenney. 2011. *Rural Women's Access to Financial Services—Credit, Savings and Insurance.* ESA Working Paper No. 11-07, FAO, Geneva.

Gammage, Sarah, Aslihan Kes, Liliane Winograd, Naziha Sultana, Sara Hiller, and Shelby Bourgault. 2017. *Gender and Digital Financial Inclusion: What Do We Know and What Do We Need to Know?* Washington, DC: International Center for Research on Women.

Gan, Christopher, and Gilbert V. Nartea. 2017. *Microfinance in Asia.* Singapore: World Scientific Publishing Co. Pte. Ltd.

Goetz, A. M., and R. Sen Gupta. 1996. "Who Takes the Credit? Gender, Power, and Control over Loan Use in Rural Credit Programmes in Bangladesh." *World Development* 24 (1): 45–63.

Grameen Foundation. 2012. *Women, Mobile Phones, and Savings: A Grameen Foundation Case Study.* Washington, DC: Grameen Foundation.

Hamm, Kathrin, Roshin Mathai Joseph, Sebastian Veit, and Sandeep Singh. 2017. *Gender Intelligence for Banks—Moving the Needle on Gender Equality.* Washington, DC: International Finance Corporation.

Hanouch, Michel, and Sarah Rotman. 2013. "Microfinance and Mobile Banking: Blurring the Lines?" CGAP Focus Note 88, World Bank, Washington, DC.

Harigaya, Tomoko. 2016. "Effects of Digitization on Financial Behaviors: Experimental Evidence from the Philippines." Working Paper, Harvard University, Cambridge, MA.

Helmore, Kristin. 2011. "Tanzania: Linking Savings Groups to Mobile Banking." Access Africa Technical Learning Series 2, Atlanta and Dar-Es-Salaam: CARE.

Hughes, Karen D., and Jennifer E. Jennings. 2012. *Global Women's Entrepreneurship Research: Diverse Settings, Questions, and Approaches.* Cheltenham: Edward Elgar Publishing.

Hughes, Nick, and Susie Lonie. 2007. "M-PESA: Mobile Money for the "Unbanked" Turning Cellphones into 24-Hour Tellers in Kenya." *Innovations: Technology, Governance, Globalization* 2 (1–2): 63–81.

Hussain, Zahid, Sheikh Tanjeb Islam, Sabiha Subah Mohona, and Shegufta Shahriar. 2017. "Bangladesh Development Update: Towards More, Better, and Inclusive Jobs." Working Paper, World Bank, Washington, DC.

International Finance Corporation and KfW Bankengruppe. 2009. "Bangladesh: Microfinance and Financial Sector Diagnostic Study—Final Report." Washington, DC and Frankfurt: IFC and KfW Bankengruppe.

International Monetary Fund. 2016. "Bangladesh: Selected Issues." IMF Country Report No. 16/28, International Monetary Fund, Washington, DC.

InterMedia. 2016. *Bangladesh Quicksights Report Fourth Annual FII Tracker Survey.* Financial Inclusion Insights, InterMedia and Bill & Melinda Gates Foundation, InterMedia.

———. 2017. "Bangladesh Wave 4 Report FII Tracker Survey Conducted August–September 2016." Financial Inclusion Insights.

Islam, Asadul. 2011. "Medium and Long-Term Participation in Microfinance: An Evaluation Using a New Panel Dataset from Bangladesh." *American Journal of Agricultural Economics* 93 (3): 847–866.

Islam, Md. Ezazul. 2016. "Financial Inclusion in Asia and the Pacific." Discussion Paper First High-Level Follow-up Dialogue on Financing for Development in Asia and the Pacific, United Nations ESCAP.

Islam, Dr. Md. Ezazul, and Md. Salim Al Mamun. 2011. "Financial Inclusion: The Role of Bangladesh Bank." Working Paper Series: WP1101, Research Department, Bangladesh Bank, Dhaka.

Islam, Asadul, Chau Nguyen, and Russell Smyth. 2015. "Does Microfinance Change Informal Lending in Village Economies? Evidence from Bangladesh." *Journal of Banking & Finance* 50: 141–156.

Kabeer, Naila. 1999. "Resources, Agency, Achievements: Reflections on the Measurement of Women's Empowerment." *Development and Change,* Blackwell Publishers Ltd. 30 (3): 435–64.

———. 2001. "Conflicts Over Credit: Re-Evaluating the Empowerment Potential of Loans to Women in Rural Bangladesh." *World Development* 29 (1): 63–84.

———. 2005. "Is Microfinance a 'Magic Bullet' for Women's Empowerment? Analysis of Findings from South Asia." *Economic and Political Weekly* 40 (44/45): 4709–18.

Kaiser, Tim, and Lukas Menkhoff. 2017. "Does Financial Education Impact Financial Literacy and Financial Behavior, and If So, When?" Policy Research Working Paper WPS 8161, World Bank, Washington, DC.

Karim, K. M. Rabiul, and Chi Kong Law. 2013. "Gender Ideology, Microcredit Participation and Women's Status in Rural Bangladesh." *International Journal of Sociology and Social Policy* 33 (1/2): 45–62.

Karim, Lamia. 2008. "Demistifying Micro-Credit. The Grameen Bank, NGOs, and Neoliberalism in Bangladesh." *Cultural Dynamics* 20 (1): 5–29.

Karlan, Dean, Jake Kendall, Rebecca Mann, Rohini Pande, Tavneet Suri, and Jonathan Zinman. 2016. "Research and Impacts of Digital Financial Services." NBER Working Paper Series w22633, National Bureau of Economic Research, Cambridge, MA.

Khalily, Baqui, and Rashid Faruqee. 2011. *Multiple Borrowing by MFI Clients.* Policy Brief, Institute of Microfinance. Dhaka: Institute of Microfinance.

Khalily, M. A. Baqui, and Pablo Mia. 2015. *Financial Literacy and Financial Inclusion in Bangladesh.* Dhaka: Institute of Microfinance (InM).

Khalily, M. A. Baqui, Rushad Faridi, and Farzana Saeed. "Does Overlapping Borrowing in Micro Credit Market Contribute to Over-Indebtedness in Bangladesh?" Working Paper 47, Institute for Inclusive Finance and Development (InM), Dhaka.

Khalily, M. A. Baqui, M. Abdul Khaleque, and S. Badruddoza. 2014. "Impact of Regulation on the Cost Efficiency of Microfinance Institutions in Bangladesh." Working Paper 22, Microcredit Regulatory Authority (MRA) and Institute of Microfinance (InM), Dhaka.

Khandker, Shahidur R., Rashid Faruqee, and Hussain A. Samad. 2013. "Are Microcredit Borrowers in Bangladesh Over-Indebted?" Policy Research Working Paper, World Bank, Washington, DC.

Khandker, Shahidur R., M. A. Baqui Khalily, and Hussain A. Samad. 2016. "Are Borrowers Overindebted?" In *Beyond Ending Poverty: The Dynamics of Microfinance in Bangladesh*, edited by Shahidur R. Khandker, M. A. Baqui Khalily, and Hussain A. Samad, 91–115. Directions in Development-Poverty. Washington, DC: World Bank.

Kumar, Dhanonjoy, Afjal Hossain, and Monto Chandra Gope. 2013. "Role of Micro Credit Program in Empowering Rural Women in Bangladesh: A Study on Grameen Bank Bangladesh Limited." *Asian Business Review* 3 (4): 114–20.

Levy Carciente, Sary. 2016. *International Property Rights Index 2016*. Property Rights Alliance.

Mahmud, Minhaj, Keijiro Otsuka, Yasuyuki Sawada, Mari Tanaka, and Tomomi Tanaka. 2017. "Women Empowerment in Bangladesh: Household Decisions under Development of Non-Farm Sectors and Microfinance Institutions." JICA-RA Working Paper 154, Japan International Cooperation Agency Reseach Institute, Tokyo.

Mahmud, Simeen, Nirali M. Shah, and Stan Becker. 2012. "Measurement of Women's Empowerment in Rural Bangladesh." *World Development* 40 (3): 610–619.

Mansur, Ahsan H. 2015. "Financial Market Development and Challenges in Bangladesh." Prepared as a background paper for the Seventh Five Year Plan, Policy Research Institute of Bangladesh.

Matin, Imran, Nuzhal Imam, and Syed Masud Ahmed. 2005. *Micro Health Insurance (MHI) Pilot of BRAC: A Demand Side Study*. BRAC Research Report, Research and Evaluation Division. Dhaka: BRAC.

Melik, James. 2010. "Microcredit 'Death Trap' for Bangladesh's Poor." *BBC News*. November 3, (accessed August 21, 2013), http://www.bbc.com/news/business-11664632.

Morawczynski, Olga, and Mark Pickens. 2009. "Poor People Using Mobile Financial Services: Observations on Customer Usage and Impact from M-PESA." CGAP Brief, World Bank, Washington, DC.

Mujeri, Mustafa K. 2015. "Improving Access of the Poor to Financial Services." A Report Prepared for the General Economics Division of the Planning Commission to Serve as a Background Study for Preparing the 7th Five Year Plan (2016–2020) of Bangladesh.

Nasher, Md. Abu. 2011. *Rural Banking and Microfinance Agencies in Bangladesh: Operations and Achievements*. Dhaka: University of Dhaka.

Nawaz, Faraha. 2015. "Microfinance, Financial Literacy, and Household Power Configuration in Rural Bangladesh: An Empirical Study on Some Credit Borrowers." *Voluntas* 26: 1100–121.

Nessa, Tasqurun, Jamal Ali, and Roslan Abdul-Hakim. 2012. "The Impact of Microcredit Program on Women Empowerment: Evidence from Bangladesh." *OIDA International Journal of Sustainable Development* 3 (9): 11–20.

Omwansa, Tonny. 2009. "M-PESA: Progress and Prospects." *Innovations/Mobile World Congress 2009*: 107–23.

Osmani, S. R., M. A. Baqui Khalily, and Mehadi Hasan. 2016. "Dynamics of Overlapping in the Microcredit Sector of Bangladesh." Working Paper 51. Institute for Inclusive Finance and Development (InM), Dhaka.

Parvez, Jaheed, Ariful Islam, and Josh Woodard. 2015. *Mobile Financial Services in Bangladesh: A Survey of Current Services, Regulations, and Usage in Select USAID Projects*. USAID, mSTAR, fhi360.

Parvin, Lovely, Jia Jinrong, and M. Wakilur Rahman. 2012. "Women Entrepreneurship Development in Bangladesh: What are the Challenges Ahead?" *African Journal of Business Management* 6 (11): 3862–71.

Population and Development Review. 2017. "Identity Systems and Civil Registration in Asia." *Population and Development Review* 43 (1): 183–88.

Prina, Silvia. 2015. "Banking the Poor via Savings Accounts: Evidence from a Field Experiment." *Journal of Development Economics* 115: 16–31.

Rabbani, Golam, and Md. Solaiman Chowdhury. "Policies and Institutional Supports for Women Entrepreneurship Development in Bangladesh: Achievements and Challenges." *International Journal of Research in Business and Social Science* 2 (1): 31–39.

Razzaque, Mohammad A., and Sayema H. Bidisha. 2012. "Does Microfinance Promote Women's Empowerment? An Empirical Investigation." *Journal of Bangladesh Studies* Special Issue: Microfinance: 11–29.

Rhyne, Elisabeth. 2012. "Microfinance in Bangladesh: It's Not What You Thought." Huffington Post, February 10, 2012.

Schnabel, Jessica A., and John Philip Mcnally. 2017. "Banking on Women: Creating Value for Banks and Boosting Economic Growth." World Bank, Washington, DC.

Shrader, Leesa. 2015. "Digital Finance in Bangladesh: Where Are All the Women?" Washington, DC: Consultative Group to Assist the Poor. http://www.cgap.org/blog/digital-finance-bangladesh-where-are-all-women.

Singh, Sanjana, Radhika Asrani, and Anupama Ramaswamy. 2016. *Study on mapping the market potential and accelerating finance for women entrepreneurs in Bangladesh*. Washington, DC: World Bank.

Sinha, Tasnuba, and Catherine Highet. 2017. "Guide to Increasing Women's Financial Inclusion in Bangladesh through Digital Financial Services." USAID and FHI 360.

Sultana, Afiya. 2012. "Promoting Women's Entrepreneurship through SME: Growth and Development in the Context of Bangladesh." *Journal of Business and Management* 4 (1): 18–29.

Suri, Tavneet, and William Jack. 2016. "The Long-Run Poverty and Gender Impacts of Mobile Money." *Science* 354 (6317): 1288–92.

Thakur, Aakanksha, Samveet Sahoo, Prabir Barooah, Isvary Sivalingam, and Grace Njoroge. 2016. "Agency Banking: How Female Agents Make a Difference." *MicroSave—Financial Inclusion in Action: Read, Share, and Discuss*. MicroSave. (accessed February 16, 2018), http://blog.microsave.net/agency-banking-how-female-agents-make-a-difference/.

Wandibba, Simiyu, Stevie M. Nangendo, and Benson A. Mulemi. 2014. "Gender Empowerment and Access to Financial Services in Machakos County, Eastern Kenya." Institute for Money, Technology and Financial Inclusion, Irvine, CA.

Women's World Banking & Credit Suisse. 2013. *From Access to Inclusion: Educating Clients*. New York: Women's World Banking.

World Bank. 2016. *Identification for Development: Strategic Framework*. ID4D, Washington, DC: World Bank.

Yousif, Fatima, Elizabeth Berthe, Jacinta Maiyo, and Olga Morawczynski. 2013. *Best Practices in Mobile Microfinance*. Grameen Foundation and Institute for Money, Technology & Financial Inclusion, Grameen Foundation.

Zaman, Hassan. 2004a. "Microfinance in Bangladesh: Growth, Achievements, and Lessons." Paper prepared for the CGAP Conference, "Scaling Up Poverty Reduction: A Global Learning Process," Shanghai, May 25–27.

———. 2004b. "The Scaling-Up of Microfinance in Bangladesh: Determinants, Impact, and Lessons." World Bank Policy Research Working Paper 3398, World Bank, Washington, DC.

5 Female Entrepreneurship

ABSTRACT *Although Bangladesh has a massive microfinance industry and women's access to credit has expanded greatly, it continues to have among the lowest levels of women's formal sector entrepreneurial activity in the world. Female entrepreneurship has grown tremendously since the 1970s, yet female-run businesses tend to start and stay small, and they are concentrated in a few sectors. The government of Bangladesh has made a number of efforts to enable female entrepreneurship, including encouraging financial institutions to provide female entrepreneurs with at least 10 percent of all credit earmarked for the small and medium enterprise (SME) sector. Implementation of current policies and schemes to facilitate affordable credit for women entrepreneurs, however, remains weak and women entrepreneurs continue to face a number of financial and technical challenges in starting and running their businesses. In addition, patriarchal norms continue to discourage women's entrepreneurial efforts. Women's entrepreneurship, however, has enormous potential to empower Bangladeshi women. There is evidence from good practices that women's entrepreneurial options can be improved by providing childcare, improving business development skills, providing sufficient and flexible credit, and increasing women's networks and market access.*

This chapter analyzes the extent, trends, nature, barriers, and good practices related to women's entrepreneurship in Bangladesh. According to statistics from Bangladesh Bank reported by Eusuf et al. (2017), micro, small, and medium enterprises comprise almost the totality of businesses in Bangladesh. The analysis in this chapter focuses primarily on such enterprises or SMEs, as defined by the Bangladesh Bank (see below). We bring in analysis of entrepreneurship and women's enterprises more broadly where relevant. There is an enormous and growing literature on women's participation in and ownership of SMEs, including in Bangladesh. Reviewing this body of work is beyond the scope of this chapter, so we discuss highlights and supplement with data from our qualitative analysis across divisions of the country.

WHAT IS A SME?

There is little agreement, either in the academic literature or among donors, about how to define "small" and "medium" enterprises. Indicators that are used to define SMEs include loan size, number of employees, and business turnover, but indicators are likely to differ across organization, country, and time period (Greene et al. 2003; Tambunan 2009; UNESCAP 2005). As a whole, SMEs are viewed as filling the space between microenterprises, on the one hand, and large enterprises, on the other, and are assumed to face different constraints and enjoy different opportunities than these other types of enterprise (Gibson and van der Vaart 2008).

Each country's government has its own definition of SMEs, primarily based on number of employees. For example, a study in 2008 finds that SME definitions range from an enterprise with a maximum of 20 employees, as defined in Tanzania, to 300 employees in Vietnam. Countries as economically diverse as Norway, Nicaragua and Ghana all consider enterprises with up to 100 employees as SMEs (Gibson and van der Vaart 2008). Some definitions exclude the informal sector, which is a concern given the importance of informal entrepreneurship, especially for women (Ayyagari, Beck, and Demirguc-Kunt 2003; Beck et al. 2005).

Bangladesh Bank recently updated Bangladesh's definition of SMEs in line with the government's National Industrial Policy 2016. This new definition increases the size of both small and medium enterprises in terms of fixed asset value and employed manpower. The current definitions for cottage, micro, small, and medium enterprises (CMSME) are detailed in table 5.1. Most of the literature reviewed for this book, however, uses a prior definition of SMEs, as defined by Bangladesh Bank in 2010 (see, for example, Singh et al. 2016, 23). In the discussion that follows, therefore, SME definitions may vary by date and usage of the research cited. Moreover, despite the different definitions below, some Bangladesh Bank documents and other recent reviews of women's entrepreneurship in Bangladesh include micro enterprises within discussions of small

TABLE 5.1 Bangladesh Bank classification of SMEs as per National Industrial Policy, 2016

SECTOR	FIXED ASSETS EXCLUDING LAND AND BUILDINGS IN BDT '000 (USD '000)			EMPLOYEES			LOAN LIMIT IN BDT '000 (USD '000)		
	MICRO & COTTAGE[a]	SMALL	MEDIUM	MICRO & COTTAGE	SMALL	MEDIUM	MICRO & COTTAGE[c]	SMALL	MEDIUM
Manufacturing	1,000–7,500 (11.8–88.8)	7,500–150,000 (88.8–1,775)	150,000–500,000 (1,775–5,917)	15 max	31–120	121–300 (garments 1,000 min.)	10,000 (118.4)[b]	200,000 (2,366.8)	750,000 (8,875.4)
Services	<1,000 (<11.8)	1,000–20,000 (11.8–236.7)	20,000–300,000 (236.7–3,550.2)	15 max	16–50	51–120	2,500 (29.6)[b]	50,000 (591.7)	500,000 (5,917)
Trading	<1,000 (<11.8)[b]	1,000–20,000 (11.8–236.7)	—	15 max	16–50	—	2,500 (29.6)[b]	50,000 (591.7)	—

Source: The Daily Star 2017, with data from Bangladesh's Industrial Policy 2016.
Notes: BDT = Bangladeshi Taka.
a. <1,000 for cottage enterprises across sectors.
b. Microenterprises only.
c. 1,000 for cottage enterprises across sectors.

enterprises in the SME classification. Thus, in this book, as well, "small" enterprises may include microenterprises.

There is also no single definition of what constitutes a woman-owned business more broadly. The definition varies by organization and country (de Haan 2016). For instance, the OECD defines a woman-owned enterprise as one that has had a sole-proprietor woman at any time (OECD 2012). Here we use the definition outlined in Bangladesh Bank's report, "Small and Medium Enterprise (SME) Credit Policies and Programmes" (Bangladesh Bank 2010a), according to which, any woman engaged in a business in her name will be considered a woman entrepreneur. In addition, the report states that "...if a woman entrepreneur owns/possesses more than 50% shares of a business, it will be deemed as a business conducted by woman entrepreneur and will be entitled for facilities under special consideration" (Bangladesh Bank 2010a, 15).

The lack of clear definitions means that policy and schemes risk being devised based on inaccurate data and analysis. That the definition of entrepreneurship, different sizes of enterprises, and what constitutes "women's entrepreneurship" all differ across country and organization and shift over time within any one country makes it difficult to assess the number and size of women's enterprises accurately. When the definition changes over time, as it has in Bangladesh, it is difficult to assess whether increased prevalence reflects growth of women's entrepreneurship or is due to expanded definitions of enterprises and women's ownership of them. In Bangladesh, additionally, different governmental agencies may use differing definitions of SMEs, and thus provide varying data on the number of SMEs. This can hamper the adoption of a set of complementary policies to support women entrepreneurs (Raihan et al. 2016).

PATTERNS AND TRENDS OF WOMEN'S ENTREPRENEURSHIP

Prevalence and growth of women entrepreneurs and women's enterprises

Bangladesh has seen tremendous growth in women's enterprises since the 1970s. Women's enterprises grew in the 1970s, and exponentially so from the 1980s to the 2000s (Singh, Asrani, and Ramaswamy 2016). Bangladesh Bank data (Bangladesh Bank 2014) from 2009 to 2013 show a growth in structural capital and thus a shift from micro to small, and small to medium enterprises run by women (figure 5.1).

Globally, Bangladesh has among the lowest levels of women's entrepreneurial activity in the formal sectors of the economy, however. The most recently available Enterprise Survey data[1] indicate that only 1.7 percent of formal firms are majority owned by women, compared to regional and global averages of 9.6 and 14.5 percent. Using the same comparator countries as in chapter 4, India is at par with two-percent majority female ownership of formal firms; Indonesia and Vietnam fare better at 18.2 and 19.3 percent, respectively. One in three formal SMEs worldwide is owned by women, according to IFC data (de Haan 2016). Of the 77 countries in the Female Entrepreneurship Index[2] calculations for 2015, Bangladesh ranks 75th in terms of an environment that is conducive to development and growth of women-owned enterprises (Terjesen and Lloyd 2015).

Within Bangladesh, women's entrepreneurship forms only a small proportion of all entrepreneurial activity, and women's enterprises tend to stay small.

FIGURE 5.1

Changes in capital (BDT), 2009–13

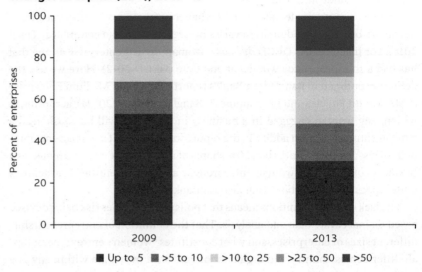

Source: Bangladesh Bank 2014.

Women own only 7.2 percent of formal-sector micro and SMEs in Bangladesh, according to Eusuf et al. (2017). Women's enterprises are also small: in 2013, about half had up to five employees, 39 percent had 5–10 employees, and a small minority were larger (Bangladesh Bank 2014). Among the women SME entrepreneurs recently surveyed by Eusuf et al. (2017) and Singh et al. (2016), most operated relatively small businesses. Women-owned SMEs have not been performing well on average, moreover: nearly one-fifth of the enterprises contacted by Singh et al. (2016) had closed, only a quarter of them were both owned and managed by women, and only 15 percent of the still-operating enterprises had taken any loans.

Women's businesses tend to be sectorally demarcated and concentrated in fewer sectors than is the case for men's businesses. An analysis of Enterprise Survey data by USAID in 2013, finds that whereas men-managed firms in Bangladesh exist in a large diversity of sectors, women-managed firms are significantly more concentrated in certain sectors, most particularly the relatively low-capital-intensive sectors, such as wholesale and garments (USAID 2014). More recent studies of women entrepreneurs or managers also find that women dominate in the wholesale and retail textile sector; at the other end of the spectrum, agricultural and food services sectors show the lowest concentration of women's SMEs (Eusuf et al. 2017; Singh, Asrani, and Ramaswamy 2016). In the Bangladeshi context, the sectors in which women predominate also are perceived by women in that sector to be female-dominated; women entrepreneurs perceive the sectors in which they have minimal presence to be male-dominated (box 5.1). These patterns are similar to global sectoral patterns for women's enterprises: an IFC study (2014) finds the largest concentration of women-owned SMEs globally to be in the retail and wholesale textile sector, while agriculture and food products are less likely to have women-owned SMEs.

Women's entrepreneurship is unevenly distributed across divisions. As of 2013, women-headed enterprises constituted a minority of formal and informal enterprises in all divisions (Bangladesh Bureau of Statistics Economic Census 2015). Chittagong had the highest proportion of enterprises headed by women,

BOX 5.1

Select characteristics of women-owned SMEs in Bangladesh

- 99 percent of SMEs are small, with 58 percent employing 1–5 workers[a]
- 80 percent have been operational for less than 6 years[a]
- Sole proprietorship ranges from 71 percent[a] to 85 percent[b] of surveyed enterprises; partnerships range from 15[b] to 28 percent[a]
- Of partnerships, most partners are male family members[a]
- The highest concentration of firms is in the wholesale and retail trade of textiles (23.8 percent). About half of the women whose SMEs fall in this sector consider this sector to be women-dominated[a]
- The lowest concentration of surveyed women-owned SMEs is in agro and food services, education, and "others" (about 5.7 percent in each)[a]
- Slightly less than half of women entrepreneurs surveyed have prior employment experience[a,b]

a. Eusuf et al. 2017.
b. Singh et al. 2016.

at 10 percent, while at the other end of the spectrum only a little over five percent of all enterprises in Sylhet and Rangpur were headed by women. Dhaka division had the largest proportion of women-headed enterprises in the country (32.5 percent), followed by Chittagong (17 percent). Barisal and Sylhet had the smallest, at 4.7 and 5 percent of women-headed enterprises, respectively. If one examines the distribution of women-headed enterprises by size of enterprise, however, the picture changes somewhat. Dhaka had the largest proportion of all women-headed enterprises that were cottage or microenterprises, while Rangpur had the largest proportion that were small or medium enterprises (figure 5.2). The Economic Census data for Bangladesh are especially valuable for research of gender gaps in entrepreneurship; unlike the Enterprise Survey data, Economic Census data include informal as well as formal firms. With the majority of Bangladeshi women-owned firms in the informal sector, the Census data allow for more accurate comparisons of women's entrepreneurship across divisions in Bangladesh, and even for comparing Bangladesh with other countries. The World Bank Group's South Asia Region has developed a spatial database that helps fill knowledge gaps about economic indicators, such as women's entrepreneurship (Li, Rama, Galdo, and Pinto 2015). Using the database, one can create maps that allow visual comparisons (of women-owned enterprise prevalence, for example) across countries and even within countries, at the division level. One such map (not pictured) suggests that shares of women-owned formal and informal enterprises in some of Bangladesh's eastern and southwestern divisions are on par with those of select East Asian countries, between 10 and 19 percent.

Recent research suggests that women entrepreneurs are younger and more educated than in past years; however, the precise age groups and education levels vary by study, since each study draws a different sample. For example, in Singh et al.'s (2016) survey of 500 women entrepreneurs across seven divisions of the country, 80 percent of their sample of women entrepreneurs was between 30 and 40 years old and a similar percentage were university graduates.

FIGURE 5.2

Distribution of women-headed enterprises by division and size, 2013

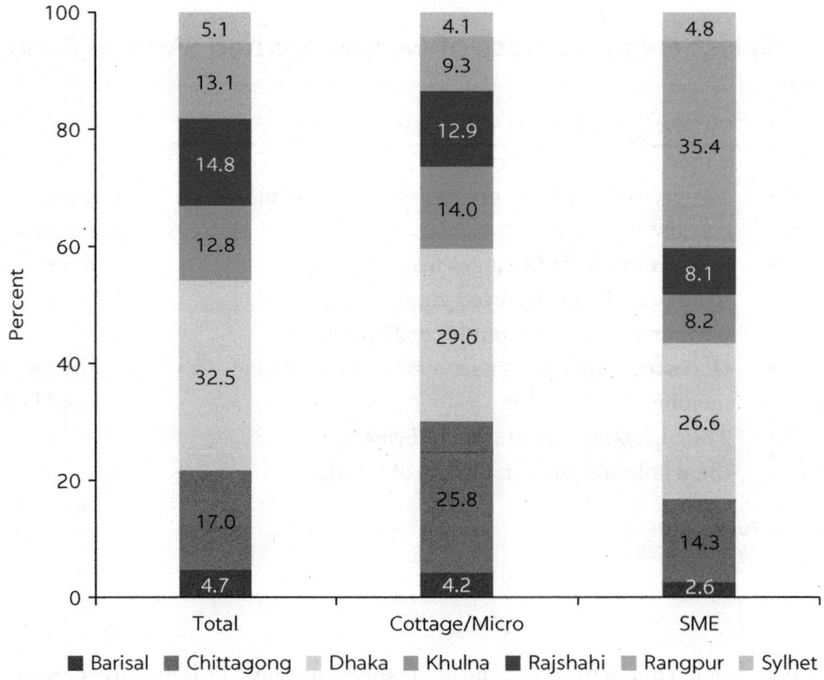

Source: World Bank calculations based on Bangladesh Bureau of Statistics 2015 data, cited in SME Foundation 2013.

Among the 300 women entrepreneurs from six divisions studied in Eusuf et al. (2017), a little more than half (56.2 percent) were between 20 and 35 years of age, and 41.3 percent had completed tertiary level education; the whole sample for this study had 12 years of schooling on average. In a 2010 survey of 400 branches of banks and NBFIs, Bangladesh Bank (2016) also finds that a little more than half (58 percent) of their sample of women owners of SMEs who had been provided credit had at least a high school degree.

The government of Bangladesh has been undertaking a range of initiatives targeted to SMEs and to women's SMEs in particular. In 2008, the Bangladeshi government established an SME Foundation with the following aims: to provide entrepreneurs with technical, capacity building and skills development services; to advocate for SME-friendly policies; to offer collateral-free loans; and to facilitate women's ownership and active participation in entrepreneurship (Bakht and Basher 2015). In 2010, for the first time in the history of the country's financial sector, a target-based program to lend to SMEs was initiated by Bangladesh Bank (Aziz and Siddique 2016). According to the National Industrial Policy 2016, banks in Bangladesh are now mandated to set aside 20 percent of their loans to SMEs, to be raised to 25 percent by 2021. At least 10 percent of this lending is earmarked for women's SME entrepreneurs, to be raised to 15 percent by 2021 (*The Daily Star* 2017). Furthermore, Bangladesh Bank has encouraged all banks and nonbank financial institutions (NBFI) to provide loans to women entrepreneurs at a 10-percent interest rate, which is about 8 percent lower than the market rate, and to establish a dedicated Women Entrepreneurs Desk (Raihan et al. 2016). Recent publications by Singh et al. (2016) and Eusuf et al. (2017) detail these and other measures. Box 5.2 summarizes some key policies.

Select government of Bangladesh policies and schemes for women's SMEs

- Women-led SMEs are to receive at least 10 percent of all credit earmarked for the SME sector[a]
- All banks and NBFIs are encouraged to provide loans at the lower-than-market interest rate of 10 percent[b]
- All banks and NBFIs are encouraged to establish dedicated Women Entrepreneurs Desks in the SME and Special Programmes Department,[b] with a lady officer officiating[c]
- Women-led SMEs are to be provided credit under initiatives, such as the Credit

- Guarantee Scheme, without requirements for collateral[a]
- Various government training institutions—such as the SME Foundation and the Bangladesh Industrial and Technical Assistance Center—are to provide training to women entrepreneurs on preparing and implementing business plans[a]
- A mechanism for women-friendly banking services is to be developed nationally, under the leadership of Bangladesh Bank[a]

a. Eusuf et al. 2017.
b. Raihan et al. 2016.
c. Bakht and Basher 2015.

Women entrepreneurs' access to finance

Singh et al. (2016) note that women entrepreneurs are growth oriented and use credit to expand their businesses, yet a minority is trained to manage these funds or enterprise growth. Nearly 75 percent of their surveyed women entrepreneurs sought credit to expand their businesses. Almost all banked with private banks, and the vast majority had some banking experience. According to data from Bangladesh Bank, by 2015 specialized banks and domestic private commercial banks were the largest sources of credit for women-owned SMEs (Singh, Asrani, and Ramaswamy 2016). At the same time, only a minority (36 percent) had undergone training to manage financial aspects of their business, and men managed the finances for two-thirds of the women's SMEs. The use of financial services, such as mobile banking, was also very limited, as was awareness of financial schemes (Singh, Asrani, and Ramaswamy 2016).

Though women entrepreneurs' access to credit has increased over time, disbursement to women entrepreneurs remains a fraction of credit disbursed to male entrepreneurs. In 2010, a little over 13,000 women-led SMEs were loaned USD 231 million by banks and other financial institutions. By 2015 there had been a dramatic increase: 188,233 women-led SMEs took loans of USD 543 million from banks and financial institutions (Eusuf et al. 2017). By this latter year, women entrepreneurs also constituted half of all women borrowers from MFIs. Statements of SME loan disbursements from the SME and Special Programmes Department of Bangladesh Bank (n.d.) show, however, that in every year between 2010 and 2017, women entrepreneurs received only about 3 percent of the total credit disbursed to cottage, micro, small and medium enterprises overall. Moreover, while the credit disbursed to male entrepreneurs exceeded the target amount in every year, credit disbursed to women entrepreneurs remained below-target each year. The largest amount disbursed to women entrepreneurs (relative to the amount targeted) was in 2015, when the financial sector as

TABLE 5.2 **Trends in credit disbursement by financial sector to CMSMEs, by sex of owner, 2010–17**

| YEAR | CUMULATIVE DISBURSEMENT OF THE YEAR | | | PERCENT OF TARGET DISBURSEMENT ACHIEVED | |
| | BDT (CRORES) | | | | |
	MALE ENTREPRENEURS	FEMALE ENTREPRENEURS	% OF TOTAL LENDING TO FEMALE ENTREPRENEURS	MALE ENTREPRENEURS	FEMALE ENTREPRENEURS
2010	51,739	1,805	3.4	147.9	46.5
2011	51,671	2,048	3.8	100.9	35.8
2012	67,529	2,224	3.2	122.8	55.4
2013	81,271	3,351	4.0	118.7	66.3
2014	96,971	3,939	3.9	117.7	59.1
2015	111,643	4,227	3.6	113.2	71.3
2016	136,590	5,346	3.8	Data not available	
2017	157,004	4,773	3.0		

Sources: Bangladesh Bank 2010b, 2011, 2012, 2013, 2014, 2015, 2016, 2017.
Notes: CMSME refers to the collection of cottage, micro, small, and medium enterprises. 1 crore BDT = 10 million BDT.

a whole disbursed about 71 percent of the target credit amount to women entrepreneurs (table 5.2).

The amount of loans disbursed to women entrepreneurs is also often insufficient for their financial needs, resulting in a financing or credit gap. Total financial need for an entrepreneurial venture includes finances required for working capital requirements estimated by a firm's receivables and payables, as well as finances needed for fixed capital requirements, such as replacement of assets (Singh, Asrani, and Ramaswamy 2016). A recent IFC (2014) survey provides estimates across regions of the average credit gap per formal SME by size of the SME and owner's sex. The survey found that South Asia was one of two world regions in which women-owned SMEs had a higher average credit gap than did men-owned SMEs. This was especially the case for small and very small enterprises, where the average gap in credit for women-owned enterprises was 28 percent higher than for those owned by men (International Finance Corporation 2014). Different studies from Bangladesh estimate varying degrees of the financing gap, making an accurate assessment difficult: the estimated financing gap for Singh et al.'s (2016) sample of women SME entrepreneurs is about 60 percent (i.e., 60 percent of women SME entrepreneurs' finance needs, regardless of SME size, are unfulfilled by banks or NBFIs), whereas Bangladesh Bank (2014) estimates a finance gap of 39.4 percent.

Gender-disaggregated data on SMEs' nonperforming assets are not available; thus, reliable data on trends in women entrepreneurs' loan repayment rates are lacking. Across several parts of the world, women entrepreneurs have high loan repayment rates; in Bangladesh, despite the lack of gender-disaggregated data on loan recovery for SMEs, Bangladesh Bank considers women entrepreneurs to have higher repayment rates than men entrepreneurs (Singh et al. 2016). Recent reports on loans to SMEs put women entrepreneurs' repayment rates at 93 percent and above (Bangladesh Bank 2014, 2016). Due to lack of gender-specific data, however, bankers do not have the requisite information; consequently, it is not surprising that credit providers have mixed beliefs regarding women's repayment rates relative to men's (Singh et al. 2016). Patriarchal attitudes that discredit women's entrepreneurial or financial capabilities—rather than hard data—thus could determine bankers' views of women's reliability on repayment.

Women's entrepreneurship and women's economic empowerment

Women's entrepreneurship is considered to have powerful potential to empower women, and women themselves seek to start businesses as a means of becoming financially independent. Almost half the Bangladeshi women entrepreneurs surveyed by Eusuf et al. (2017) started a business either to be economically empowered or to do "something independently" (p. 17). About one-third noted that their decision to be an entrepreneur and choice of business was influenced by prior family business experience, whereas other individuals or businesses inspired about 28 percent. Similarly, a little more than half (55 percent) of the women entrepreneurs surveyed by Bangladesh Bank (2014) reported being self-motivated to start their businesses to become financially independent, while a little under one-third (31.5 percent) were motivated by a family business.

Women entrepreneurs are also eager to expand their businesses, which in theory should boost their economic empowerment further. About three-quarters of the SME entrepreneurs surveyed by Singh et al. (2016) reported eagerness to expand. A higher 89 percent of those surveyed by Bangladesh Bank (2014) were eager to expand, while 82.7 percent of those sampled for a subsequent study by Bangladesh Bank (2016) prioritized the use of their profits into future business expansion. The care and other household roles that women have to perform whether or not they are entrepreneurs, however, can inhibit the growth potential of women's enterprises (de Haan 2016) because of the demands they place on women's time.

The effectiveness of entrepreneurship as a promoter of women's economic empowerment is likely to differ for women who become entrepreneurs from poverty and necessity compared to those who become entrepreneurs by choice. In some cases, women choose to start or grow an enterprise because they see a market or business opportunity, while in other cases women who turn to entrepreneurship—particularly of the micro and small variety—may do so out of necessity arising either from poverty constraints (Buvinić and O'Donnell 2016) or mobility constraints or both (Kabeer 2012). When women turn to self-employment as a "default option" (p. 27) or based on a "survivalist" (p. 25), or mobility-constraint motivation (Kabeer 2012) these businesses are less likely to grow and may have less empowerment potential.[3] On the other hand, for women pursuing entrepreneurship by design and choice, running a business may indeed be empowering, as illustrated by Nupur's story from qualitative data collected for this book (box 5.3).

The empowering potential of entrepreneurship for women depends also on several other factors, and, even putting aside motivation, research argues that women's enterprise development cannot by itself enhance women's empowerment. In fact, women entrepreneurs themselves may be gender-biased: one-quarter of formal-sector women entrepreneurs who participated in the 2013 Enterprise Survey felt that hiring women could cause disruption in the working environment. Nonetheless, women entrepreneurs are much less gender-biased than are men entrepreneurs, almost half of whom agreed with the same statement in the survey.[4]

In general, enterprise development for women can only enhance their empowerment if, in addition to increasing women's income and control over income, it addresses power relations in the household and society that disempower women (Mayoux 2001), as well as the many other barriers women entrepreneurs face from their households, communities and institutions (Buvinić and Furst-Nichols 2014). Next, we analyze such barriers.

BOX 5.3

Nupur's story

Nupur Begum[a] grew up in a poor family with three siblings in a minority area of Rangamati district. They lived on their father's income, but he died in an accident when Nupur was 13 years old. She and her siblings quit school and she started sewing to earn money, while her brothers worked in carpentry. Nupur was determined, however, to do better in life. She married a man of her choice, because of which her family disowned her. She and her husband moved to Dhaka. Nupur's husband was supportive of her aspirations and willingly paid for her to get training in manufacturing ladies' handbags. Acting on her suggestion, her husband set up a shop for handbags in Dhaka. Nupur started expanding her business: she bought three sewing machines and hired three local women to work for her. Now, she has a wholesale store for handbags and purses next to her husband's shop, and she supplies handbags to a showroom in Dhaka, as well. Her husband also aided her in raising the capital she needed to expand, and her business handles all stages of the value chain. Nupur and her husband save business profits in a bank, and Nupur also saves some independently in a local shamity (a local association or cooperative). Nupur believes that she is successful because of her determination, as well as her husband's support.

Source: Case study conducted for this book in 2016.
a. Not actual name.

BARRIERS TO WOMEN'S ENTREPRENEURSHIP

Both men and women consider lack of adequate infrastructure and political instability to be major barriers[5] to starting and/or running an enterprise. One-third of men and women formal-sector business owners interviewed for the 2013 Enterprise Survey reported that political instability was the biggest obstacle affecting the operation of their business (figure 5.3). About one-quarter of men and women business owners cited infrastructure problems, primarily with electricity, as another major obstacle. Surprising in light of other literature is the small—and equivalent—share of both men and women who cited access to finance as a barrier. This could be an artifact of the sample, however. Not surprisingly, women were more likely to cite lack of education as a barrier than were men, though this was not among the major reported barriers.

Bangladeshi women SME entrepreneurs, specifically, are dissatisfied with the debt ecosystem within which they seek credit. Three-quarters (76 percent) of those surveyed by Bangladesh Bank (2014) said they faced one or more problems in receiving their loans. Entrepreneurs in other surveys echo these sentiments: Singh et al. (2016) used an index developed by the IFC to gauge satisfaction among the 500 women SME entrepreneurs they surveyed. Bangladesh scored 46 on a 100-point scale of this index (where higher scores reflect greater satisfaction) and 39 for the process of getting loans from the financial system. These low scores did not vary much by division or industry, suggesting that women entrepreneurs in general perceived multiple barriers in accessing the financial system.

In fact, women who want to start a business face a chain of barriers (figure 5.4) that starts with patriarchal attitudes with which they must contend in the very decision to start a business, combined with often negative attitudes and poor implementation of government schemes at every step of the way.

FIGURE 5.3

Biggest reported obstacles to running an enterprise

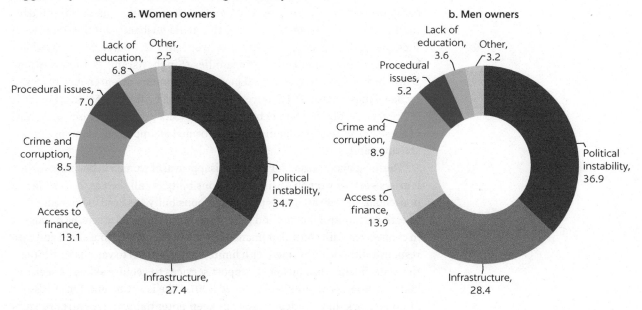

a. Women owners

b. Men owners

Source: World Bank calculations based on 2013 Enterprise Survey data.

FIGURE 5.4

Chain of barriers inhibiting women's entrepreneurship

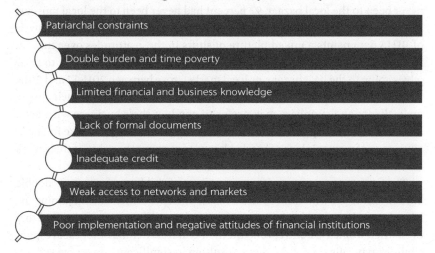

Barriers continue with financial, knowledge, and other constraints in getting started with a new business, and persist with lack of access to networks, markets and credit to grow their enterprises. Below we examine each of these in some detail.

The role of patriarchy and purdah

The evidence on the extent to which familial attitudes towards women's entrepreneurship are patriarchal and constraining for would-be entrepreneurs is mixed. For instance, women entrepreneurs interviewed in several studies reviewed by Ara and Hamid (2011) reported that family members, relatives, and neighbors advised them against starting a business, at least in part due to perceptions that having a woman engaged in business will reflect badly on her family. In a survey conducted in 2009, almost one-quarter (22.4 percent) of respondents noted that their husbands did not approve of them being an entrepreneur, but just over half (52.4 percent) reported not facing any opposition from their families (Singh, Asrani, and Ramaswamy 2016). More recently, close to 40 percent of women entrepreneurs surveyed by Bangladesh Bank (2014) were either inspired by family to start a business (7.7 percent) or by the family business itself (31.5 percent). Among one-third of these entrepreneurs, family support formed an important element of their starting capital.

The most likely reason for familial disapproval of women in business—when it arises—is that women's primary responsibility is still seen as focused in the household. In contrast, men's primary responsibility—as head of household—is to earn and control income and other household financial assets, as discussed in connection with control of financial assets in chapter 4. Household and care responsibilities leave women with limited time to travel to various institutions to obtain finance, use business support services to acquire skills, or seek out better customers or suppliers (Ahmed 2001). The isolation and time pressure of housework and childcare also can keep potential women entrepreneurs unaware of their products' market potential (Rahaman 2010). The institution of *purdah*, or enforced female seclusion, raises another barrier by limiting women's mobility and thus access to both credit and markets. Among women in rural Bangladesh surveyed by Anderson and Eswaran (2009), 93 percent had never been to the local bazaar, 92 percent had never been to the local mosque, and 68 percent left their residential compound at most once a week. Analysis of BIHS data paints a mixed picture of shifts in these attitudes over time, at least in rural areas. While the proportion of men who did not object to their wives going to the haat bazaar, or local market, rose between 2011–12 and 2015, the proportion who insisted on purdah also increased. Because of such norms, male clients and suppliers may prefer to conduct their business with men. Male middlemen, suppliers, contractors, and exporters may also take financial advantage of women's lack of market knowledge about the value of their work (Sultana 2012).

The focus on women as primary caretakers of children can create a "double burden" for those who want to also become entrepreneurs. As with joining the labor force (described in chapter 2), studies from different countries find that even when women are entrepreneurs, their childrearing and other care responsibilities typically do not decrease, resulting in significant "time poverty" for such women (Kabeer 2012, 16). A key consequence of this double burden is a tremendous increase in women's work if they decide to also start a business. Another consequence of having the primary (or sole) responsibility for childcare is that women may be confined to business activities that have minimal risks for children and that do not require much time, so that they can attend to children whenever needed; it also restricts their mobility (Dolan 2005). These constraints, in turn, limit the types, size, and location of women's enterprises, for example, by steering women toward home-based, informal activities that allow them the greater flexibility that their care responsibilities require. The likely consequent limited market and credit access can result in women's enterprises remaining concentrated in lower-value and lower-return activities (OECD 2006).

Low levels of financial literacy

Women borrowers' low levels of financial literacy, discussed in chapter 4, have implications for successful entrepreneurship, as well. Low financial literacy suggests that women are not aware of the range of financial products and schemes for their businesses, and it exacerbates their noncompetitiveness by diminishing their ability to maintain business and financial records (Rabbani and Chowdhury 2013).

A lack of awareness of laws, such as business registration, government policies, or programs designed to help them, constrains women entrepreneurs, particularly from entering the formal sector, which requires registration. For instance, Singh et al. (2016) finds that three-quarters (76 percent) of surveyed SME entrepreneurs were unaware of government or bank-related schemes to assist them in their entrepreneurial ventures. Such awareness varies by sector and across divisions: women SME owners engaged in trade of textiles and garments are most aware about financial assistance schemes (24 percent), while less than 10 percent of entrepreneurs in the agro-food processing and education industries are aware of loan schemes being offered by banks. Regionally, awareness of financial laws, programs and schemes is lowest in Barishal, Sylhet, and Khulna (Singh, Asrani, and Ramaswamy 2016). Bangladesh Bank (2016) finds also that women entrepreneurs often do not take advantage of the lower interest rate of 10 percent mandated for them, as they are not aware of this policy.[6]

Women also have limited awareness and understanding of specific procedures, such as loan application processes, and struggle to maintain documentation and records required for such procedures. Of the women entrepreneurs interviewed by Singh et al. (2016), 55 percent were unclear about loan processes. About one-quarter of them (29 percent) found it challenging to submit a completed loan application form. Respondents also stated that banks fail to provide all the information needed to make a full application. At the same time, a large proportion of women themselves were unable to maintain the paperwork needed in a business. Only 38.2 percent of women entrepreneurs interviewed by Bangladesh Bank (2014) reported maintaining a balance sheet. According to Singh et al. (2016), only 50 percent of women SME entrepreneurs generate regular financial statements, and three-quarters (77 percent) cite this task as a challenge. As a result, women may cede control and have husbands or other male relatives manage their businesses, which in turn feeds into the patriarchal norms of masculine and feminine roles. For instance, a majority (66 percent) of women entrepreneurs interviewed by Singh et al. (2016) left it to male members of their household to manage the financial aspects of their business, while an even larger proportion (81 percent) relied on them to evaluate financing options.

Limited financial literacy and resultant lack of records and documentation serve to increase financial institutions' reluctance to lend to women entrepreneurs. In the Singh et al. (2016) study, most bankers perceived women to have very poor financial literacy; this was not considered to be the case for men. Banks assume that women's lower financial literacy (compared to men) would increase loan processing costs because women would need more assistance in identifying appropriate financial products, developing their business plans and completing documentation requirements. Incomplete business records add to the problem: almost two-thirds (62 percent) of surveyed SME women owners perceived their lack of documentation as an additional reason for loan rejection (Singh, Asrani, and Ramaswamy 2016).

Limited business development knowledge, experience, and training

Few women specialize in nontraditional, but higher-earning fields of tertiary education, such as science, technology, and business (Rahaman 2010). In combination with limited financial literacy, this low level of education and skills can severely constrain women's entrepreneurial options. Of the entrepreneurs interviewed by Eusuf et al. (2017), 21 percent reported their lack of technical knowledge to be a major barrier to their successful engagement in business activities. Similarly, 45 percent of women entrepreneurs participating in another study started their businesses without any experience (Bangladesh Bank 2014).

Women also generally have fewer training opportunities than men, and the training that they do receive tends to reinforce traditionally female-oriented skills (Kabeer 2012), such as in garment and food production. In a 2014 study, Bangladeshi female entrepreneurs identified lack of training programs and technical support, as well as lack of managerial experience, as critical hurdles to starting their businesses (Afroze et al. 2014). In a more recent survey, 35 percent of respondents perceived the lack of training opportunities as a significant hurdle impeding their ability to start a business (Eusuf et al. 2017).

Similarly, women have limited access to—and are often unlikely to use—business development services. In some cases, shortage of manpower and resources among financial providers limits the provision of nonfinancial services, such as business development (Singh, Asrani, and Ramaswamy 2016); when business development services are provided, they are not structured to account for women's particular constraints with time, mobility, etc. Other institutions that do provide support services to female entrepreneurs, such as MFIs, may focus on women's rights rather than business development per se (Rabbani and Chowdhury 2013). Finally, even where training and skills development services are available, women tend not to use them. Huq and Moyeen (2008) suggest that this may be due to the generally mixed-gender nature of many learning programs, as well as their location, timing, or duration—all of which may be inimical for women's participation.

Inadequate credit

Notwithstanding the other issues cited by the Enterprise Survey's sample of firms (figure 5.3), problems in accessing timely, adequate credit and the consequent lack of financial capital are still among the largest barriers to women's entrepreneurship. Despite the increase in overall numbers of women SMEs accessing credit, formal financial institutions continue to lend miniscule portions to women-owned SMEs: between 2010 and 2014, loans to women-owned enterprises remained at 3–4 percent of total SME loan portfolios of formal financial institutions (Singh, Asrani, and Ramaswamy 2016). Even when women entrepreneurs do access credit, the amount is inadequate. Singh et al. (2016) estimate that, among their sample, almost two-thirds of women SME entrepreneurs' financing needs (60.2 percent) were unmet by banking or nonbanking financial institutions. Close to the same percentage of respondents in the survey of women entrepreneurs (58 percent) by Eusuf et al. (2017) said that lack of capital was their main constraint to starting a business, while 29 percent reported that access to credit was the limiting factor.

Micro and small enterprises—which make up the majority of women's enterprises—find it particularly difficult to get sufficient loans from banks. Among women SME owners surveyed by Singh et al. (2016), almost all enterprises were small; of those successful in accessing finance, one-third (36 percent) could not get adequate credit and two-thirds were unable to finance more than 75 percent of their business requirements. Efforts to mandate banks to provide credit to such enterprises—for example Bangladesh Bank mandated a lower interest rate of 9 percent for women's small and cottage industries (Mehedi and Sumon 2017)—may create problems; financial institutions may eschew lending to women altogether in favor of loaning to men at higher interest rates (Asian Development Bank 2015). The inability to access enough credit because of small business size creates a perverse circularity where a successful small business is then unable to grow larger, as illustrated by Monika's story from qualitative data collected for this book (box 5.4).

One reason for limited credit availability is women's lack of collateral in the form of assets owned by them, as detailed in chapter 3. A large 87.9 percent of female entrepreneurs in Bangladesh suffered from a lack of capital in 2009 (Ara and Hamid 2011). For rural women, the lack of ownership of physical assets—including land—means they have little or nothing that can be used as collateral for loans (*The Financial Express* 2012). About half (52 percent) of women SME entrepreneurs surveyed by Singh et al. (2016) reported independent access to collateral, primarily in the form of personal property; yet, over two-thirds (69 percent) faced challenges in meeting collateral requirements for loans. Further, despite smaller loan sizes and Bangladesh Bank guidelines that encourage banks to provide collateral-free loans up to 25 lakh BDT (USD 32,000) to women, about one-third (38 percent) of women owners of SMEs reported their loans being rejected because of inadequate collateral. The same study notes, however, that when collateral-free lending is available, women SME entrepreneurs benefit more (22 percent) than the SME sector overall, at 12 percent (Singh, Asrani, and Ramaswamy 2016).

Other procedures to access formal sources of credit, such as paperwork for bank account records and guarantees required for bank loans, are also a barrier

---

BOX 5.4

Monika's story

Monika[a] is a 34-year old Christian who lives in a village in Rajshahi district. The eldest of three, she went to school until grade 10, at which point she had to drop out to help her mother with housework. Monika was married at the age of 14, and now has four children. After her marriage, she worked as a paddy farmer, but it was too difficult for her to do this work and manage her household responsibilities. With her husband's encouragement, she decided to start a grocery shop near her house, which would also then enable her to fulfill her household responsibilities. She used the couple's savings, as well as an NGO loan her husband received to get started. The shop has remained smaller than she would like, however, and she is unable to get enough financial help to expand her business. Whatever savings they had they have since used in building their own house after their extended household split into separate units. At this point, Monika says the biggest barrier for her is the lack of capital with which to invest in the shop.

Source: Case study conducted for this book in 2016.
a. Not actual name.

to women accessing credit and may be more of a barrier than for men (Rabbani and Chowdhury 2013). The documentary requirements for accessing finance in Bangladesh are substantial and are not always made explicit by bankers (Choudhury and Raihan 2000). Identification, proof of domicile, and reference letters are often required to open a checking or savings account in Bangladesh, yet many people lack such documentation (Islam 2016). Utility bills may be required as proof for loan applications, which is a problem when these are in men's names rather than in women's or both partners' names. Many women also lack trade licenses. Even accessing collateral-free loans requires a long list of documents that women may or may not have, such as a nationality certificate, voter ID card or Tax Identification Number (TIN) (Hughes and Jennings 2012). Even with the paperwork and required collateral, securing a loan takes a large amount of time, as discussed in chapter 4.

Weak access to networks and markets

Access to markets to sell their products remains a major challenge for Bangladeshi women entrepreneurs. According to a 2009 Midas study, 21.3 percent of female entrepreneurs lacked good marketing opportunities (Ara and Hamid 2011). Especially in rural areas and for lower-income entrepreneurs there is a general lack of physical space to sell goods or services, for instance in the Local Haat Bazaars[7] at the upazila level, despite these bazaars having a committee tasked with mobilizing women's business promotion.[8] Where there is space, sufficient infrastructure is lacking, including women's bathrooms and security, which *de facto* limits women's market presence. Harassment of women in the marketplace is commonly reported, as well. This dearth of women's market facilities has led female entrepreneurs to often fail to get proper prices for their products from customers (*The Financial Express* 2012).

Limited information on appropriate markets is another problem for Bangladeshi women entrepreneurs. Women may be less aware of market potential for their products than are men because of their relative isolation in the home and limited time to search for markets after they have fulfilled their household responsibilities (Rahaman 2010). A combination of poor financial literacy, low levels of education and lack of time because of household work may also disallow women to increase their knowledge of markets: a 2008 Bangladesh Women Chamber of Commerce study shows that over 60 percent of women entrepreneurs did not conduct any form of feasibility study on markets or sectors prior to starting their business (Bangladesh Women Chamber of Commerce 2008). Middlemen, suppliers, contractors, and exporters are known to take advantage of women's isolation at home and lack of market knowledge about the value of their work, resulting in suppliers selling goods to women entrepreneurs for higher prices than their male counterparts and wholesalers buying goods from them at lower prices (Sultana 2012).

Women entrepreneurs also have weaker access than do men to peer, business or support networks that could help in starting or growing an enterprise. More relegated to the domestic domain than men, women entrepreneurs have weaker connections to organized business networks. Groups started by MFIs have played an active role in increasing women's access to at least peer mentors, as through Grameen Bank's programs. Although Bangladesh has several associations for women entrepreneurs, most women SME owners are not members and cannot benefit from such networking opportunities (Asian Development Bank 2015).

Implementation and attitudinal issues on the part of financial institutions

Though a host of policies and schemes are mandated to facilitate affordable credit for women entrepreneurs, implementation remains weak. For the most part, mechanisms are lacking to monitor activities of commercial banks and to evaluate the efforts of formal financial institutions in providing affordable, accessible finance for women entrepreneurs, creating an "accountability deficit" (Eusuf et al. 2017, 26). Moreover, although policies specify which governmental bodies are tasked with identifying and assisting women entrepreneurs, each one's specific role and how they are to liaise across organizations are not clearly defined. As a result, they often cannot help their target clients effectively (Eusuf et al. 2017).

Poor implementation manifests in multiple ways. Several women entrepreneurs surveyed by Bangladesh Bank (2014) reported not using the lower interest rate the government mandated for them, because the concerned commercial banks did not subscribe to this facility. Thus, the lower rate was not available for entrepreneurs seeking credit at these banks. Banks themselves may suffer delays and other procedural barriers in efforts to obtain Bangladesh Bank's sanction for particular financial schemes with women's SMEs; one example is Bangladesh Bank's refinance schemes for women entrepreneurs (Singh, Asrani, and Ramaswamy 2016). Yet another is the Women Entrepreneur Dedicated Desks, which are supposed to be established in all bank branches and headed by trained women to make credit provision more women-friendly. Recent assessments by Bangladesh Bank, however, noted that several of these were not led by women (Bangladesh Bank 2014); in other cases, they did not disburse funds to women entrepreneurs (Bangladesh Bank 2016).

Banks' negative and discriminatory attitudes towards women entrepreneurs seeking credit are also a problem. Almost three-quarters (71 percent) of the women SME entrepreneurs interviewed by Singh et al. (2016) reported being unhappy with their interactions with bank staff; in particular, the respondents pointed to bank staff's gender bias and indifference to women applicants' needs. Other studies also find that bank officials are not always helpful to women seeking credit for their entrepreneurial ventures (Bangladesh Bank 2014). It is possible that some of this lack of interest may stem not from gender discriminatory attitudes per se, but because of a shortage of manpower, lack of training, or limited resources for raising awareness about the specific needs of women-owned SMEs (Singh, Asrani, and Ramaswamy 2016). Yet, patriarchal attitudes are also at work: Singh et al. (2016) find that 85 percent of their entrepreneur respondents were required to provide a male signatory as part of their loan application.

GOOD PRACTICES AND RECOMMENDATIONS

Chapter 4 recommends good practices related to financial literacy and addressing negative and discriminatory attitudes of financial service providers, which are also relevant for women entrepreneurs. The examples below provide additional recommendations for good practices to address either women's entrepreneurship specifically, or women's entrepreneurship alongside financial inclusion.

Interventions or policies need to keep in mind that there is no one-size-fits-all solution to improve women's entrepreneurship. Rather, interventions need to be designed keeping in mind the characteristics of intended beneficiaries, the context, and the outcomes the intervention intends to impact. This is the conclusion arrived at by Cho and Honorati (2014) in their meta-analysis of more than 20 rigorously evaluated entrepreneurship programs across a range of countries, types of beneficiaries, and six different outcomes. At the same time, the analysis finds that, for women as a whole, the largest positive effects on a range of business improvement outcomes arise from providing credit, confirming other study findings that financing constraints are a key barrier for women's entrepreneurship. Figure 5.5 summarizes some other key findings from Cho and Honorati's (2014) analysis across evaluated interventions relevant for structuring entrepreneurship programs for women.

Interventions need to consider women's motivation to start or grow a business as that motivation matters for the success of efforts to improve business outcomes. In a review of evaluated interventions, Buvinić and O'Donnell (2016) note that women who became microentrepreneurs because they saw a market were more likely to benefit from programs (like credit) to improve business outcomes than women who went into micro enterprise work because of necessity. They suggest that this differential might reflect greater motivation, interest and entrepreneurial ability among women who choose to seize an opportunity. In contrast, for women who are "necessity" microentrepreneurs (Buvinić and O'Donnell 2016, 10), credit could play a different role, namely, allowing them

FIGURE 5.5

Recommended good practices to structure women's entrepreneurship programs

Interventions need to be customized

- Designed keeping in mind the outcomes of interest and the particular constraints most active for the target population
- Likely to work better if delivered by providers that know the local context and already have strong connections with the target population
- Engaging the private sector improves several business outcomes

What works in financial programs?

- Financial support seems more effective than other interventions to improve women entrepreneurs' business performance
- Longer time period is needed to measure success, as it may take time for the use of a loan or grant to yield benefits

What works in training programs?

- Vocational training offers the best chance of program success, especially if combined with counseling or financial services
- Business training is more effective than financial training
- Duration of training matters: optimal are intensive, short training, or substantially long training

Choice between financial and training programs depends on the context and outcomes of interest

- Overall, financial programs that also have a training component perform better than stand-alone financial programs on a range of business improvement outcomes
- Training-only programs improve business knowledge and practice
- Finance-only programs enhance business performance by easing credit constraints

It is important to give interventions time to mature

- Program effects measured over a longer time period are stronger than those measured over a shorter period
- In the short term, an intervention can more easily change business knowledge and practice, but not behavior or income

Source: Based on information from Cho and Honorati 2014.

greater financial flexibility to find the wage or other work they may prefer. Of course, there is also always a question of some level of selection bias in that women who choose to seize a market opportunity may be more knowledgeable, entrepreneurial, skilled or otherwise suited to entrepreneurship in ways that affect success ex ante (Kabeer 2012). When it comes to market opportunity, regional integration and cross-border trade could open new opportunities for female entrepreneurs (box 5.5).

BOX 5.5

Cross-border trade and women's economic empowerment

Women play an important role in Bangladesh's trade value chains, but their direct involvement in trade continues to be far below its potential. For example, women account for a large share of workers in the apparel and textile sectors (the two sectors with the highest export value in Bangladesh). Women entrepreneurs participate heavily in these sectors: 28 percent of female entrepreneurs are in the clothing and accessories sectors, while 13 percent of female entrepreneurs are owners of knitwear and ready-made garments businesses. Less than two percent of all formal firms are owned by women, however. More importantly, women-owned firms are far less likely than men-owned firms to be directly involved in overseas trade. One of the reasons for this is that female-owned firms are smaller than male-owned firms, and thus are unable to capture export opportunities to the same extent as their male counterparts (Sultan, Alam, and Nora 2018).

At the grassroots level, cross-border trade could offer great opportunities for women entrepreneurs. A recent study on the newly developed border haats (border markets) along the India-Bangladesh border suggests that, despite the small trade volumes involved, this type of trade can play an important role in fostering female entrepreneurship (Kathuria 2018). At the Meghalaya State-Bangladesh border haat, for example, women are engaged as entrepreneurs, as well as buyers who sell the purchased products subsequently in their respective communities. The proactive efforts of local institutions have been crucial in promoting women's participation at this border haat. More specifically, a deliberate decision by the border haat committee in Balat, Meghalaya, India, to distribute 12 of 25 vendor cards to women resulted in women making up one-half of all vendors and buyers. In contrast, at Kalaichar, another border haat in the same state where

vendor cards were not distributed to women, women's participation is not as strong, despite a similar cultural context. The initiative in Balat, Meghalaya is being replicated in Feni, Bangladesh.

Constraints on female traders at border haats include negative gender norms, poor infrastructure, and cumbersome permit procedures. First, sociocultural norms undermine the participation of some groups of women. In Tripura, for example, Hindu Bengali women are expected to play a traditional role, as are Muslim Bengalis on the other side of the border. On the other hand, women from the Chittagong Hill Tracts in Bangladesh, and Meghalaya in India, find greater opportunities in entrepreneurial roles.

Second, poor infrastructure deters women's participation (in trade, work, or entrepreneurship in general). For example, the absence of functioning toilets and other facilities is a major constraint for women on both sides of the border. The lack of public transport also affects women more adversely than it does men, as they are more likely to rely on public transportation than men. Finally, cumbersome trade procedures and requirements to obtain permits affect poor women disproportionately. Even after obtaining permits, women traders face difficulties in maintaining vendor cards due to the lack of capital investment and the small size of their businesses.

The benefits of cross-border trade for women extend beyond financial transactions. The border haat study reveals that cross-border exchange between people and communities may have changed attitudes toward women's economic roles. Upon seeing substantial participation of women traders in Baliamari haat, Meghalaya, men and women interviewed for the study remarked that they have a greater understanding and realization of women's economic potential.

Sources: Kathuria 2018; Sultan, Alam, and Nora 2018.

Programs and policies also need to consider the entrepreneurial ability of target groups, as this ability can influence women's success as entrepreneurs. For instance, interventions or policies seeking to introduce improved business practices need to consider whether or not women entrepreneurs are willing and able to adopt proposed new processes and practices required to grow a business. Calderon et al. (2013) test the importance of women's entrepreneurial ability in their randomized control experimental analysis of a business development training program in rural Mexico. They hypothesize that participating entrepreneurs' decisions on whether to adopt the new practices taught in the program would at least in part be influenced by their ability, measured here by pre-intervention profits. They find that women with lower ability are more likely to quit their entrepreneurial ventures after the training than are other women, and that those with the "best" abilities derived the greatest benefits.

In addition to the above recommendations on how to structure entrepreneurship programs, several good practices from Bangladesh and elsewhere provide evidence on how to address specific barriers to entrepreneurship faced by Bangladeshi women. Chapter 4 describes several studies that address barriers to financial inclusion, including interventions that tackle patriarchal norms; improve financial literacy; and address providers' gender-biased attitudes. Discussed below are good practices to improve women's entrepreneurial options by providing childcare, improving business development skills, providing sufficient and flexible credit, and increasing women's networks and market access.

Address constraints arising from patriarchal norms

The same societal patriarchal constraints underlie all aspects of women's economic engagement, and thus the same kinds of interventions already discussed for other aspects are likely also to benefit women's entrepreneurship. Among these, programs that increase women's mobility, access and control of financial resources, and financial security through ownership of physical assets are likely to be particularly effective: increased mobility can allow women more freedom to explore different markets, while increased financial flexibility gives entrepreneurs the space in which to grow and expand.

In addition, providing childcare services can aid women entrepreneurs in managing the double burden of care responsibilities and entrepreneurship. Chapter 2 discusses the importance of childcare to increase female labor force participation. Affordable childcare can have a similarly salubrious effect on women's ability to become entrepreneurs or grow their enterprises. An evaluation of the universal child care program in China (Wang 2015) shows that use of the program, which households consider affordable, is associated with increased numbers of women entrepreneurs. Unfortunately this evaluation does not examine which specific aspects of the childcare program were more or less strongly associated with the observed beneficial impact.

Improve business development knowledge, experience, and training

Two main features of programs and policies are important for developing business training: (1) training needs to be of long duration to have an impact; and (2) among the different aspects of training, improving business practices appears to be key. Below we discuss good practices to address both issues.

High-quality business development training needs to be relatively long in duration to improve the performance of women-owned businesses, according to a review of interventions by Buvinić and O'Donnell (2016). A randomized control trial in Mexico of women entrepreneurs who received no other input (i.e., no other targeted credit or microfinance activities) manages to disentangle the effect of business training from those of other inputs. The authors (Calderon, Cunha, and De Giorgi 2013) find that in-class training indeed contributes to increased profits, revenue, and number of clients for participating women. They credit the program's success to the unusually long length of the training course, with 48 hours of in-class time over 6 weeks. Similarly, Valdivia's (2015) intervention study in Peru was implemented over 36 three-hour group sessions delivered three times a week; the author emphasizes the importance of the program's intensity. In contrast, several shorter-duration programs in multiple countries see no positive effect on women-owned businesses (Buvinić and O'Donnell 2016; Valdivia 2015). This difference may at least in part arise because shorter training programs are not as effective as longer ones in offsetting deep-seated patriarchal constraints women face in engaging in productive economic activity, as Giné and Mansuri (2014) posit for their experiment in Pakistan.

Among the range of inputs business development training provides, improving business practices is considered critical to improving outcomes for women entrepreneurs. Calderon et al. (2013) posit that the main contributions to the success of their business training intervention likely were women's improved and increased use of formal accounting practices and registration with the government. Valdivia (2015) finds that those who received general business training perform as well over a two-year period following the intervention as do participants who additionally received technical education with individual counseling. He concluded that "managerial capital" (p. 26) is often more critical to improve than is technical knowledge. In their review of business practice and performance of micro and small firms between 2008 and 2014, almost half of which were women-owned, McKenzie and Woodruff (2016) also find that improving business practices (akin to "managerial capital") is paramount to improving performance.

Provide sufficient credit to entrepreneurs

In addition to the good practices recommended in chapter 4, providing flexible credit to women entrepreneurs is critical to improving their business performance and earnings, as it encourages more financial risk-taking, Buvinić and O'Donnell (2016) find in their review of credit programs for women entrepreneurs. For instance, a field experiment in India by Field et al. (2013) tested whether the typical MFI model of inflexible, short replacement times for loans actually inhibited entrepreneurship among poor, urban women in Kolkata, compared to flexible replacement rules. Their analysis reveals that microfinance clients who receive the flexible grace period terms to repay their loans are more than twice as likely to start a new enterprise as are clients with the regular contract and, nearly three years later, continue to report significantly higher profit and capital increases. The authors speculate that this might reflect clients' greater willingness to experiment with flexible loans, compared to loans with a strict repayment guideline. This may be at least in part because inflexible loans, particularly those with short recovery times, do not lend themselves to experimentation. In fact, as described in chapter 4, such inflexible, short-recovery loans may not be used for entrepreneurial purposes at all.

Addressing procedural costs is also important. A range of global examples provides good practices on how to address costs arising from lack of a credit history (such as among first-time women entrepreneurs), for instance. One experiment uses alternative means of credit testing that do not require traditional credit-related documentation, such as a psychometric credit tool developed and tested in Peru by Arráiz et al. (2015). Their pilot evaluation compares repayment behavior of different groups of creditors whose creditworthiness had been measured using different methods, including the psychometric application. When combined with traditional credit-scoring methods, they find this tool was effective in identifying risky entrepreneurs among a financial institution's existing clients. The study also reveals that this tool works as an alternate mechanism to providing credit to unbanked entrepreneurs who may be rejected by traditional credit-scoring methods, and without increasing default rates. As such, it could be tested in the Bangladeshi context for women and specifically rural women without a formal credit history.

Providing microcredit alone may, however, be insufficient to boost women's business productivity; rather, it needs to be accompanied by a bundle of other activities and services for women entrepreneurs. In a panel analysis of 20 years of microfinance in Bangladesh, Khandker and Samad (2014) find that over time, the income-generating potential of microcredit diminishes. In the case of their study population, most of the credit was given to entrepreneurs in the trading sector, and the authors suggest that market saturation creates diminishing returns. To be productive over the long run, credit needs to be accompanied by other efforts to overcome market saturation, such as skills training and market diversification.

Address the paucity of networks and markets

The Bangladesh Women's Chambers of Commerce and Industry (BWCCI) is a promising avenue to increasing Bangladeshi women entrepreneurs' professional networks and markets. Established in 2001, the BWCCI[9] was the first chamber of commerce to focus on women in Bangladesh. Since then, Women's Chambers have been established at the district level in multiple districts. Although we were unable to find any exhaustive evaluation, documentation from the Asian Development Bank (ADB) and the Center for International Private Enterprise, which have partnered with the BWCCI, conveys its potential to address various advocacy and networking barriers. Because of its growing membership of over 3,500 women and its scope across the country, BWCCI has engaged in strong advocacy with the government on the institution and implementation of a number of reforms for its members (Schleifer and Nakagaki 2014; Nakagaki 2013). Moreover, through membership in the national and divisional Chambers, women entrepreneurs have formed a mutual support group for personal, social, and business networking (Asian Development Bank 2015; Eusuf et al. 2017). A recent assessment notes that, to reach its potential, BWCCI, along with its divisional branches, still requires much capacity building and support (Eusuf et al. 2017).

Studies find that including role models, mentors and networking opportunities in other interventions can enhance their effect on outcomes for women entrepreneurs. Such networks provide social support, as well as sources of information, although it is admittedly difficult to isolate the effect of the mentorship or peer activities from the rest of the intervention activities that they complement (Buvinić and O'Donnell 2016). Field et al. (2016) in India posit that bringing a friend to classroom-based financial literacy and business skills training can create a more supportive environment for a woman entrepreneur, increase her social network during and after the training, or, conversely, increase the competitive pressure to perform well; in either case, business training with friends is found to be more effective than without in their experiment, though the authors are unable to unequivocally isolate how exactly peer effects operate.

Policy makers and programmers can additionally explore the use of microfranchising to address market barriers, especially for very poor women entrepreneurs, as it connects them directly to companies and their markets. Microfranchising can be defined as a business model that combines a product or service with social value (for instance, nutrition or hygiene) with a business opportunity to sell these products (de Haan 2016). A distinctive feature of this approach is its multisectoral nature, since it is typically a collaboration between multinational companies, "market facilitators," such as large nonprofits (de Haan 2016, 19), and MFIs to provide appropriate financial services to participants. A case-study evaluation of such a program in India called Shakti, run by Hindustan Unilever in partnership with CARE, finds that women microfranchisees' income tripled; some who were shopkeepers prior to joining the Shakti program saw their profits double (Thekkudan and Tandon 2009). According to the case study, most participants were happy to be part of the project and found increased status and self-confidence because of their increased earnings. A case study of a similar program, JITA, in Bangladesh, finds that participating saleswomen's incomes more than tripled between 2005 when the program started and 2008 (McKague and Tinsley 2012). More rigorous evaluation studies are needed to unequivocally determine impacts, however.

DATA GAPS

The data gaps related to financial inclusion that are identified in chapter 4 in areas such as credit, financial literacy, and service provision are important to address in encouraging women's entrepreneurship in Bangladesh. In addition to these, there are data gaps specific to understanding the situation facing the country's female entrepreneurs—particularly those who are operating in the informal sector.

The lack of a commonly agreed-upon definition of SMEs throughout the country is a problem, as it makes it impossible to estimate the trends and progress of SMEs, including women's SMEs. Similarly, the lack of clarity on what constitutes a "woman-owned" or "woman-managed" SME is problematic.

There are no reliable national statistics on the prevalence, characteristics, sectoral or geographic spread of women's SMEs. All studies reviewed comprise samples of SMEs, and several do not specify whether they are focused on enterprises in the formal, informal, or both sectors. What is needed is a national accounting of the number, scale, scope, sectoral and geographic distribution of women's SMEs—similar to the case for women's labor force participation (LFP) or use of formal financial institutions—so that policy making can be better targeted.

In Bangladesh and elsewhere there are myriad programs to provide entrepreneurship services or training or funds to women entrepreneurs; however, rigorous evaluations are limited. Most programs are not evaluated, in particular training programs for either financial literacy or business development training. This makes it difficult to isolate what it is about such training that does or does not work. The least evaluated perhaps are programs that seek to encourage mentorship or role models. Overall, however, more rigorous evaluation and documentation is necessary to isolate which aspects of good practices are most critical, and how these can be replicated or scaled up successfully.

NOTES

1. http://www.enterprisesurveys.org/data/exploretopics/gender. The Enterprise Survey includes only firms in the formal sectors of the economy.
2. Produced by the Global Entrepreneurship and Development Institute, the Female Entrepreneurship Index compiles data from the Global Entrepreneurship Monitor database, and is a normalized, weighted index based on a series of criteria and conditions that are considered important for women's entrepreneurship to thrive. Rankings are based on the value of the index. See Terjesen and Lloyd (2015), appendix B for more details.
3. Also possible is a selection process wherein women motivated by choice to invest in and grow an enterprise are ex ante more empowered and less poor than women who do so by necessity (Kabeer 2012).
4. Analysis based on data from the 2013 Enterprise Survey.
5. Barriers discussed here are in addition to the barriers women face in accessing finance (see chapter 4).
6. In contrast, almost all of the different sample of women entrepreneurs responding to an earlier survey by Bangladesh Bank (2014) reported that they knew all terms and conditions of loans available to them. This difference between the two Bangladesh Bank studies may be an artifact of the samples picked for each; however, it is not possible to verify this.
7. The local marketplace.
8. This finding comes from the World Bank's Nordic Trust Fund (NTF) Gender, Social Protection, and Human Rights Project in Bangladesh, which funded various activities in 9 villages in Dinajpur and Rangpur to complement existing efforts towards local women's economic empowerment.
9. http://www.bwcci-bd.org/.

REFERENCES

Asian Development Bank. 2015. *Bangladesh Quarterly Economic Update, March-June 2015.* Mandaluyong City, Philippines: Asian Development Bank, 2015.

Ahmed, Nilufer Karim. 2001. "Jobs, Gender and Small Enterprises in Bangladesh: Factors Affecting Women Entrepreneurs in Small and Cottage Industries in Bangladesh." SEED Working Paper 14, Series on Women's Entrepreneurship Development and Gender in Enterprises—WEDGE, International Labour Organization, Geneva and Dhaka: International Labour Organization.

Afroze, Tania, Md. Kashrul Alam, Eliza Akther, and Nahid Sultana Jui. 2014. "Women Entrepreneurs in Bangladesh: Challenges and Determining Factors." *Journal of Business and Technology (Dhaka)* IX (2): 27–41.

Anderson, Siwan, and Mukesh Eswaran. 2009. "What Determines Female Autonomy? Evidence from Bangladesh." *Journal of Development Economics* 90 (2): 179–91.

Ara, Jinnat, and Syed Abdul Hamid. 2011. "Against the Odds." D+C Development and Cooperation, German Federal Ministry for Economic Cooperation and Development publication.

Arráiz, Irani, Miriam Bruhn, and Rodolfo Stucchi. 2015. "Psychometrics as a Tool to Improve Screening and Access to Credit." Working Paper Series No. IDB-WP-625, Office of the

Multilateral Investment Fund, Inter-American Development Bank, Washington, DC: Inter-American Development Bank.

Ayyagari, Meghana, Thorsten Beck, and Asli Demirguc-Kunt. 2003. "Small and Medium Enterprises across the Globe: A New Database." Policy Research Working Paper No. 3127, World Bank, Washington, DC.

Aziz, Tarek, and Md. Nur-E-Alom Siddique. 2016. "The Role of Bangladesh Bank in Promoting SMEs' Access to Finance in Bangladesh." *International Journal of SME Development* 2: 103–18.

Bakht, Zaid, and Abul Basher. 2015. *Strategy for Development of the SME Sector in Bangladesh.* Dhaka: Bangladesh Institute of Development Studies.

Bangladesh Bank. 2010a. *Small and Medium Enterprise (SME) Credit Policies & Programmes.* Dhaka: Bangladesh Bank.

——. 2010b. *Bank Categorywise Quarterly SME Loan Statement as on 31.12.2010.* Dhaka: Bangladesh Bank.

——. 2011. *Bank Categorywise Quarterly SME Loan Statement as on 31.12.2011.* Dhaka: Bangladesh Bank.

——. 2012. *Bank Categorywise Quarterly SME Loan Statement as on 31.12.2012.* Dhaka: Bangladesh Bank.

——. 2013. *Bank Categorywise Quarterly SME Loan Statement as on 31.12.2013.* Dhaka: Bangladesh Bank.

——. 2014. *Quarterly SME Loan Statement as on 31.12.2014.* Dhaka: Bangladesh Bank, 2014.

——. 2015. *Bank Categorywise Quarterly SME Loan Statement as on 31.12.2015.* Dhaka: Bangladesh Bank.

——. 2016. *Bank Categorywise Quarterly SME Loan Statement as on 31.12.2016.* Dhaka: Bangladesh Bank.

——. 2017. *Prudential Guidelines for Agent Banking Operation in Bangladesh.* Dhaka: Bangladesh Bank.

Bangladesh Bureau of Statistics. 2015. *Population and Housing Census 2013, Report of Economic Census 2013, Abridged Form.* Statistics and Informatics Division, Ministry of Planning, Dhaka: Bangladesh Bureau of Statistics.

Bangladesh Women Chamber of Commerce and Industry. 2008. *Building Women in Business: A Situation Analysis of Women Entrepreneurs in Bangladesh.* Dhaka: BWCCI.

Beck, Thorsten, Asli Demirguc-Kunt, and Ross Levine. 2005. "SMEs,Growth, and Poverty: Cross-Country Evidence." *Journal of Economic Growth* 10 (3): 197–227.

Buvinić, Mayra, and Rebecca Furst-Nichols. 2014. "Promoting Women's Economic Empowerment: What Works?" Policy Research Working Paper 7087, World Bank, Washington, DC.

Buvinić, Mayra, and Megan O'Donnell. 2016. *Revisiting What Works: Women, Economic Empowerment and Smart Design.* Center for Global Development, Washington, DC.

Calderon, Gabriela, Jesse M. Cunha, and Giacomo De Giorgi. 2013. "Business Literacy and Development: Evidence from a Randomized Controlled Trial in Rural Mexico." NBER Working Paper 19740, National Bureau of Economic Research, Cambridge.

The Daily Star. "BB Updates SME Terms." July 3, 2017.

de Haan, Arjan. 2016. *Enhancing the Productivity of Women-Owned Enterprises: The Evidence on What Works, and a Research Agenda.* Canada: International Development Research Centre.

Dolan, Catherine. 2005. *Gender and Pro-Poor Growth: Tools & Key Issues for Development Specialists.* Washington, DC: USAID.

Eusuf, M. Abu, Asif Mohammad Shahan, Md. Abdul Khaleque, and Ebney Ayaj Rana. 2017. *The Shared Roles of the Central Bank, Commercial Banks and Women Chambers in Promoting Innovative Financing Models for Women-Led SMEs.* Center on Budget and Policy, The Asia Foundation.

Field, Erica, Rohini Pande, John Papp, and Natalia Rigol. 2013. "Does the Classic Microfinance Model Discourage Entrepreneurship among the Poor? Experimental Evidence from India." *American Economic Review* 103 (6): 2196–2226.

The Financial Express. "Financial Inclusions Scales New Peak—Farmers Figure Prominently in Opening Bank Accounts." August 12, 2012.

Gibson, Tom, and H. J. van der Vaart. 2008. "Defining SMEs: A Less Imperfect Way of Defining Small and Medium Enterprises in Developing Countries." The Brookings Institute, Washington, DC.

Giné, Xavier, and Ghazala Mansuri. 2014. "Money or Ideas? A Field Experiment on Constraints to Entrepreneurship in Rural Pakistan." Policy Research Working Paper 6959, World Bank, Washington, DC.

Greene, Patricia G., Myra M. Hart, Elizabeth J. Gatewood, Candida G. Brush, Nancy M. Carter. 2003. "Women Entrepreneurs: Moving Front and Center: An Overview of Research and Theory." *Coleman White Paper Series* 3 (1): 1–47.

Hughes, Karen D., and Jennifer E. Jennings. 2012. *Global Women's Entrepreneurship Research: Diverse Settings, Questions, and Approaches.* Cheltenham: Edward Elgar Publishing.

Huq, Afreen, and AFM Abdul Moyeen. 2008. "Addressing Gender in Enterprise Development Programs: Current Practices and a Proposed Approach." Presented at the 2008 International Council for Small Business World Conference, June 22–25, 2008, Halifax, Canada.

International Finance Corporation. 2014. *Women-Owned SMEs: A Business Opportunity for Financial Institutions—A Market and Credit Gap Assessment and IFC's Portfolio Gender Baseline.* Washington, DC: International Finance Corporation.

Kabeer, Naila. 2012. "Women's Economic Empowerment and Inclusive Growth: Labour Markets and Enterprise Development." Discussion Paper 29/12, School of Oriental and African Studies, University of London, London.

Kathuria, Sanjay, ed. 2018. *A Glass Half Full: The Promise of Regional Trade in South Asia.* South Asia Development Forum. Washington, DC: World Bank.

Khandker, Shahidur R., and Hussain A. Samad. 2014. "Dynamic Effects of Microcredit in Bangladesh." World Bank Policy Research Working Paper 6821, World Bank, Washington, DC.

Li, Yue, Martin Rama, Virgilio Galdo, and Maria Florencia Pinto. 2015. "A Spatial Database for South Asia." World Bank, Washington, DC.

Mayoux, Linda. 2001. *Poverty Elimination and the Empowerment of Women.* Geneva: International Labour Organization.

McKague, Kevin, and Sarah Tinsley. 2012. "Bangladesh's Rural Sales Program: Towards a Scalable Rural Sales Agent Model for Distributing Socially Beneficial Goods to the Poor." *Social Enterprise Journal* 8 (2): 16–30.

McKenzie, David, and Christopher Woodruff. 2016. "Business Practices in Small Firms in Developing Countries." *Management Science* 63 (9): 2967–81.

Mehedi, Fakhruddin, and R. H. Sumon. 2017. "9% Interest on Loan for Business Women." *The Asian Age,* April 5.

Nakagaki, Maiko. 2013. "Closing the Implementation Gap for Women Entrepreneurs in Bangladesh." *CIPE Blog.* September 30.

OECD (Organisation for Economic Co-operation and Development). 2006. "Enhancing Women's Market Access and Promoting Pro-poor Growth." In *Promoting Pro-Poor Growth: Policy Guidance for Donors,* edited by OECD, 111–20. Paris: OECD Publishing.

———. 2012. *Entrepreneurship at a Glance 2012.* OECD-Eurostat Entrepreneurship Indicators Programme, Paris: OECD Publishing.

Parvin, Lovely, Jia Jinrong, and M. Wakilur Rahman. 2012. "Women Entrepreneurship Development in Bangladesh: What Are the Challenges Ahead?" *African Journal of Business Management* 6 (11): 3862–71.

Rabbani, Golam, and Md. Solaiman Chowdhury. 2013. "Policies and Institutional Supports for Women Entrepreneurship Development in Bangladesh: Achievements and Challenges." *International Journal of Research in Business and Social Science* 2 (1): 31–39.

Rahaman, Md. Mojibur. 2010. "Barriers of Women Entrepreneurs in Bangladesh." BRAC University.

Raihan, Selim, Bazlul Haque Khondker, Shaquib Quoreshi, and Abdur Rahim. 2016. *Trade Winds of Change—Women Entrepreneurs on The Rise in South Asia: Background Country*

Study—Bangladesh. UNDP Regional Bureau for Asia and the Pacific, Bangkok Regional Hub. Bangkok: UNDP.

Schleifer, Marc, and Maiko Nakagaki. 2014. "Supporting the Bangladesh Women's Chamber of Commerce and Industry: Organizational Transformation and Policy Advocacy." *Public-Private Dialogue*. CIPE. October 30.

Singh, Sanjana, Radhika Asrani, and Anupama Ramaswamy. 2016. *Study on Mapping the Market Potential and Accelerating Finance for Women Entrepreneurs in Bangladesh*. Washington, DC: World Bank.

SME Foundation. 2013. *Ownership (Male Headed/Female Headed) - (Division Wise)*. http://smedata.smef.org.bd/index.php/report/ownerships (accessed May 2, 2018).

Sultan, Maheen, Rita Alam, and Luiza Nora. Forthcoming. *Diagnosis and Scoping Study on Increased Integration for Bangladesh Women in Regional Trade*. Washington, DC: World Bank.

Sultana, Afiya. 2012. "Promoting Women's Entrepreneurship through SME: Growth and Development in the Context of Bangladesh." *Journal of Business and Management* 4 (1): 18–29.

Tambunan, Tulus. 2009. "Women Entrepreneurship in Asian Developing Countries: Their Development and Main Constraints." *Journal of Development and Agricultural Economics* 1 (2): 27–40.

Terjesen, Siri, and Ainsley Lloyd. 2015. *Female Entrepreneurship Index: Analyzing the Conditions that Foster High-Potential Female Entrepreneurship in 77 Countries*. Washington, DC: The GEDI Institute.

Thekkudan, Julie, and Rajesh Tandon. 2009. "Women's Livelihoods, Global Markets and Citizenship." IDS Working Paper 336, Brighton: Institute of Development Studies at the University of Sussex.

UNESCAP (United Nations Economic and Social Commission for Asia and the Pacific). 2005. *Developing Women Entrepreneurs in South Asia: Issues, Initiatives and Experiences*. Trade and Investment Division. Thailand: UNESCAP.

USAID (United States Agency for International Development). 2014. *Bangladesh: Inclusive Growth Diagnostic*. USAID and DFID Inclusive Growth Diagnostic Team. Dhaka: USAID and DFID.

Valdivia, Martin. 2015. "Business Training Plus for Female Entrepreneurship? Short and Medium-Term Experimental Evidence from Peru." *Journal of Development Economics* 113: 33–51.

Wang, Qing. 2015. *Child Care, Work-Family Policy and Female Entrepreneurship*. Shenzhen, China: Peking University HSBC Business School.

6 Economic Empowerment Patterns among Ethnic Minority Groups in Bangladesh

ABSTRACT *Relatively little is known about patterns of economic empowerment among Bangladesh's ethnic minority populations. As data collected at the national level are not disaggregated by ethnicity, the number of ethnic groups and size of the country's ethnic and religious minority population remain unknown. Studies find that ethnic and religious minorities in Bangladesh experience frequent violent attacks and high levels of exclusion by various actors on the grounds of their ethnic and religious minority identities. The greater vulnerability of minorities compared to the general population is exacerbated for minority women, who also contend with strongly patriarchal traditions and disproportionately fall victim to discrimination, violence, and rape. Higher-than-average poverty and illiteracy rates among minority communities and minority women's need for increased household income are associated with higher probabilities of minority women's labor force participation (LFP), compared to those of rural women generally. Yet, the potential for economic empowerment from paid work is tempered as ethnic minority women suffer from wage discrimination and other forms of economic disempowerment in the workplace, compared to the majority population.*

OVERVIEW: SITUATION OF KEY MINORITY AND ETHNIC GROUPS

Bangladesh is largely ethnically homogeneous, with over 98 percent of the population identifying as ethnically Bengali. The remaining population is comprised of ethnic groups with linguistic and/or cultural backgrounds that are different from the majority population. Bangladesh had no official state religion when it became independent in 1971, and equality was granted to citizens of all faiths,

161

creeds, and ethnicities. Bengali nationalism is, however, a cornerstone of the Constitution, with Article 3 declaring Bengali the sole official language. With the rise of military rule in place of democracy between 1976 and 1990, certain changes were introduced to increase the role of religion in national and political life. In 1988, Islam was declared the state religion and incorporated into the Constitution. According to a global study of minority rights, these constitutional declarations outline a clear Bangladeshi identity based on Bengali ethnicity, culture, and language—with Islam as the official and state-recognized religion—thus de facto excluding from recognition the country's ethnic, linguistic, and religious minorities (Minority Rights Group International 2016).

Current national and international provisions to protect minority populations are not well enforced in Bangladesh; the government has multiple agencies overseeing different ethnic minority populations, which may present challenges to coordinated approaches, according to Vinding and Kampbel 2012.[1] Although a constitutional reform process initiated in 2010 encouraged public recognition of ethnic minority rights, minority issues continue to have limited visibility in Bangladesh (Vinding and Kampbel 2012).

There is a dearth of demographic and economic data on minority groups. The government of Bangladesh officially recognizes 27 ethnic minority groups in Bangladesh (see appendix F), whereas researchers and Bangladeshi organizations generally believe that the number falls between 45 and 73 (Ali and Sikder n.d.; Chakma and Maitrot 2016; Gain 2015a; Kapaeeng Foundation 2012; Rafi 2006). There also is disagreement over the size of Bangladesh's ethnic population. The 2011 Census reports an ethnic population of 1.6 million, constituting 1.1 percent of Bangladesh's total population (Bangladesh Bureau of Statistics 2015). According to the Census, the three largest ethnic minority groups in Bangladesh are the Chakma, Marma, and Santal. It is widely believed, however, that official numbers are far below actual numbers of ethnic minorities. Various ethnic communities estimate the number at closer to 3 million (Barman and Neo 2012). This chapter compares ethnic women's economic empowerment with that of rural women overall. Because most ethnic minority communities reside in rural areas, comparing minority data with overall rural data is valid.

Ethnic minorities largely live in the Chittagong Hill Tracts (CHT) in southeast Bangladesh and through the plains of the country (United States Department of State 2011) (see appendix F for a presentation of data on the geographical concentration of ethnic minority groups in Bangladesh). Discussions of Bangladeshi minorities tend to differentiate between those in the CHT and those in "the plains," which refers to all parts of the country outside of the CHT's three districts. This distinction is due to the unique character of the CHT, with its greater concentration of minority populations, long history of insurgencies, own peace treaty (the 1997 Chittagong Hill Tracts Treaty), and particular government policies and actions, such as special provisions and a separate Ministry of Chittagong Hill Tracts Affairs.

Bangladesh also has several religious minority groups (appendix F). About 90 percent of Bangladesh's population is Muslim, with an estimated 8.5 percent Hindu, 0.6 percent Buddhist, and 0.3 percent Christian. Represented in even smaller numbers, the indigenous Mro practice animism. Muslim groups not identified as part of Bangladesh's mainstream Sunni Muslim majority are viewed as minorities, including the Shia Muslims, Ahmadi community, and Sufi Muslims (Minority Rights Group International 2016). Finally, whereas Bangladeshi

Hindus are primarily ethnically Bengali, most Bangladeshi Buddhists identify as ethnic minorities (appendix F), and over 80 percent of ethnic minority groups in the CHT are Buddhist (Minority Rights Group International 2016). A significant number of minorities are Christian—more than 36 percent of all ethnic minorities in the plains (Toufique et al. 2016).

Despite the diversity among Bangladesh's minorities, most have in common outcomes that are below national levels of health, education, household income, food consumption, community participation and women's empowerment (Toufique et al. 2016). Many groups face double exclusion on religious and ethnic grounds. Chakma and Maitrot (2016) suggest that low economic opportunity, unfavorable geographical location, exclusion, deprivation, and dispossession of land are the main operators of poverty among Bangladesh's minorities.

The current dearth of data, absence of legal protections, limited government attention, and (according to Minority Rights Group International 2016) restrictive religious nationalism are contributing to the marginalization of Bangladeshi ethnic and religious minorities. Minorities are reported to disproportionately experience political marginalization, social prejudice, low access to services, employment and wage discrimination, economic opportunism, land dispossession, arson, forced abduction, as well as various forms of violence including sexual assault of minority women (Minority Rights Group International 2015, 2016). Exposed to vulnerabilities rooted in gender, as well as minority status, ethnic and/or religious minority women often experience severe marginalization and discrimination in Bangladesh, more so than majority women and minority men.

DIFFERENTIALS IN WOMEN'S LABOR FORCE PARTICIPATION

Female minorities carry a double burden, as women—with all the disadvantages that women in Bangladesh face—and because they belong to a marginalized ethnic or religious group (Shakil 2013). As members of religious and/or ethnic minority groups, minority women are believed to face higher rates of discrimination, as illustrated, for instance, by high levels of sexual and gender-based violence (Human Rights Watch 2016; Shakil 2013; United Kingdom Home Office 2018), and fewer opportunities for income-generating activities than minority men and majority females (Toufique et al. 2016).

Little is known about the labor situation of Bangladesh's minorities and minority women in particular. National data are not collected or disaggregated by ethnic group, and very little information has been gathered or rigorous analysis conducted on labor-related issues as pertaining to Bangladesh's minority communities. The LFS does collect data disaggregated by religion, which can be used as a weak proxy to identify some of the country's minorities and understand their economic situation. A 2016 Bangladesh Institute of Development Studies (BIDS) study (Toufique et al. 2016) of 10,000 ethnic minority households across Bangladesh provides a useful picture of the specific ethnic minority groups' economic situations. The primary qualitative data collected for this book offer further insight into minority employment challenges in Bangladesh. We use these data to analyze differences between minority women and majority women; gender gaps within minority groups as a whole; and disparities in economic engagement between women from different minority groups.

Labor force participation and employment

Whereas male labor force participation (MLFP) rates are comparable across all religious groups at just above 80 percent, female labor force participation (FLFP) rates vary substantially, with higher LFP rates among women from minority religious communities (Buddhists and Christians) than among Bengali women (Hindus and Muslims). Furthermore, there is less of a gender difference in LFP rates among religious minorities compared to the religious majority (figure 6.1). Hindu and Muslim women appear to participate in labor markets at about the same rate, with about 47 percent lower participation rates than their male counterparts. Religious minority women, on the other hand, have higher LFP rates, with a gender gap of 35 percent among Christians and only 16 percent among Buddhists. These differences likely arise, at least in part, from less patriarchal cultural (and particularly religious) norms among at least some minority groups.

Within ethnic minorities, LFP rates are higher for men than women in both the CHT and the plains. BIDS data explain gender gaps in LFP rates across ethnic groups. At 62.8 percent, the LFP rate among sampled ethnic minority households is higher than the national rural average of 58.7 percent (Toufique et al. 2016; Bangladesh Bureau of Statistics 2017). Across all ethnic minority groups, men are more likely to be in the labor force than are women (table 6.1). There are significant variations across minorities: among the CHT groups, the largest gender gaps in LFP are among the Chakma and Tripura minorities, with 30 percentage points higher MLFP than FLFP. More of the plains tribes than those in the CHT show similarly large gender gaps in LFP. A key measure of demand for labor in the economy, the employment-to-population ratio (EPR) suggests much greater employment opportunities in the plains than in the CHT (Toufique et al. 2016). These variations may in part explain both, the substantial variation in LFP rates among ethnic groups, as well as the range of gender gaps across ethnic groups.

LFS data suggest that women from religious minorities are more responsive to economic factors than women from the religious majority. We analyze LFS data in a restricted scenario where households are likely to be in dire need of additional income from women, limiting the sample to those with less than five

FIGURE 6.1

Labor force participation by religion and gender, 2016

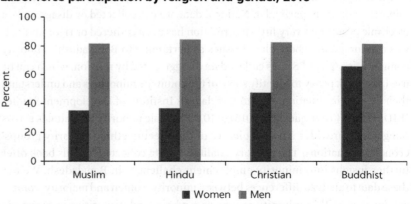

Source: World Bank calculations based on LFS 2016 data.

TABLE 6.1 **Sampled ethnic minority labor force statistics, 2016**

ETHNIC MINORITY	LFPR		
	TOTAL	MALE	FEMALE
Chakma	54.32	71.88	36.51
Marma	51.45	60.55	42.72
Tripura	53.65	73.60	33.15
Tanchaynga	57.35	66.29	47.65
Murong	50.97	50.93	51.01
Other CHT	56.81	55.86	57.71
Total CHT	**53.88**	**66.60**	**41.10**
Garo	60.57	75.85	45.14
Khasia	75.44	76.98	73.79
Monipuri	51.37	67.58	35.11
Hajong	58.56	78.20	39.82
Barmon	55.01	77.14	31.11
Santal	67.85	76.97	58.44
Munda	56.38	60.48	52.35
Orao	68.78	75.04	62.54
Pahan	66.19	72.61	59.92
Kuch	62.46	79.78	44.12
Other plains	68.54	80.09	56.96
Total plains	**65.05**	**75.99**	**53.95**
Total	**62.76**	**74.08**	**51.30**

Source: Toufique et al. 2016.
Note: LFPR = labor force participation rate.

TABLE 6.2 **LFPR of women with less than 5 years of education, by religion and socioeconomic status quintile, 2016**

	LOWEST QUINTILE (%)	TOP 2 QUINTILES (%)
Christian	66	44
Buddhist	72	41
Hindu	47	46
Muslim	38	43

Source: World Bank calculations based on LFS 2016 data.
Notes: The top two quintiles are used to represent the wealthiest household groups; two quintiles are used, instead of one, to increase the sample size due to the small sample of religious minorities.

years of education and breaking those down by socioeconomic status (SES) quintiles as a proxy for income level.[2] Table 6.2 shows little difference in LFP rates between the poorest and wealthiest Muslim and Hindu women—that is, the Bengali ethnic majority—in this scenario, whereas there is a considerable difference between the poorest and wealthiest women from the Buddhist and Christian minority groups, whose LFP rates roughly double as income falls. Although the sample sizes of these different groups and subgroups are too small to give this pattern much weight, it is borne out in the qualitative analysis.

Unemployment

Though unemployment is significantly lower among ethnic minority households than the general rural population, minority women have higher unemployment rates than minority men. The average unemployment rate of BIDS' sampled ethnic minority households is 0.37 percent compared to the higher national rural unemployment rate of 4.13 percent (Bangladesh Bureau of Statistics 2017). Despite very low unemployment among minority women, it is higher than that of men in all of the surveyed ethnic minority groups for which there is data (table 6.3). Moreover, lower unemployment among minority women compared to majority women may be less a reflection of greater economic empowerment than of poverty compelling minority women to work for even minimal income.

Formal versus informal employment

The large majority of ethnic minorities work in the informal sector, especially minority women. Reflecting the overall informality of Bangladesh's total rural employment (see chapter 2), the 2016 BIDS study finds that 89.84 percent of all surveyed employed ethnic minority households work in the informal sector (Toufique et al. 2016), more so in the CHT compared to

TABLE 6.3 Unemployment rate of sampled ethnic minority labor force, by sex, 2016

	UNEMPLOYMENT RATE		
ETHNIC MINORITY	**TOTAL %**	**MALE %**	**FEMALE %**
Chakma	0.69	0.66	0.76
Marma	1.65	1.43	1.95
Tripura	0.50	—	1.65
Tanchaynga	—	—	—
Murong	—	—	—
Other CHT	0.52	1.08	—
Total CHT	**0.78**	**0.70**	**0.91**
Garo	0.73	0.58	0.98
Khasi	—	—	—
Monipuri	0.36	0.54	—
Hajong	0.79	1.21	—
Barmon	0.34	0.31	0.41
Santal	0.25	0.18	0.34
Munda	1.05	1.98	—
Orao	0.08	0.15	—
Pahan	0.06	—	0.13
Kuch	0.46	0.70	—
Other plains	0.16	0.07	0.29
Total plains	**0.28**	**0.26**	**0.30**
Other	0.21	—	—
Total	**0.37**	—	**0.40**

Source: Toufique et al. 2016.
Note: — indicates no evidence of unemployment in this group.

the plains. Almost all agricultural employment and the majority share of employment in manufacturing and services is in the informal sector (Toufique et al. 2016). A higher share of minority women than men appears to work in the informal sector. Among BIDS' surveyed ethnic minority households, 91.15 percent of women are in informal employment compared to 88.96 percent of men (Toufique et al. 2016). Pahan, Orao, and Hjang women have the highest shares of informal employment (99.11, 97.71, and 95.45 percent, respectively).

Qualitative data also reveal that work in the formal sector is limited among women in the studied ethnic communities. In the CHT study area, educated women work mostly in local garment and textile industries. Many also work as school teachers, NGO workers, and sales girls in business show rooms. Less educated minority women mainly engage in traditional employment, working as day laborers in fields, processing crops, making handicrafts, running small businesses, and selling products at nearby markets. Some work as day laborers in nearby urban areas or travel in a group to other areas to work in the construction sector. Growth in tourism in the CHT may have increased opportunities for women to find local jobs; however, unlike in Chittagong, low or unskilled women from Rajshahi's Santal community have few work opportunities outside the farming season, when they commonly work as informal day laborers.

Wage differentials

There are substantial wage differences between Bangladesh's minority groups and the Muslim Bengali majority, and large gender differences, with minorities, especially minority women, appearing to earn significantly less. BIDS' 2016 survey finds that the average monthly wage of minority men and women (BDT 2,445 and BDT 1,697, respectively) is almost five times lower than the average monthly wages of men and women (BDT 10,576 and BDT 10,379, respectively) among the total rural population (Toufique et al. 2016). Our qualitative data lend insight into gender wage differentials within minority communities. A Santal woman in Rajshahi said that local women, "get lower wages than their male counterparts doing the same labor for the same time. The male laborer gets BDT 200 but a female laborer gets BDT 150 when working from 8:00am until 2:00pm." Interestingly, some of the minority women in the Rajshahi Santal community do not see their lower wages as a form of discrimination, but rather due to working less than their male counterparts. A 36-year old Santal woman from Rajshahi explained, "the women cannot work in the field as much as a man can, we, therefore, accept this slight difference in wages."

Employment by industry, occupation, and status of minority women

As the majority of Bangladesh's total rural population continues to work in agriculture (see chapter 2), so too does an even higher relative share of BIDS' sampled ethnic minority labor force. A larger share of ethnic minority women (75 percent) is employed in agriculture than the 72 percent of the total sampled minority population, though more so in the plains (77.42 percent) than in the CHT (65.13 percent). A larger share of minority women (11.67 percent) also work in manufacturing than do minority men (Toufique et al. 2016). In the CHT, 14 percent of employed women are in manufacturing compared to 11 percent of women in the plains. Ethnic groups with the highest shares of female employment in manufacturing are the Monipuri (70.16 percent), Munda (39.33 percent), and Kuch (29.33 percent), all residing in the plains.

The main occupation of ethnic minority groups is wet rice cultivation, poultry, livestock (Chakma 2011), fishing, and small entrepreneurship business in teak plantation (Khisa and Mohiuddin 2015). Minorities in the plains are more involved in these occupations than those in the CHT (Toufique et al. 2016). Ethnic minority women appear to be concentrated in typically female occupations, working as agricultural labor in cultivating and processing crops, producing handicrafts, running small businesses, and selling products at nearby markets. A much larger proportion of the employed minority women are agricultural day laborers (55.24 percent) than men (43.4 percent). Among women, 17.85 percent in the CHT are agricultural day laborers, compared to 62.59 percent in the plains. Among men, 16.11 percent of those employed in the CHT are agricultural day laborers, whereas 49.48 percent are in the plains.

Traditionally engaged in an array of agricultural jobs, Bangladeshi minority populations' loss of land (see "Barriers to ownership and control over assets" section) and subsequent loss of income has forced many households to seek wage labor instead of—or in addition to—traditional occupations (Inter-Agency Support Group on Indigenous Issues (IASG) 2014). Many ethnic minority women today work as domestic workers, in beauty parlors, and in the garment industry, with an estimated 3,000 working in Export Processing Zones (EPZ) near Dhaka and 10,000 in the EPZ near Chittagong (Vinding and Kampbel 2012). Focus group discussions find that many minority women work in textile industries and handloom factories while more educated women work as local teachers, NGO employees, and sales workers. Self-employment is much less prevalent among minority women than men at 28.37 percent and 35.27 percent, respectively.

The concentration of minority women in low-level jobs is, in part, the result of their high levels of poverty. Extreme poverty among minority communities sometimes forces a choice between education and employment. The need for children to supplement household income can curtail their educational achievement, which in turn stems their ability to access higher paid, and formal jobs. Minority women from the qualitative research report that poverty constrains their education more than do social barriers (see appendix F). Still, relatively higher education levels are found among certain religious minority women; Hindu and Christian women have higher rates of receiving at least some college education, completing school with a diploma, and completing grade 12 than do Muslim and Buddhist women (see figure F.1 in appendix F).

DIFFERENTIALS IN OWNERSHIP AND CONTROL OVER ASSETS

Ownership and control over household assets

Unfortunately, no gender-disaggregated data on ethnic minority ownership and control of assets exist. Overall, however, most of the ethnic minority households (73 percent) surveyed in BIDS' 2016 study own the houses in which they live. Yet, minority home ownership is lower than the national rural ownership rate of 88 percent as reported by the 2016 LFS (Bangladesh Bureau of Statistics 2017). Although ethnic minority households in Bangladesh traditionally possess customary land rights (Barkat et al. 2009), most are not able to regularize their land ownership documents through official registration processes. BIDS also finds limited access to public land among minority households. Minority households in the plains are thus highly dependent on accessing land through leasing (appendix F). Government declarations of reserved forests, implementation of commercial cultivation in the CHT, and most importantly land grabbing by the elite and security forces (see "Barriers to ownership and control over assets" section) have further decreased minorities' access to land (Chakma and Maitrot 2016).

Despite the lack of gender-disaggregated data, it may be assumed that minority women are even less likely than Muslim women to own land since, as per the customary laws of many indigenous groups, women generally do not inherit property (see "Barriers to ownership and control over assets" section and table 6.4).

Access to and control over financial assets

There is a complete lack of data on financial assets gender-disaggregated by ethnic group. Studies suggest, however, that minority women have even more

TABLE 6.4 Inheritance systems among different ethnic groups in Bangladesh

	WHO INHERITS PROPERTY			
INDIGENOUS GROUP	WIFE	SON	DAUGHTER	WHETHER CUSTOMARY LAWS ARE FOLLOWED FULLY
Chakma	Widow	Yes	No	Not always
Marma	Widow, but not if remarried	5/8 property	3/8 property	Not always
Tripura	No	Yes	No, but movable property	Varies clan-to-clan
Mro	No	Yes	No	Father can "will" a portion to daughter
Tanchangya	No	Yes	No	Father can "will" a portion to daughter
Bawm	No	Youngest son gets most	No	Customs are changing
Lushai	No	Youngest son gets most	No	Youngest son responsible for caring for parents
Pankhu	No	Youngest son gets most	No	Customs are changing
Khyang	Widow gets small share	Yes	No	Customs are changing
Chak	No	Divided equally among sons	No	Needy daughter may get small portion
Khumi	No	Youngest son gets most	No	—
Khasi	10%	10%	80%	—
Orao	No	Yes	No	—
Garo	Yes	No	Yes	Male family member maintains property
Santal	No	Yes	No	—

Source: Vinding and Kampbel 2012.

limited access to credit than Muslim Bengali women, if any (Kapaeeng Foundation and Bangladesh Indigenous Women's Network 2016). Overall, the limited financial data for ethnic minorities disaggregated by location suggests that ethnic minorities in the CHT have higher levels of savings than those in the plains and higher savings with commercial banks, MFIs and informal organizations and co-operatives (Toufique et al. 2016) (appendix F). BIDS also finds that CHT minorities have higher overall levels of debt than those in the plains (appendix F), and are more likely to be indebted to informal sources than commercial banks (Toufique et al. 2016).

This book's qualitative data suggests that minority women's financial control is limited. Most working women from the minority study sites have some control over their earnings, which they usually spend on household needs, including children's education. Minority Santal respondents in Rajshahi say that it is customary for women to be able to spend their earned money after discussing it with the family. Upon closer examination, their control over finances seems very limited, as financial decision-making requires husbands' permission. Minority women report not being allowed to support their parents with their earnings without husbands' and often in-laws' approval, or to own or increase their assets with their own money. As a man from the Rajshahi Santal community explained, "If a woman buys any property with her money, it must be in her husband's name, since men are the heads of families and properties are distributed among male members for generations." Women report handing over large shares of earnings to their husbands, albeit not all voluntarily. Minority women's control over savings and owned land is also rare. Analysis of responses from minority women show that improvements in their control over income in the past decade were not very significant.

BARRIERS TO MINORITY WOMEN'S ECONOMIC EMPOWERMENT

Barriers to formal, higher-paid employment

Mobility restrictions limit minority women's access to jobs outside the community. As an adolescent girl in the Rajshahi Santal community explained, "It is our tradition where both men and women work at the farm land. Women continue to work even after their marriage, but in such context, women have to obtain permission from their in-laws. However, if any woman intends to work in an NGO that requires frequent field visits, family members do not appreciate that." Another woman in the same community said, "being members of an ethnic community, Santal women have little access to work in the neighboring Muslim society." Perceptions of women's mobility, however, appear to be changing (see "Perceptions of female employment among minority groups" section), and a few Santal women do work outside their own community, either in NGOs or as teachers in their community schools.

Minority women's limited access to education has contributed to their overwhelming participation in the informal sector, which increases their vulnerability. Census data suggest that the average literacy rate of 39.9 percent among Bangladesh's ethnic minorities (aged 7 years and above) is substantially lower than that of the general population at 51.8 percent (Bangladesh Bureau of Statistics 2015). The literacy gender gap is also larger within ethnic populations, with minority women having literacy rates more than 10 percent lower than minority men, compared to a national literacy gender gap of less than five percent. The typically low-wage informal jobs of low-educated minority women provide little employment security and thus high levels of vulnerability (Vinding and Kampbel 2012) due to the insecurity, lower wages, as well as absence of contracts, benefits, and regulations in the informal sector.

Various religious and ethnic minorities have reported wage discrimination in Bangladesh, particularly in the private sector (United States Department of State 2015). Bangladesh's labor laws and policies, including the 2004 EPZ Worker Association and Industrial Relations Act, have proved insufficient in protecting the rights of workers (Kapaeeng Foundation and Bangladesh Indigenous Women's Network 2016). This is a problem for all workers, but particularly minorities. Management of garment factories in the EPZs near Dhaka and Chittagong, for instance, reportedly tend to prefer hiring ethnic minorities over Bengalis since the former are not unionized and thus have minimal power to demand better wages or benefits (Vinding and Kampbel 2012). Whereas all minority members may face wage discrimination based on their ethnicity and/ or religion, minority women may additionally experience wage discrimination due to their gender. Minority women are among the most likely to experience wage discrimination as there are fewer of them, they are not united across minority groups, and they do not work as a cohesive pressure group to bargain. Ethnic minority women working in agriculture in the north appear to experience wage discrimination, as do Garo women working in beauty parlors (Kapaeeng Foundation and Bangladesh Indigenous Women's Network 2016). The lower average wages of minority women compared to their majority counterparts as well as minority men stem their economic empowerment (see "Wage differentials" section).

Barriers to ownership and control over assets

Although relevant data are not gender-disaggregated, land grabbing in the CHT and plains has contributed to overall low levels of minority land and home ownership. Attacks on Bangladesh's ethnic and religious minority populations are generally linked to attempts to grab their lands (Chowdhury and Chakma 2018). Ethnic minorities' tendency to possess customary land rights without their properties being registered (see "Ownership and control over household assets" section) has rendered them vulnerable to land grabbing. Minority women are victimized by physical, sexual, and verbal violence, often as a part of communal aggression on their ancestral lands (Chowdhury and Chakma 2018). According to Amnesty International (2013), land grabbing and resulting displacement are currently the main threat to ethnic minorities living in the CHT (Chakma and Maitrot 2016). About 22 percent of ethnic minority households in the CHT have lost their lands, with minority households losing an average of 115 decimals (a decimal is equal to approximately 1/100th of an acre), of land over three generations compared to 58 decimals for Bengali households (Barkat et al. 2009). Land grabbing is a major challenge to minorities in the plains as well, with land grabbers often using violence against minorities—including rape and gang rape of minority women—as a weapon to scare minorities out of their ancestral lands (Chowdhury and Chakma 2018).

Mainstream assimilation of traditionally matriarchal minority groups is further undermining women's ability to own land. Unlike the Muslim Bengali majority as well as most minority groups, which are heavily patriarchal, the

Garo and Khasi in Bangladesh as well as some subgroups of the Marma are matrilineal (Khaleque and Gain 1995). In some of these communities, women have higher levels of ownership and control over assets, such as land, houses, and other properties than men; however, some matrilineal indigenous communities, such as the Koch, are assimilating into mainstream society, with possession of property increasingly following patriarchal Bengali customs and laws (Gain 2015b). In other cases where prior Hindu groups have converted to Christianity, such as the Santal community in Rajshahi included in our qualitative study, they still follow Hindu inheritance laws under which sons inherit land from their father while daughters only inherit land if they have no brothers, or if their husbands die. Furthermore, among Hindus, property inherited by a woman is not considered property of which she is the absolute owner (Zahur 2016).

Many ethnic communities' residence in the remote CHT grants them limited financial access. Despite the government's enabling policies, even where there is physical access to finance, financial institutions and cooperatives in Bangladesh appear to view loans to ethnic minority women farmers as too risky, fearing inability to repay the installments on time (ActionAid 2016). Furthermore, as is the case for Bangladeshi women in general (see chapter 4), focus group discussions with minority women confirm the unsuitability of typical loan terms and conditions, with requirements to pay the first installment right after receiving the loan proving a major obstacle to accessing finance.

ENABLING FACTORS FOR MINORITY WOMEN'S ECONOMIC EMPOWERMENT

Perceptions of female employment among minority groups

Gender norms restricting women's labor force participation may not be as strong in minority ethnic communities as in the general population. Focus group discussions conducted suggest that female respondents from the studied minority communities may enjoy greater flexibility and independence to work outside the household compared to respondents from the studied urban and rural majority communities. In the focus group discussion of ethnic working women in urban Chittagong, participants explained that women in the minority Assam slum "have no obstacles for working after the marriage or becoming a new mother. New brides in this area can work if they work at home or beside the home. In the case of new mothers, they can seek work outside the house if their families have people to look after the baby. But new mothers that come from families that have no one to look after the baby make bags at home....The work of women is never taken negatively by anyone."

Qualitative data also suggest that perceptions of women's mobility and work beyond the immediate community may be changing, as some women have had to take jobs outside the community due to limited local employment opportunities. In a focus group discussion among Santal women in Rajshahi one respondent explained, "Earlier everyone thought we could not adjust with the people outside our community and we would not be able to communicate with them. But now as we can earn money by doing various activities going beyond our community, none from the community makes any negative comment. Now the community appreciates women going out to work for money." Another participant added that acceptance of outside work is growing, as witnessed by the fact that "It's the people of our community who have helped to get this job."

Ethnic communities may be supportive of women's income-generating activities due to their dire financial situation. The two ethnic study sites in which qualitative data were gathered are very poor. Most minority women respondents in both areas believe that the support from family members is largely rooted in the household's need for additional income. A minority adolescent girl in the Chittagong study site mentioned in this context that, "Many women from poverty stricken families work after marriage. Almost all family members engage in income-generating activities. Women work for financial solvency in the family. It is an example of self-reliance; therefore, neither the family nor the society see it negatively." A focus group discussion with Santal women in rural Rajshahi highlighted that financial need is driving women's employment as well as societal support for it. One participant explained, "If the women do not work alongside men, they and the children will have to starve." Similarly, another Santal woman said, "The women have to work to provide education to their children. Hence they have the permission from their family to work outside for a living."

In recognition of their financial contributions, ethnic women in the study sites report receiving various types of support from family and community members. Help is provided to learn a particular type of work, and services are available from local NGOs and financial organizations that provide access to finance. Female minority respondents, however, noted that the terms and conditions of available loans do not suit their needs; these minority women flagged the difficult requirement of having to pay the first installment right after taking out the loan, a challenge shared with Bangladeshi women more generally (see chapter 4).

Education and employment generally appear to increase the social status of minority women. Although the number of educated women in the ethnic Rajshahi Santal study site is low, the community appears to attach high value to education. A male focus group discussion respondent explained that parents increasingly regard girls' education as a positive development for the family that can lead to improved social status. The qualitative research provides many examples of uneducated women feeling undervalued, in part due to their illiteracy. A working woman from the Rajshahi Santal community noted, "The community values the opinions expressed by educated and working women. Husbands also consult with them on many issues. Women make decisions about the education of children. However, women who work as day laborers have relatively low status in society. People do not listen to their opinions, assuming that they do not understand things very well."

Respondents in the CHT generally believe that education is critical for obtaining regular monthly paid employment. For almost all available jobs in the area, a certain level of education is compulsory. In Rangamati, for instance, even a sales girl at a clothing store needs to at least have completed the 8th grade. In studied ethnic communities, education is perceived as extremely important, with participants reporting that not one single girl in their community is staying home instead of attending school. Participants of the focus group discussions expressed great pride in the fearlessness of girls from the "Hills," that is, the CHT. Women mentioned that girls are becoming more self-reliant due to education, as well as awareness campaigns led by NGOs and government organizations, which is in turn contributing to lower incidence of claiming dowry, fewer items claimed, lower value of dowry, or some combination of these. These women respondents explained that the jobs of employed women are increasingly thought of in terms of a potential source of income for the future in-laws and as a substitute for dowry at the time of marriage.

The qualitative research suggests that women in the ethnic minority study sites do contribute to household decision-making, though the extent is unclear. An ethnic minority woman respondent in Chittagong suggested that, "Women living in ethnic communities enjoy greater independence in decision-making processes compared to women from Bengali communities. In some cases, the society of ethnic communities encourages and approves of women taking part in decision-making processes, whether they work or not." A respondent interviewed in Rajshahi noted that since most Santal women are employed for part of the year, they can often contribute to the decision-making process in their family. Despite some female decision-making power within the studied ethnic minority communities, however, approval by the men in the household still appears to remain critical for women to enjoy such decision-making power. Also, for ethnic women in Rajshahi and Chittagong to continue or initiate employment after marriage generally requires permission from their families with regard to working outside of their own community; it also requires compliance with social norms and restrictions on women's mobility, such as wearing very conservative clothing and using head scarves.

GOOD PRACTICES AND RECOMMENDATIONS

A number of laws, policies, and programs in Bangladesh and globally provide good practice examples of how minorities overall may be supported. Unfortunately, however, many do not provide adequate evaluated insight into how specifically to address the double disadvantage of gender and ethnicity faced by minority women. Still, several of these examples can be considered opportunities to adapt not only for the Bangladesh context but also to address ethnic women's vulnerabilities explicitly.

Good practice examples of national laws and policies

Various countries have taken steps to develop national strategies or plans to protect their indigenous communities. For instance, Bulgaria has a National Roma Integration Strategy 2012–20; Vietnam has a National Strategy on Gender Equality 2011–20 that seeks to increase the access of poor rural and ethnic minority women to economic resources and the labor market; and Panama is currently preparing a National Indigenous Peoples Development Plan with its indigenous communities and with assistance from the World Bank. Bangladesh can follow these good practices and develop a national approach to guide priorities, policies, and programs to reduce marginalization of the country's ethnic and religious minority women and support their empowerment.

Programs for Bangladesh's minority communities are split between the Prime Minister's office and the Ministry of Chittagong Hill Tracts Affairs. Vietnam has a Committee on Ethnic Minority Affairs, a ministry-level agency responsible for managing ethnic minority affairs throughout the country. The Vietnamese parliament also created the Council of Ethnic Minorities, the primary duties of which are to contribute to, investigate, and oversee legal documents and procedures regarding ethnic affairs; the Council has helped pass various pieces of legislation targeting the interests of ethnic minorities (Panter et al. 2017). These institutions may have contributed to the relatively greater policy attention to minorities in Vietnam and help enable international programs for minority communities, including CARE's projects focused on minority women. In other countries—such as in India—political reservation for minorities may have contributed to lowering rural poverty (Chin and Prakash 2010). Yet there has been no evaluation of the extent to which these benefits may have influenced minority women's economic engagement and empowerment specifically.

Select countries have passed antidiscrimination laws and created supportive policies and institutions to protect their minorities, yet there is a distinct lack of attention to minority women and their particular challenges. Bulgaria, Mexico, and the Netherlands have taken steps to stem discrimination in the labor market specifically, including shifting the onus to the employer to prove that discrimination did *not* take place once an employee brings a claim for discrimination (Panter et al. 2017). Yet, none of these efforts speak specifically to the double discrimination that ethnic minority women face.

Affirmative action policies that provide minorities a leg up in accessing education are likely to benefit minority women and can be assessed and adapted for the Bangladeshi context. Vietnam's Education Act 2005 establishes quotas for ethnic minority admission into secondary and higher-level educational institutions, waives the requirement of taking the enrollment examination for ethnic minorities, and calls for the government to prioritize budget allocations to schools for ethnic minority children below the university level (Panter et al. 2017). China also has preferential education quotas for ethnic minorities, granting "bonus points" to the National College Entrance Examination scores of minority applicants, as determined by individual provinces. Such laws have increased the ability of minority children and young adults to access education and build skills as well as enhance their competitiveness in the labor market (Panter et al. 2017). Bulgaria and Mexico have introduced laws requiring that school curricula be updated to ensure removal of prejudicial language against minorities, and that teachers at the primary and secondary levels receive nondiscrimination training (Panter et al. 2017). Other programs, such as a CCT program in Mexico examined by Lopez-Calva and Patrinos (2015), can help offset potential loss of income-generating opportunities due to increased time spent in school—and incentivize families to send minority girls to school. Efforts to improve ethnic minorities' educational attainment would likely benefit minority women and girls, as well, given the apparent lack of cultural barriers to girls' education among most minority communities.

Adapting good practices for gender equality to minorities

Efforts to elevate ethnic minority communities overall would, however, not necessarily improve the situation of minority women. Approaches that have been used globally to close gender gaps could be adapted for minority women and complement overall efforts to empower minority communities, including: conditional cash transfers (CCTs) for girls to attend school and promoting girls' enrollment in science, technology, and other subjects not considered typically female; vocational training for women in higher paid, nontraditional livelihoods, and developing their connections to markets and networks; training in business management and finance; programs to formally register land and properties in a woman's name or jointly with her husband; as well as efforts to raise awareness among husbands and communities of women's rights, their abilities, and the unpaid work burdens related to domestic responsibilities.

Adapting good practices for minorities specifically to women minorities

Some programs have been effective in increasing the incomes of minority groups beyond low-paying jobs and could be adapted to include a focus on minority women. The Juventud y Empleo Project in the Dominican Republic provided low-income marginalized youth with life skills to strengthen self-esteem and work habits, technical job training to meet the needs of local job markets, and internships in private sector firms. After an experimental evaluation by Card et al. (2011) found little impact, the program was re-oriented to focus on components that employers identified as essential—including closer collaboration with the private sector and a stronger life skills component. Subsequent assessments show greater positive impacts on earnings and the quality of employment (World Bank 2014). Bangladesh could adapt this model to strengthen linkages between area employers and civil society organizations to better orient minorities' job and life skills—with a focus on minority women's particular opportunities and constraints—to specific, local labor market needs.

Several countries have worked to address their indigenous communities' land-related vulnerability by working to establish formal land rights which could improve ethnic minorities' economic position overall; yet, it is unclear how this would positively affect ethnic women's land rights given indigenous tradition that does not favor women's ownership of land. Countries have addressed ethnic communities' land rights in a variety of ways, including constitutionally (Mexico), through regularization of community held land (Romania) and through laws (Nicaragua) (Duchicela et al. 2015; Panter et al. 2017). Bangladesh could assess how to implement such efforts, modifying them to address also traditional customs that currently hamper ethnic minority women's ownership of land.

Good practice examples in directly empowering minority women

Bangladesh's minorities—and minority women in particular—could benefit from programs directly focused on expanding their educational and employment opportunities. The 2004–09 Nepal Poverty Alleviation Fund (PAF) supported excluded communities—mostly women, Dalits (untouchable castes), and Janajatis (ethnic minorities)—by mobilizing local partner organizations to establish sub-project proposals, create community organizations (COs), and provide grants for community-selected income-generating activities, product development, and/or market linkages in CO households. An impact evaluation of the Nepal PAF finds a number of statistically significant impacts, including a 19 percent growth of real per capita consumption, and a 19-percentage point decline in incidence of food insecurity, with a relatively greater 24-percentage point decline among minority households (Parajuli et al. 2012). The evaluation also finds a significant 15-percentage point increase in school enrollment rate among 6–15 year-olds, and attributes this in part to increases in income that reduced barriers to sending children to school. The project had a relatively greater impact on girls, who experienced a 21-percentage point increase in school enrollment rate.

In an evaluation of CARE projects in the Mekong region, Taylor and Gillingham (2015) identify practical-based training and learning approaches as particularly successful in supporting ethnic minority women's economic empowerment. CARE used peer-to-peer and cascading learning through villages, which established minority women as teachers and thought leaders to both enhance learning as well as women's status throughout the village. The projects also sought women's active participation in project study visits and activities. Vietnam has implemented a particularly large number of programs to economically empower its ethnic minorities, including minority women. However, while assessments by Nguyen, Phung, and Westbrook (2013) and Nguyen Viet (2014) point to overall positive outcomes for targeted minority groups, it is unclear to what extent these have explicitly addressed the double discrimination minority women face.

CARE's Vietnam Ethnic Minority Women's Empowerment Project (EMWE) provides a promising example of how to directly empower minority women. The EMWE focused on improving economic and other conditions for ethnic minority women farmers in remote areas by helping them adapt their farming practices and earn a better living in the context of climate change. EMWE established women's only Village Savings and Loans Associations (VSLA) to improve minority women's financial access, and Livelihood and Rights Clubs (LARC) in which small groups of women came together regularly to learn financial and leadership skills, share knowledge about farming and livestock management, and discuss household and community needs to be shared with local government authorities. The project also worked with local government officials and male family members to support women's participation and voice. CARE (2017) finds that over the course of the project, women's savings doubled from USD 10 to USD 20 per month, in part due to use of new animal husbandry techniques; rice yields also increased by 40–60 percent and became more climate resilient as a result of meteorological advice on the best times to plant based on the seasonal forecast. Local partners have started creating their own ethnic women's financial groups after witnessing the success of the CARE model. The LARC groups, which enabled ethnic minority women's first ever participation in local level planning discussions for 2016–20, have already affected change in the government; ethnic minority women have gained a voice in government and spurred action after raising the need for seedlings and upgraded irrigation channels to avoid the annual floods that destroy their crops. Efforts to engage ethnic men in the project areas also appear to have led to small but significant changes in perception and behavior, with husbands increasingly caring for children, cooking, and cleaning while their wives participate in meetings, and encouraging their wives to expand their livelihoods.

In their assessment of EMWE and another of CARE's Vietnam projects—the Civil Action for Socio-Economic Inclusion Project (CASI)—Henriksen and Thøgersen (2015) note distinct benefits of engaging minority women in women-only groups and mixed-gender groups. EMWE utilized women-only groups while CASI utilized mixed-gender groups that included minority women's male relatives. The mixed-gender groups had particular benefits in that the groups and their activities were less isolated from society as they better reflected the community, and the groups appeared to affect greater and faster change in men's perceptions of women as valuable and respected individuals. A significant benefit of women-only groups, however, was that they managed to engage *all* women in the village whereas the mixed-gender groups ended up engaging only those already active in the community (Henriksen and Thøgersen 2015).

A number of studies globally find ethnic minority women to be good financial clients, with high repayment rates and positive outcomes from borrowing. Whereas financial institutions and cooperatives in Bangladesh often view loans to ethnic minority women farmers as risky (ActionAid 2016), this assumption is not borne out in much of the research. Lyngdoh and Pati (2013), for instance, find that microfinance provided to matrilineal tribal women in north-east India has had a positive impact on income, expenditure, savings, access to livestock, micromachines, family wealth, family savings, and other credit. Similar findings have been noted for female minority participation in self-help groups (SHGs), or village-based financial intermediary committees where members make small interest bearing loans to one another. An evaluation of the economic empowerment of Mising tribal women in Assam, India, finds significant increases in monthly income, expenditure, and savings of tribal women after joining SHGs (Bori 2017). Lenka and Mohanta (2015) also find that SHG membership contributes to the economic empowerment of tribal women in Odisha: participants experienced improvements in economic independence and living standards, 90 percent gained knowledge about banking, and 70 percent reported reduced social, religious, and cultural barriers. In an evaluation of CARE projects, Taylor and Gillingham (2015) find that the participation of ethnic minority women in VSLA in the Mekong Delta, coupled with activities to promote enhanced production and access to markets, has been successful in enhancing minority women's access to finance, stimulating income-generating activities, and also providing a community of support and learning for these generally excluded women. These success stories could be used to encourage financial institutions in Bangladesh to focus more on reaching minority women with their financial products.

Recommendations

Despite limited understanding of the opportunities and barriers facing ethnic minority women in Bangladesh, addressing several clear hurdles would contribute to creating an enabling environment for their economic empowerment.

All Bangladeshi ethnic communities would welcome being recognized in the national census, and this would address—among other issues—the problem of potential undercounting of many ethnic groups identified as living in the country, low levels of attention to the status of and challenges facing minority groups, and insufficient amounts of funds allocated to them.

Bangladesh should also systematically collect national data disaggregated by ethnicity and gender. Doing so in the census and LFS will improve understanding of the particular situation and challenges facing women belonging to different minority groups in different parts of the country. It would also provide invaluable information that would assist the government of Bangladesh, civil society organizations, and development partners in developing economic empowerment programs tailored to specific groups—and to women within these groups—given the great diversity across minority communities.

Bangladesh may consider signing international conventions protecting ethnic minorities and enact nondiscrimination laws to address the economic vulnerability of its minorities. Bangladesh can work towards adopting the 2007 United Nations Declaration on the Rights of Indigenous Peoples as well as ratifying the Indigenous and Tribal Peoples Convention (ILO Convention 169) and Rome Convention for the Protection of Human Rights and Fundamental Freedoms. To create a supportive enabling environment for ethnic minority women's economic empowerment, the government of Bangladesh can also look to the experience of other countries to develop and pass comprehensive nondiscrimination laws providing protections from discrimination on ethnic grounds.

Developing a national approach for the country's ethnic and religious minorities is another important action the Bangladeshi government needs to consider seriously. The government can also look to countries that have established strategies for supporting their vulnerable minority populations and policies and programs to remove barriers and enable their empowerment. Strategies will need to be modified to address also gender gaps that make minority women additionally vulnerable.

Government institutions need to be strengthened to develop policies and coordinate multisectoral efforts to protect and empower ethnic minorities. The country would benefit from a holistic, centralized framework and approach to minorities to help address discrimination, set priorities, and inform policy as well as programmatic support to reduce exclusion by addressing the current vulnerabilities and economic disempowerment experienced by minorities. Any holistic approach should, however, include the Ministry of Women and Children Affairs as a partner so that a focus on ethnic women and their vulnerabilities is highlighted.

To protect minorities' land ownership, efforts need to be made to regularize ethnic minority property rights or provide alternative property rights systems, so as to reduce minorities'—and particularly minority women's—land-related economic vulnerability. Bangladesh could improve ethnic minorities' access to public khas land as well as examine the provision of legal assistance to its ethnic communities to establish formal titles or leases to the land on which they reside. This could also enable promotion of female-only and joint property titles.

DATA GAPS

Knowledge of the varying levels of exclusion and economic disempowerment facing specific ethnic minority populations is sparse. The current practice of not disaggregating data collected at the national level by ethnicity has made it difficult to identify and analyze issues pertaining to minority groups' labor force participation, asset ownership, and financial access, and to determine how to best overcome the barriers to their economic empowerment. With so little data collected on ethnic minorities in Bangladesh—by the government, development organizations, academics, and civil society—even less is known about the economic situation of minority women and the dynamics surrounding their economic empowerment.

NOTES

1. The Special Affairs Division under the Prime Minister's office undertakes programs for minorities in the plains, while the Ministry of Chittagong Hill Tracts Affairs undertakes programs for minorities in the CHT (Toufique et al. 2016).
2. It should be noted that due to income effect, individuals in more affluent households are generally less likely to work.

REFERENCES

ActionAid. 2016. "Women's Resilience Index." ActionAid Bangladesh, Dhaka.

Ali, Md. Ayub, and Shourav Sikder. n.d., "Counting the Peoples' Voice: MLE the Intrinsic Means of Inclusive Education." Oxfam.

Amnesty International. 2013. *Pushed to the Edge: Indigenous Rights Denied in Bangladesh' Chittagong Hill Tracts*. London: Amnesty International Secretariat.

Bangladesh Bureau of Statistics. 2015. *Population and Housing Census 2011, National Report, Vol: 1*. Dhaka: Ministry of Planning, Government of the People's Republic of Bangladesh.

———. 2017. *Bangladesh Quarterly Labour Force Survey (LFS) 2015-16*. Statistics and Informatics Division, Ministry of Planning, Dhaka: Bangladesh Bureau of Statistics.

Barkat, Abul, Sherly Halim, Avijit Poddar, B. Zaman, Abdelkarim Osman, Sarzamin Khan, M. Rahman, Muhammad Norhisham Majid, G. Mahiyuddin, S. Chakma, and S. Bashir. 2009. "Socio-Economic Baseline Survey of Chittagong Hill Tracts." A project financed by the European Union, HDRC, UNDP Bangladesh, Prepared for Chittagong Hill Tracts Development Facility (CHTDF).

Barman, D. C., and M. S. Neo. 2012. *Human Right Reports 2012 on Indigenous Peoples in Bangladesh*. Dhaka: Kapaeeng Foundation.

Bori, Bhumika. 2017. "Economic Empowerment of Tribal Women through Self Help Groups: A Case Study of Gulung Temera Gaon Panchayat under Bokakhat West Development Block, Golaghat District of Assam, India." *Journal of Humanities and Social Science* 22 (11): 01–10.

Card, David, Pablo Ibarrarán, Ferdinando Regalia, David Rosas-Shady, and Yuri Soares. 2011. "The Labor Market Impacts of Youth Training in the Dominican Republic." *Journal of Labor Economics* 29 (2): 267–300.

CARE. 2017. *Impact Brief: Supporting Ethnic Minority Women and Their Communities in Vietnam*. Melbourne: CARE Australia.

Chakma, Nikhil, and Mathilde Maitrot. 2016. "How Ethnic Minorities Became Poor and Stay Poor in Bangladesh: A Qualitative Enquiry." Working Paper 34, EEP/Shiree, Dhaka.

Chakma, Sugata. 2011. "The Chakma." In *Survival of the Fringe: Adivasis of Bangladesh*, edited by Philip Gain, 81–89. Dhaka: Society for Environment and Human Development.

Chin, Aimee, and Nishith Prakash. 2010. "The Redistributive Effects of Political Reservation for Minorities: Evidence from India." NBER Working Paper No. 16509, Cambridge: National Bureau of Economic Research.

Chowdhury, Mong Shanoo, and Pallab Chakma. 2018. *Human Rights Report 2017 on Indigenous Peoples in Bangladesh*. Dhaka: Kapaeeng Foundation.

Duchicela, Luis Felipe, Svend Jensby, Jorge Uquillas, Jelena Lukic, and Karen Sirker. 2015. *Our People, Our Resources: Striving for a Peaceful and Plentiful Planet*. Case Studies Report, Washington, DC: World Bank.

Gain, Philip. 2015a. "Excluded Groups and Democratization." SEHD.

———. 2015b. "Koch of Modhupur, A Demographic Survey of a Marginal Ethnic Community." SEHD.

Henriksen, Anna, and Silja Thøgersen. 2015. *Empowering Women & Communities A Study of Women Empowerment Outcomes and Best Practices of EMWE & CASI*. CARE Vietnam.

Human Rights Watch. 2016. "Bangladesh: Events of 2016." *Human Rights Watch* (accessed June 11, 2018), https://www.hrw.org/world-report/2017/country-chapters/bangladesh.

Inter-Agency Support Group on Indigenous Issues (IASG). 2014. "Indigenous Peoples' Access to Decent Work and Social Protection." Thematic paper towards the preparation of the 2014 World Conference on Indigenous Peoples. United Nations Inter-Agency Support Group (IASG) on Indigenous Issues, New York.

Kapaeeng Foundation. 2012. *Human Rights Report 2012 on Indigenous Peoples in Bangladesh*. Dhaka: Kapaeeng Foundation and OXFAM.

Kapaeeng Foundation and Bangladesh Indigenous Women's Network. 2016. *Annual Situation Report 2015 on Indigenous Women in Bangladesh*. Dhaka: Kapaeeng Foundation.

Khaleque, Kibriaul, and Philip Gain. 1995. *Bangladesh: Land, Forest, and Forest People*. Dhaka: Society for Environment and Human Development (SEHD).

Khisa, Sudibya Kanti, and Mohammad Mohiuddin. 2015. "Shrinking *Jum* and Changing Livelihoods in the Chittagong Hill Tracts of Bangladesh." In *Shifting Cultivation, Livelihood and Food Security: New and Old Challenges for Indigenous Peoples in Asia*, edited by Christian Erni, 41–96. Bangkok: FAO, International Work Group For Indigenous Affairs, and Asia Indigenous Peoples Pact.

Lenka, Chandrashree, and Yasodhara Mohanta. 2015. "Empowerment of Women through Participation Inself-Help Groups—A Study in Tribal Area." *International Journal of Home Science Extension and International Communication Management* 2 (2): 126–31.

Lopez-Calva, Luis F., and Harry Anthony Patrinos. 2015. "Exploring the Differential Impact of Public Interventions on Indigenous People: Lessons from Mexico's Conditional Cash Transfers Program." *Journal of Human Development and Capabilities* 16 (3).

Lyngdoh, Benjamin F., and Ambika P. Pati. 2013. "Impact of Microfinance on Women Empowerment in the Matrilineal Tribal Society of India: An Analysis Using Propensity Score Matching and Difference-in-Difference." *International Journal of Rural Management* 9 (1): 45–69.

Minority Rights Group International. 2015. *State of the World's Minorities and Indigenous Peoples 2015: Events of 2014*. London: Minority Rights Group International.

———. 2016. "Under Threat: The Challenges Facing Religious Minorities in Bangladesh." London: Minority Rights Group International.

Nguyen, Cuong, Tung Phung, and Daniel Westbrook. 2013. "Do the Poorest Ethnic Minorities Benefit from a Large-Scale Poverty Reduction Program? Evidence from Vietnam." MPRA Paper No. 50689, Munich Personal RePEc Archive.

Nguyen Viet, Cuong. 2014. "Impact Evaluation of Development Programmes and Policies: Experiences from Viet Nam." MPRA Paper 60919, Munich Personal RePEc Archive.

Panter, Elaine, Tanya Primiani, Tazeen Hasan, and Eduardo Calderon Pontaza. 2017. "Antidiscrimination Law and Shared Prosperity: An Analysis of the Legal Framework of Six Economies and Their Impact on the Equality of Opportunities of Ethnic, Religious, and Sexual Minorities." Policy Research Working Paper 7992, World Bank, Washington, DC.

Parajuli, Dilip, Gayatri Acharya, Nazmul Chaudhury, and Bishnu Bahadur Thapa. 2012. *Impact of Social Fund on the Welfare of Rural Households: Evidence from the Nepal Poverty Alleviation Fund*. Policy Research Working Paper 6042, World Bank, Washington, DC.

Rafi, Mohammad. 2006. *Small Ethnic Groups in Bangladesh: A Mapping Exercise*. Dhaka: Panjeree Publications.

Shakil, Md. Rajib Hasnat. 2013. "Systematic Persecution of Religious Minorities: Bangladesh Perspective." *IOSR Journal of Humanities And Social Science (IOSR-JHSS)* 7 (3): 9–17.

Taylor, Georgia, and Sarah Gillingham. 2015. *Promote Women's Economic Empowerment with Ethnic Groups in the Mekong: Evaluation Highlights*. CARE.

Toufique, Kazi Ali, Abdul Hye Mondal, Mohammad Yunus, Sinora Chakma, and Sami Farook. 2016. "Baseline Assessment of Skills and Employment of Indigenous and Tribal Peoples in Bangladesh." BIDS.

United Kingdom Home Office. 2018. *Country Policy and Information Note Bangladesh: Women Fearing Gender Based Violence*. London, UK: Home Office.

United States Department of State. 2011. "International Religious Freedom Report—Bangladesh, July–December, 2010." Bureau of Democracy, Human Rights, and Labor, Washington, DC: United States Department of State.

———. 2015. "2014 Country Reports on Human Rights Practices—Bangladesh." Washington, DC: United States Department of State.

Vinding, Diana, and Ellen-Rose Kampbel. 2012. "Indigenous Women Workers with Case Studies from Bangladesh, Nepal and the Americas." Working Paper 1, International Labour Office, ILO's International Labour Standards Department (PRO 169), ILO Bureau for Gender Equality, ILO, Geneva: ILO.

World Bank. 2014. "Handbook for Improving the Living Conditions of Roma." Working Paper 92395, World Bank, Washington, DC.

Zahur, Mahua. 2016. "Hindu Women's Property Rights: Bangladesh Perspective." *BRAC University Journal* (BRAC) XI (1): 79–87.

7 Taking Action to Improve Women's Economic Empowerment in Bangladesh

Earlier chapters have explored gender gaps in four key domains of economic empowerment—labor market outcomes, household asset ownership, ownership and control over financial nonhousehold assets, and entrepreneurship—while tracking changes in these gender gaps over time. In addition, the previous chapter considers these gaps among Bangladesh's ethnic and religious minority groups, for whom existing data are scant. Although the country has other important minority groups to consider— such as the physical and mentally disabled population, as well as lesbian, gay, bisexual, trans, and queer (LGBTQ) individuals—the lack of economic data on these groups unfortunately makes related analysis extremely difficult and thus beyond the scope of this book.

This concluding chapter is organized as follows. First, findings from chapters 2–6 are briefly summarized with a focus on the degree to which women have become more economically empowered in the four domains over the past 10–15 years, if at all. Using the definition of economic empowerment that Golla et al. (2011) propose, we consider whether women not only are able to succeed and advance in economic terms, but have the power to make economic decisions and act on them, as well. For each domain of economic empowerment, we list the main areas of interventions needed to close gender gaps within the domain, details and good practices for which can be found in the earlier chapter dedicated to that domain. The "Recommended Roles and Responsibilities of Various Stakeholder Groups" section summarizes some of these details, organized by each type of stakeholder—namely, the government of Bangladesh (GoB), the private sector, NGOs and civil society organizations (CSOs), research institutions, media and entertainment, development and donor partners—and the recommended actions each can take to help close gender gaps in economic empowerment. The discussion on development partners includes recommendations for specific activities in the World Bank Group's Bangladesh portfolio.

WOMEN'S ECONOMIC EMPOWERMENT HAS INCREASED, BUT CHOICES REMAIN LIMITED

More improvement in basic labor market outcomes than in decisions about own labor

Bangladesh's female labor force participation (FLFP) rate has risen substantially—a full 10 percent between 2003 and 2016. Yet, women's participation still is only 44 percent that of men. Among Bangladeshi women age 15–65, those who are least likely to be in the labor force—with their odds continuing to fall over time—are urban women (though rural women have the highest unemployment rates), women living in Sylhet, women who complete their educations at the 10th grade (girls who leave school before and after the 10th grade have higher labor force participation (LFP) rates than those leaving at the 10th grade), and women from the wealthiest (top 20 percent) of households. While women ages 30–39 enjoy the highest LFP rates, those ages 15–34 have the highest unemployment rates. Those who drop out of school after grade 10 face a double penalty: they have the lowest odds of participating in labor markets, but the highest odds of unemployment if they do participate (compared to women at all other levels of education, including those with no schooling at all).

Married women are in Bangladesh's labor force at much higher rates than they were a decade ago, but many still need permission—and even active support—from husbands or parents-in-law to work outside the home after marriage, according to our qualitative research. Obtaining marital family support to continue education after marriage is even more difficult and rare. This has concerning implications for women's work choices: only 7 percent of women who complete their educations at grade 10—and 3 percent or less of those who leave school earlier—work in the formal sector. The lower the age at marriage, the more a woman's education is truncated to the point where, even if she receives family support, her work choices will be limited to low-skill and low-pay jobs. Lower age at marriage also implies the earlier absorption of young women into the responsibilities of housework and childcare, which is associated with a penalty on the likelihood of joining the labor market. Although marriage of girls under age 18 dropped by 6 percentage points between 2004 and 2014, it remains very high at 59-63 percent, depending on the source of data. This suggests that for more than half of adolescent and younger girls, their educations—and by extension, decent and well-paying job prospects—are shut down early in their lives. The fact that more than one-fourth of Bangladeshi girls are married before age 15 speaks volumes about the remaining barriers to more and better jobs for women in Bangladesh.

Women appear still to have very limited choices with regards to work options across broad sectors, although many industries have seen a decline in sex segregation. The quadrupling of the share of women working in mixed female-male industries between 2003 and 2016, along with the more than two-thirds reduction of the share working in female-dominated industries, indicates this decline. However, women's opportunities in industry and services—that is, outside of agriculture, where women have little chance of occupying positions with decision-making authority—have not increased as much as men's. In fact, smaller shares of women in 2016 work in both the industry and service sectors than in 2003. Overall, the degree of occupational sex-segregation in Bangladesh remains high, due in part to sex-based streaming into different education fields: boys gravitate more toward STEM fields (which build marketable skills for job markets), while girls overwhelmingly do not. Qualitative data reveal that girls who express interest in male-dominated fields may be steered away from them. Sex-segregated occupational choice that is driven by gender norms appears to be more common in rural than in urban areas; urban women from the middle class, in particular, are able to choose from a broader set of occupations than are urban poor and rural women.

The raw gender wage gap has decreased dramatically, which is another positive sign of improving gender equality in Bangladesh's labor markets. Gender differences in endowments, such as level of schooling, explain only a small fraction of the remaining pay gap, however. Most is explained by the difference (bias) in how markets value men's and women's endowments, especially in the informal sector. In other words, gender norms and bias in labor markets increasingly explain the remaining gender pay gap, especially on the demand side of labor. In 2016, female workers earned roughly three-fourths of what men did, with a 24 percent gap, whereas the earlier gap, in 2013, was 43 percent. This is another positive sign of improving gender equality in Bangladesh's labor markets; however, persistent gender biases manifest as both institutional and statistical forms of discrimination in ways that compound the effects of streaming young women into fields of study and training that do not provide marketable skills. Segregation of women into lower-paying, nonmanagement positions (as is the case in the garment sector), is one facet of institutional bias; direct discrimination by employers and managers is evident from the 2013 Enterprise Survey finding that nearly half of all employers and managers—and 100 percent of those in microenterprises—regard women's mere presence as potentially disruptive to the work environment.

Further closure of gender gaps in labor markets requires practical interventions that both (a) address constraints on women's LFP and gainful employment, and (b) improve working conditions for those who do secure employment. The latter helps create a virtuous cycle of attracting more women into the labor force. The main categories of recommended interventions, for which details and good practice examples are given in chapter 2, are listed below. More specific recommended actions for the GoB and other stakeholders can be found in the "Recommended Roles and Responsibilities of Various Stakeholder Groups" section.

- Continue to lower rates of child marriage and address other barriers to girls' education beyond grade 10
- Improve women's technical (especially STEM) skills to prepare them for jobs in higher-paying industries and occupations
- Improve working conditions, workplace and transport safety, and female-friendly benefits to draw more women into sustained private sector employment.

Women's ownership and control over household assets: increased choice through partial rights

Women own land, one of the four most valuable household assets, at much lower rates than do men in rural Bangladesh. Among rural women, 12 percent solely or jointly own agricultural land and 7 percent own nonagricultural land, compared to 69.3 percent and 86.5 percent of rural men, respectively. Despite qualitative findings that women—both rural and urban—own more land than they did a decade ago, the data indicate that 96 percent of household land in rural areas still is owned by husbands alone (Quisumbing, Kumar, and Behrman 2018). The gender gap in land ownership is primarily attributable to male-biased practices in inheritance, the main channel through which land is acquired. The more devoutly religious a family is—among the vast majority of households, which are Muslim—the more likely it is to allow daughters to inherit their share of natal family assets, as dictated by the Quran or religious prescription, or inheritance as per respective religious laws. FGDs and interviews with imams suggest, however, that it is much more common for daughters not to receive and claim their share, due to the prevalence of customary norms around men's role as breadwinners and household wealth owners.

Given the lack of quantitative data on inheritance patterns in urban Bangladesh, we draw from our qualitative research to estimate that rural women inherit land much less frequently (one in five women inherit) than do urban women (especially middle-class urban women, who inherit at roughly equal rates as middle-class urban men do). Household wealth is positively associated with women's inheritance; there simply is "more to go around" and families can afford to move beyond strict gender norms. Even when women do inherit land, however, they face more obstacles than men in registering and legally owning their inheritance, such as high fees for registering land, for which they have to ask husbands; procedural obstacles; limited mobility to travel to government offices, etc. Families know this and sometimes use it to justify not giving shares to daughters, rather than acknowledging how much more productive women could be with their inherited assets. Qualitative data suggest that this practice is yet another effect of discriminatory gender norms. Natal families also worry about losing land if given to daughters who could register the land in names of husbands or children. At the same time, agricultural land ownership is not positively associated with greater economic empowerment of women, according to multivariate analysis, which finds a more robust relationship between women's economic activities and accumulation of assets other than agricultural land. Qualitative data lend insight into this finding: women's agricultural land ownership appears to be more determined by their relationships with men (fathers, brothers, husbands) than does their ownership of other assets. Many of these other assets owned by women are highly likely to be sold in case of economic shocks, however.

Although most women may not own land and major productive assets, many exert greater economic control over agricultural land and the three other valuable assets (cattle, house, and nonagricultural land) than ownership patterns suggest. Few women meet the full criteria of direct ownership of land (that is, having the full range of economic rights over assets: the right to sell, mortgage, rent, and retain the revenue the asset generates), yet many possess some of these rights. Among rural women whose households own any assets, 43 percent have rights to sell, give, rent or buy agricultural land (compared to 88 percent of men with household assets). Considering all four assets, 38 percent of rural women from households with any assets have full or joint ownership (compared to 96 percent of rural men), but 58 percent have economic rights (compared to 97 percent of men).

The only asset ownership gender gaps that favor women are for a few small, lower-value household assets, namely, poultry (chickens, ducks, and turkeys) and small consumer durables. In addition, women own small livestock at only slight lower rates than do men, at 59 and 70 percent, respectively. One drawback to owning small assets, however, is that these assets are more likely to be sold in times of economic shocks, making women asset-owners more economically vulnerable than men who own assets.

Despite these gaps, there has been marked improvement in society's attitude toward women's asset ownership. Women are claiming their inheritance at increasing rates over time, due in part to a change in attitudes; qualitative data suggest that brothers are more supportive than they were 10 years ago of their sisters claiming their inheritance. Married women have more of their own funds thanks to their rising FLFP and employment rates; multivariate analysis finds asset ownership to be positively correlated with LFP. Although they still rarely do so, women also are more likely than before to register and own land that they purchased with their own funds, as owning land through this channel is more acceptable than through inheritance.

Further closure of gender gaps in land and other household asset ownership requires policy change and practical interventions, which can be organized into the main recommendation areas listed below. Specific recommended actions and good practice examples can be found in chapter 3, as well as in the "Recommended Roles and Responsibilities of Various Stakeholder Groups" section later in this chapter, where select examples are organized according to the responsible stakeholder.

- Institute legal reform for women's inheritance of land
- Address social norms against women's land ownership and registration
- Draw from successful practices elsewhere to inform programs on how to improve women's land rights

Women's ownership and control of financial assets: Improving over time, but products and services not sufficiently well-suited

Bangladesh has since the 1970s led the way in the developing world in innovative financial service provision for the poorest women. Roughly four-fifths of microfinance institution (MFI) clients are poor women from the country's rural areas. Although the growing urban population—which is increasingly targeted by MFIs—constitutes a minority of MFI borrowers, most of these are women.

Women's use of financial assets is increasing over time, but it is not increasing rapidly enough to close gender gaps. In fact, stubborn gaps in the use of some financial products have expanded. Between 2014 and 2017, men's account ownership grew by 30 percentage points to reach 65 percent, while women's grew by only 10 percentage points to 36 percent. As a consequence, Bangladesh substantially underperforms comparator countries in the size of these gaps. Bangladesh also has among the lowest rates of borrowing—by both women and men—from a financial institution among the same comparator countries. Bangladeshis' shift away from financial institutions to borrow and save between 2011 and 2017 is particularly evident among rural women, more than three-fourths of whom save in an NGO or shamity. Only about one-fourth of men save there; the bulk of their savings (61.3 percent) are in banks or other government financial institutions or in land leased from others. They also save at home or with relatives and in "other" locations at higher rates than women do. Rural women also are far more likely (72 percent) to borrow from an NGO or shamity than men (13.5 percent), who have higher rates of borrowing from all four alternative sources.

Women in Bangladesh thus appear to have less diversity—in other words, fewer choices—than men in *where* they save and borrow money. They also have a smaller range than men in *which types* of financial products they typically use. Most women clients use credit, typically provided by MFIs through group loans that do not require traditional forms of collateral (which women lack due to their low ownership rates of high-value household assets). The next most commonly used product is savings, which is increasing among women due to mobilization by MFIs, though not as much as for men. Less common is insurance: women traditionally have been excluded from insurance markets, although MFIs have started offering life and health insurance to their female savers and borrowers. Still, the use rates among the poorest women are extremely low.

Loans to women continue to be of lower value and shorter duration—and have stricter terms—than loans to men, on average (the gender gap in loan size increased between 2007 and 2010), despite financial institutions' incipient efforts to become more flexible toward female clients. Historically, the narrow terms of women's credit is related, in part, to their lack of collateral and low financial literacy, as well as to binding gender norms that deem men more responsible and better suited than women to controlling finances. As women have become more educated, more exposed to work environments, more engaged in household decisions, and confident, MFIs are increasingly unable to meet women's demand for loans.

Loans are more likely to economically empower women if they are larger and of longer duration than the typical microloan, and the evidence on whether microcredit economically empowers women in Bangladesh is mixed. Too often these microloans to women end up under the control of husbands or other male household members, reinforcing women's minimal decision-making power in the household. In these cases, when loans are used for productive purposes (i.e., to start, operate, or expand a farm or business), they increase the capital of existing household business rather than promote women's entrepreneurship. Most microloans and savings, moreover, are not even used productively by men and women alike, but rather for household expenditures, such as groceries, and emergency purposes. In 2017, only 9 percent of men and 7 percent of women used savings productively, though both rates had increased slightly since 2014. The gender gap in rural areas is especially large: 21 percent of men's savings and 6 percent of women's savings were used to buy land or a house or for productive purposes in 2017. Our qualitative research confirms that in both urban and rural areas, women are more likely than men to use savings and loans for family consumption needs.

Regardless of residential area, few women are the sole decision-makers on household financial issues (12–16 percent) or even on their own use of financial services (14 percent). Their spouses continue to make the majority of these decisions, and joint decision making is the next most common. Even parents or guardians have greater decision-making power than women over household assets and financial services. There is evidence, however, that for rural women, sole decision making is at least increasing over time (accompanied by a decrease in joint decision making), though men's rates of sole decision making are increasing even more. The 2015 finding that 70 percent or less of rural women control income spent on their own needs (for their own medicines, clothes, toiletries and food)—up from 50 percent or less in 2011–12—suggests that women are gaining decision-making power over some—but not all—kinds of household finance. Families that strictly observe purdah—curtailing or even disallowing altogether women's mobility outside the home—as well as the high household demands on women's time reinforce barriers to women's choice and freedom to control and make household expenditures.

Constraints on women's access to and control over finances emanate from outside the family, as well. Limited geographical coverage of financial institutions, especially in rural areas; minimum account balances and other fees in banks (and high-interest fees in MFIs); necessary paperwork and formal documents; and collateral requirements all are more likely to derail women's than men's efforts to open accounts. This is because, compared to men, women on average have lower wages, less mobility, less ownership of high-value assets, and a lower frequency of having their names on formal documents, such as national certificates, voter ID cards, tax ID numbers and even utility bills. Mobile banking and other digital technologies for accessing financial institutions have the potential to ease many of these constraints on women. Unfortunately, the technical gender gap in Bangladesh is large. Women comprise only 18–32 percent of all users of mobile banking services or other digital finance, including debit and credit cards and accounts—even among those who are aware of mobile money options.

Chapter 4 presents a number of recommendations regarding policy change and good practice interventions to close gender gaps in ownership and control of financial assets, as summarized by the main recommendation areas listed below. Select recommended actions and good practice examples also can be found in the "Recommended Roles and Responsibilities of Various Stakeholder Groups" section, where they are organized by responsible stakeholder group.

- Tackle patriarchal norms that undermine women's ability to use and control financial services
- Expand the types and flexibility of financial services available for women
- Improve the ease of documentation and other procedural barriers
- Raise women's rates of financial literacy
- Reduce financial and transaction costs, and increase flexibility by addressing multiple constraints simultaneously
- Address women's low use of mobile and digital technologies for finance

Women's entrepreneurship: Growing, but gender gaps continue to impede women's economic empowerment

It is important that the GoB, Bangladesh's financial institutions, and other stakeholders recognize that entrepreneurship endows women with much greater economic empowerment than does mere access to and use of credit. Roughly half of Bangladeshi women entrepreneurs surveyed in 2014 and 2017 reported starting a business in order to become financially independent and/or more economically empowered. In spite of the government's and Bangladesh Bank's laudable efforts to promote women entrepreneurs through policy and schemes that target women SMEs, gender gaps in entrepreneurship remain larger than gender gaps in use and control over financial assets. Numerous layers of obstacles must be addressed before women can more easily advance in creating and sustaining successful SMEs, which comprise the vast majority of enterprises in the country.

In 2015, Bangladesh ranked 75 out of 77 countries in providing an environment that encourages development and growth of women-owned firms. This is despite tremendous increases in both the number of women's enterprises since the 1970s and the rates of women's graduation from owning small to medium, and medium to large, enterprises. Women comprise only 10 percent of all business owners, and female majority-owned enterprises comprise a mere 1.7 percent of formal enterprises; moreover, their firms are smaller, have lower survival rates, and are concentrated in fewer sectors (primarily wholesale and retail trade of textiles) than firms in the formal sector that are owned by male entrepreneurs. Women-owned enterprises also are unevenly geographically distributed: Dhaka division hosts the greatest share with nearly one-third of the country's women-led enterprises, while Barisal and Sylhet have the smallest share, at roughly 5 percent each. Finally, although women entrepreneurs' access to credit has risen over time, the total value of credit disbursed to them annually from 2010 to 2017 was only 3 percent of the value disbursed to men entrepreneurs.

Differences between female and male entrepreneurs' demand for credit and aspirations to expand businesses *do not* explain this gender gap in disbursement amounts. Women business owners aspire to have larger-value loans and to expand their businesses more quickly than their circumstances allow. The heavy time burden of household responsibilities, lack of education and financial literacy, and onerous procedural requirements all hamper female entrepreneurs' aspirations more than they hamper men's.

In addition to these barriers, other obstacles to women's use and control over finance tend to hinder women's entrepreneurship, as well. Patriarchal constraints—on women's mobility; on their access to markets, networks, and financial institutions; on family and community approval of women being entrepreneurs; and on opportunities beyond fulfilling family roles of wife and mother, for example—keep even women who manage to start businesses closely tied to the household, with enterprises often confined to home-based and informal activities that typically generate low value and low returns.

The lack of consistent definitions of SMEs in Bangladesh complicates efficient policy making and undermines the efficacy of existing schemes to support women entrepreneurs and would-be entrepreneurs. Still, it is clear that improving rates of female entrepreneurship, as well as growth and survival rates of women-owned firms, will depend upon expanding the range of choices available to women who aspire to create and grow businesses. Bangladeshi women need more options available to them in terms of size and flexibility of loans, up-to-date financial literacy and business development training, customized interventions, industries in which they are welcome to produce and sell goods and services, and—more generally—alternatives to being providers of care and housework in their homes.

As detailed in chapter 5, improving women's rates of starting and sustaining enterprises will require supportive interventions that fall under the main recommendation areas listed below. Many of these recommendations can be found organized by responsible stakeholder group in the "Recommended Roles and Responsibilities of Various Stakeholder Groups" section.

- Enforce policies and schemes that support women entrepreneurs, and customize selected interventions
- Maximize success of business development training with complementary training, and pay attention to the timing and length of such training

- Address constraints arising from patriarchal norms that are binding for entrepreneurs
- Ensure that credit meets the demand of women entrepreneurs
- Address women entrepreneurs' poor access to networks and markets
- Reach more women by providing a women-friendly financial environment

Exclusion of ethnic and religious minority women: little choice and rights, but high potential

The dearth of gender-disaggregated economic data on ethnic and religious minorities—itself a sign of their marginalization from labor and other markets in Bangladesh—makes analysis of economic empowerment of women in these groups exceedingly difficult. The scant available data suggest that ethnic minority women are doubly marginalized in select domains. For instance, they have lower literacy rates than all women and compared to ethnic minority men, although the gender gap in minority literacy rates is narrowing over time. Given ethnic minorities' overall lower rates of land and other household asset ownership, financial access, and entrepreneurship compared to the general population, it may be surmised that minority women's levels of ownership and control in these areas as well are lower than those for majority women. The data from our qualitative research indicate that minority women have very limited control over household finances, and that minority women who come into any property—inheriting it or even buying it with their own funds—hand it over to husbands to register in men's names and keep property in the male line. Average monthly wages for minority groups are about one-fifth of those for the total rural population, and there are much greater gender wage gaps within minority groups that favor men than among the total rural population. The large majority of ethnic minorities—especially minority women—work in the informal sector. Unlike other women who participated in the primary qualitative research, minority women did not express a sense of their economic empowerment improving over time.

Minority women's higher rates of LFP—and in some cases, of educational attainment—than majority women may, however, suggest a high potential for women of some ethnic and religious minority groups to make rapid gains in economic empowerment, so long as they are sufficiently targeted by supportive policies and interventions. As discussed in chapter 6, when the small Bangladesh Institute of Development Studies (BIDS) sample is disaggregated by ethnic group, we find LFP rates for both women and men in ethnic minority households to be greater than national rural household averages. High poverty rates among minority groups—and the accompanying economic pressure to take any kind of paying job—may only partly explain their greater participation in labor markets, especially among minority women. Ethnic minority women appear to be more responsive to economic factors than nonminority women, suggesting that the former may be less hampered by social restrictions on women's mobility and their confinement to family roles. LFS data indicate little difference in labor force participation rates between the poorest and wealthiest Muslim and Hindu (that is, religious majority) women, whereas there is a considerable difference between the poorest and wealthiest women from the Buddhist and Christian minority groups, whose LFP rates roughly double as income falls (table 6.2). Poverty also does not explain the greater relative education achieved by women in some of the minority religious groups, compared to that achieved by majority women. The primary qualitative research as well finds that the studied minority women may have greater flexibility and independence to work outside the household, compared to urban and rural women in majority groups, even after marriage and childbirth.

Together, the quantitative and qualitative data suggest that sustainable interventions to improve the economic empowerment of women from ethnic and religious minority groups in Bangladesh could have especially high returns. We find almost all examples of good practices related to ethnic minority communities to be activities that are directly funded by development partners. When implemented, these examples have yielded positive results; however, their sustainability remains problematic. Unlike those in the majority population, ethnic and religious minority citizens (women in particular) have yet to attain their individual and community-level capabilities to sustain development interventions beyond the project period. For ethnic minority populations in the Chittagong Hills Tract (CHT) region, geographical remoteness creates an additional barrier. For ethnic minorities living in other parts of the country, social exclusion impedes their agency. Nonetheless, the government's and development partners' initiative of introducing primary education using five indigenous languages may open possibilities of introducing more inclusionary practices in the future. Minorities in Bangladesh are still very much struggling to achieve greater voice, as many of these groups may remain unrecognized or undercounted, as experts on the subjects believe.

The particularly few documented interventions for minorities, coupled with the lack of data at the national level disaggregated by ethnicity, contribute to a very limited understanding of specific challenges facing different minority groups. This makes it difficult to design policies and programs that would help enable minorities' advancement and economic empowerment. Many minorities face double exclusion due to their ethnic and religious minority identities, and minority women contend with an additional level of vulnerability as women in a highly patriarchal country.

Chapter 6 presents in detail a number of policy and practice recommendations to close ethnicity gaps, and gender gaps within ethnic minority groups, in the labor market, as well as in ownership and control of nonfinancial and financial assets, as summarized by the main recommendation areas listed below. Select recommended actions and good practice examples also can be found in the "Recommended Roles and Responsibilities of Various Stakeholder Groups" section, where they are organized by responsible stakeholder group.

- Improve understanding of all ethnic minorities residing throughout Bangladesh
- Strengthen the national framework to address minority issues
- Remove barriers to minority women's education and asset accumulation

RECOMMENDED ROLES AND RESPONSIBILITIES OF VARIOUS STAKEHOLDER GROUPS

There are myriad tested and evaluated policies and programs by CSOs, governments and private sector actors across the globe and in Bangladesh that illustrate how to effectively address women's lack of economic empowerment, as detailed in chapters 2–6. While adapting global and older Bangladeshi interventions to the current imperatives of women's economic empowerment in Bangladesh, certain principles need to be kept in mind. First, it will be important to assess the cost and cost effectiveness of potential interventions before choosing between them. It also is clear from the range of promising interventions that *one size does not fit all*. Global examples may thus have to be modified and targeted such that they are appropriate for Bangladesh, and all programs need to be structured to respond to women's economic and other constraints and opportunities in the target communities within the country. For instance, it is likely important to design interventions somewhat differently for minorities than for other groups, for the very poor versus not-so-poor women entrepreneurs, for urban versus rural women, and so on. Even the most successful global interventions need to be piloted and tested in Bangladesh and in different communities before being rolled out on a large scale. Finally, global experience makes clear that *political will*—among the government (which already has conveyed its will at the national level, with the National Women Development Policy, as shown in box 7.1), civil society and private sector—to shift the needle on gender equality and women's economic empowerment is essential for success, as is the active engagement of women and their communities in achieving these goals.

The following sections briefly summarize the roles and responsibilities of government and other stakeholders in Bangladesh, based on good practices described in prior chapters. Yet, there are certain actions that *all* stakeholders need to keep in mind while designing or testing programs or policies to address any of the domains of women's economic engagement and empowerment. Most critically, and as this book has emphasized, all actors need to recognize that multiple aspects of women's economic empowerment—rights over productive assets, employment, access to finance, and control over income—are connected. Policy interventions should aim to improve not only a single dimension, but, rather, multiple dimensions of women's economic empowerment. Second, policy and programmatic attempts need to be based in an acknowledgement of the role of gender-unequal patriarchal norms in perpetuating women's economic disengagement and disempowerment. Recognizing the existing unequal power dynamics between women and their spouses, families, and community, as well as attempting to shift this balance of power, would help to achieve sustainable gender equality. As part of this effort, stakeholders will likely need to invest in raising awareness of the benefits of women's economic participation and the costs of excluding women.

BOX 7.1

The National Women Development Policy

In 2011, Shirin Sharmin Chowdhury, Speaker of the Bangladesh Parliament, announced plans to draw up a national action plan that would "Provide women with full control over their right to land, earned property, health, education, training, information, inheritance, credit, technology and opportunity to earn…And enact necessary new laws to put these rights into practice." The policy also aims to "Ensure women's rights in formulation and implementation of economic policies [for sectors like trade, currency and tax]."

Source: Adapted from Tusher (2011).

There are other, specific barriers common across domains of economic empowerment that all stakeholders will likely need to address, whether in terms of the job market, financial institutions, or assets. These include sexual harassment and other safety issues; mobility constraints; high financial, procedural, transactional, and other costs that raise an often insurmountable barrier for women with few financial means in their control; and the lack of childcare. Finally, it is incumbent on all stakeholders to collect or maintain—to the extent feasible for each type of stakeholder—accurate gender-disaggregated data on their efforts to improve women's economic engagement, so that progress can be tracked across economic domains and over time.

Beyond these overarching actions, there are specific roles and responsibilities for which particular stakeholders—or groups of stakeholders—are best placed to take the lead. We describe these in the paragraphs below. Table 7.1 first presents priority actions for all stakeholders, with the most urgent listed first, and then summarizes interventions that each type of stakeholder can take in closing select gender gaps in economic empowerment. "Low-hanging fruit"—that is, priority interventions that can be implemented within the next 1–2 years to see short- and near-term results—are identified by an asterisk (*).

Government of Bangladesh

Law and policy

At the level of international policy compliance and in recognition of the importance of women's economic empowerment, the government has taken a range of appropriate actions. Bangladesh is committed to the Convention on the Elimination of All Forms of Discrimination against Women (CEDAW) and the Beijing Platform for Action. Further, Article 29 of the Bangladeshi Constitution mandates "equal opportunity" for all citizens. As described across chapters 2–6, several national-level policies also exist.

TABLE 7.1 **Stakeholder roles in reducing gender gaps in Bangladesh, by area/outcome of economic empowerment**

GENDER GAP	KEY RECOMMENDATIONS	ACTIONS AND ROLES FOR SPECIFIC STAKEHOLDERS (BASED ON EVIDENCE FROM BANGLADESHI AND GLOBAL GOOD PRACTICES)		
		GOVERNMENT OF BANGLADESH	PRIVATE SECTOR	OTHER STAKEHOLDERS
Priority actions for all stakeholders to adopt in addressing gender gaps in all domains of economic engagement and empowerment				

1. Launch multimedia awareness campaigns about benefits of women's economic participation and costs of women's low economic empowerment

2. Lower procedural costs of women's ownership of land, formal financial accounts, and enterprises

3. Collect gender-disaggregated data that can be compared over time and covers all aspects of economic engagement and empowerment

4. Address sexual harassment and other safety concerns in workplaces, public spaces, and transportation

5. Provide childcare through public-private partnerships (PPPs) and private sector firms

6. Address social norms that underlie and perpetuate gender gaps in economic opportunity and control

continued

TABLE 7.1, *continued*

GENDER GAP	KEY RECOMMENDATIONS	ACTIONS AND ROLES FOR SPECIFIC STAKEHOLDERS (BASED ON EVIDENCE FROM BANGLADESHI AND GLOBAL GOOD PRACTICES)		
		GOVERNMENT OF BANGLADESH	PRIVATE SECTOR	OTHER STAKEHOLDERS
Key gender gaps in labor market outcomes • Female labor force participation • Gender wage gap	1. Address barriers to girls' education beyond 10th grade 2. Improve women's access to technical education and other marketable skills* 3. Improve women's working conditions* 4. Provide female-friendly benefits like childcare* 5. Address gender norms to expand choices beyond traditional household roles 6. Further lower rates of child marriage	• Better enforce existing supportive laws • Review and improve policy and practice on quotas for women's employment in public sector* • Scale up tested education-related conditional cash transfers aimed at keeping girls and minorities in school beyond grade 10, and encouraging their acquisition of STEM skills* • Scale up CCTs and other established methods to further raise age at marriage • Better align TVET and other curricula to skills demanded by the market • Explore PPP options for childcare* • Consider extending school day to minimize need for childcareᵇ • Improve gender-disaggregated economic data collection*	• Pilot employer-provided childcare good practices* • Proactively partner with Ministry of Labor and Employment, Ministry of Education, Ministry of Primary Education, and TVET providers to ensure their training curricula are imparting high-level technical skills that private sector employers are seeking, following enactment of the National Skills Development Act*	**NGOs** • Increase awareness of barriers to women's labor force participation and equal wages* • Engage men and community leaders in efforts to change gender norms around women in the workplace • Increase awareness of and experiment with programs to increase age at marriage **WB operations** • Transforming Secondary Education for Results* • Safety Net Systems for the Poorest (AF)* • Bangladesh Jobs Programmatic DPC*
		• Provide safe, accessible and affordable transportation for women between home and workplace (* for private sector only)		**WB operations** • Dhaka Public Transport Improvement Project
		• Address risks of sexual harassment and other gender-based violence in the workplace and provide redressal mechanisms • Provide clean, functional, and separate sanitation facilities for women and men • Share costs through PPPs to provide high-quality, affordable, accessible childcare either in addition to or as alternatives to private childcare		
				WB operations • Dhaka City Neighborhood Upgrading Project* • Dhaka Sanitation Improvement Project • Bangladesh Municipal Water Supply and Sanitation Project*

* Indicates a "quick win"; that is, an intervention to undertake in the next 1–2 years to yield near- and medium-term results.

continued

TABLE 7.1, *continued*

GENDER GAP	KEY RECOMMENDATIONS	ACTIONS AND ROLES FOR SPECIFIC STAKEHOLDERS (BASED ON EVIDENCE FROM BANGLADESHI AND GLOBAL GOOD PRACTICES)		
		GOVERNMENT OF BANGLADESH	PRIVATE SECTOR	OTHER STAKEHOLDERS
Gender gaps in ownership and control of household assets • Land ownership • Economic rights over land • Nonagricultural land and smaller household assets	1. Institute legal reform for women's inheritance of land 2. Address social norms against women's land ownership and registration	• Bring women's land inheritance and ownership rights into national dialogue about development • Offer discounted land registration fees for women[b] • Streamline property registration procedures* • Establish legal protection of marital property • Promote joint titling of land and property • Institute automatic mechanisms that register inheritance in daughters' names • Amend law with "cooling-off period" after division of land as per laws[a] • Land grants to landless[b]		**Legal aid associations** • Provide legal (including pro bono) services for women to use their inheritance rights • Provide dispute-resolution training* **Other NGOs** • Work with women advocates, including locally elected women, to raise issues of women's land rights **WB operations** • Integrated Digital Government Project • Livestock and Dairy Development Project* • Bangladesh Sustainable Coastal and Marine Fisheries* • Sustainable Forests and Livelihood Project*
		• Engage community and religious leaders in addressing social norms against women's asset ownership and inheritance by daughters per Muslim Personal Law		
Gender gaps in financial inclusion • Accounts in financial institutions • Loans & savings in formal financial institutions • Use and control of credit	1. Tackle patriarchal norms that undermine women's ability to use and control financial services 2. Expand the types and flexibility of financial services available for women* 3. Improve the ease of documentation and other procedural barriers 4. Raise women's rates of financial literacy	• Provide financial products (accounts, savings, loans, credit, wages, etc.) solely in women's names to enable women's control[b]* • Address the inflexibility of financial services that lead to high monetary and transaction costs for women • Experiment with alternate forms of evaluating creditworthiness since women often do not own land or other assets necessary for traditional credit rating[b] • Invest in secure national biometric identification to reduce the burden of documentation-related barriers • Train bank staff in how to work with women clients and engage more women bank staff to create women-friendly environments in financial institutions[b]* • Experiment with tested methods, such as agent banking, to increase access to banking and other financial services*		**Media** • Use television and other popular media to spread awareness of financial products and services, for example, through TV drama and theater[b]* **MFIs** • Provide collateral-free credit with more flexible repayment options[b]* • Bundle programs for skills training and market diversification along with microcredit **WB operations** • Cash Transfer Modernization Project • Integrated Digital Government Project

* Indicates a "quick win"; that is, an intervention to undertake in the next 1–2 years to yield near- and medium-term results.

continued

TABLE 7.1, *continued*

GENDER GAP	KEY RECOMMENDATIONS	ACTIONS AND ROLES FOR SPECIFIC STAKEHOLDERS (BASED ON EVIDENCE FROM BANGLADESHI AND GLOBAL GOOD PRACTICES)		
		GOVERNMENT OF BANGLADESH	PRIVATE SECTOR	OTHER STAKEHOLDERS
	5. Address high financial and transaction costs, and increase flexibility, by addressing multiple constraints simultaneously 6. Address women's low use of mobile and digital technologies for finance	• Engage with men and other community leaders to address patriarchal constraints, such as mobility and women's control of finance • Collaborate to create multifaceted programs to address financial illiteracy that combine financial education with financial services and community awareness-raising • Government, private sector and MFIs can collaborate to systematically increase women's use of mobile and digital technologies informed by good practices in other countries and in Bangladesh[b]		
Gender gaps in entrepreneurship • Enterprise ownership, growth and management	1. Enforce policies and schemes that support women entrepreneurs, customize interventions 2. Maximize success of business development training with complementary training, timing 3. Address constraints arising from patriarchal norms that are binding for entrepreneurs 4. Ensure that credit meets the demand of women entrepreneurs 5. Address women entrepreneurs' poor access to networks and markets 6. Reach more women by providing a women-friendly financial environment		• Provide high-quality training in business practices, such as formal accounting practices, registration practices, and managerial skills[b] • Business development training has to be intensive and of long duration to be effective[b] • Provide microfranchising opportunities (with NGOs)[b]*	**WB operations** • Sustainable Enterprise Project • Livestock and Dairy Development Project* • Bangladesh Sustainable Coastal and Marine Fisheries* • Sustainable Forests and Livelihood Project*
		• Address risks of sexual harassment and other forms of gender-based violence and provide redressal mechanisms • Provide credit that aligns with women entrepreneurs' needs, that is: flexible credit which accommodates women's lack of credit history and is bundled with other financial services to improve business performance and earnings[b]* • All other actions by the governmental and private financial sectors to improve financial inclusion would also improve women's entrepreneurship opportunities and growth		
		• There is no one-size-fits all approach. • Design interventions keeping in mind participating women's skills, constraints, motivations for entrepreneurship and other characteristics • Experiment with and evaluate a range of childcare provision interventions and scale up successful efforts		

* Indicates a "quick win"; that is, an intervention to undertake in the next 1–2 years to yield near- and medium-term results.

continued

TABLE 7.1, *continued*

GENDER GAP	KEY RECOMMENDATIONS	ACTIONS AND ROLES FOR SPECIFIC STAKEHOLDERS (BASED ON EVIDENCE FROM BANGLADESHI AND GLOBAL GOOD PRACTICES)		
		GOVERNMENT OF BANGLADESH	PRIVATE SECTOR	OTHER STAKEHOLDERS
		• Combine microcredit with other services, such as skills training and market diversification		
		• Create, encourage and increase awareness of women's professional networks[b]		
		• Provide high-quality, affordable, accessible childcare either in addition to or as alternatives to private childcare		
Exclusion of minority ethnic women • Labor market outcomes • Land and household assets • Financial inclusion • Entrepreneurship	1. Improve understanding of all ethnic minorities residing throughout Bangladesh* 2. Strengthen the national framework to address minority issues 3. Remove barriers to minority education and asset accumulation	• Address lack of official recognition of several minority groups • Regularize ethnic minorities' customary land titles and/or provide alternative nationally recognized property rights • Disaggregate all national data by ethnicity*		**WB operations** • Safety Net Systems for the Poorest (AF)* • Transforming Secondary Education for Results Operation*
		• Consider affirmative action and incentive programs, such as CCTs (e.g., for education) • Create programs to specifically expand employment opportunities for minority women • Collaborate to better orient minorities' job skills to specific, local labor market needs		

Notes: CCT = conditional cash transfer; TVET = Technical and Vocational Education and Training; NGO = nongovernmental organization; MFI = microfinance institution; STEM = science, technology, engineering, and mathematics.
a. For rural areas only.
b. Evaluated good practice.
* Indicates a "quick win"; that is, an intervention to undertake in the next 1–2 years to yield near- and medium-term results.

To reduce gender gaps in education, skills development, LFP, and employment opportunities, GoB has the opportunity to ensure better enforcement of laws that support girls' and women's progress in these areas. Given an already strong policy framework that addresses risks of sexual harassment related to the workplace, Bangladesh would benefit from a thorough review of whether—and how—the policies are enforced. It could follow the review with implementation of good practice examples (tailored to fit Bangladesh's particular needs) of strengthening enforcement, such as the AASHA movement in Pakistan and "safety audits" in India. More broadly, GoB could strengthen enforcement of labor regulations, including benefits. Female workers are often deprived not only of proper protection from sexual harassment, but of legally guaranteed maternity and family leave as well. The Department of Inspections of Factories and Establishments (DIFE) needs to enhance its capacity building, increase its pool of labor inspectors, and modernize its systems.

GoB also would benefit from a review of both policy and practice regarding its experience—since 1976—with quotas for women's employment in the public sector, which is more welcoming to women's employment than other sectors. A review would help identify both means of improving the efficacy of quotas (for example, by highlighting needs for capacity building and, perhaps, placement of women in higher decision-making positions to increase attention to gender inequities in labor markets) and laws and policies that require better enforcement to support women's public sector employment and related benefits, given the time required to improve women's job opportunities in the private sector.

To institute legal reform for women's inheritance of land, GoB can draw from the experience of different countries on several continents, as detailed in chapter 3, which have brought women's right to inherit and other ownership rights over land into national dialogue or constitutions. Among these, Nigeria incorporated women's land titling rights into its development agenda through its National Gender Policy in 2006; the Philippines, Vietnam, and Bolivia all have successfully used joint titling laws to ensure that married women can legally protect their rights in owning property. India's experience with the Hindu Succession (Amendment) Act of 2005 emphasizes the importance of not only creating but enforcing laws that protect daughters from discrimination in land inheritance practices and allow them to *de facto* inherit land. In urban and rural communities, among men and women alike, the government can help raise awareness of laws that support women's rights to inherit, own, and make decisions about land and other productive household assets. The NGO sector has proven quite successful at implementing outreach and awareness-raising programs, and examples may exist that the government could scale up (see NGO/ CSO section, below).

Similarly, the government also needs to ensure greater awareness and more effective implementation of existing, potentially excellent policies and schemes to improve women's access to finance, including for successful entrepreneurship. To raise awareness and improve implementation of schemes would necessitate several simultaneous actions, including better training of government and implementing partners' staff, simpler design of products, improved geographic accessibility, and more effective use of awareness campaigns—such as the example given in chapter 3—to spread messages and encourage participation (see Financial sector section below for more detailed recommendations regarding financial inclusion and women's entrepreneurship).

In terms of greater social inclusion, Bangladesh could start with the various as-yet unsigned international conventions, including the 2007 United Nations Declaration on the Rights of Indigenous Peoples, the Indigenous and Tribal Peoples Convention (ILO Convention 169), and the Rome Convention for the Protection of Human Rights and Fundamental Freedoms. GoB also can look to the experience of other countries to develop and pass comprehensive national nondiscrimination laws that provide protections from discrimination on ethnic grounds, as has occurred in Bulgaria, Mexico, and the Netherlands. Bulgaria's National Roma Integration Strategy 2012–20 and Panama's National Indigenous Peoples Development Plan are two examples that GoB could use to develop a national approach to better include the country's ethnic and religious minorities in its economic opportunities. Bangladesh would benefit from expanding the role of the Ministry of Chittagong Hill Tracts Affairs to cover all citizens (in both the hills and the plains) belonging to ethnic minority groups. The Human Rights Commission also should have a separate cell to address human rights violation complaints and other issues for minority groups. Similar institutional efforts in Vietnam have laid the groundwork for greater policy attention to minorities and helped enable international programs for minority groups.

Programming by government sector (nonfinancial)

Education. An urgent priority is to raise the average age at marriage, so that girls can continue their education past early adolescence. The Multi-Sectoral Programme on Violence Against Women, implemented under the Ministry of Women and Children Affairs, has been a pioneering force in government efforts to address violence against women and girls. Among the many important services it provides is the National Helpline Centre for Violence Against Women and Children (NHCVAWC), dedicated to violence treatment and prevention. NHCVAWC also serves as a means of raising awareness about and reporting—and possibly preventing—incidents of violence against women and girls, including child marriages. It is important to sustain and, as needed, scale up the Helpline Centre and other components of the program, with concerted efforts to map, harmonize, and coordinate with the many NGO initiatives in Bangladesh that aim to mitigate child marriage. Now in its fourth phase (2016–21), the multi-sectoral program is implemented jointly by GoB and the government of Denmark through the Ministry of Women and Children Affairs and in collaboration with the Ministries of Education; Health and Family Welfare; Home Affairs; Information; Law, Justice and Parliamentary Affairs; Labour and Employment; Local Government; Posts; Religious Affairs; Rural Development and Cooperative; Social Welfare; Telecommunications and Information Technology; and Youth and Sports (Ministry of Women and Children Affairs 2018).

GoB also can incentivize girls' education among minorities and other poor groups to increase these groups' educational attainment and, consequently, expand job opportunities. Programs such as conditional cash transfers can offset the potential loss of income and/or cost of childcare due to increased time spent in school by girls.

Closing gender gaps in technical skills training will improve the gender balance in tertiary education. Together with modifying curricula to emphasize content that responds to labor market demands, this will increase young women's qualifications for higher-paying job opportunities. In so doing, GoB can address the stubborn pattern of considerable occupational sex segregation in Bangladesh and even reduce gender wage gaps, to the extent that gender wage disparities are determined by gender differences in human capital attainment. GOB's ongoing TVET program, implemented in collaboration with the EU, does aim to remove gendered barriers to women's training in a range of nonconventional sectors for women and to better align itself with the private sector in public-private partnerships (see Private sector section below, for more details). The current program may well benefit from some additional review and adjustment with the following principles in mind:

- *Encourage girls and young women toward STEM fields and, beyond that, careers,* by working with female role models, school counselors, and in-school support groups. Doing so will help (a) raise awareness and encourage girls and their families toward this broader spectrum of potential occupations; and (b) retain female students and workers, with particular attention to those from minority groups, once they join STEM educational and occupational fields.
- *Better align school curricula—particularly in TVET—to skills demanded by growth sectors of the economy* (see Republic of Korea example in chapter 2).

- *Improve female and male students' acquisition of STEM skills, including minority students, to better prepare them for job markets*—for example, through STEM-pathway focused programs (Hallman et al. 2003; Lyon et al. 2012; Ruel et al. 2002) or by mandating universal computer training in secondary school or even earlier—or variations thereof, as implemented by several countries (Passey 2017).

The education system also can join other stakeholders to offer alternatives to private childcare services (see chapter 2 for a broader discussion of good practice examples; see "Private sector (other than financial)" section below regarding such services offered by the private sector). Affordable, accessible childcare can benefit multiple aspects of women's economic empowerment, including entrepreneurship and other paid work, and can ease women's double burden of care responsibilities and employment. Government, civil society and the private sector could join hands in sharing the costs to provide high-quality childcare that women and their households would use, which is especially needed in lower-income communities. There are several ways in which Bangladesh's education system could help provide parents of school-age children with time to work or seek work, including (a) Early childhood education programs for young children (see Head Start example in chapter 2); (b) Public-private partnerships to provide on-site or near-site childcare for private firm employees; (c) Partnerships with high-quality private childcare services to provide school-based aftercare for school-age children; (d) Provision of educators to carry out psycho-pedagogical activities in community-based child care models (as Guatemala's Hogares Communitarios Program has done, for example), (e) Extended the length of the school day (see example from Chile in chapter 2).

Land. To ensure that women receive inheritance as per Muslim Personal and civil laws—and, in particular, prevent women from renouncing their inheritance shares and giving up their property to male relatives—the government may consider implementing innovative policies, such as automatic mechanisms that register inheritance in daughters' names, as well as imposing a "cooling-off" period (see example from Jordan) after the division of an inheritance during which heirs cannot renounce their rights. The government could also do the following:

- *Offer discounted land registration fees for women.* The government must recognize that land registration fees are one of the obstacles for women to register land in their own names, and should look into developing policies that waive such fees or provide discounts for women who register property in their name.
- *Streamline property registration procedures.* As women suffer from cumbersome bureaucratic processes more than men due to their greater lack of agency, mobility constraints, and purdah practices, government streamlining of procedures could help further narrow the gender gap in property registration.
- *Establish legal protections of marital property.* Women are vulnerable to losing legal rights to property when their marital status changes due to divorce or death of husbands. Legal solutions can be categorized into three broad groups, namely promoting joint ownership of property, remedying the marital property regime, and instituting gender equal property rights in higher laws.

- *Address social norms against women's land ownership and registration.* Engaging women, other household members (especially husbands and in-laws), communities, and community religious leaders through community mobilization and similar efforts has proven effective in changing norms and increasing women's land rights.
- *Use community mobilization also to improve land registration processes* (see chapter 3 for good practices).

Minority women need additional attention. The government could establish nationally recognized property rights for minority groups (with special measures to ensure women minorities' rights) by developing a public program to regularize ethnic minorities' customary land titles and/or provide alternative property rights to reduce land-related economic vulnerability. Providing vulnerable minorities with public khas land (as in Vietnam), assisting with formal titles or leases to the land on which they reside (as in the World Bank CESAR Project in Romania), and promoting female-only and/or joint property titles could reduce ethnic and religious minority women's exclusion and expand their economic opportunity.

Labor and Employment. GoB's Ministry of Labour and Employment will need to play more of a convening and coordinating role in bringing together industry leaders, educators (in secondary education, tertiary education, and the TVET system), and job search mechanisms and networks. With the recent submission to Parliament of the National Skills Development Act, now is the time to develop a system that maximizes efficient collaboration across the concerned stakeholders. Close and regular communication among these four entities will ensure alignment between employers' labor needs and the advanced skills—such as in STEM fields—being taught in secondary schools, universities, and vocational training programs. The Ministry can help target women who have just completed their skills training to link them with the kinds of jobs that help close gender gaps in access to the same job search mechanisms—for instance, in local media, on job search websites, through networks of mentors—that are useful to male job seekers. This, in turn, will help close gender gaps in the quality of work and wages paid for that work.

To ensure firms' compliance with the various laws and policies that support women's safety in the workplace, the Ministry's Inspector of Factories and Establishments will need to expand its monitoring and compliance efforts to better enforce firms' compliance with laws. This could include actions such as instituting and enforcing sexual harassment mitigation measures required by law; ensuring implementation of maternity leave policies; providing separate toilet facilities for women; ensuring safe conditions for women in workplaces and public spaces, on transport, and in work-provided dormitories and other housing for women workers; and providing other women-friendly workplace benefits and amenities. At the same time, however, the Ministry needs to be cognizant of—and monitor—whether it then becomes more expensive for firms to hire women to the extent that they are reluctant to do so.

Transport. The country's transportation system is in dire need of improvement to ensure that women and girls—as well as men and boys—have safe and affordable access to public transportation to school and work, whether they live in urban centers or in more remote areas of Bangladesh. Even for those who can physically access and afford public transportation, its current unsafe conditions of travel and the high rates of sexual harassment and other gender-based violence against women and girls on public transport are simply unacceptable. From national to local levels of government, the responsible agencies can immediately start exploring options to adapt to the Bangladeshi context and pilot good practice interventions from other countries. Such interventions will require holistic approaches that address both concrete and near-term needs (such as training transportation personnel in safe operating practices) as well as longer-term and less-tangible requirements, such as improving social support for women's safety in the public sphere. Given the multifaceted, cross-sectoral nature of effective interventions, GoB should partner with relevant stakeholders in the private sector, NGO, and media. Each stakeholder can bring its comparative advantage to collaborative efforts. This multipronged approach was largely responsible for the success of the Hazme el Paro program in Mexico (see details in chapter 2).

Financial sector (government and private sector)

The financial sector can contribute to addressing patriarchal norms that undermine women's ability to use and control financial services by offering products in women's own names, global examples show. An effective "quick win" in this area is to offer women savings other financial products that are solely in their names—as opposed to in husbands' names or joint owner-ship. Evaluations of such efforts in countries as varied as Brazil, India, Mexico, Pakistan, and the Philippines indicate that when financial savings or income is in women's own names, they have much greater control over these finances. Similarly, experiments from Kenya detailed in chapter 4 illustrate the power of mobile technology to increase women's control over finances. Creating a more women-friendly environment or women-friendly banks can address women's mobility constraints, which also hamper their use of financial services.

The financial sector needs to collaborate with nonfinancial government and nongovernment sectors to improve women's financial literacy. Some of the nonfinancial sectors with which partnership can yield positive results, evaluations show, include the media, community organizations, and organizations that provide classroom-based financial education. The evidence is clear: only through cross-sectoral programs that respond to clients' needs and combine financial literacy with financial services can women's financial literacy improve notably.

Addressing the wide range of high financial and transaction costs is also important, and it is possible to do so effectively. There are multiple types of costs, however, that the financial system would need to consider. These include costs that arise from inflexibility of financial services relative to women's needs; procedural and documentation-related costs because often women do not have adequate official identification documents; and a range of transaction and transport costs because of poor access. As with the other changes to the financial system recommended here, evaluated examples from across the world provide a template for experimentation in Bangladesh, as detailed in chapter 4. Bangladeshi organizations, such as the Grameen Bank, lead the way in providing collateral-free, flexible credit to women to address transaction and financial costs women would otherwise have to incur. Other microfinance institutions in Bangladesh and elsewhere illustrate different aspects of cost reduction, such as providing door-to-door services to decrease transport and access-related costs.

Financial systems globally are becoming more digitized; the challenge is to increase women's currently low use of mobile and digital technologies for finance. Although there is less evaluated evidence in this area than for other aspects of financial inclusion, experiments and large-scale programs from Kenya, other Sub-Saharan countries, India, and Bangladesh itself offer lessons on how best to design digitization and increase specifically women's use of mobile technology for finance, including the following:

- *Start with feasibility studies* rather than rushing to put new technology in place;
- *Conduct and evaluate a pilot* before rolling out new mobile or digital money services;
- *Choose carefully* the relevant partners and model of digitization most applicable for the intended audience;
- *Start small* and simple and build as experience grows;
- *Take the time* to fully integrate new mobile financial services with pre-existing systems;
- *Secure support and provide training* to staff and current and potential users;
- *Ensure continuous communication and good relations with all stakeholders* to promote use of technology, get feedback, and address problems;
- *Be ready to wait* if the current research suggests that the market is not ready for a viable program.

The actions above serve the purpose also of enabling women to reach beyond use of finance to become successful entrepreneurs. However, the financial sector likely needs to reach beyond these recommendations to take additional actions specifically for problems women face in creating, managing and growing their own enterprises.

High-quality business development training is an important input to women entrepreneurs that the financial sector could take the lead in providing. In particular, as evaluated experiments across the developing world illustrate, improving women's business practices is key. These include formal accounting practices, registration practices, and managerial skills. Evaluated models of business development training from Mexico, Peru and other countries also emphasize that, given the urgent need to improve the performance of women-owned businesses, effective training needs to be intensive and of relatively long duration. Although there is no consensus on just how long training has to be so that it is effective, evidence leans toward multiple, hour-long classes spread over several weeks.

The financial sector can take a number of specific actions to improve women entrepreneurs' business performance and earnings. These actions include offering flexible credit, addressing prohibitive costs and lacunae, such as a lack of credit history, and linking credit offers with a bundle of other services and activities. Available evidence suggests, for instance, that women entrepreneurs who receive flexible credit may be more willing to experiment with trying new ways to grow their businesses. The use of alternate credit mechanisms—such as those tested in Peru and detailed in chapters 4 and

5—can help the financial sector reach additional women entrepreneurs in need of credit. The experience of Bangladesh's MFIs themselves suggests that the financial sector needs to combine credit with other efforts to ensure profitability, such as skills training and market diversification.

All stakeholders can play a part in addressing the paucity of professional networks, mentors and markets that women entrepreneurs face. As discussed in chapter 5, the Bangladesh Women's Chambers of Commerce and Industry (BWCCI) is a good example of one kind of national and local network opportunity. Programs from India and elsewhere show that networking, mentorship and marketing opportunities do not have to be stand-alone structures—which are costly to set up—but can also be introduced as part of other interventions. In this, the GoB could tap into its links with the financial sector, MFIs and other NGOs that already have programs or policies to reach out to women entrepreneurs; together, all stakeholders could provide mentoring, networking and other such opportunities to participants.

Private sector (other than financial)

Ideally, expanded opportunities for women's employment in the private sector would help rapidly shift women from informal to formal sector jobs. Given the enormous share of informal employment among all paid employment in Bangladesh (especially among women), however, near-term improvements in private sector employment will need to occur in informal sector firms just as much as—if not more so than—in formal firms. Attracting more women to private sector jobs will hinge not only on improving women's technical skills and other qualifications for working in these jobs (see Education section, above), but also on improving work conditions and female-friendly benefits to attract women and retain them. Sexual harassment and poor working conditions discourage competent candidates and productive employees. As a first step, private firms need to comply with employee treatment and working condition requirements that the government already has put in place. Efforts to improve such conditions in the RMG sector—such as the formation of the Accord, the Alliance, and Better Work Bangladesh (box 2.1)—can be emulated in other sectors. The private sector should aim not only to implement government-required actions thoroughly, but also to go "above and beyond" such requirements in order to improve conditions to sufficiently attract and retain a much larger share of working-age women. As discussed in detail in chapter 2, this would involve the following areas of action:

- *Address risks of sexual harassment and other GBV at workplaces:* Bangladesh's strong policy framework must be better implemented and enforced; a renewed focus on implementation efforts should draw from the relevant well-evaluated good practices, executed mostly by NGOs
- *Ensure safe and comfortable workspaces for all employees,* which includes access to safe, clean, and separate water and sanitation facilities for women
- *Provide women with safe and affordable transportation to and from the workplace:* In the near term, before public transportation systems have been upgraded to sufficient levels of safety and accessibility, large-scale private sector firms need to provide women workers with private transportation—for example, in buses or vans—operated by individuals who have been trained in recognizing and responding to incidents of sexual harassment and other forms

of GBV. Costs of private transportation should at least be subsidized, if not fully covered, by the employing enterprise. Smaller-scale firms should explore options to share costs of privately provided transportation.

- *Provide childcare*: The private sector should be held accountable in complying with the Bangladesh Labor Act of 2006 (Sec. 94), which requires all factories and other workplaces with 40 or more workers to have a daycare center for workers' children under the age of 6. Employers can look to the IFC report, *Tacking Childcare: The Business Case for Employer-Supported Childcare* (2017) for good practice examples of private sector employers providing a range of childcare options, some of which are described in chapter 2. The IFC also will be leading collaborative market research in Bangladesh, to be launched in 2019, that aims to promote the business case for employer-supported childcare services in Bangladesh. The research also will offer potential solutions, so that childcare-providing employers can improve their business outcomes, while also encouraging greater compliance with legal requirements.

- *Inform workforce development*: Large companies can work with GoB to inform the focus of workforce development programs in secondary, tertiary, and vocational education and training institutions to ensure that these programs are much better aligned with firms' immediate hiring needs and longer-term staffing goals. Similarly, smaller-scale private sector employers can work with NGOs operating at local levels that can provide guidance on (i) how to make training programs targeting women more available and accessible; and (ii) career advice provided at educational institutions to help girls and women develop skills to match local market needs.

Nongovernmental organizations and civil society organizations

Bangladesh is known for its strong and vast network of NGOs that reach millions of people throughout the country. CSOs are similarly important, though they are not necessarily formally registered as NGOs are. Both have played an enormous role in implementing programs and enforcing policies and laws that support women's economic empowerment in the various domains.

Around the globe, NGOs have provided awareness outreach and many other services to mitigate barriers to women's LFP and to promote sustainable, comfortable, and safe employment.

The large and well-run NGOs in Bangladesh—with their close relationship with the government—could scale up their own (BRAC's, for instance) and also study other countries' examples of CSO-provided community-based child care center programs, which have been especially helpful to working women in rural areas.

The Safe Cities Intervention in Delhi, Jagori and GEMS interventions in India (with GEMS replicated in other countries already) are successful examples of how to change attitudes about gender roles and create safer spaces related to women's work—and their travel to and from work. Importantly, NGO programs aiming to change gender norms need to engage stakeholders across the board and to work with men and community leaders alongside local women.

Women's land inheritance has also been supported by NGOs in Bangladesh. The Madaripur Legal Association and the Khan Foundation have been instrumental in helping women claim property and realize other inheritance rights.

Such organizations have employed a range of innovative methods—such as interactive media campaigns; street theater and folk songs; dispute resolution training; leveraging religious leaders' influence over community attitudes and practices; and engaging women advocates to mobilize and train networks of women, including locally elected women—to raise awareness, advocate for women's inheritance rights, and help redress violations of women's property rights. Effective approaches also can be found in the evaluated Community-based Legal Aid (CBLA) program in Tanzania, in which an NGO's professional legal staff trained paralegals from program-covered villages to conduct outreach and raise awareness about legal rights over land and productive assets, help with lawyer referral, and advocate for women community members in disputes.

NGOs in Bangladesh also have long played a critical role in financial provision for women, especially for entrepreneurs in SMEs. Evidence from Bangladesh and elsewhere suggests how to improve their role further: providing flexible credit is a key element. NGOs providing microcredit to entrepreneurs need to shift their approach somewhat to provide additional services, such as skills training and market diversification; a range of experiments across the world suggest that microcredit alone is not an effective input into entrepreneurship development for women. In addition, NGOs are particularly well structured to take the lead on the recommended actions (described in the following paragraphs) to improve women's use and control of financial assets.

Make efforts to provide a greater set of options around financial provision and support to reflect women borrowers' and entrepreneurs' financial needs. Although this recommendation is applicable to any kind of institution—including public and private—that provides services to women financial clients and entrepreneurs, NGO-MFIs are especially well-designed and well-partnered to include a broader set of options in terms of repayment schedules (i.e., offering larger windows to make loan payments than is traditional for MFIs); providing women assistance in "graduating" to larger loan sizes without traditional collateral; as well as connecting women borrowers to broader financial support services, such as NGO-organized efforts (for instance, in schools and with women borrowers' husbands) to raise awareness around women's ownership of loans and women's ability to use and manage funds productively.

Establish programs directly focused on expanding the employment opportunities of Bangladesh's minorities, and minority women in particular. Bangladesh may, for instance, wish to explore the benefits of mobilizing local partner organizations to assist minority households to develop subproject proposals and provide grants for community-selected activities (see the Nepal Poverty Alleviation Fund example in chapter 6); providing job training for minorities and facilitating their access to markets (for example, see the Brazil Salto Caxias Hydropower Project in chapter 6); building minorities' market-oriented agricultural production capacity (as undertaken in Vietnam's P135-II); establishing minority women as teachers and thought leaders in villages to enhance learning and women's status (as CARE projects did in the Mekong region); and helping minority women earn a better living by adapting their farming practices through the establishment of women's only Livelihood and Rights Clubs (LARC) as well as Village Savings and Loans Associations (VSLA) (as in Vietnam's EMWE).

Strengthen the linkages between area employers and CSOs to better align minorities' job and life skills to specific, local labor market needs. The Juventud y

Empleo Project in the Dominican Republic is a good example that may be modifiable for the Bangladeshi context. This project provided low-income marginalized youth with life skills, technical job training, and private sector internships to meet the needs of local job markets.

Entertainment industry and other media

Raise awareness of women's decision-making roles about work and finances in households, and of women's rights over land and productive assets. The media could provide interesting and innovative ways of engaging women, men, and their broader communities to raise awareness about women's rights over land and productive assets (see example in chapter 3). Television and movies are effective vehicles through which to introduce more contemporary narratives about women working for pay, while also sharing family care and other housework with men in the household.

Address patriarchal norms that undermine women's ability to use and control financial services. The media can play an effective role in changing attitudes and behavior to enhance financial inclusion, experiences from around the world suggest. Local media can experiment with TV dramas and other edutainment programs. Media can raise awareness around norms that frown on women's control over finance; the practice of purdah that can result in women's seclusion or otherwise constrains their mobility; and women's time constraints due to the heavy burdens of household roles and responsibilities. In particular, if designed keeping in mind specific financial products and processes, such programs have been shown to not only increase awareness but also change financial behavior for viewing women and their households.

Research in academia, research institutions, development partners, others

The importance of collecting gender-disaggregated data cannot be overemphasized. Such data is critical to better understand the barriers to and opportunities for women's economic empowerment. In partnership with researchers working in academia, NGOs, and bilateral and multilateral development partners, the government should take steps to systematically collect and analyze data related to gendered constraints, such as asset ownership, time use, mobility, and perceptions of safety in upcoming household surveys (such as the HIES) to fill knowledge gaps.

Gender-disaggregated data on portfolio statistics and quality related to women's access to and use of various financial products and services is also needed. For timely data collection that can be useful for policy making the government needs to (a) maintain gender-based data on credit disbursement and dissemination of information on credit opportunities; (b) conduct annual studies to ensure that data are compared and progress is measured until the specific targets and quotas for women-owned businesses are met; and (c) strengthen the statistical basis for carrying out gender-related cross-country analyses and longitudinal studies on the impact of financial developments and relevant policies. Due to the nationally representative nature of these data, these efforts will need to be spearheaded by the government, but could include partnerships with the many research organizations in Bangladesh.

Empowerment of Bangladesh's minorities hinges in part on the government recognizing all of the country's ethnic groups and systematically collecting national data disaggregated by ethnicity and gender. Government must systematically collect national data disaggregated by ethnicity and gender in the census, ensuring that all minority individuals are counted in the census and other surveys, such as the LFS, including those working in the tea estates. The lack of official recognition of many minority groups as well as the undercounting of the country's minority population are contributing to current low levels of attention to minority issues.

Donor and development partners

Donor and development partners are involved in myriad ways—in partnerships with GoB and NGOs, in particular—in various programs across the country that aim to improve many aspects of women's economic engagement and empowerment, such as female students' acquisition of more advanced technical skills (especially in STEM fields), higher rates of women's labor force participation and paid employment, workplace safety and comfort, enhanced ownership and rights over land and financial assets, etc. In addition, we find almost all examples of good practices related to ethnic minority communities to be direct activities of projects funded by development partners. When implemented, these examples have yielded positive results; however, their sustainability remains problematic. To this end, it is important that donor and development partners supporting programs in Bangladesh allow financial support to be great enough and program duration to be long enough to see results and test piloted interventions for scalability. The amount and length of the funding also need to allow for rigorous evaluation to fill a vast knowledge gap about "what works" to economically empower women—particularly minority women—in Bangladesh and, more broadly, South Asia.

The World Bank Group's portfolio in Bangladesh

There are a number of operations in the World Bank Group's (WBG) lending portfolio in Bangladesh that are well placed and well designed to directly incorporate recommendations from this book to close gender gaps in the relevant arenas of economic empowerment, as project timelines allow. Relevant operations are organized below chronologically, by date of World Bank Board of Executive Directors approval, and the areas of potential intervention are listed beside each. The authors of this book and the Gender Platform for Bangladesh, Bhutan, and Nepal are available upon request to provide project teams with specific guidance for each intervention area.

Safety Net Systems for the Poorest (AF: P163677): This operation could prepare project beneficiaries for graduation from the program—with particular attention to women and ethnic minorities—by helping them, for example, to acquire technical skills needed for private sector jobs; achieve greater financial inclusion through national identity cards and mobile banking; or gain access to financial literacy and business development training.

Transforming Secondary Education for Results Operation (P160943): If timing permits, this project could be scoped for the potential to incorporate recommendations and good practices for increasing rates of girls' enrolment, retention, and completion of STEM courses; or for mandating computer training for all students, male and female.

Cash Transfer Modernization Project (P160819): There are potential entry points for actions to close gender gaps in financial inclusion, particularly through mobile banking, asset ownership, advanced skills education and training, and even entrepreneurship. Special efforts could be made to target populations from minority ethnic groups.

National Strategy for Development of Statistics Implementation Support (P157987): This task has the potential to help Bangladesh address lacunae in gender-disaggregated economic and financial data, including among ethnic minority populations.

Sustainable Enterprise Project (P163250): Depending on timing, this now ongoing operation might be able to incorporate one or a number of recommendations about closing gender gaps in enterprise ownership and growth.

Bangladesh Integrated Digital Government Project (P161086): Having already incorporated actions and indicators to close the gender digital divide, while improving digital integration across GoB agencies and catalyzing digital public services, this project is a key opportunity to ensure that more women and ethnic minorities are recognized in national digital systems for citizenship, land registration, and even accounts in public sector banks.

Rural Bridges Improvement and Maintenance Program (P161928): This project already has identified a gender gap in high-skill employment in the transport sector and proposes promoting women's work in this sector by developing Labor Contracting Societies (LCSs), with targets for female-led and female-majority LCSs. The project will utilize the LCS structure to train employed women in technical, management, and leadership skills.

Dhaka City Neighborhood Upgrading Project (P165477): There are several potential entry points for improving girls' and women's safe access to education and employment, not least of which are interventions to mitigate the risk of sexual harassment and other GBV in public spaces—especially near schools, workplaces, and points of entry to public transportation.

Sustainable Forests and Livelihoods Project (P161996): The operation may present possibilities worth exploring to close gender gaps in all areas of economic empowerment that are most relevant to rural women: ownership and control of agricultural land and other household assets; access to and use of finance; and micro, and small and medium enterprise (SME) creation and expansion for women entrepreneurs. The setting also suggests the opportunity to support ethnic minority women in these three areas.

Livestock and Dairy Development Project (P161246): This project presents the same possibilities as the one above, with a particular focus on women, who already are heavily involved in livestock and dairy value chains.

Bangladesh Sustainable Coastal and Marine Fisheries (P161568): This project already has mainstreamed gender across all of its components. It is supporting women's employment and entrepreneurship in coastal and marine fisheries value chains, starting with establishing women's savings groups in all villages covered by the project, which eventually will scale up nationwide. Project design and preparation phases received technical support from members of this report team.

Bangladesh Jobs Programmatic DPC (P167190): This project directly supports GoB's program of reforms to tackle Bangladesh's jobs challenges. One of its components aims to improve policies and programs in the country to expand vulnerable populations' access to jobs. Its attention to women's needs in this arena includes a range of measures that address multiple barriers to women's paid work and entrepreneurship. By reengaging with GoB on development policy lending, the operation will be implementing select findings from the recent *Bangladesh Jobs Diagnostic* (Farole and Cho 2017), as well as from this book.

Bangladesh Municipal Water Supply and Sanitation Project (P161227) and Dhaka Sanitation Improvement Project (P161432): In both of these operations, there are likely opportunities to improve girls' and women's access to clean, safe, and separate toilet facilities in schools and training centers, workplaces, transport hubs, and heavily trafficked public spaces.

Dhaka Public Transport Improvement Project (P166435): This operation is a crucial entry point for improving female students' and working women's access to safe and affordable transportation. On a more general level, this project ideally will improve dramatically the poor safety conditions of public transportation for all its users.

CONCLUSION

There is increasing urgency to improve women's economic participation and empowerment. At the same time, there are multiple examples of good practices by government, CSOs and the private sector, from Bangladesh and other countries, which could be tested, adapted and implemented for Bangladeshi women. In the arena of improving female labor force participation, interventions fall into two broad buckets—that is, efforts to remove constraints to women's meaningful employment, and programs to improve workplace conditions for working women. Efforts to improve women's ability to own and control their rightful share of inherited and other land include legal reform and attention to proper enforcement; addressing social norms that prevent women from claiming their inheritance; and a range of other interventions. Organizations seeking to increase women's financial inclusion have tested interventions to expand the type and flexibility of financial services for women; address procedural barriers to accessing formal finance; and reach more women with a women-friendly environment in financial institutions. Across the board, however, rigorous evaluations are rare and urgently needed. Yet, formal and informal assessments suggest that political will (by governments and the private sector) and engagement of women and their communities are essential elements in the success of any endeavor to improve women's economic empowerment.

Women's economic opportunities are improving—some more than others—but their range of choices is still far too narrow. The different arenas of economic engagement are not evolving rapidly enough to accommodate women's greater aspirations derived from greater presence in the public sphere, greater awareness of potential opportunities, and greater educational attainments over time. Although women are very resourceful in finding ways around constraints that originate both in and outside the household (for instance, registering land they inherit in their children's names), they should not have to do so. This book has offered recommendations for improving incentives and conditions in these arenas to improve systems, better accommodate women's aspirations, and close gender gaps.

REFERENCES

Farole, Thomas, and Yoonyoung Cho. 2017. "Bangladesh Jobs Diagnostic." World Bank, Washington, DC. https://openknowledge.worldbank.org/handle/10986/28498.

Golla, Anne Marie, Anju Malhotra, Priya Nanda, and Rekha Mehra. 2011. *Understanding and Measuring Women's Economic Empowerment: Definition, Framework and Indicators.* Washington, DC: International Center for Research on Women.

Hallman, K., A. R. Quisumbing, M. T. Ruel, and B. de la Briere. 2003. "Childcare and Work: Joint Decisions among Women in Poor Neighborhoods of Guatemala City." FCND Discussion Paper No. 151, IFPRI, Washington, DC.

Lyon, Gabrielle H., Jameela Jafri, and Kathleen St. Louis. 2012. "Beyond the Pipeline: STEM Pathways for Youth Development." *Afterschool Matters* 16 (Fall): 48–57.

Ministry of Women and Children Affairs. 2018. *Multi-Sectoral Programme on Violence Against Women.* Ministry of Women and Children Affairs Multi-Sectoral Programme on Violence Against Women, (accessed September 10, 2018), http://www.mspvaw.gov.bd/.

Passey, Don. 2017. "Computer Science (CS) in the Compulsory Education Curriculum: Implications for Future Research." *Education and Information Technologies* 22 (2): 421–43.

Quisumbing, Agnes R., Neha Kumar, and Julia A. Behrman. 2018. "Do Shocks Affect Men's and Women's Assets Differently? Evidence from Bangladesh and Uganda." *Development Policy Review* 36 (1): 3–34.

Ruel, MT., B. de la Briere, K. Hallman, A. Quisumbing, and N. Coj. 2002. "Does Subsidized Childcare Help Poor Working Women in Urban Areas? An Evaluation of a Government-Sponsored Program in Guatemala City." FCND Discussion Paper 131, IFPRI, Washington, DC.

Appendix A
Bangladesh Country Gender Statistical Profile

INTRODUCTION

Bangladesh has performed well in select aspects of gender equality, as the country supports a gender-neutral legal and political context in a number of areas, including access to institutions. There is room for improvement in other realms, however, such as supportive working conditions for women; other aspects of economic empowerment, such as rights and practices in asset inheritance and ownership; and protecting women from violence—particularly intimate partner violence. Similarly, although Bangladesh performs better than the rest of the region in its total fertility rate (TFR) and contraceptive prevalence, other key health indicators, such as adolescent fertility rates, need improvement. Gross female enrollment rates at the primary and secondary levels are higher than those of males; however, female labor force participation rates remain lower than those of males, for both the broader working-age population (age 15+) and younger cohorts (age 15–29) of the population. Some voice and agency indicators are comparable to regional averages, such as the proportion of seats held by women in national parliament.

As a whole, there is sufficient data available to support analysis and policy in key development areas, but more research is essential in certain domains, such as on gender-based violence, as well as on certain aspects of women's economic participation, as detailed in the chapters of this book.

LEGAL AND POLITICAL CONTEXT

Bangladesh has been successful in providing gender-neutral laws for areas that pertain to institutional access, according to the World Bank's *Women, Business and the Law* (2016). For instance, the constitution of Bangladesh contains clauses on nondiscrimination and equality. Although both customary and personal laws are recognized as valid sources of law, they are invalidated if they contradict the constitutional provisions listed above. There is also no legally sanctioned gender discrimination in terms of choices surrounding travel, registering a business, opening a bank account, getting a job, pursuing a trade or profession, choosing where to live, or conferring citizenship to children. Married women are not required by law to obey their husbands. Gender equality in laws governing access to justice also display some egalitarian features, for instance, a woman's testimony in court carries the same weight as that of a man. Access to property is more ambiguous. While unmarried and married women and men have equal rights to property ownership, this may not be exercised in practice; also, sons and daughters do not have equal rights to inherit property from their parents. Similar ambivalence exists for multiple aspects of violence against women. There is legislation on domestic violence, but marital rape is not explicitly criminalized and, though legislation on sexual harassment in the workplace exists, no civil remedies or criminal penalties are prescribed.

There is room for improvement in the domain of women's economic engagement. Although the law mandates equal remuneration for work of equal value, there are several legal gaps that can enable gender discrimination in hiring, as well as within the workplace. For example, there are currently no laws to prohibit gender-based discrimination in hiring or to prohibit prospective employers from asking about family status.[1] Furthermore, laws do not prohibit the dismissal of pregnant workers; nor do the laws prohibit creditors from discriminating on the basis of gender or marital status.

ENDOWMENTS: HEALTH AND NUTRITION

Summary of current status

Bangladesh performs well on several health and nutrition indicators (table A.1). For example, the rate of contraceptive prevalence among women who are married or in union is slightly higher (62.4 percent) than the regional average of 52.1 percent, while TFR is lower. In 2015, the maternal mortality ratio in Bangladesh was 176 deaths per 100,000 live births compared to the South Asian regional average of 182. In contrast, Bangladesh's 2016 adolescent fertility rate of 84.4 births per 1,000 women ages 15–19 years remains significantly higher than the regional average of 33.7. Similarly, antenatal care and the percentage of births attended by skilled health staff are lower than the regional averages. Prevalence of underweight girls under 5 years of age is higher in Bangladesh than in any other South Asian country.

Trends over time

Bangladesh has gradually improved its TFR from close to 3 in 2001 to closer to 2 births per woman in 2016. This reduction in fertility rate is even more remarkable considering TFR was close to 7 births per woman in 1960. The adolescent fertility rate, while still higher than South Asia as a whole, decreased from 98.6 in 2005 to 84.4 births per thousand women ages 15–19 years in 2016, while the percentage of births attended by skilled health staff has risen from 20.1 percent in 2006 to 49.8 percent in 2016, and prenatal care has increased from 47.7 percent

TABLE A.1 **Key health and nutrition indicators, by sex**

INDICATOR NAME	TOTAL/AVERAGE (% OF AGE-RELEVANT POPULATION)	FEMALE	MALE	REGIONAL AVERAGE/FEMALE AVERAGE
Life expectancy at birth (years)—2016[a]	72.5	74.3	70.9	68.7 (70.3 female)
Under-five mortality rate (per 1,000 live births) by sex—2017[a]	32.4	30.0	34.7	44.8 (44.5 female)
Fertility rate, total (births per woman)—2016[a]	—	2.1	—	2.5
Adolescent fertility rate (births per 1,000 women, ages 15–19)—2016[a]	—	84.4	—	33.7
Women who were first married by age 18 (% of women ages 20–24)—2014[a]	—	58.6	—	NA
Pregnant women receiving prenatal care[a]	—	63.9 (2014)	—	73.7 (2013)
Births attended by skilled health staff (% of total)[a]	—	49.8 (2016)	—	75.9 (2014)
Maternal mortality ratio-modelled estimate (per 100,000 live births)—2015[a]	—	176	—	182
Contraceptive prevalence rate (% of women ages 15–49)—2014[a]	—	62.4	—	52.1
Percentage of children 12–23 months who had received specific vaccines by the time of the survey, by sex, all basic vaccines—2014[b]	—	84.1	83.6	—
Underweight prevalence, weight for age (% of all children under 5)—2014[a]	32.6	33.5	32.3	—
Stunting prevalence, height for age (% of all children under 5)—2014[a]	36.1	35.9	36.9	—
Women's share of population ages 15+ living with HIV (%)—2017[a]	—	33.9	—	36.2

a. World Bank (World Development Indicators database).
b. National Institute of Population Research and Training (NIPORT), Mitra and Associates, and ICF International 2016.

in 2006 to 63.9 percent in 2014. Most remarkably, the under-five female mortality rate decreased from 84.9 per thousand in 2000 to 30.0 per thousand in 2017, with the under-five male mortality rate dropping from 91 per thousand to 34.7 per thousand in the same time period. The percent of girls less than 5 years of age stunted has also come down in recent years from 42 percent in 2011 to 35.9 in 2014, as has the prevalence of underweight female children under 5 years of age: from 38.8 in 2011 to 33.5 in 2014.

ENDOWMENTS: EDUCATION

Summary of current status

Bangladesh performs better than the region in gender gaps in literacy, gross primary and gross secondary enrollment rates (table A.2). Additional improvement in gender parity is needed at the tertiary level, however. The ratio of female-to-male gross tertiary enrollment rates is 0.7 compared to the regional average of 1.0.

TABLE A.2 **Key education indicators, by sex**

INDICATOR NAME	COUNTRY RATE OR F/M RATIO	FEMALE	MALE	REGIONAL AVERAGE FEMALE	MALE
Literacy					
Youth literacy rate (% of population 15–24)—2016	92.2	93.5	90.9	85.9	90.4
Literacy rate, youth (ages 15–24), gender parity index (GPI)—2016	1.0	—	—	0.9	
Literacy rate, adult total (% of people ages 15 and above)	72.8	69.9	75.6	62.2	79.4
Enrollment					
Primary					
Total gross primary enrollment rate (% of age-relevant population)—2016	118.6	122.1	115.2	118.1	107.8
School enrollment, primary (gross), gender parity index—female to male (GPI) (F/M ratio)—2016	1.06	—	—	1.1	
Secondary					
Total gross secondary enrollment rate (% of age-relevant population)—2016	69.0	72.5	65.6	70.9	71.0
School enrollment, secondary (gross), gender parity index—female to male (GPI) (F/M ratio)—2016	1.1	—	—	1.0	
Tertiary					
Total tertiary gross enrollment rate (% of age-relevant population)—2016	17.3	14.2	20.3	22.8	23.7
School enrollment, tertiary (gross), gender parity index—female to male (GPI) (F/M ratio)—2016	0.7	—	—	1.0	
Completion					
Completion rate, primary (% of total age-relevant population)	98.1 (2015)	106.6 (2015)	89.9 (2015)	94.4 (2016)	92.4 (2016)
Ratio of female-to-male primary completion rates	1.1 (2015)	—	—	1.0 (2016)	
Male-female gap in primary completion rates (male minus female rates)	−16.7 (2015)	—	—	−2.0 (2016)	
Completion rate, lower secondary (% of total age-relevant population)—2016	76.5	84.1	69.3	81.8	77.9
Ratio of female-to-male lower-secondary completion rates—2016	1.2	—	—	1.1	
Male-female gap in lower-secondary completion rates (male minus female rates)—2016	−14.8	—	—	−3.9	

Source: World Bank (World Development Indicators database).
Note: GPI = Gender parity index. GPI refers to the ratio of females to males in the given outcome.

Trends over time

Bangladesh has done well in maintaining and improving its performance on key education indicators. The ratio of youth female-to-male literacy rates increased from 89.7 in 2001 to 102.8 percent in 2016, while the ratio of adult female-to-male literacy rates increased from 75.7 in 2001 to 92.5 percent in 2016. Since 2005, the ratios of female-to-male primary and secondary enrollment have also remained consistently above 100 percent, while the ratio at the tertiary level increased from 52.1 percent in 2005 to 69.9 percent in 2016. The ratio of female-to-male primary completion rates has also increased from 108.4 percent in 2005, to 118.6 percent in 2015, while the ratio at lower secondary has risen from 112.7 to 121.4 percent between 2005 and 2016.

ECONOMIC OPPORTUNITY: LABOR FORCE PARTICIPATION, EMPLOYMENT, AND ACCESS TO FINANCE

Summary of current status

The male labor force participation rate for those in the 15-year plus age group is more than twice that for women. This gender gap also holds true for the 15–29 years age group. The unemployment rate is also higher for women, with women more than twice as likely as men to be unemployed (table A.3).

TABLE A.3 **Key economic opportunity indicators, by sex**

INDICATOR NAME	TOTAL/AVERAGE (% OF AGE-RELEVANT POPULATION)	FEMALE	MALE	REGIONAL AVERAGE	
				FEMALE	MALE
Labor force participation					
Proportion of labor force	—	34.6 (2016)[a]	69.3 (2016)[a]	25.5 (2017)[b]	74.5 (2017)[b]
Labor force participation rate by sex (%, ages 15+)	58.5 (2016)[a]	35.6 (2016)[a]	81.9 (2016)[a]	28.5 (2017)[b]	79.5 (2017)[b]
Labor force participation rate for ages 15–29, (%)—2016[a]	49.9	32.3	69.6	—	—
Employment					
Employed persons as a percentage of working age population, ages 15+, by sex	56.1 (2016)[a]	33.2 (2016)[a]	79.4 (2016)[a]	27.1 (2017)[b]	76.8 (2017)[b]
Employed persons as a percentage of working-age population, youth ages 15-29, by sex—2016[a]	45.6	28.6	64.5	—	—
Unemployment					
Unemployment by sex (% of total labor force)	4.2 (2016)[a]	6.8 (2016)[a]	3.0 (2016)[a]	4.8 (2017)[b]	3.4 (2017)[b]
Ratio of female-to-male unemployment rate	226.7 (2016)[a]	—	—	141.2 (2017)[b]	
Unemployment, youth, by sex (% of total labor force ages 15–17)—2016[a]	10.5	12.0	10.0	—	—
Ratio of youth female-to-male unemployment rate (ages 15–17)—2016[a]	120	—	—	—	—
Type (status) of employment					
Employees (% of employed ages 15+) by sex—2016[a]	39.1	8.5	30.6	—	—
Vulnerable employment (i.e., own-account or contributing family workers) (% of employed ages 15+), by sex—2011[b]	57.7	70.7	52.2	—	—
Percent of employed who are own-account workers (ages 15+), by sex—2016[a]	43.2	33.1	47.6	—	—
Percent of employed who are contributing family workers (ages 15+), by sex—2016[a]	14.5	37.6	4.6	—	—
Percent of employed who are employers (ages 15+), by sex	2.7 (2016)[a]	0.1 (2016)[a]	2.6 (2016)[a]	0.5 (2017)[b]	2.0 (2017)[b]
Sector of employment					
Employment in agriculture (percentage of employed)	42.7 (2015–16)[a]	63.1 (2015–16)[a]	34.0 (2015–16)[a]	59.3 (2017)[b]	37.7 (2017)[b]
Employment in services (percentage of employed)	36.9 (2015–16)[a]	20.8 (2015–16)[a]	43.7 (2015–16)[a]	24.0 (2017)[b]	37.3 (2017)[b]
Employment in industry (percentage of employed)	20.5 (2015–16)[a]	16.1 (2015–16)[a]	22.3 (2015–16)[a]	16.7 (2017)[b]	25.0 (2017)[b]
Access to finance					
Account ownership at a financial institution or with a mobile-money provider, by sex (% ages 15+)—2017[b]	50.0	35.8	64.6	—	—

a. Bangladesh Bureau of Statistics 2017.
b. World Bank (World Development Indicators database).

Trends over time

Nationally, the female labor force participation rate decreased from 55.9 percent in 2000 to 35.6 percent in 2016 while the male labor force participation rate dropped from 87.2 to 81.9 percent between 2000 and 2016. This period thus saw an increase in the gender gap in labor force participation.

VOICE AND AGENCY: POLITICAL REPRESENTATION, GENDER-BASED VIOLENCE AND LAND OWNERSHIP

Summary of current status

Bangladesh has achieved a level of women's political participation roughly on par with the regional average (table A.4). The proportion of seats held by women in the Bangladeshi national parliament is 20.3 percent, slightly higher than the regional average of 19.4 percent (2016).

TABLE A.4 **Key indicators, by sex, for voice and agency, gender-based violence, and land ownership**

INDICATOR NAME	BANGLADESH (%)	REGIONAL AVERAGE (%)
Political representation		
Proportion of seats held by women in national parliaments—2017[a]	20.3	19.4
Voice and agency		
Women participating in the three decisions (own health care, major household purchases, and visiting family) (ages 15–49)—2014[a]	47.2	—
Female-headed households—2014[a]	12.5	—
Women who were first married by age 18 (ages 20–24)—2014[a]	58.6	—
Gender-based violence		
Ever-married women who have experienced physical violence by their husbands in the last 12 months/ever in their lifetime—2015[b]	20.8/49.6	—
Ever-married women who have experienced sexual violence by their husbands in the last 12 months/ever in their lifetime—2015[b]	13.3/27.3	—
Ever-married women experiencing acts of controlling, economic and emotional behavior during the last 12 months/ever in their lifetime (includes United National standard and Bangladesh-specific types of behavior)—2015[b]	56.7/70.9	—
Women who have experienced physical violence from nonpartners in the last 12 months/ever in their lifetime—2015[b]	6.2/27.8	—
Beliefs about when intimate partner violence is justified		
Women who believe a husband is justified in beating his wife when she argues with him—2014[a]	19.9	—
Women who believe a husband is justified in beating his wife when she burns the food—2014[a]	4.3	—
Women who believe a husband is justified in beating his wife when she goes out without telling him—2014[a]	14.4	—
Women who believe a husband is justified in beating his wife when she neglects the children—2014[a]	14.9	—
Women who believe a husband is justified in beating his wife when she refuses sex with him—2014[a]	7.2	—
Women who believe a husband is justified in beating his wife (any of five reasons)—2014[a]	28.3	—

continued

TABLE A.4, *continued*

INDICATOR NAME	BANGLADESH (%)	REGIONAL AVERAGE (%)
Land ownership		
Distribution of agricultural holders by sex (females)—2008 Agricultural Census[c]	4.6	—
Distribution of agricultural landowners by sex (female-documented ownership)—2011–12 Bangladesh Integrated Household Survey[c]	22.6	—
Incidence of female agricultural landowners (sole- or jointly documented ownership)—2011–12 Bangladesh Integrated Household Survey[c]	8.5	—
Distribution of agricultural land area owned by sex (female-sole documented ownership)—2011–12 Bangladesh Integrated Household Survey[c]	10.1	—
Distribution of agricultural land area owned by sex (female-jointly documented ownership)—2011–12 Bangladesh Integrated Household Survey[c]	2.2	—

a. World Bank (World Development Indicators database).
b. Bangladesh Bureau of Statistics 2016.
c. Food and Agriculture Organization (Gender and Land Rights Database [GLRD]).

Agricultural land ownership data from the Food and Agriculture Organization (FAO) indicates that women account for 22.6 percent of agricultural landowners in Bangladesh. Women are the sole owners of only 10.1 percent of total agricultural land, and an even smaller amount (2.2 percent) of such land is owned jointly by women with men. Also, women constitute only 4.6 percent of total agricultural landholders,[2] suggesting that while women own agricultural land, they may not necessarily make major decisions regarding its use.

Research suggests that gender-based violence remains pervasive in Bangladesh, however. According to the Violence against Women Survey by the Bangladesh Bureau of Statistics (2016), over one-fifth of ever-married women have experienced physical violence by their husbands in the past 12 months. This number was 13.3 percent for sexual violence and 56.7 percent for acts of controlling, economic and emotional behavior.

Trends over time

Between 2000 and 2017, the proportion of women in Bangladesh's national parliament increased from 9.1 percent to 20.3 percent. The percentage of women married by the age of 18 has decreased slightly, from 65.3 percent in 2000 to 58.6 percent in 2014.

DATA AND KNOWLEDGE GAPS—AREAS FOR MORE RESEARCH

Overall, there exists enough data on key gender indicators to sufficiently support analysis and policy direction in Bangladesh. Data is available for most indicators, including health, education, economic participation, some aspects of voice and agency, and intimate partner violence. However, there are several areas that continue to have serious data gaps. Available data on employment (for example, vulnerable employment) is largely outdated and needs to be updated. Data on forms of violence other than intimate partner violence, such as trafficking and sexual harassment in public or work spaces, is limited. Finally, there is very little data on women's political participation, voice, or agency.

NOTES

1. Family status refers to both whether the applicant is married or has children.
2. An agricultural holder is defined as the civil or judicial person who makes the major decisions regarding resource use and exercises management control over the agricultural holding operation.

REFERENCES

Bangladesh Bureau of Statistics. 2016. *Report on Violence Against Women (VAW) Survey 2015.* Dhaka: Bangladesh Bureau of Statistics (BBS), Statistics and Informatics Division (SID), Ministry of Planning, Government of the People's Republic of Bangladesh.

——.2017a. *Bangladesh Quarterly Labour Force Survey (LFS) 2015–16.* Statistics and Informatics Division, Ministry of Planning, Dhaka: Bangladesh Bureau of Statistics.

——. 2017b. *Report on Quarterly Labour Force Survey (QLFS) 2015-16.* Dhaka: Bangladesh Bureau of Statistics.

Iqbal, Sarah. 2015. *Women, Business, and the Law 2016: Getting to Equal.* Washington, DC: World Bank.

National Institute of Population Research and Training (NIPORT), Mitra and Associates, and ICF International. 2016. *Bangladesh Demographic and Health Survey 2014.* Dhaka, Bangladesh NIPORT, Mitra and Associates, and ICF International.

Appendix B
Full Regression Results for
Labor Outcomes

TABLE B.1 **Labor force participation regressions, 2016 (marginal effects)**

LABOR FORCE PARTICIPATION	(1) ALL	(2) ALL FEMALES	(3) ALL MALES	(4) URBAN-ALL	(5) URBAN-FEMALES	(6) URBAN-MALES	(7) RURAL-ALL	(8) RURAL-FEMALES	(9) RURAL-MALES
Household characteristics									
Number of children ages 5 and under	−0.00232*	−0.0282***	0.00268	−0.0104***	−0.0516***	0.00338	0.000698	−0.0188***	0.00237
	(0.00134)	(0.00219)	(0.00170)	(0.00210)	(0.00357)	(0.00269)	(0.00166)	(0.00267)	(0.00209)
Number of children ages 6–10	0.00479***	0.00681***	0.00442***	−0.00230	−0.00532*	0.00624**	0.00797***	0.0134***	0.00381**
	(0.00125)	(0.00199)	(0.00153)	(0.00200)	(0.00315)	(0.00249)	(0.00153)	(0.00244)	(0.00185)
Number of children ages 11–14	−0.00989***	−0.0112***	0.00479***	−0.0184***	−0.0203***	0.000516	−0.00485***	−0.00533*	0.00714***
	(0.00135)	(0.00221)	(0.00152)	(0.00218)	(0.00348)	(0.00246)	(0.00166)	(0.00272)	(0.00185)
Number of elderly male	0.00132	0.0182***	0.0184***	0.00230	0.0284***	0.0282***	0.000817	0.0115**	0.0154***
	(0.00267)	(0.00419)	(0.00300)	(0.00448)	(0.00677)	(0.00483)	(0.00322)	(0.00508)	(0.00366)
Number of elderly female	0.0224***	0.0155***	0.0176***	0.0111**	0.0159**	−0.00222	0.0266***	0.0196***	0.0209***
	(0.00303)	(0.00470)	(0.00347)	(0.00505)	(0.00759)	(0.00550)	(0.00363)	(0.00567)	(0.00414)
Female-headed household	−0.00948***	−0.0152***	−0.0162***	−0.00330	−0.00824	−0.0176***	−0.0127***	−0.0201***	−0.0155***
	(0.00237)	(0.00373)	(0.00244)	(0.00372)	(0.00550)	(0.00371)	(0.00298)	(0.00474)	(0.00312)
Individual characteristics									
Female dummy	−0.445***			−0.455***			−0.440***		
	(0.00112)			(0.00140)			(0.00153)		
Female head of household	0.106***	0.125***		0.129***	0.160***		0.0956***	0.110***	
	(0.00406)	(0.00526)		(0.00606)	(0.00746)		(0.00517)	(0.00679)	
Age	0.0348***	0.0320***	0.0302***	0.0334***	0.0224***	0.0346***	0.0359***	0.0371***	0.0289***
	(0.000342)	(0.000641)	(0.000391)	(0.000564)	(0.00102)	(0.000611)	(0.000416)	(0.000784)	(0.000478)
Age-squared	−0.000436***	−0.000437***	−0.000377***	−0.000438***	−0.000360***	−0.000441***	−0.000440***	−0.000476***	−0.000357***
	(4.07e-06)	(8.12e-06)	(4.40e-06)	(6.84e-06)	(1.33e-05)	(7.05e-06)	(4.91e-06)	(9.83e-06)	(5.29e-06)
Married	0.0997***	−0.0112***	0.132***	0.0745***	−0.0640***	0.138***	0.109***	0.0217***	0.128***
	(0.00249)	(0.00404)	(0.00328)	(0.00395)	(0.00573)	(0.00507)	(0.00311)	(0.00521)	(0.00411)
Education									
1–5 years of education dummy	0.0238***	−0.00678*	0.0713***	0.0235***	−0.0222***	0.0907***	0.0252***	−0.00103	0.0667***
	(0.00234)	(0.00372)	(0.00352)	(0.00396)	(0.00579)	(0.00607)	(0.00282)	(0.00454)	(0.00418)

continued

TABLE B.1, *continued*

LABOR FORCE PARTICIPATION	(1) ALL	(2) ALL FEMALES	(3) ALL MALES	(4) URBAN-ALL	(5) URBAN-FEMALES	(6) URBAN-MALES	(7) RURAL-ALL	(8) RURAL-FEMALES	(9) RURAL-MALES
6–9 years of education dummy	-0.0256***	-0.0572***	-0.00361	-0.0610***	-0.135***	0.0120**	-0.00755**	-0.0159***	-0.00704*
	(0.00238)	(0.00387)	(0.00303)	(0.00377)	(0.00581)	(0.00510)	(0.00296)	(0.00485)	(0.00364)
SSC dummy	-0.153***	-0.148***	-0.113***	-0.186***	-0.248***	-0.105***	-0.131***	-0.0808***	-0.114***
	(0.00296)	(0.00527)	(0.00286)	(0.00428)	(0.00737)	(0.00470)	(0.00390)	(0.00695)	(0.00351)
HSC dummy	-0.0236***	-0.0632***	-0.00886	-0.0630***	-0.137***	-0.00948	0.0140*	0.00486	-0.00159
	(0.00458)	(0.00796)	(0.00564)	(0.00568)	(0.00976)	(0.00792)	(0.00720)	(0.0122)	(0.00791)
Diploma training dummy	-0.161***	-0.0409**	-0.127***	-0.150***	-0.109***	-0.114***	-0.165***	0.0106	-0.130***
	(0.00847)	(0.0169)	(0.00555)	(0.0115)	(0.0204)	(0.00826)	(0.0118)	(0.0267)	(0.00737)
Above HSC dummy	-0.0403***	0.0366***	-0.0817***	-0.0452***	-0.0207***	-0.0765***	-0.0464***	0.0657***	-0.0810***
	(0.00403)	(0.00642)	(0.00340)	(0.00515)	(0.00783)	(0.00514)	(0.00626)	(0.0104)	(0.00458)
Location characteristics									
Urban dummy	-0.0226***	-0.0553***	-0.00353**						
	(0.00168)	(0.00273)	(0.00179)						
Chittagong dummy	0.0172***	0.0516***	-0.0148***	0.00643	0.0185**	-0.0124***	0.0204***	0.0603***	-0.0170***
	(0.00366)	(0.00607)	(0.00415)	(0.00426)	(0.00726)	(0.00478)	(0.00453)	(0.00739)	(0.00512)
Dhaka dummy	0.00809**	0.00392	0.00733*	0.0282***	0.0408***	0.00161	-0.00954**	-0.0322***	0.00691
	(0.00337)	(0.00573)	(0.00385)	(0.00403)	(0.00685)	(0.00455)	(0.00413)	(0.00704)	(0.00471)
Khulna dummy	0.0730***	0.120***	0.0237***	0.0408***	0.0664***	0.0120**	0.0814***	0.131***	0.0272***
	(0.00383)	(0.00627)	(0.00429)	(0.00462)	(0.00779)	(0.00507)	(0.00463)	(0.00749)	(0.00520)
Rajshahi dummy	0.110***	0.181***	0.0310***	0.0426***	0.0823***	0.00759	0.128***	0.208***	0.0379***
	(0.00381)	(0.00614)	(0.00425)	(0.00486)	(0.00804)	(0.00534)	(0.00460)	(0.00731)	(0.00512)
Rangpur dummy	0.0734***	0.106***	0.0416***	0.0552***	0.0705***	0.0354***	0.0775***	0.112***	0.0439***
	(0.00388)	(0.00639)	(0.00440)	(0.00503)	(0.00831)	(0.00574)	(0.00460)	(0.00753)	(0.00520)
Sylhet dummy	-0.0307***	-0.0790***	-0.00201	-0.0646***	-0.140***	-0.0247***	-0.0219***	-0.0646***	0.00432
	(0.00420)	(0.00761)	(0.00479)	(0.00458)	(0.00886)	(0.00516)	(0.00507)	(0.00896)	(0.00584)
Observations	339,010	171,541	167,469	168,352	85,360	82,992	170,658	86,181	84,477

Source: World Bank calculations based on LFS 2016 data.
Notes: Standard errors in parentheses. *** p<0.01, ** p<0.05, * p<0.1. The reference dummies are illiterate dummy and Barisal dummy. HSC = Higher secondary school; SSC = Secondary School Certificate.

TABLE B.2 **Labor force participation regressions, 2003 (marginal effects)**

LABOR FORCE PARTICIPATION	(1) ALL	(2) ALL FEMALES	(3) ALL MALES	(4) URBAN-ALL	(5) URBAN-FEMALES	(6) URBAN-MALES	(7) RURAL-ALL	(8) RURAL-FEMALES	(9) RURAL-MALES
Household characteristics									
Number of children ages 5 and under	-0.00273**	-0.0161***	-0.00193	0.00341	-0.0150***	0.00246	-0.00472***	-0.0170***	-0.00285*
	(0.00123)	(0.00212)	(0.00130)	(0.00210)	(0.00364)	(0.00242)	(0.00145)	(0.00251)	(0.00147)
Number of children ages 6–10	-0.00780***	-0.00662***	0.00274*	-0.00931***	-0.0137***	0.00252	-0.00730***	-0.00436	0.00253
	(0.00146)	(0.00245)	(0.00159)	(0.00256)	(0.00428)	(0.00296)	(0.00173)	(0.00289)	(0.00183)
Number of children ages 11–14	-0.0151***	-0.00671**	-0.00130	-0.0145***	-0.0104**	0.00408	-0.0154***	-0.00607*	-0.00308
	(0.00172)	(0.00289)	(0.00164)	(0.00281)	(0.00477)	(0.00285)	(0.00209)	(0.00349)	(0.00194)
Number of elderly male	-0.0179***	0.00155	6.24e-05	-0.0135**	-0.0119	0.0189***	-0.0194***	0.00455	-0.00522
	(0.00355)	(0.00567)	(0.00325)	(0.00591)	(0.00962)	(0.00562)	(0.00428)	(0.00677)	(0.00384)
Number of elderly female	0.0128***	-0.00209	0.0174***	0.0127*	0.00890	0.00859	0.0125***	-0.00635	0.0185***
	(0.00390)	(0.00648)	(0.00376)	(0.00653)	(0.0109)	(0.00621)	(0.00466)	(0.00775)	(0.00448)
Female-headed household	0.0481***	0.0650***	-0.00911*	0.0729***	0.0923***	0.00602	0.0379***	0.0545***	-0.0151**
	(0.00962)	(0.0111)	(0.00492)	(0.0133)	(0.0159)	(0.00732)	(0.0128)	(0.0146)	(0.00637)
Individual characteristics									
Female dummy	-0.500***			-0.489***			-0.503***		
	(0.00100)			(0.00178)			(0.00123)		
Female head of household	0.138***	0.163***		0.118***	0.139***		0.143***	0.170***	
	(0.0114)	(0.0131)		(0.0165)	(0.0194)		(0.0148)	(0.0169)	
Age	0.0148***	-0.00261***	0.0275***	0.0232***	0.00755***	0.0363***	0.0123***	-0.00574***	0.0246***
	(0.000443)	(0.000786)	(0.000555)	(0.000765)	(0.00146)	(0.000841)	(0.000522)	(0.000912)	(0.000667)
Age-squared	-0.000207***	-4.68e-05***	-0.000331***	-0.000294***	-0.000158***	-0.000428***	-0.000181***	-1.29e-05	-0.000299***
	(5.12e-06)	(9.71e-06)	(6.11e-06)	(9.02e-06)	(1.86e-05)	(9.33e-06)	(5.97e-06)	(1.11e-05)	(7.29e-06)
Married	0.122***	0.00447	0.109***	0.119***	-0.00248	0.118***	0.121***	0.00525	0.104***
	(0.00370)	(0.00547)	(0.00451)	(0.00580)	(0.00889)	(0.00764)	(0.00457)	(0.00671)	(0.00536)
Education									
1–5 years of education dummy	-0.00658**	-0.0380***	-0.00233	-0.00244	-0.0445***	0.0233**	-0.00968***	-0.0385***	-0.00926*
	(0.00313)	(0.00542)	(0.00440)	(0.00544)	(0.00916)	(0.00907)	(0.00372)	(0.00649)	(0.00485)

continued

TABLE B.2, continued

LABOR FORCE PARTICIPATION	(1) ALL	(2) ALL FEMALES	(3) ALL MALES	(4) URBAN-ALL	(5) URBAN-FEMALES	(6) URBAN-MALES	(7) RURAL-ALL	(8) RURAL-FEMALES	(9) RURAL-MALES
6–9 years of education dummy	-0.0809***	-0.0949***	-0.0967***	-0.0734***	-0.0976***	-0.0902***	-0.0862***	-0.0972***	-0.0984***
	(0.00316)	(0.00546)	(0.00287)	(0.00489)	(0.00828)	(0.00595)	(0.00394)	(0.00687)	(0.00320)
SSC dummy	-0.142***	-0.108***	-0.149***	-0.138***	-0.121***	-0.160***	-0.143***	-0.0992***	-0.144***
	(0.00543)	(0.00931)	(0.00354)	(0.00692)	(0.0120)	(0.00621)	(0.00781)	(0.0138)	(0.00441)
HSC dummy	-0.123***	-0.0702***	-0.153***	-0.129***	-0.0914***	-0.184***	-0.115***	-0.0504***	-0.139***
	(0.00643)	(0.0114)	(0.00422)	(0.00806)	(0.0141)	(0.00694)	(0.00966)	(0.0178)	(0.00557)
Diploma training dummy	0.0350	-0.0438	-0.0151	0.0421	-0.00110	-0.0748*	0.0469	-0.0712	
	(0.0368)	(0.0771)	(0.0338)	(0.0509)	(0.104)	(0.0386)	(0.0527)	(0.110)	
Above HSC dummy	0.00363	0.0965***	-0.128***	0.0168*	0.0843***	-0.152***	-0.0189	0.105***	-0.123***
	(0.00816)	(0.0120)	(0.00546)	(0.00904)	(0.0136)	(0.00863)	(0.0146)	(0.0239)	(0.00764)
Location characteristics									
Urban dummy	0.00635***	0.0160***	-0.00852***						
	(0.00242)	(0.00384)	(0.00217)						
Chittagong dummy	0.00418	0.0134*	-0.00956**	-0.0149*	-0.0403***	-0.00330	0.0101*	0.0289***	-0.0115**
	(0.00468)	(0.00792)	(0.00447)	(0.00811)	(0.0133)	(0.00741)	(0.00557)	(0.00949)	(0.00536)
Dhaka dummy	0.00490	0.00398	0.00109	-0.00442	-0.0260**	0.00552	0.00803	0.0131	0.000601
	(0.00437)	(0.00751)	(0.00431)	(0.00759)	(0.0123)	(0.00689)	(0.00522)	(0.00910)	(0.00526)
Khulna dummy	-0.00834*	-0.0115	-0.00894*	-0.00727	-0.0196	-0.00901	-0.0103*	-0.0113	-0.00978*
	(0.00481)	(0.00830)	(0.00475)	(0.00829)	(0.0134)	(0.00789)	(0.00576)	(0.0102)	(0.00573)
Rajshahi dummy	-0.000480	0.0115	-0.0149***	0.00258	-0.00296	-0.00369	-0.00237	0.0144	-0.0188***
	(0.00497)	(0.00834)	(0.00490)	(0.00863)	(0.0138)	(0.00810)	(0.00591)	(0.0101)	(0.00588)
Rangpur dummy	0.00796	0.0143*	0.00119	0.00773	0.00750	-0.000351	0.00760	0.0164	0.00121
	(0.00505)	(0.00856)	(0.00505)	(0.00914)	(0.0145)	(0.00842)	(0.00591)	(0.0102)	(0.00604)
Sylhet dummy	0.0153**	0.0391***	-0.0178***	-0.00746	-0.0255	0.000747	0.0215***	0.0559***	-0.0222***
	(0.00619)	(0.00994)	(0.00596)	(0.0108)	(0.0176)	(0.00959)	(0.00728)	(0.0117)	(0.00708)
Observations	117,766	57,790	59,976	42,943	21,072	21,871	74,823	36,718	38,076

Source: World Bank calculations based on LFS 2003 data.

Notes: Standard errors in parentheses. *** p<0.01, ** p<0.05, * p<0.1. The reference dummies are illiterate dummy and Barisal dummy. HSC = Higher secondary school; SSC = Secondary School Certificate.

TABLE B.3 **Oaxaca decomposition of increase in female labor force participation between 2003 and 2016**

OVERALL	VALUE	STD. ERR.
Female LFP in 2003	0.261	0.002
Female LFP in 2016	0.356	0.001
Difference in LFP from 2003 to 2016	−0.095	0.002
Due to endowments	0.002	0.001
Due to coefficients	−0.087	0.003
Due to interaction	−0.010	0.002

If female in 2016 coefficients is taken as base

	AMOUNT	PERCENT OF TOTAL DIFFERENCE
Difference in LFP from 2003 to 2015	−0.09494	100
Due to endowments	−0.00842	8.9
Due to coefficients	−0.08652	91.1

	ENDOWMENTS		COEFFICIENTS		INTERACTION	
	VALUE	STD. ERR.	VALUE	STD. ERR.	VALUE	STD. ERR.
Number of children ages 5 and under	−0.012	0.001	0.007	0.001	0.006	0.001
Number of children ages 6 to 10	0.002	0.000	−0.009	0.001	−0.003	0.000
Number of children ages 11 to 14	0.000	0.000	−0.001	0.001	0.000	0.000
Number of elderly males	0.000	0.000	0.001	0.001	0.000	0.000
Number of elderly females	0.000	0.000	−0.001	0.001	0.000	0.000
Female-headed household	0.002	0.000	0.019	0.003	−0.013	0.002
Female head of household	−0.006	0.000	0.005	0.001	−0.002	0.001
1-5 years of education dummy	0.000	0.000	−0.007	0.001	0.002	0.000
6-9 years of education dummy	0.003	0.000	−0.009	0.001	0.002	0.000
SSC dummy	0.010	0.000	0.004	0.001	−0.002	0.001
HSC dummy	0.000	0.000	0.000	0.000	0.000	0.000
Diploma training dummy	0.000	0.000	0.000	0.001	0.000	0.000
Above HSC dummy	−0.002	0.000	0.004	0.001	−0.003	0.000
Age	−0.026	0.002	−0.915	0.027	0.035	0.002
Age-squared	0.024	0.002	0.411	0.013	−0.025	0.002
Married	0.000	0.000	−0.006	0.005	0.000	0.000
Urban	0.002	0.000	0.021	0.001	−0.003	0.000
Chittagong dummy	0.000	0.000	−0.007	0.002	0.000	0.000
Dhaka dummy	0.000	0.000	0.000	0.003	0.000	0.000
Khulna dummy	0.003	0.000	−0.016	0.001	−0.004	0.000
Rajshahi dummy	−0.001	0.000	−0.024	0.001	0.001	0.000
Rangpur dummy	0.000	0.000	−0.010	0.001	0.000	0.000
Sylhet dummy	0.000	0.000	0.007	0.001	0.000	0.000
Constant			0.442	0.016		

Sources: World Bank calculations based on LFS 2003 and 2016 data.
Notes: HSC = Higher secondary school; SSC = Secondary School Certificate; LFP = Labor force participation. The reference dummies are illiterate dummy and Barisal dummy.

TABLE B.4 **Mincer regression monthly earnings, 2016—formal employment**

	(1)	(2)	(3)
	ALL WORKERS	**MALE WORKERS**	**FEMALE WORKERS**
Sector			
Agriculture dummy	−0.432***	−0.404***	−0.639***
	(0.0939)	(0.109)	(0.195)
Manufacturing dummy	0.110**	0.126***	−0.00793
	(0.0463)	(0.0475)	(0.158)
Construction dummy	0.145**	0.179***	−0.367
	(0.0679)	(0.0690)	(0.246)
Occupation group			
Managerial dummy	0.0353	0.0200	−0.111
	(0.0583)	(0.0633)	(0.146)
Skilled-worker dummy	−0.00180	−0.00940	−0.176
	(0.0607)	(0.0649)	(0.156)
Education			
1–5 years of education dummy	0.299***	0.204**	0.388**
	(0.0827)	(0.0941)	(0.165)
6–9 years of education dummy	0.350***	0.310***	0.146
	(0.0722)	(0.0811)	(0.184)
SSC dummy	0.580***	0.492***	0.688***
	(0.0727)	(0.0836)	(0.166)
HSC dummy	0.779***	0.668***	0.930***
	(0.0700)	(0.0810)	(0.150)
Diploma training dummy	0.896***	0.809***	0.982***
	(0.0775)	(0.0898)	(0.161)
Above HSC dummy	0.990***	0.914***	1.067***
	(0.0696)	(0.0802)	(0.149)
Individual characteristics			
Male dummy	0.0772***		
	(0.0259)		
Age	0.0454***	0.0432***	0.0482***
	(0.00718)	(0.00833)	(0.0144)
Age-squared	−0.000402***	−0.000382***	−0.000404**
	(8.75e-05)	(0.000100)	(0.000183)
Spatial			
Urban dummy	0.267***	0.281***	0.222***
	(0.0211)	(0.0248)	(0.0409)
Chittagong dummy	0.0962***	0.141***	−0.0437
	(0.0361)	(0.0404)	(0.0720)

continued

TABLE B.4, *continued*

	(1)	(2)	(3)
	ALL WORKERS	**MALE WORKERS**	**FEMALE WORKERS**
Dhaka dummy	0.221***	0.225***	0.195***
	(0.0323)	(0.0395)	(0.0497)
Khulna dummy	0.0183	0.0330	−0.0129
	(0.0351)	(0.0419)	(0.0594)
Rajshahi dummy	0.0653*	0.0536	0.0726
	(0.0383)	(0.0481)	(0.0522)
Rangpur dummy	0.0250	0.0443	−0.0564
	(0.0444)	(0.0525)	(0.0826)
Sylhet dummy	0.0268	0.0559	−0.0411
	(0.0451)	(0.0536)	(0.0795)
Constant	9.709***	9.909***	9.756***
	(0.166)	(0.197)	(0.314)
Observations	6,301	4,578	1,723
R-squared	0.291	0.261	0.394

Source: World Bank calculations based on LFS 2016 data.
Notes: Robust standard errors in parentheses. *** $p<0.01$, ** $p<0.05$, * $p<0.2$. The reference dummies are service-sector dummy, unskilled-worker dummy, illiterate dummy, and Barisal dummy.
HSC = Higher secondary school; SSC = Secondary School Certificate.

TABLE B.5 Oaxaca decomposition of gender gap in monthly earnings, 2016

	TOTAL EFFECT
Aggregated effect	
Ln(earnings) of women	11.88
Ln(earnings) of men	11.96
Difference in earnings	−0.0791
Difference due to endowments	0.0104
Difference due to coefficients	−0.103
Difference due to interaction	0.0131

	PERCENT OF TOTAL DIFFERENCE
If male coefficient is taken as base	
Difference	100
Due to endowments	1.5
Due to coefficients	99.5

Source: World Bank calculations based on LFS 2016 data.

Appendix C
Full Regression Results for Relationship of Child Marriage with FLFP and Women's Education

TABLE C.1 **Full logit regression analysis: Relationship of marriage under age 18 to working for pay**

DHS YEAR	2004	2007	2011	2014
	OUTCOME: WORKS FOR PAY			
Demographic characteristics				
Married under age 15	−0.0319**	0.00873	−0.0335***	0.00922
	(0.0131)	(0.0147)	(0.00668)	(0.0117)
Current age	0.000752	0.00238*	0.00201***	0.00708***
	(0.000982)	(0.00126)	(0.000703)	(0.00116)
Highest education level	0.00230	−0.00343	0.0161***	0.00348
	(0.00696)	(0.00812)	(0.00455)	(0.00743)
Partner characteristics				
Partner's age	0.000406	−0.00179*	−0.00234***	−0.00383***
	(0.000765)	(0.000994)	(0.000572)	(0.000886)
Partner's highest education level	−0.0235***	−0.0118*	−0.0108***	−0.0240***
	(0.00570)	(0.00684)	(0.00379)	(0.00632)
Whether partner is employed	−0.00205	0.0335	−0.0194	0.0569*
	(0.0236)	(0.0341)	(0.0155)	(0.0300)
Whether partner lives elsewhere	−0.0557***	−0.0426*	−0.00647	−0.103***
	(0.0210)	(0.0228)	(0.0117)	(0.0189)
Household characteristics				
Household wealth quintile	−0.0205***	−0.0359***	−0.0128***	−0.0260***
	(0.00382)	(0.00488)	(0.00270)	(0.00444)
Whether head of household is female	0.0778***	0.0199	0.0154	0.0729***
	(0.0204)	(0.0230)	(0.0131)	(0.0196)

continued

TABLE C.1, *continued*

DHS YEAR	2004	2007	2011	2014
	OUTCOME: WORKS FOR PAY			
Number of children under age 5	−0.0420***	−0.0413***	−0.0355***	−0.0459***
	(0.00770)	(0.00920)	(0.00549)	(0.00975)
Number of women over age 50	−0.0517***	−0.0455***	−0.0217***	−0.0183
	(0.0119)	(0.0136)	(0.00720)	(0.0117)
Residence characteristics				
Distance to the nearest market	−0.00910	−0.0204***	−0.0139***	0.00601
	(0.00611)	(0.00772)	(0.00408)	(0.00677)
Urban residence (ref: rural)	0.0639***	0.0474***	0.0802***	0.0299**
	(0.0114)	(0.0133)	(0.00748)	(0.0116)
Respondent's division (ref: Dhaka)				
Barisal division	−0.0714***	−0.108***	−0.0405***	−0.0727***
	(0.0136)	(0.0149)	(0.00917)	(0.0168)
Chittagong division	−0.0542***	−0.0842***	−0.0264***	−0.0705***
	(0.0121)	(0.0146)	(0.00839)	(0.0147)
Khulna division	0.0148	0.0597***	−0.0125	−0.0451***
	(0.0142)	(0.0166)	(0.00895)	(0.0144)
Rajshahi division	0.0617***	0.0894***	−0.00200	0.0306**
	(0.0132)	(0.0163)	(0.00924)	(0.0154)
Sylhet division	−0.0215	−0.140***	−0.00491	0.00180
	(0.0167)	(0.0159)	(0.00957)	(0.0177)
Rangpur division			−0.0289***	−0.173***
			(0.00981)	(0.0147)
Observations	9,594	9,491	15,662	15,892

Sources: World Bank calculations based on DHS 2004, 2007, 2011, and 2014 data.
Notes: Robust standard errors in parentheses. *** $p<0.01$, ** $p<0.05$, * $p<0.1$. Sample for each DHS is all ever-married women in that DHS.

TABLE C.2 Full logit regression analysis: Relationship of marriage under age 15 to working for pay

DHS YEAR	2004	2007	2011	2014
	OUTCOME: WORKS FOR PAY			
Demographic characteristics				
Married under age 15	3.59e−05	0.0271**	0.000297	0.0221**
	(0.00946)	(0.0112)	(0.00628)	(0.0102)
Current age	0.000950	0.00249**	0.00248***	0.00717***
	(0.000986)	(0.00126)	(0.000719)	(0.00116)
Highest education level	0.00538	−0.000985	0.0201***	0.00498
	(0.00696)	(0.00810)	(0.00462)	(0.00737)
Partner characteristics				
Partner's age	0.000247	−0.00198**	−0.00265***	−0.00395***
	(0.000772)	(0.00100)	(0.000591)	(0.000893)
Partner's highest education level	−0.0227***	−0.0111	−0.00903**	−0.0236***
	(0.00571)	(0.00685)	(0.00376)	(0.00637)

continued

TABLE C.2, *continued*

DHS YEAR	2004	2007	2011	2014
	OUTCOME: WORKS FOR PAY			
Whether partner is employed	−0.00172	0.0352	−0.0194	0.0562*
	(0.0236)	(0.0342)	(0.0156)	(0.0297)
Whether partner lives elsewhere	−0.0568***	−0.0425*	−0.00538	−0.103***
	(0.0213)	(0.0228)	(0.0118)	(0.0188)
Household characteristics				
Household wealth quintile	−0.0205***	−0.0356***	−0.0130***	−0.0262***
	(0.00382)	(0.00487)	(0.00270)	(0.00444)
Whether head of household is female	0.0785***	0.0198	0.0143	0.0727***
	(0.0206)	(0.0229)	(0.0132)	(0.0195)
Number of children under age 5	−0.0423***	−0.0413***	−0.0356***	−0.0449***
	(0.00772)	(0.00917)	(0.00554)	(0.00976)
Number of women over age 50	−0.0499***	−0.0448***	−0.0194***	−0.0180
	(0.0119)	(0.0135)	(0.00720)	(0.0117)
Residence characteristics				
Distance to the nearest market	−0.00952	−0.0206***	−0.0144***	0.00606
	(0.00611)	(0.00773)	(0.00411)	(0.00678)
Urban residence (ref: rural)	0.0647***	0.0478***	0.0812***	0.0301***
	(0.0114)	(0.0132)	(0.00749)	(0.0116)
Respondent's division (ref: Dhaka)				
Barisal division	−0.0719***	−0.107***	−0.0433***	−0.0724***
	(0.0135)	(0.0149)	(0.00907)	(0.0168)
Chittagong division	−0.0523***	−0.0820***	−0.0256***	−0.0691***
	(0.0122)	(0.0146)	(0.00846)	(0.0147)
Khulna division	0.0133	0.0588***	−0.0154*	−0.0462***
	(0.0141)	(0.0165)	(0.00889)	(0.0144)
Rajshahi division	0.0609***	0.0888***	−0.00421	0.0294*
	(0.0131)	(0.0162)	(0.00921)	(0.0154)
Sylhet division	−0.0175	−0.136***	−0.00764	−8.28e−06
	(0.0169)	(0.0161)	(0.00953)	(0.0177)
Rangpur division			−0.0234**	−0.171***
			(0.0102)	(0.0148)
Observations	9,594	9,491	15,662	15,892

Sources: World Bank calculations based on DHS 2004, 2007, 2011, and 2014 data.
Notes: Robust standard errors in parentheses. *** $p<0.01$, ** $p<0.05$, * $p<0.1$. Sample for each DHS is all ever-married women in that DHS.

TABLE C.3 **Full Ordinary Least Squares (OLS) regression analysis: Relationship of child marriage to years of schooling**

DHS YEAR	2004	2007	2011	2014
	OUTCOME: YEARS OF SCHOOLING			
Age at marriage (ref: over 18 years)				
Age at marriage: 15 to 18	−0.261***	−0.304***	−0.305***	−0.290***
	(0.0899)	(0.0972)	(0.0648)	(0.0736)
Age at marriage: <15	−1.317***	−1.227***	−1.218***	−1.290***
	(0.0706)	(0.0841)	(0.0569)	(0.0685)
Respondent's age				
Age	−0.330***	−0.266***	−0.113***	−0.0469*
	(0.0250)	(0.0301)	(0.0222)	(0.0275)
Age-squared	0.00393***	0.00275***	0.000426	−0.000587
	(0.000370)	(0.000437)	(0.000323)	(0.000394)
Respondent's partner characteristics				
Partner's age	−0.0321***	−0.0398***	−0.0366***	−0.0348***
	(0.00451)	(0.00585)	(0.00441)	(0.00511)
Partner's education (ref: none)				
Partner's education: primary	0.798***	1.237***	1.086***	1.376***
	(0.0672)	(0.0861)	(0.0622)	(0.0754)
Partner's education: secondary	2.415***	2.864***	2.853***	3.023***
	(0.0846)	(0.102)	(0.0718)	(0.0936)
Partner's education: tertiary	5.906***	6.699***	6.215***	6.209***
	(0.117)	(0.137)	(0.0952)	(0.109)
Whether partner is employed	−0.127	−0.675***	0.216*	−0.151
	(0.139)	(0.192)	(0.128)	(0.149)
Respondent's household characteristics				
Household wealth (ref: poorest quintile)				
Second poorest quintile	0.589***	0.450***	0.621***	0.697***
	(0.0774)	(0.105)	(0.0720)	(0.0950)
Middle wealth quintile	0.967***	0.830***	1.251***	1.386***
	(0.0837)	(0.110)	(0.0764)	(0.0994)
Fourth wealth quintile	1.537***	1.434***	1.660***	1.593***
	(0.0890)	(0.117)	(0.0813)	(0.104)
Richest quintile	2.565***	2.582***	2.757***	2.849***
	(0.108)	(0.138)	(0.0966)	(0.119)
Whether household is female-headed	−0.0186	0.137	0.0959	−0.0695
	(0.118)	(0.126)	(0.0933)	(0.0955)
Number of children under age 5	−0.0784*	−0.0113	0.0245	0.0744
	(0.0433)	(0.0599)	(0.0436)	(0.0576)
Number of women over age 50	0.239***	0.335***	0.189***	0.269***
	(0.0707)	(0.0848)	(0.0583)	(0.0644)

continued

TABLE C.3, *continued*

DHS YEAR	2004	2007	2011	2014
	OUTCOME: YEARS OF SCHOOLING			
Respondent's residence				
Urban (ref: rural)	−0.0650	−0.196**	−0.193***	−0.235***
	(0.0690)	(0.0833)	(0.0618)	(0.0658)
Respondent's division (ref: Dhaka)				
Barisal division	0.627***	0.791***	0.914***	1.033***
	(0.0944)	(0.112)	(0.0797)	(0.101)
Chittagong division	−0.0435	0.0673	0.199***	0.152*
	(0.0850)	(0.103)	(0.0744)	(0.0880)
Khulna division	0.239***	0.476***	0.477***	0.615***
	(0.0898)	(0.105)	(0.0747)	(0.0848)
Rajshahi division	0.0403	0.279***	0.211***	0.559***
	(0.0764)	(0.0994)	(0.0771)	(0.0861)
Sylhet division	−0.694***	−0.473***	0.365***	0.665***
	(0.100)	(0.121)	(0.0774)	(0.0988)
Rangpur division			−0.222***	−0.133
			(0.0851)	(0.0999)
Constant	9.006***	9.314***	6.193***	5.514***
	(0.422)	(0.523)	(0.368)	(0.483)
Observations	9,595	9,478	15,681	15,899
R-squared	0.597	0.567	0.595	0.578

Sources: World Bank calculations based on DHS 2004, 2007, 2011, and 2014 data.
Notes: Robust standard errors in parentheses. *** $p<0.01$, ** $p<0.05$, * $p<0.1$. Sample for each DHS is all ever-married women in that DHS.

Appendix D
Full Regression Results
for Assets

TABLE D.1 **Determinants of land ownership and rights**

VARIABLES	(1) FEMALE JOINTLY OWNS MOST OF AGRICULTURAL LAND	(2) FEMALE JOINTLY HAS AT LEAST ONE RIGHT OVER AGRICULTURAL LAND	(3) MALE JOINTLY OWNS MOST OF AGRICULTURAL LAND	(4) MALE JOINTLY HAS AT LEAST ONE RIGHT OVER AGRICULTURAL LAND
Education: some primary (grades 1–4)	−0.01	0.04	0.18**	0.02
	(0.105)	(0.063)	(0.081)	(0.105)
Education: primary (grade 5)	0.09*	0.02	0.28***	0.18**
	(0.049)	(0.059)	(0.058)	(0.076)
Education: some secondary (grades 6–9)	−0.10	−0.12**	0.34***	0.33***
	(0.071)	(0.057)	(0.094)	(0.124)
Education: secondary and above (grades 10+)	0.09	−0.05	0.68***	0.56***
	(0.146)	(0.200)	(0.068)	(0.137)
Age in years	0.01*	−0.00	0.01***	0.01**
	(0.004)	(0.005)	(0.002)	(0.003)
Age at first marriage	−0.03***	−0.01	0.01**	−0.01
	(0.007)	(0.015)	(0.006)	(0.008)
Household size	−0.04**	−0.03***	0.03*	0.03
	(0.020)	(0.008)	(0.018)	(0.025)
Per capita household expenditure '000 BDT	0.02	0.00	0.12***	0.08***
	(0.017)	(0.012)	(0.027)	(0.023)
Division: Chittagong	−0.51***	−0.66***	−0.90***	−0.37***
	(0.020)	(0.039)	(0.034)	(0.024)

continued

TABLE D.1, *continued*

VARIABLES	(1) FEMALE JOINTLY OWNS MOST OF AGRICULTURAL LAND	(2) FEMALE JOINTLY HAS AT LEAST ONE RIGHT OVER AGRICULTURAL LAND	(3) MALE JOINTLY OWNS MOST OF AGRICULTURAL LAND	(4) MALE JOINTLY HAS AT LEAST ONE RIGHT OVER AGRICULTURAL LAND
Division: Dhaka	−0.01	0.43***	0.12***	−0.01
	(0.012)	(0.029)	(0.016)	(0.014)
Division: Khulna	0.23***	−0.16***	0.13***	−0.23***
	(0.019)	(0.014)	(0.019)	(0.019)
Division: Rajshahi	−0.20***	−0.43***	−0.32***	−0.23***
	(0.019)	(0.023)	(0.022)	(0.025)
Division: Rangpur	−0.24***	−0.04	−0.37***	0.55***
	(0.026)	(0.025)	(0.027)	(0.037)
Division: Sylhet	0.49***	0.64***	−0.51***	−0.46***
	(0.036)	(0.057)	(0.026)	(0.041)
Value asset brought at marriage (inflated to 2015 values)	0.00**	0.00**		
	(0.000)	(0.000)		
Was in job market including raising poultry with pay	−0.04	0.21**	−0.33	−0.04
	(0.176)	(0.102)	(0.235)	(0.147)
Woman has control of money to buy food from the market	0.12	0.23**		
	(0.218)	(0.106)		
Constant	−0.89***	−0.26	−0.59*	0.64*
	(0.286)	(0.249)	(0.330)	(0.356)
Observations	2,441	2,441	2,623	2,623

Source: World Bank calculations based on BIHS 2015 data.
Notes: Robust standard errors in parentheses. *** $p<0.01$, ** $p<0.05$, * $p<0.1$. Reference variables: no education dummy and Barisal Division dummy.

TABLE D.2 Asset ownership and female labor force participation

VARIABLES	(1) IN JOB MARKET	(2) IN JOB MARKET	(3) IN JOB MARKET	(4) IN JOB MARKET
Education: some primary (grades 1–4)	−0.05	−0.10	−0.19**	−0.19**
	(0.070)	(0.069)	(0.091)	(0.091)
Education: primary (grade 5)	0.04	−0.00	−0.04	−0.04
	(0.086)	(0.105)	(0.118)	(0.121)
Education: some secondary (grades 6–9)	−0.12	−0.14	−0.15	−0.14
	(0.142)	(0.135)	(0.146)	(0.144)
Education: secondary and above (grade 10+)	−0.28	−0.30	−0.48	−0.49*
	(0.198)	(0.191)	(0.295)	(0.284)
Age in years	0.00	0.00**	0.00	0.00
	(0.002)	(0.002)	(0.006)	(0.005)

continued

TABLE D.2, *continued*

VARIABLES	(1) IN JOB MARKET	(2) IN JOB MARKET	(3) IN JOB MARKET	(4) IN JOB MARKET
Age at first marriage	0.00	0.00	0.00	0.00
	(0.013)	(0.013)	(0.015)	(0.014)
Number of children ages 5 years or less	−0.19*	−0.20*	−0.25**	−0.25**
	(0.103)	(0.103)	(0.100)	(0.100)
Number of children ages 6–18 years	0.18***	0.18***	0.16***	0.16***
	(0.062)	(0.052)	(0.044)	(0.045)
Number of men ages 19–50 years	−0.07	−0.06	−0.08	−0.08
	(0.061)	(0.059)	(0.069)	(0.068)
Number of women ages 19–50 years	0.08	0.07	−0.05	−0.05
	(0.050)	(0.052)	(0.049)	(0.048)
Number of men ages 51 years and above	−0.14	−0.15	−0.12	−0.12
	(0.172)	(0.152)	(0.151)	(0.154)
Number of women ages 51 years and above	−0.06	−0.06	−0.21**	−0.20**
	(0.077)	(0.078)	(0.098)	(0.092)
Per capita household expenditure/month	−0.00	−0.00	−0.00	−0.00
	(0.000)	(0.000)	(0.000)	(0.000)
Division: Chittagong	0.03	0.01	−0.07	−0.03
	(0.031)	(0.040)	(0.054)	(0.064)
Division: Dhaka	0.46***	0.39***	0.61***	0.59***
	(0.023)	(0.035)	(0.032)	(0.041)
Division: Khulna	0.56***	0.58***	0.51***	0.50***
	(0.029)	(0.024)	(0.015)	(0.020)
Division: Rajshahi	1.11***	1.09***	1.05***	1.07***
	(0.052)	(0.032)	(0.029)	(0.023)
Division: Rangpur	1.79***	1.70***	1.64***	1.65***
	(0.059)	(0.033)	(0.049)	(0.044)
Division: Sylhet	−0.41***	−0.44***	−0.24***	−0.28***
	(0.080)	(0.071)	(0.090)	(0.079)
Value asset brought at marriage (inflated to 2015 values)	−0.00**	−0.00**	−0.00*	−0.00*
	(0.000)	(0.000)	(0.000)	(0.000)
Owns any of agricultural land, large livestock, house, and other land	1.07***			
	(0.139)			
Right over any of agricultural land, large livestock, house, and other land		0.75***		
		(0.101)		
Jointly owns most of agricultural land			−0.19	
			(0.193)	

continued

TABLE D.2, *continued*

VARIABLES	(1) IN JOB MARKET	(2) IN JOB MARKET	(3) IN JOB MARKET	(4) IN JOB MARKET
Jointly has AT LEAST ONE right over agricultural land				0.10
				(0.090)
Household size				
Constant	−0.67	−0.71**	0.51	0.43
	(0.430)	(0.353)	(0.361)	(0.324)
Observations	3,688	3,688	2,441	2,441

Source: World Bank calculations based on BIHS 2015 data.
Notes: Robust standard errors in parentheses. *** $p<0.01$, ** $p<0.05$, * $p<0.1$. Reference variables: no education dummy and Barisal Division dummy.

Appendix E
Full Regression Results for Women's Control over Credit (Rural Bangladesh)

TABLE E.1 Factors associated with rural women's control over credit

	SELF MADE DECISION TO BORROW MONEY FROM AT LEAST ONE SOURCE			SELF DECIDED HOW TO USE ANY BORROWED MONEY FROM AT LEAST ONE SOURCE			SELF MADE DECISION TO BORROW MONEY FROM AT LEAST ONE SOURCE AND DECIDED HOW TO USE BORROWED MONEY FROM AT LEAST ONE SOURCE		
	ODDS RATIO	STANDARD ERROR	P VALUE	ODDS RATIO	STANDARD ERROR	P VALUE	ODDS RATIO	STANDARD ERROR	P VALUE
Respondent's demographic characteristics									
Age (years)	0.979	0.004	0.000	0.978	0.004	0.000	0.978	0.004	0.000
Age at marriage (years)	0.963	0.013	0.007	0.964	0.013	0.006	0.963	0.013	0.006
Years of education	0.973	0.013	0.038	0.975	0.013	0.057	0.972	0.013	0.036
Household asset score (baseline)	1.000	0.000	0.000	1.000	0.000	0.008	1.000	0.000	0.001
Respondent's public participation									
Is not a member of any group	0.572	0.062	0.000	0.563	0.061	0.000	0.550	0.059	0.000
Is not comfortable speaking in public in at least one context	0.693	0.069	0.000	0.732	0.070	0.001	0.703	0.069	0.000
Who decides if respondent can go to haat (ref: other)									
Self decides	1.347	0.215	0.063	1.332	0.200	0.057	1.309	0.200	0.078
Self and husband decide	1.370	0.143	0.003	1.429	0.151	0.001	1.337	0.139	0.005
Respondent's economic engagement at baseline									
Owns any of agricultural land, large livestock, house, and other land	0.988	0.097	0.899	1.051	0.101	0.605	1.007	0.097	0.945
Rights over any of agricultural land, large livestock, house, and other land	1.341	0.126	0.002	1.219	0.110	0.028	1.285	0.119	0.007
Works for pay	1.154	0.123	0.181	1.142	0.118	0.201	1.155	0.124	0.179
Division (ref: Dhaka)									
Barisal	0.511	0.117	0.004	0.469	0.116	0.002	0.504	0.112	0.002
Chittagong	0.568	0.089	0.000	0.572	0.096	0.001	0.580	0.093	0.001
Khulna	0.688	0.118	0.031	0.677	0.118	0.026	0.757	0.125	0.093
Rajshahi	0.725	0.124	0.061	0.754	0.122	0.082	0.713	0.119	0.044
Rangpur	0.974	0.170	0.880	1.065	0.177	0.705	1.013	0.178	0.941
Sylhet	0.907	0.167	0.598	0.999	0.175	0.994	0.917	0.169	0.639
Constant	10.747	3.540	0.000	9.059	2.955	0.000	11.588	3.758	0.000
Total observations	3,209			3,209			3,209		

Sources: World Bank calculations based on BIHS 2012 and 2015 data.

Notes: Source of data is two rounds of the Bangladesh Integrated Household Survey, conducted in rural Bangladesh in 2011–12 and 2015. Sample includes women between the ages of 20 and 73. The lower bound is selected, so that there is no censoring on education. The upper bound is female life expectancy.

Appendix F
Ethnic and Religious Minorities

OVERVIEW

In 1972, Bangladesh became a signatory to the International Labor Organization (ILO) Indigenous and Tribal Populations Convention of 1957 (No. 107), the Discrimination (Employment and Occupation) Convention of 1958 (No. 111), and the Equal remuneration Convention of 1951 (No. 100). Bangladesh has yet to sign a number of international instruments protecting minorities. It has neither ratified the ILO's Indigenous and Tribal Peoples Convention of 1989 (No. 169), nor the Employment Policy Convention of 1964 (No. 122) and the Human Resources Development Convention of 1975 (No. 142), which provide minorities with employment-related protections.

DESCRIPTIVE CHARACTERISTICS OF KEY MINORITY GROUPS CONSIDERED IN THIS BOOK

Bangladesh's ethnic minorities

There is no consensus on the number of ethnic minority groups in Bangladesh. Different understandings of the terms "ethnicity," "ethnic communities," "tribe," "tribal groups," "adivasis," and "indigenous people" have led to disagreement among government, academics, nongovernmental organizations, and community groups about the number of distinct minority groups in the country. The government of Bangladesh officially recognized 27 ethnic groups under its 2010 Cultural Institution for Small Anthropological Groups Act and in its 2011 Population and Housing Census (Bangladesh Bureau of Statistics 2015). The 2011 Census named the Chakma, Marma, Tripura, Mro, Tanchaynga, Bom, Pankhoya, Chak, Khyang, Khumi, Lusai, Koch, Santal, Dalu, Usai/Usui, Rakhain, Monipuri, Garo, Hajong, Khasia, Mong, Orao/Oraon, Barman, Pahari, Malpahari, Munda, and Kol minority groups. However, three ethnic groups are double counted, with this mis-categorization resulting in the Census' 27 ethnic minority groups actually identifying only 24 groups, and possibly including an individual

TABLE F.1 **Top ten minority ethnic groups in Bangladesh, 2011**

RANK	ETHNIC GROUP	SHARE OF BANGLADESHI POPULATION (%)
1	Bengali	98.89
2	Chakma	0.30
3	Others	0.23
4	Marma	0.14
5	Santal	0.10
6	Tripura	0.08
7	Garo	0.05
8	Orao	0.05
9	Barmon	0.03
10	Mro	0.03

Source: Bangladesh Bureau of Statistics 2015.

person in more than one group (Gain 2016). For instance, Marma and Mong are the same ethnic group, as are the Malpahari and Pahari. According to the Census, the three largest ethnic minority groups in Bangladesh are the Chakma, Marma, and Santal (table F.1).

Whereas Bangladesh's ethnic minority population appears to be increasing—the 2001 census reported 1.41 million and the 1991 census 1.21 million—ethnic minorities represent a decreasing share of the country's total population. The 2011 Census suggests a 1.18 percent annual growth rate for Bangladesh's ethnic population, as compared to 1.47 percent growth for the total population (Bangladesh Bureau of Statistics 2015). In Chittagong, this shift results at least in part from the ethnic majority population moving into the area at a faster rate than that of the local ethnic population growth.

Geographic concentration of ethnic minorities

The 2011 Census collects data on the location of individuals that fall under the 27 government-identified minority groups. Government data suggest that few districts in Bangladesh have substantial populations of ethnic minorities. Out of the 64 districts in the country, only 11 have ethnic minority groups that represent more than one percent of the total district population including concentrated minority populations in the three districts of the CHT. The largest concentration of ethnic population in Bangladesh is in Rangmati district, where 356,153 ethnic minorities reside, accounting for 32.7 percent of total population. Two other districts with high ethnic populations are Khagrachhari and Bandarban, both in CHT (map F.1).

Whereas the 2011 Census includes no data on the distribution of different ethnic groups across the country, community reports for each of the 64 districts include the number of ethnic households. These community data find Chakma to be the dominant ethnic group in the CHT, followed by Marma. There are a number of ethnic minority groups located in the plains and hills of the north and northwest (Vinding and Kampbel 2012). The government community reports find Swantal and Orao to be the dominant ethnic groups in the western part of Rajshahi and Rangpur (map F.2). The Koch, Munda, Oraon, Paharia, Rajbansi, and Santal have traditionally inhabited parts of Bogra, Dinajpur, Kusthia, Pabna, Rajshahi, and Rangpur Districts on the northern border (Khaleque and

MAP F.1

Concentration of ethnic minorities, 2011

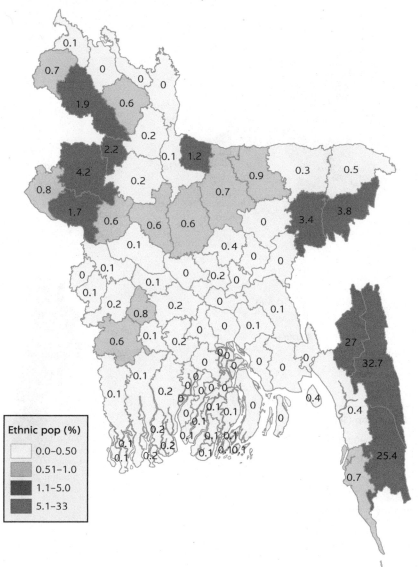

Source: Illustration based on Bangladesh Bureau of Statistics 2014.
Note: Concentration of ethnic minorities is presented by the ratio of ethnic minority individuals to total population; the ratios (in percentages) are displayed in the map for each district.

Gain 1995). The Garo, Koch, and Hajong ethnic groups are concentrated in Mymensingh and Jamalpur Districts in the north and in the north-central Tangail District (Khaleque and Gain 1995). Many, if not most, minority populations in the northeast are members of small ethnic minority groups, such as Almik, Bhuiya, Barak, Soura, Bauri, Manraji, Mudi, Rabidash, Gour, Bhumij, Layek, Goala, Rikhmon, and Rikshan (Toufique et al. 2016). The 2011 census finds that of the two districts in this region, 45 percent of ethnic minority households in Moulvibazar and 93 percent in Sunamganj are from the census category "others."[1] The Khasi, Manipuri, Pathor, and Tipra tend to live in the northeastern Sylhet district (Khaleque and Gain 1995), and the Meithei-speaking Meitei are also concentrated in Sylhet.

MAP F.2

Dominant ethnic groups by district, 2011

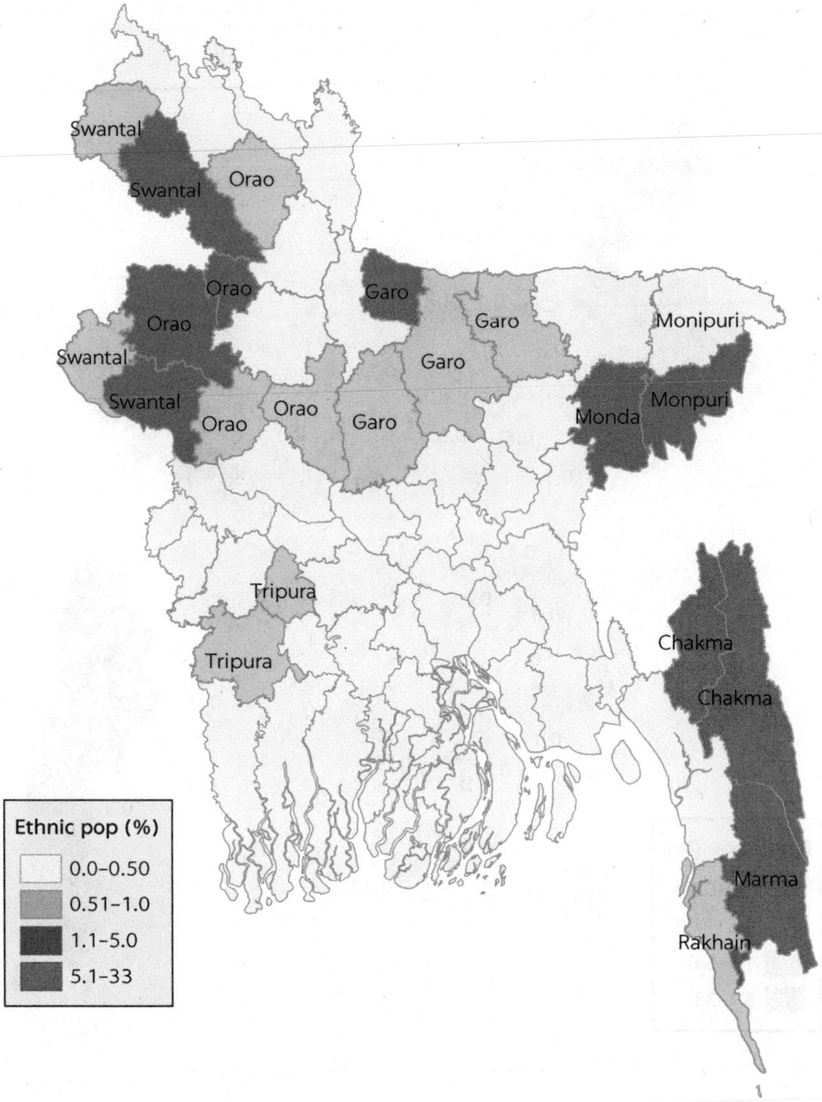

Source: Illustration based on Bangladesh Bureau of Statistics 2014.
Note: Ethnic groups are shown only in districts with "substantial" ethnic minority populations, defined as constituting more than 0.5 percent of the total population of the district.

Educational profile of ethnic minorities

The scant available data suggest that Bangladeshi minorities have low educational achievement compared to the overall population. For instance, this is suggested by government data indicating lower literacy rates for ethnic minorities (table F.2). Certain minorities and those in certain geographical areas, however, appear to have higher than average levels of education as compared to other minority groups, as well as the general population. Research by Barkat et al. (2009) notes high overall primary and secondary school enrollment in the CHT (with 82 percent of all surveyed children ages 5–16 enrolled), marginally higher than for Bengali children. Secondary quantitative data paint a bleaker picture, with Barkat et al. (2009) finding that 65 percent of surveyed children in the CHT

TABLE F.2 **Literacy rate of ethnic population, seven years and above, by sex, 1991-2011**

Years

SEX	1991		2001		2011	
	TOTAL POPULATION	ETHNIC POPULATION	TOTAL POPULATION	ETHNIC POPULATION	TOTAL POPULATION	ETHNIC POPULATION
Male	38.90	31.6	50.27	39.3	54.11	45.8
Female	25.45	17.9	41.80	24.8	49.44	34.1
Total	32.40	24.9	46.15	32.2	51.77	39.9

Source: Bangladesh Bureau of Statistics 2015.

had dropped out before completing their primary education, while another 19 percent had dropped out after primary completion. Interestingly, the study finds primary education dropout rates to be higher among Bengali children than indigenous children, at 71 percent and 59 percent, respectively. Two-thirds to three-quarters of both boys and girls drop out due to financial challenges. Also, despite relatively high enrollment in the CHT, educational institutions are generally few and far between. Recent developments in certain areas have, however, resulted in improved access. Respondents from focus group discussions conducted in Chittagong for this book mentioned that the developed transport network in their area has allowed them to attend schools far from their locality. The ethnic minority respondents in Chittagong also noted that support and incentive programs run by the government and NGOs have contributed to increasing access to girls' education. In the Rajshahi ethnic study site—where poverty is a major problem—girls' educational access seems to have benefitted from the support of the NGO World Vision.

Marriage profile of ethnic minorities

While there are no nationwide data on early marriage disaggregated by ethnicity or religion, research suggests that child marriage may be prevalent among ethnic communities in the studied areas, as it is throughout Bangladesh. The relative openness of the Santal community in Rajshahi—as illustrated, for instance, by the practice of co-education, contrasting with Muslim counterparts' strict segregation of boys and girls in educational institutions—has enabled very young boys and girls to enter relationships and start co-habitating as early as age 13. These young couples "marry" under their indigenous religion, forming unions that are socially recognized in their communities but not approved of, or legally recognized by the church or nationally. In contrast, ethnic communities in the CHT marry later than the general population, with the average age of marriage for girls being around 22 or 23.

Whereas parents throughout Bangladeshi society usually make marital decisions for their children, ethnic minority youth may have greater decision-making power with regard to their marriages than their majority counterparts. The qualitative research undertaken for this book finds that minority parents—especially educated ones—often ask for their daughters' opinions about potential partners, which informs the final marital decision. Santal boys and girls in Rajshahi choose their partners for co-habitation without parental involvement. Many parents do not discourage these relationships as they view them as early commitments to partners within the community to avoid future marriage outside of it.

Bangladesh's religious minorities

Religious minorities today constitute 9.6 percent of the country's total population, down from 23.1 percent in 1951. The out-migration of Hindus—in many cases to the state of West Bengal in India—has driven Bangladesh's decline in religious diversity. India's partition—which created Pakistan in 1947—Bangladesh's independence from Pakistan in 1971, and the passing of the Vested Property Act in 1974 all were accompanied by substantial waves of Hindu migration to West Bengal.

The Hindu minority

An estimated 219,000 Hindus left Bangladesh annually between 1964 and 2001 (Minority Rights Group International 2016). Hindu out-migration from Bangladesh continues today, albeit at a much slower pace. While they are part of a religious minority, most Hindus in Bangladesh are not ethnic minorities, as they usually share the same language and general culture with the Muslim majority population. The Hindus remaining in Bangladesh have migrated across regions within the country—mainly in response to threats of, or actual attacks by, other communal groups—and are concentrated in the north and southwest of the country (Minorities at Risk Project 2006; Minority Rights Group International 2016).

The Buddhist minority

Geographically, Bangladesh's Buddhists are quite localized, living mostly in Chittagong division and to a lesser extent in the northern areas of Bangladesh. In the CHT, the large majority of people belonging to ethnic minority groups are Buddhist (80.7 percent). Most Bangladeshi Buddhists identify as members of the Chakma and Marma ethnic groups from the CHT (Minority Rights Group International 2016).

The Christian minority

Mostly Roman Catholic, in smaller numbers Protestant, and also represented in some indigenous tribal communities, such as the Lushei and Bawm, Bengali Christians primarily live in the urban areas of Barisal, Khulna, and Gazipur (Minority Rights Group International 2016). In the CHT, about 22 percent of members of the Tripura and 6 percent of the Murong ethnic groups are Christian (Toufique et al. 2016). In the plains, 36.6 percent of ethnic minority group members are Christian—mostly from the Garo, Khasia, and Santal groups.

Other minorities

In addition to Bangladesh's more clear-cut ethnic and religious minorities, there are other excluded communities—many of whom are identified by their trade—that may be members of religious and/or ethnic minority groups, but may also be part of the Muslim Bengali population. These include the Rishis (cobblers), Kawra (pig-rearing community), tea workers, Teli (oil pressers), Napit (barbers), Dhopas (washer-men), Tati (weavers from Pakistan who speak Urdu), Hajam (unqualified doctors for circumcision), Mazi (boatmen), Bhera (carriers of bridal carriages), Kasai (butchers), and Hijra (transgender individuals who have gained official governmental recognition as a third gender) (Gain 2015).

Scattered across the country, these communities are among the most disadvantaged and excluded despite being part of the ethnic and religious majority (Gain 2015). There are furthermore a number of minority groups who are not officially recognized by the government of Bangladesh. Unrecognized groups include the Biharies (marooned Muslims of Pakistan), Bede (water gypsies), Bawali, Mawali, Patra (a small community in Sylhet), Jaladash (traditional fisherman), and Rohingya refugees. These communities are not counted in the national census, rendering them largely unnoticed and undercounted in society and in public programs.

Ownership and control over household assets

There are no national data disaggregated by ethnic group and gender in Bangladesh on ownership and control of assets. Secondary research suggests, however, that many ethnic minority households possess customary land rights (Barkat et al. 2009) and few of them are able to regularize their land to make ownership recognized officially. Minorities also appear to have limited access to public land, all of which together makes leasing an important part of minorities' access to land (figure F.1).

Furthermore, there is a complete lack of data on financial assets gender-disaggregated by ethnic group. Overall, the limited financial data suggest that ethnic minorities in the CHT have higher levels of savings than those in the plains, and higher savings with commercial banks, MFIs, and informal organizations/co-operatives (table F.3). Minorities in the CHT also have higher overall levels of debt than those in the plains, and are more likely to be indebted to informal sources than to commercial banks (Toufique et al. 2016).

FIGURE F.1

Ethnic minority land ownership and use by area of residence

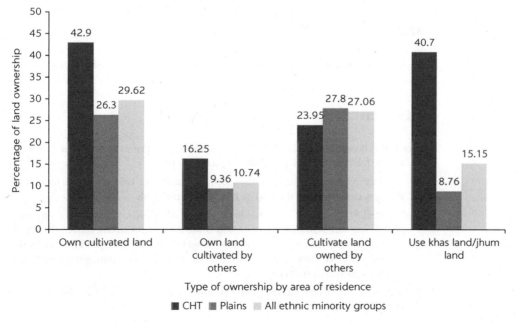

Source: Toufique et al. 2016.

TABLE F.3 **Average savings by sampled ethnic minority groups, BDT**

ETHNIC MINORITY	SAVINGS IN COMMERCIAL BANKS	SAVINGS IN MICROCREDIT ORGANIZATION/ NGOS	SAVINGS IN INFORMAL ORGANIZATIONS/ COOPERATIVES	SAVINGS (POST OFFICE, AT HOME)	LOANS GIVEN TO OTHER INDIVIDUALS/ INSTITUTIONS	SAVINGS IN INSURANCE SCHEME	MONEY INVESTED IN OTHER WAYS
Chakma	46,444	8,854	14,926	2,971	8,050	14,811	37,639
Marma	55,301	7,398	10,066	3,188	57,333	18,700	600
Tripura	35,431	11,808	2,450	1,953	4,000	10,806	39,883
Tanch-aynga	41,500	8,156	3,280	2,820	111,000	18,000	100,000
Murong	31,022	5,310	1,600	2,024	2,000	—	2,000
Other CHT	63,781	7,392	4,214	3,319	28,000	44,506	—
Total CHT	**48,728**	**8,263**	**10,049**	**2,872**	**37,645**	**30,061**	**37,756**
Garo	34,081	6,852	11,481	2,932	36,206	21,263	89,025
Khasia	35,118	7,899	9,480	4,919	1,000	95,250	200,000
Monipuri	82,270	6,920	3,233	4,389	58,000	26,871	69,650
Hjang	13,459	5,575	12,022	1,966	75,000	—	70,385
Barmon	41,874	8,181	3,306	2,498	6,505	9,009	85,680
Sawntal	32,845	4,617	7,388	1,604	37,513	9,714	36,295
Munda	13,786	3,921	1,400	1,164	45,000	13,560	1,600
Orao	36,536	6,828	8,920	3,169	13,961	10,900	63,686
Pahan	35,627	5,927	3,804	1,997	9,828	12,566	76,019
Kuch	46,292	6,239	4,700	2,556	—	11,629	53,786
Other plains	18,945	4,671	4,990	1,562	16,115	13,763	52,450
Total plains	**41,423**	**5,822**	**7,919**	**2,311**	**22,223**	**16,110**	**73,763**
Other total	33,478	4,926	4,821	1,799	18,553	20,351	52,450
Total	**44,029**	**6,047**	**8,239**	**2,445**	**23,264**	**17,674**	**70,953**

Source: Toufique et al. 2016.
Note: NGO = nongovernmental organization.

NOTE

1. That is, not members of one of the 27 ethnic minority groups listed in the census.

REFERENCES

Bangladesh Bureau of Statistics. 2014. *Population and Housing Census 2011, Community Report, Various Districts.* Dhaka: Bangladesh Bureau of Statistics.

———. 2015. *Population and Housing Census 2011, National Report, Volume 1.* Dhaka: Ministry of Planning, Government of the People's Republic of Bangladesh.

Barkat, Abul, Sherly Halim, Avijit Poddar, B. Zaman, Abdelkarim Osman, Sarzamin Khan, M. Rahman, Muhammad Norhisham Majid, G. Mahiyuddin, S. Chakma, and S. Bashir. 2009. "Socio-Economic Baseline Survey of Chittagong Hill Tracts." A Project Financed by the European Union, HDRC, UNDP Bangladesh, Prepared for Chittagong Hill Tracts Development Facility (CHTDF).

Gain, Philip. 2015. "Excluded Groups and Democratization." Society for Environment and Human Development (SEHD).

——. 2016. "Mapping of the Little-Known Ethnic Communities of the Plains." In *Lower Depths; Little Known Communities of Bangladesh*, edited by Philip Gain, 3. Dhaka: Society for Environment and Human Development (SEHD).

Khaleque, Kibriaul, and Philip Gain. 1995. *Bangladesh: Land, Forest, and Forest People*. Dhaka: Society for Environment and Human Development (SEHD).

Minorities At Risk Project. 2006. "Data—Assessment for Hindus in Bangladesh." Center for International Development and Conflict Management, University of Maryland.

Minority Rights Group International. 2016. "Under Threat: The Challenges Facing Religious Minorities in Bangladesh." London: Minority Rights Group International.

Toufique, Kazi Ali, Abdul Hye Mondal, Mohammad Yunus, Sinora Chakma, and Sami Farook. 2016. "Baseline Assessment of Skills and Employment of Indigenous and Tribal Peoples in Bangladesh." Bangladesh Institute of Development Studies.

Vinding, Diana, and Ellen-Rose Kampbell. 2012. *Indigenous Women Workers with Case Studies from Bangladesh, Nepal and the Americas*. International Labour Standards Department (PRO169) and ILO Bureau for Gender Equality, International Labour Organization (ILO). Geneva: ILO.